尾田栄一郎

I saw an unusual panda on TV the other day.
You know the parts that are supposed to be
black? They were all white! I guess it was
one of those freaks of nature. And what was
more, this panda lived in the Arctic! What
an incredible panda! (*Laugh*) Now let's begin
One Piece Volume 21, *Utopia*.

—Eiichiro Oda, 2001

Eiichiro Oda began his manga career at the age of
17, when his one-shot cowboy manga **Wanted!**
won second place in the coveted Tezuka manga
awards. Oda went on to work as an assistant to
some of the biggest manga artists in the industry,
including Nobuhiro Watsuki, before winning the
Hop Step Award for new artists. His pirate
adventure **One Piece**, which debuted in
Weekly Shonen Jump in 1997, quickly became
one of the most popular manga in Japan.

ONE PIECE VOL. 21
The SHONEN JUMP Manga Edition

This volume contains material that was originally published in English in **SHONEN JUMP** #74-76. Artwork in the magazine may have been slightly altered from that presented here.

STORY AND ART BY EIICHIRO ODA

English Adaptation/Lance Caselman
Translation/JN Productions
Touch-up Art & Lettering/Vanessa Satone
Additional Touch-up/Rachel Lightfoot
Design/Sean Lee
Editor/ Yuki Murashige

Editor in Chief, Books/Alvin Lu
Editor in Chief, Magazines/Marc Weidenbaum
VP, Publishing Licensing/Rika Inouye
VP, Sales & Product Marketing/Gonzalo Ferreyra
VP, Creative/Linda Espinosa
Publisher/Hyoe Narita

Printed in the U.S.A.

Published by VIZ Media, LLC
P.O. Box 77010
San Francisco, CA 94107

SHONEN JUMP Manga Edition
10 9 8 7 6 5 4 3 2 1
First printing, June 2009

PARENTAL ADVISORY
ONE PIECE is rated T for Teen and is recommended for ages 13 and up. This volume contains fantasy violence and tobacco usage.
ratings.viz.com

THE WORLD'S
MOST POPULAR MANGA

www.viz.com

www.shonenjump.com

BAROQUE WORKS

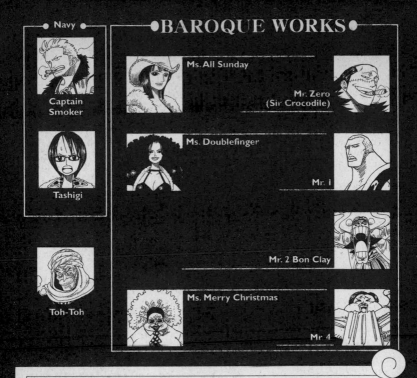

Captain Smoker

Tashigi

Toh-Toh

Ms. All Sunday

Mr. Zero (Sir Crocodile)

Ms. Doublefinger

Mr. 1

Mr. 2 Bon Clay

Ms. Merry Christmas

Mr. 4

Monkey D. Luffy started out as just a kid with a dream—to become the greatest pirate in history! Stirred by the tales of pirate "Red-Haired" Shanks, Luffy vowed to become a pirate himself. That was before the enchanted Devil Fruit gave Luffy the power to stretch like rubber, at the cost of being unable to swim—a serious handicap for an aspiring sea dog. Undeterred, Luffy set out to sea and recruited some crewmates: master swordsman Zolo, treasure-hunting thief Nami, lying sharpshooter Usopp, the high-kicking chef Sanji, and the latest addition, Chopper—the walkin' talkin' reindeer doctor.

On the Grand Line, Luffy and crew struggle to help Princess Vivi save her war-torn and drought-ravaged kingdom from the evil Sir Crocodile and his secret criminal organization, the Baroque Works. Now the climactic showdown between the rebels and the King's forces is at hand! While Luffy lies half-dead in the Alabasta desert following his defeat by Sir Crocodile, the rest of the crew enters Alubarna to help Vivi put an end to the bloodshed. Usopp and Chopper outmaneuver Ms. Merry Christmas and Mr. 4 in a deadly game of baseball, while Sanji squares off against the eccentric but formidable Mr. 2 Bon Clay. Will the Straw Hats have what it takes to overcome the best of the Baroque Works?!

Vol. 21
Utopia

CONTENTS

Chapter 187:
STALEMATE

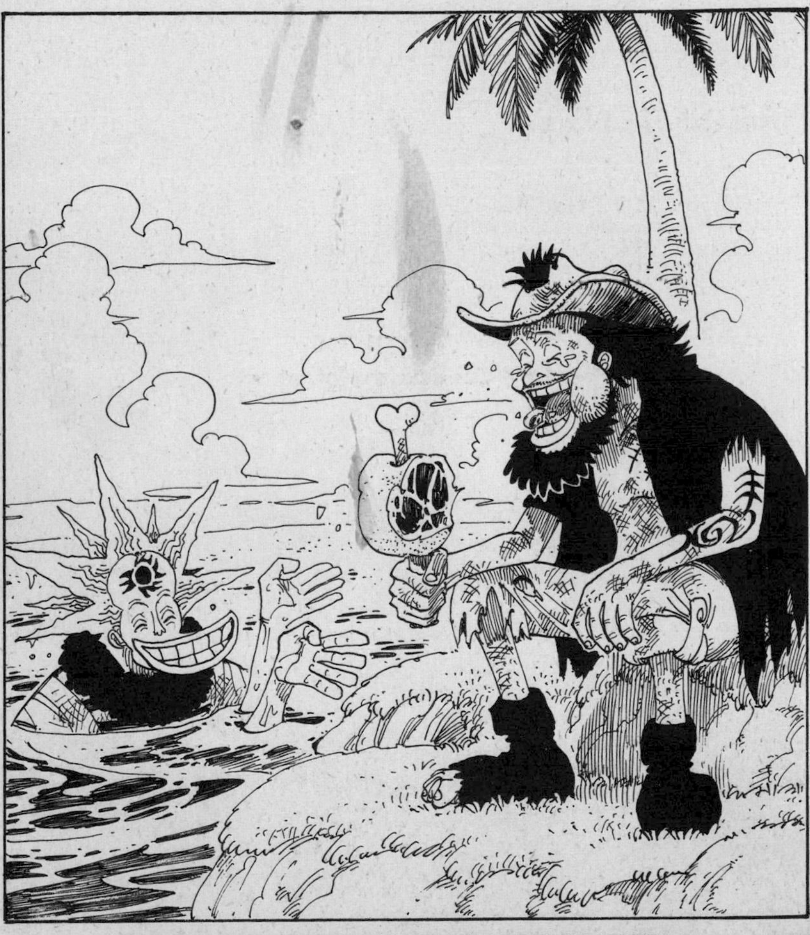

HACHI'S WALK ON THE SEAFLOOR, VOL. 5:
"HACHI ENCOUNTERS A HUNGRY MAN"

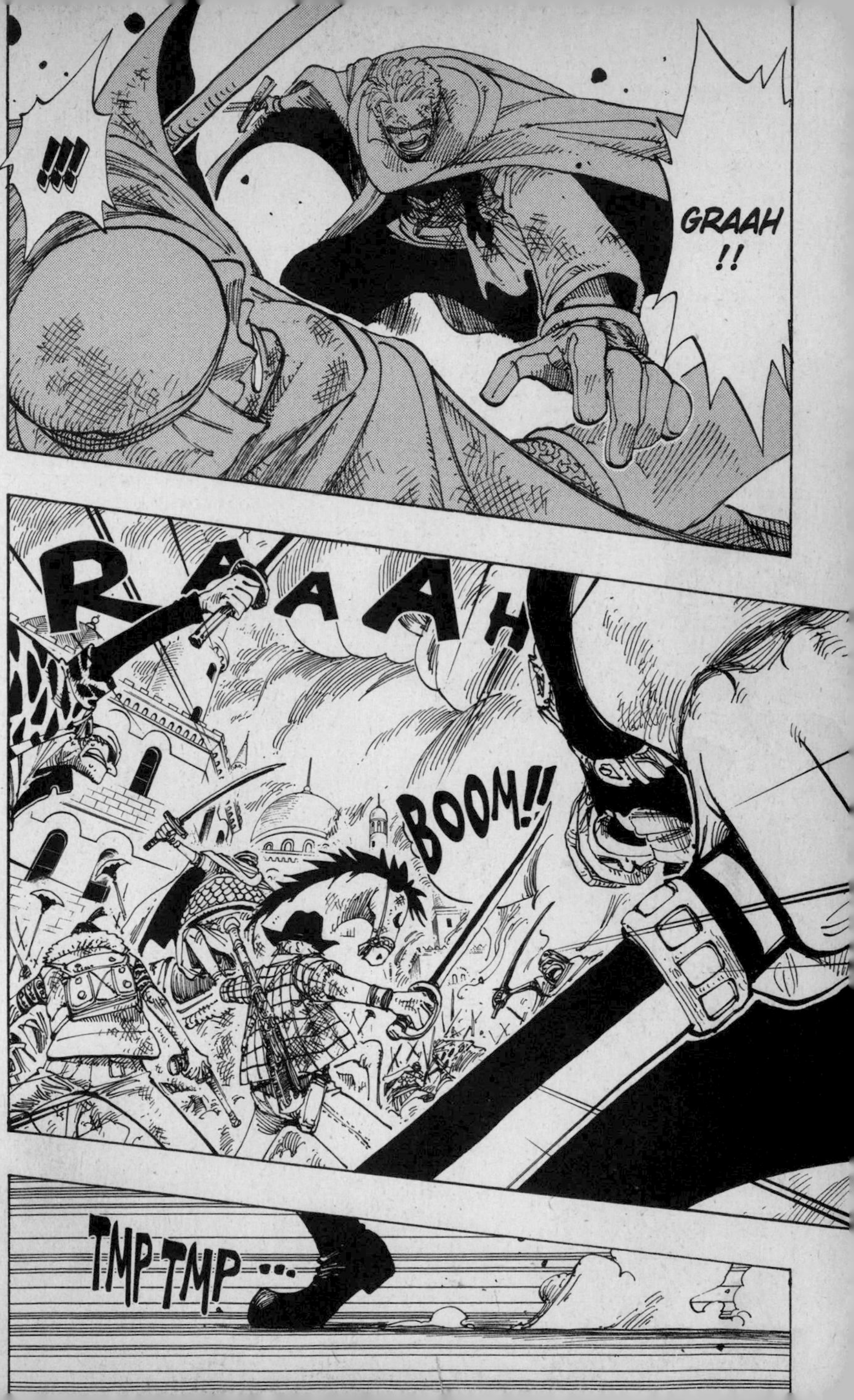
GRAAH !!
!!!!
RAAAH
BOOM!!
TMP TMP ...

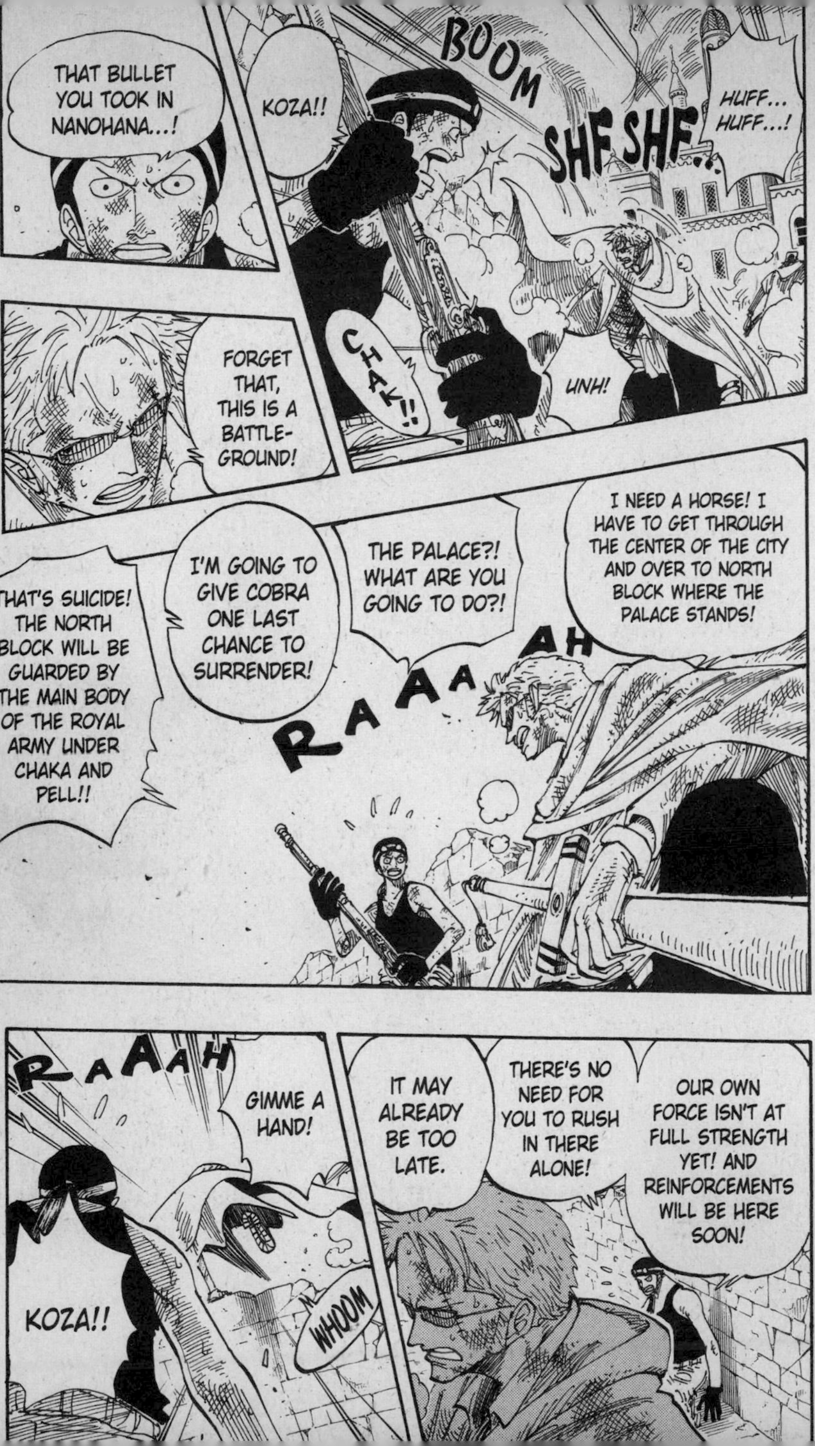
HUFF... HUFF...!
BOOM
SHF SHF
KOZA!!
CHAK!!
UNH!
THAT BULLET YOU TOOK IN NANOHANA...!
FORGET THAT, THIS IS A BATTLE-GROUND!
I NEED A HORSE! I HAVE TO GET THROUGH THE CENTER OF THE CITY AND OVER TO NORTH BLOCK WHERE THE PALACE STANDS!
THE PALACE?! WHAT ARE YOU GOING TO DO?!
I'M GOING TO GIVE COBRA ONE LAST CHANCE TO SURRENDER!
THAT'S SUICIDE! THE NORTH BLOCK WILL BE GUARDED BY THE MAIN BODY OF THE ROYAL ARMY UNDER CHAKA AND PELL!!
RAAAAAH
OUR OWN FORCE ISN'T AT FULL STRENGTH YET! AND REINFORCEMENTS WILL BE HERE SOON!
THERE'S NO NEED FOR YOU TO RUSH IN THERE ALONE!
IT MAY ALREADY BE TOO LATE.
WHOOM
RAAAH
GIMME A HAND!
KOZA!!

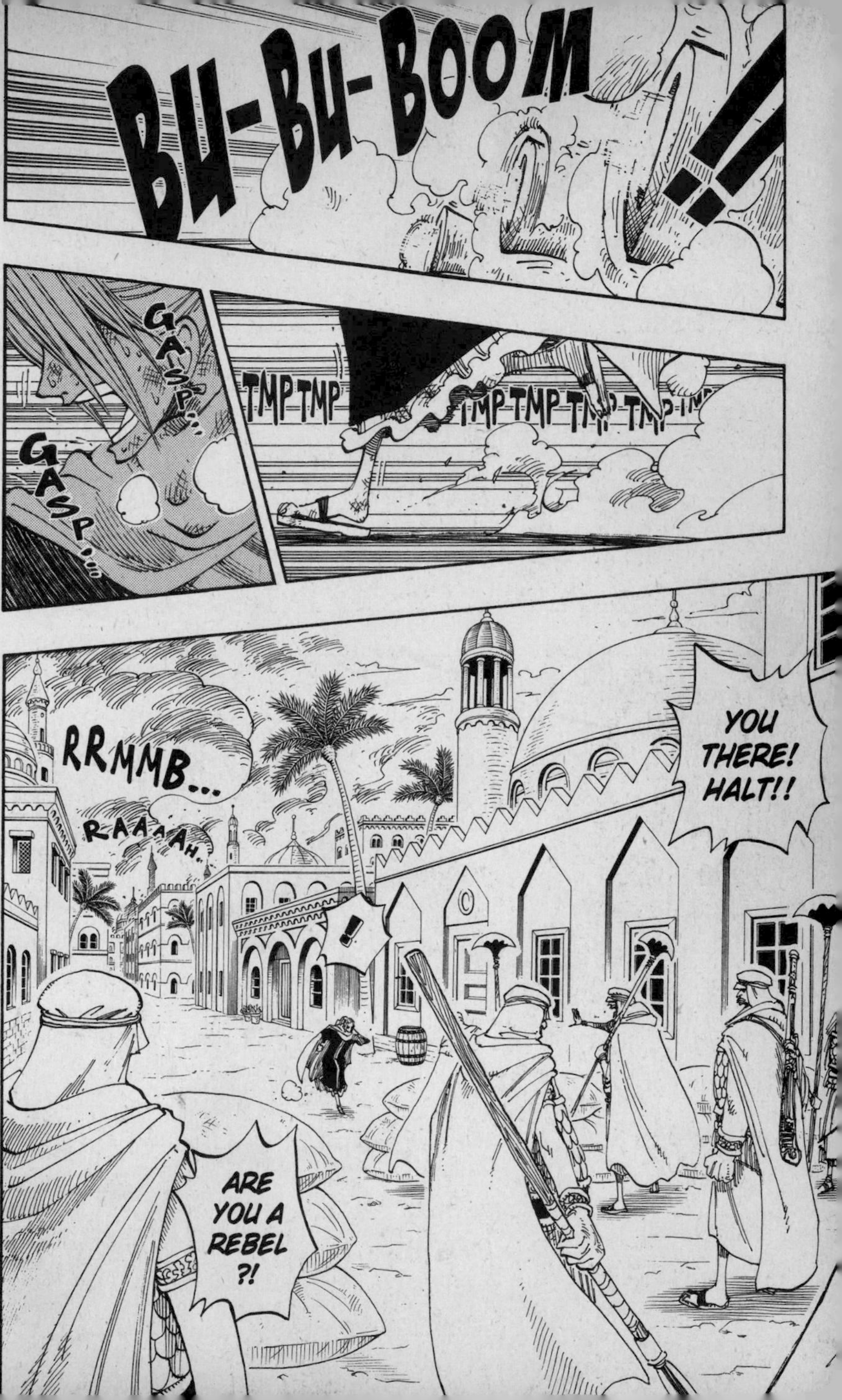
BU-BU-BOOM!!
TMP TMP TMP TMP
TMP TMP
GASP...
GASP...
YOU THERE! HALT!!
!
RRMMB...
RAAAAAH...
ARE YOU A REBEL?!

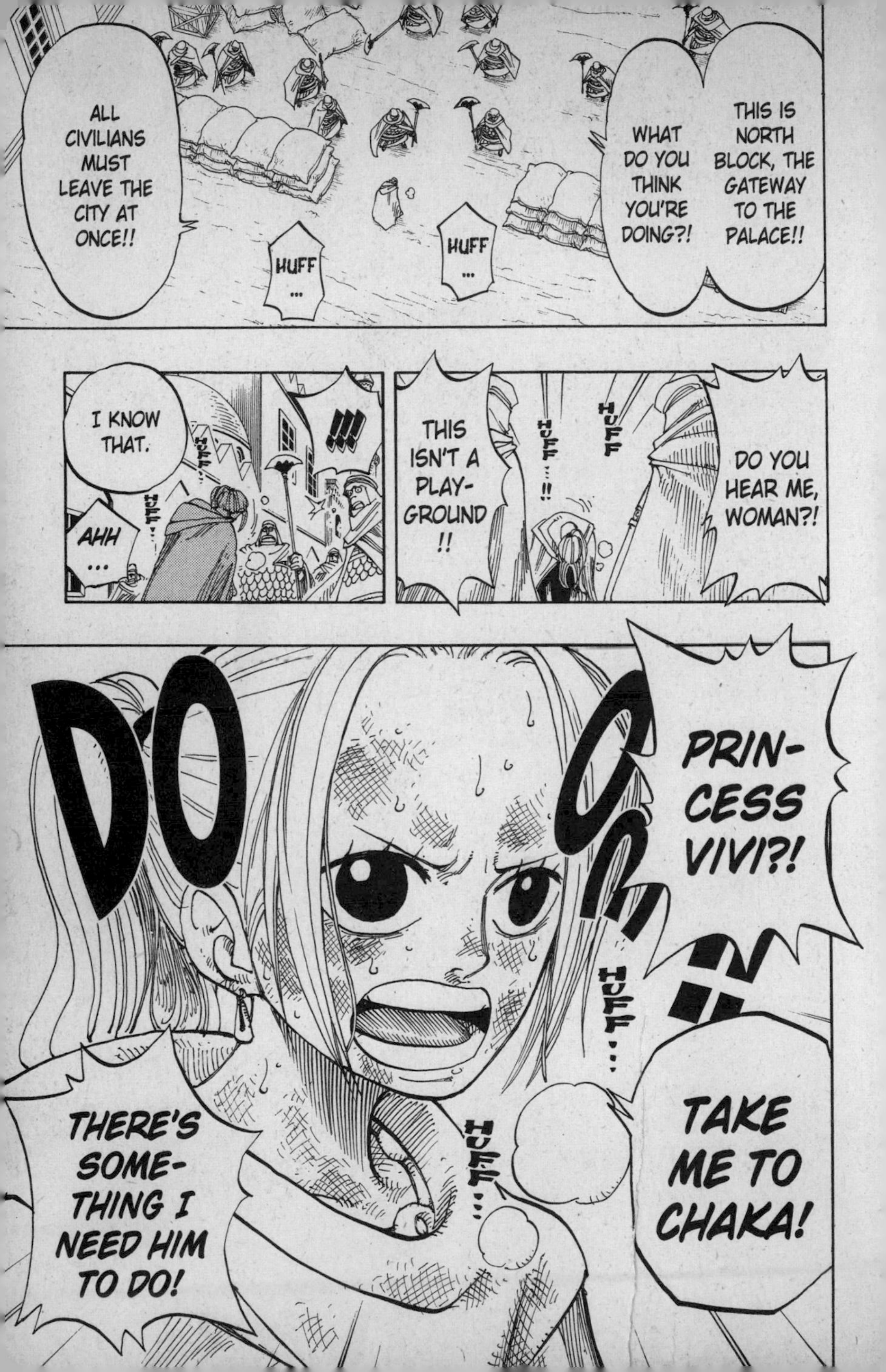
THIS IS NORTH BLOCK, THE GATEWAY TO THE PALACE!!
WHAT DO YOU THINK YOU'RE DOING?!
HUFF ...
HUFF ...
ALL CIVILIANS MUST LEAVE THE CITY AT ONCE!!
HUFF
DO YOU HEAR ME, WOMAN?!
HUFF ... !!
THIS ISN'T A PLAY-GROUND !!
!!!
HUFF ...
I KNOW THAT.
HUFF ...
AHH ...
PRIN-CESS VIVI?!
DOOM!!
HUFF ...
TAKE ME TO CHAKA!
HUFF ...
THERE'S SOME-THING I NEED HIM TO DO!

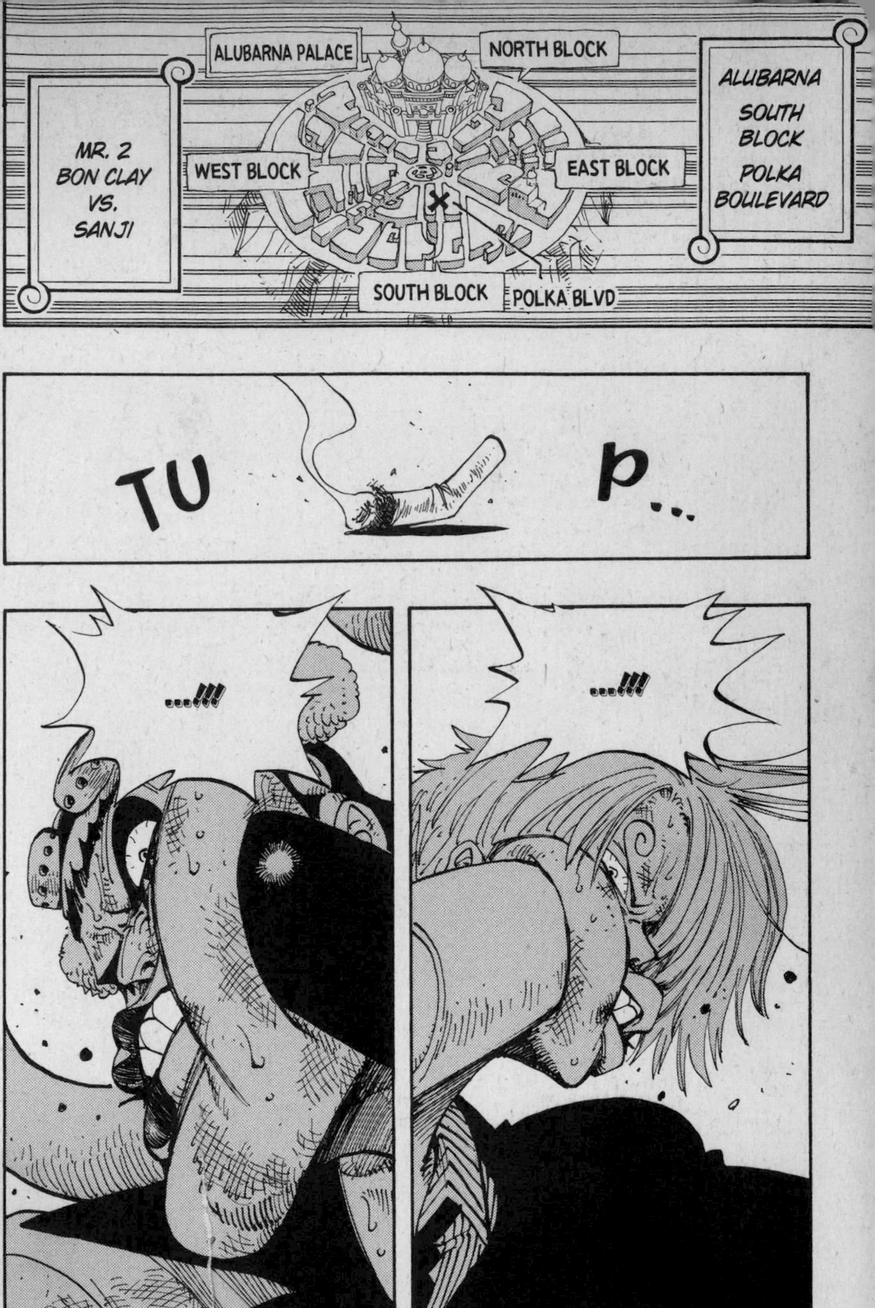
ALUBARNA SOUTH BLOCK POLKA BOULEVARD
NORTH BLOCK
ALUBARNA PALACE
EAST BLOCK
WEST BLOCK
POLKA BLVD
SOUTH BLOCK
MR. 2 BON CLAY VS. SANJI
TU p...
...!!!
...!!!

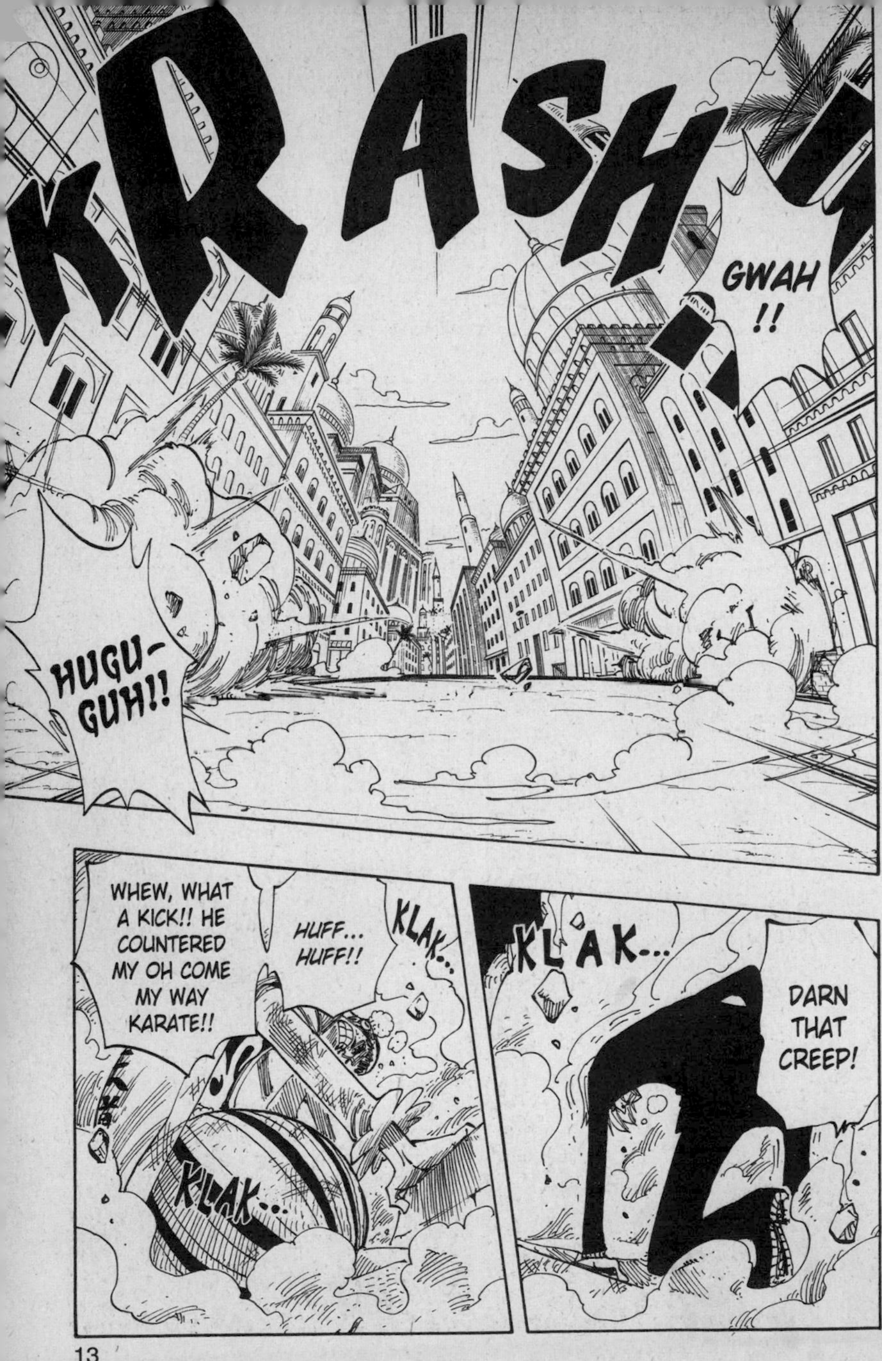
KRASH
GWAH !!
HUGU-GUH!!
KLAK...
DARN THAT CREEP!
KLAK...
HUFF... HUFF!!
WHEW, WHAT A KICK!! HE COUNTERED MY OH COME MY WAY KARATE!!
KLAK...

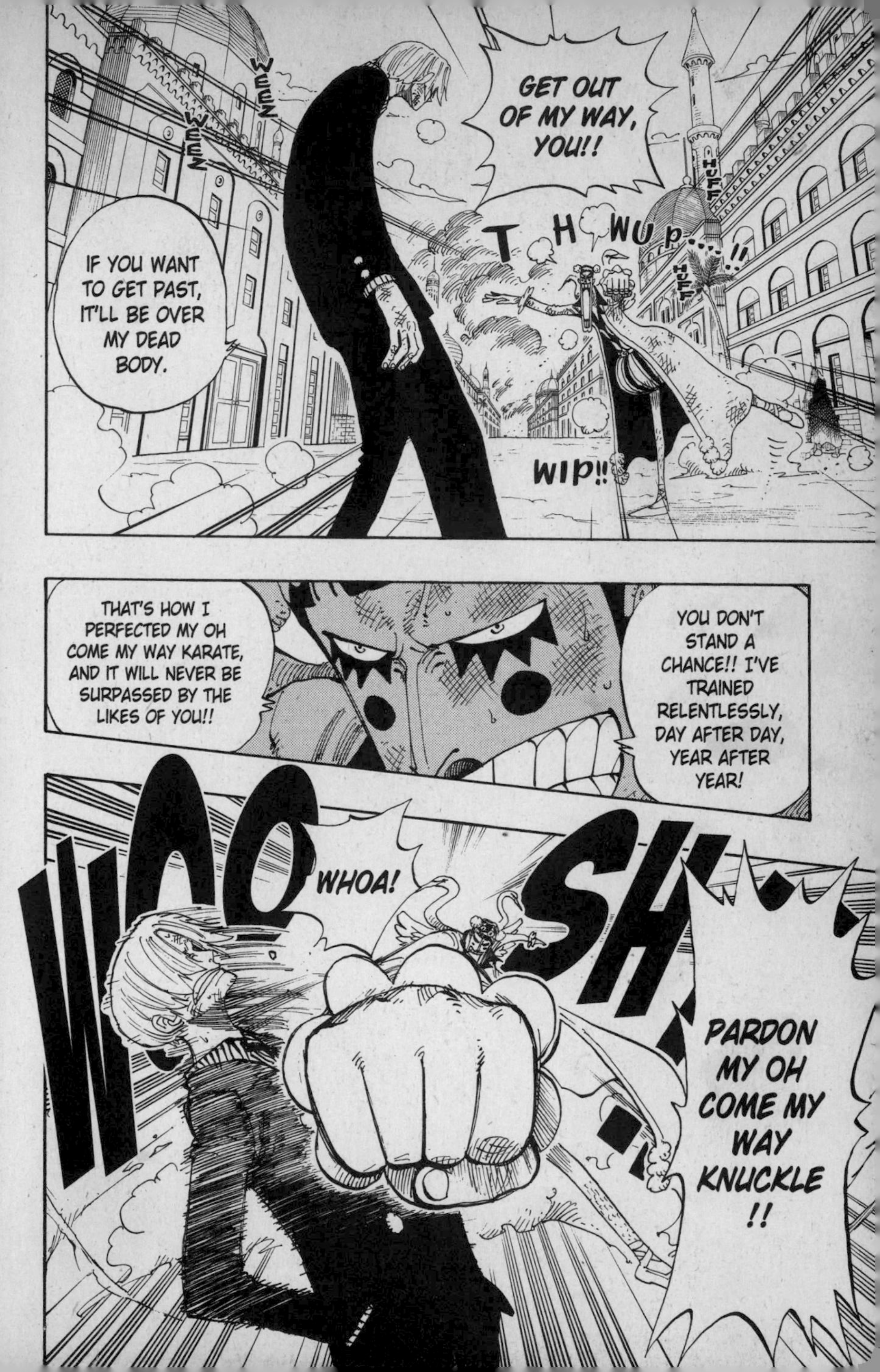
HUFF
HUFF
GET OUT OF MY WAY, YOU!!
THWUP...!!
WEEZ
WEEZ
IF YOU WANT TO GET PAST, IT'LL BE OVER MY DEAD BODY.
WIP!!
YOU DON'T STAND A CHANCE!! I'VE TRAINED RELENTLESSLY, DAY AFTER DAY, YEAR AFTER YEAR!
THAT'S HOW I PERFECTED MY OH COME MY WAY KARATE, AND IT WILL NEVER BE SURPASSED BY THE LIKES OF YOU!!
PARDON MY OH COME MY WAY KNUCKLE!!
WOOSH!!
WHOA!

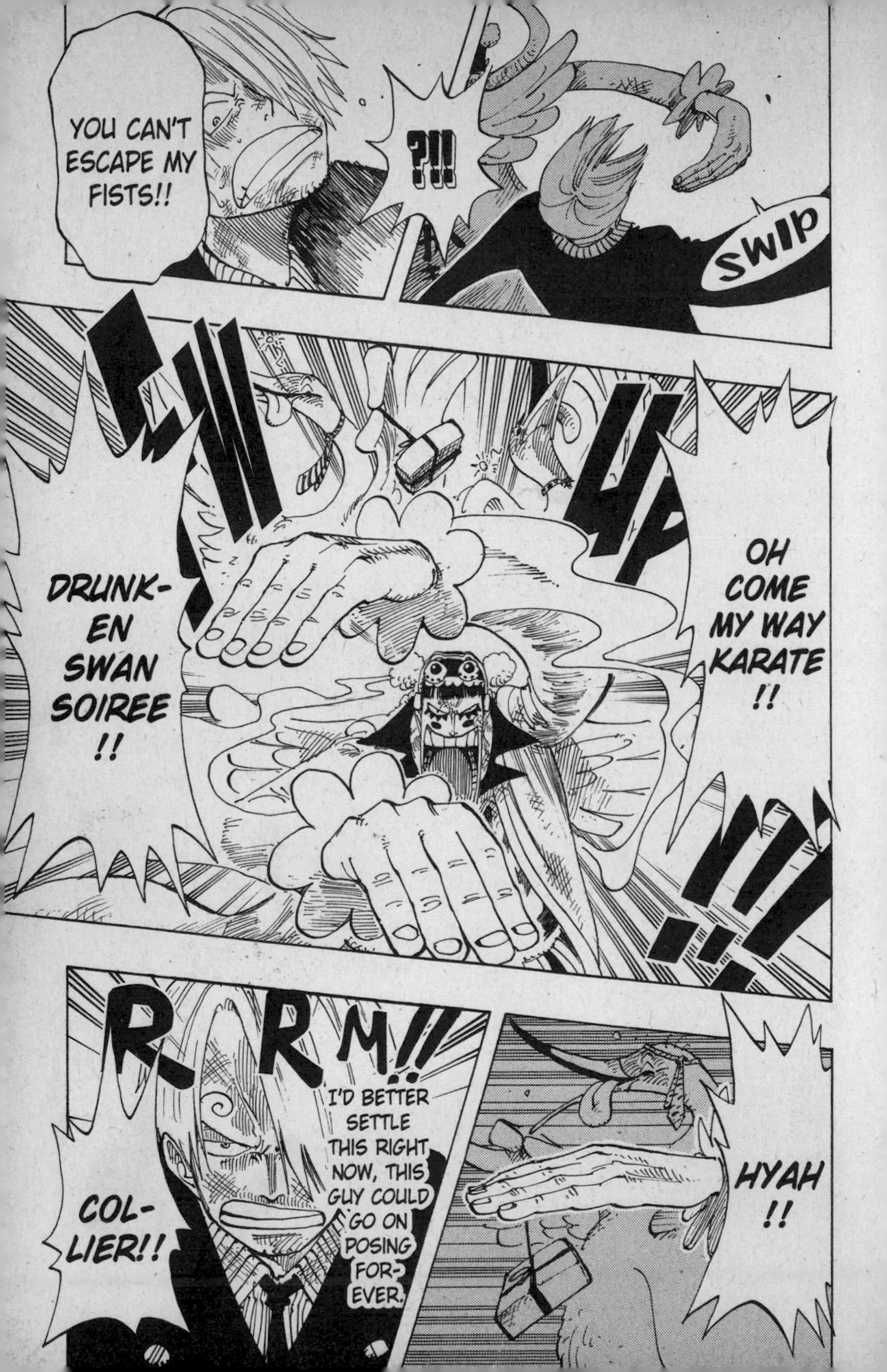
SWIP
?!!
YOU CAN'T ESCAPE MY FISTS!!
OH COME MY WAY KARATE !!
DRUNKEN SWAN SOIREE !!
HYAH !!
R-RM!!
I'D BETTER SETTLE THIS RIGHT NOW, THIS GUY COULD GO ON POSING FOREVER.
COLLIER!!

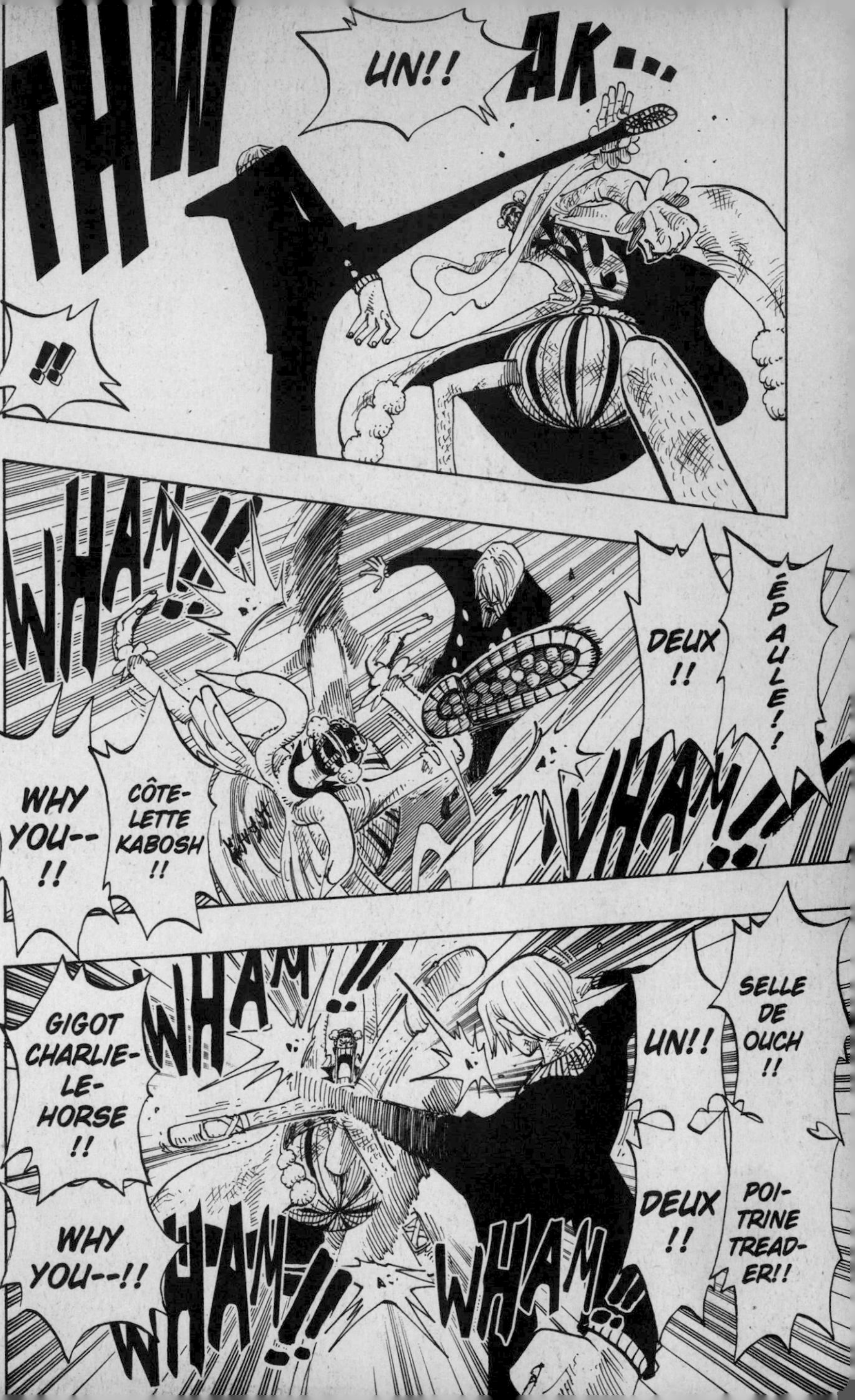

UN!!
THW AK...
!!
ÉPAULE!!
DEUX!!
WHAM!!
WHAM!!
CÔTE-LETTE KABOSH!!
WHY YOU--!!
SELLE DE OUCH!!
UN!!
WHAM!!
GIGOT CHARLIE-LE-HORSE!!
POITRINE TREADER!!
DEUX!!
WHAM!!
WHAM!!
WHY YOU--!!

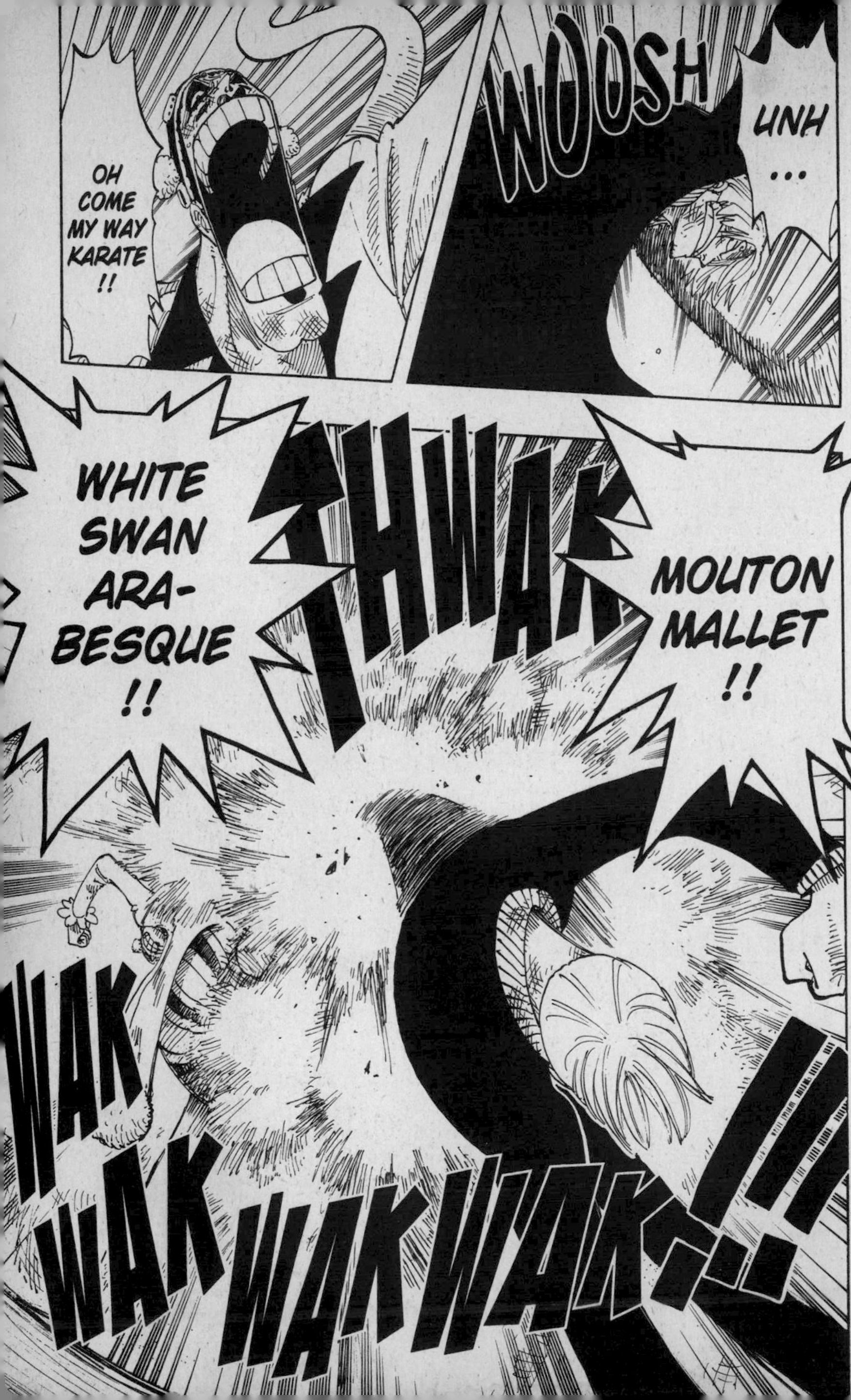
WOOSH
UNH ...
OH COME MY WAY KARATE !!
MOUTON MALLET !!
THWAK
WHITE SWAN ARA-BESQUE !!
WAK WAK WAK WAK...!!!

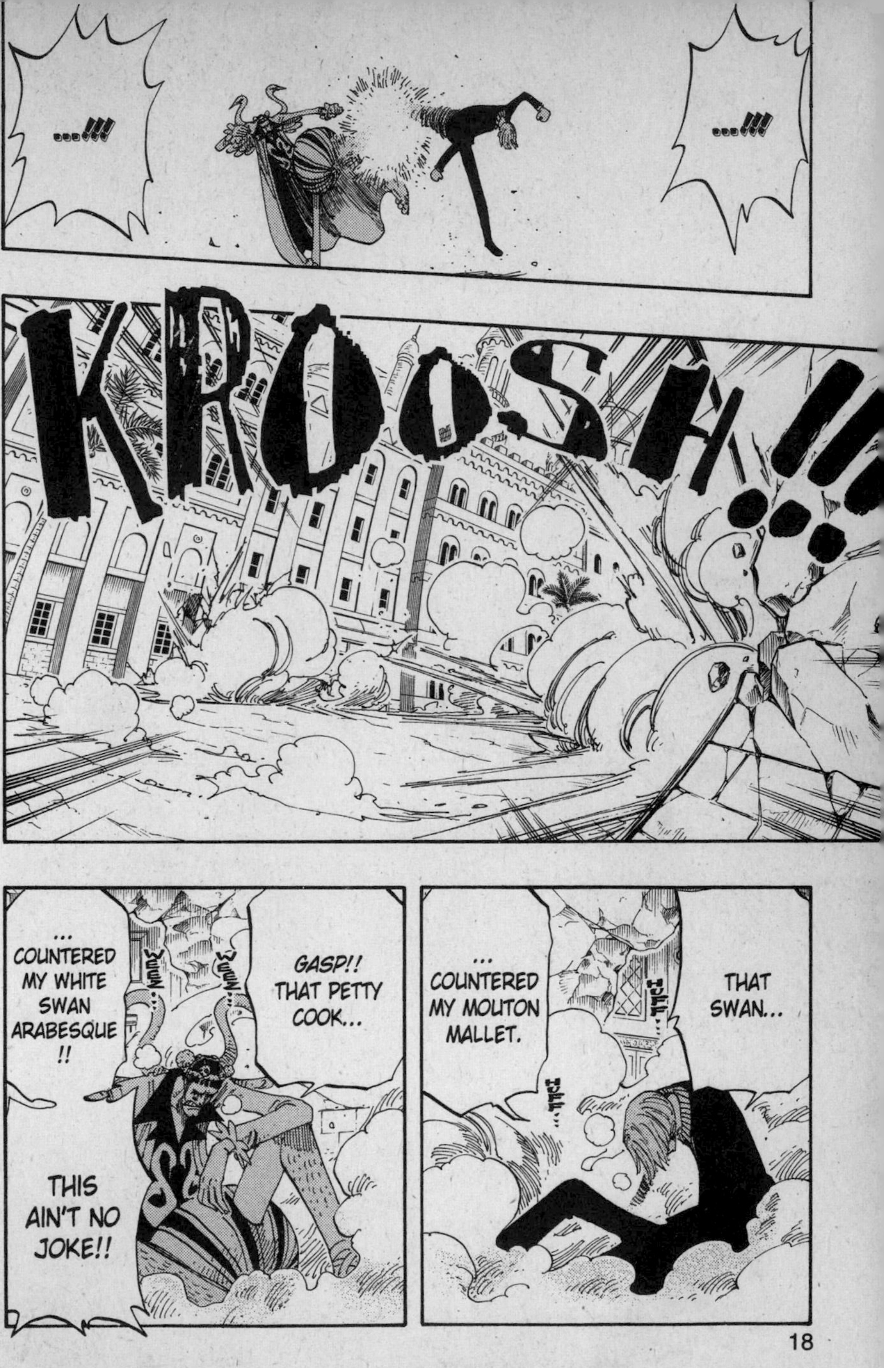

...!!!
...!!!
KROOSH!!!
THAT SWAN...
HUFF...
HUFF...
... COUNTERED MY MOUTON MALLET.
GASP!! THAT PETTY COOK...
WEEZ...
WEEZ...
... COUNTERED MY WHITE SWAN ARABESQUE !!
THIS AIN'T NO JOKE!!

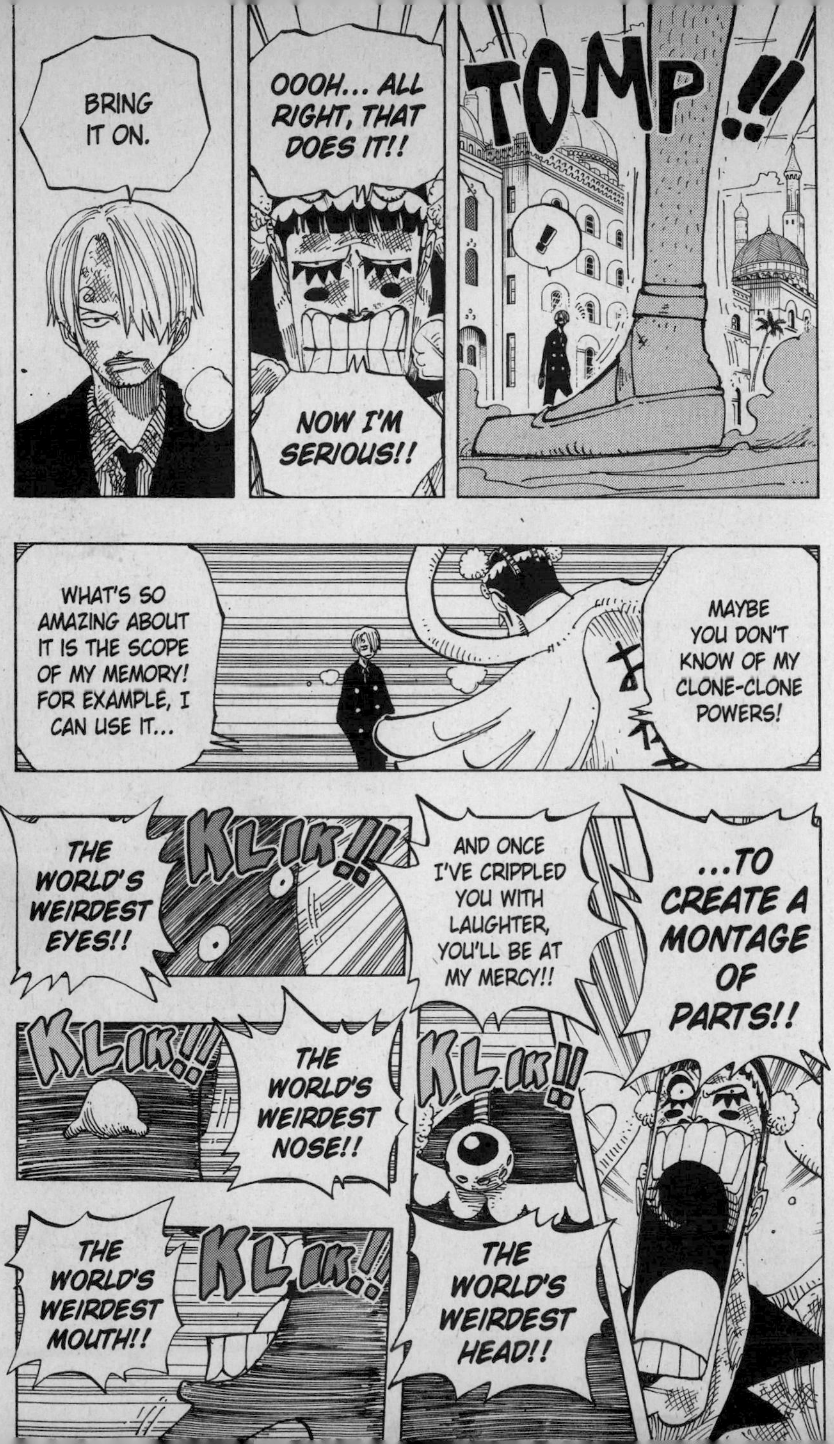
TOMP!!
!
OOOH... ALL RIGHT, THAT DOES IT!!
NOW I'M SERIOUS!!
BRING IT ON.
MAYBE YOU DON'T KNOW OF MY CLONE-CLONE POWERS!
WHAT'S SO AMAZING ABOUT IT IS THE SCOPE OF MY MEMORY! FOR EXAMPLE, I CAN USE IT...
...TO CREATE A MONTAGE OF PARTS!!
AND ONCE I'VE CRIPPLED YOU WITH LAUGHTER, YOU'LL BE AT MY MERCY!!
KLIK!!
THE WORLD'S WEIRDEST EYES!!
KLIK!!
THE WORLD'S WEIRDEST HEAD!!
KLIK!!
THE WORLD'S WEIRDEST NOSE!!
KLIK!!
THE WORLD'S WEIRDEST MOUTH!!

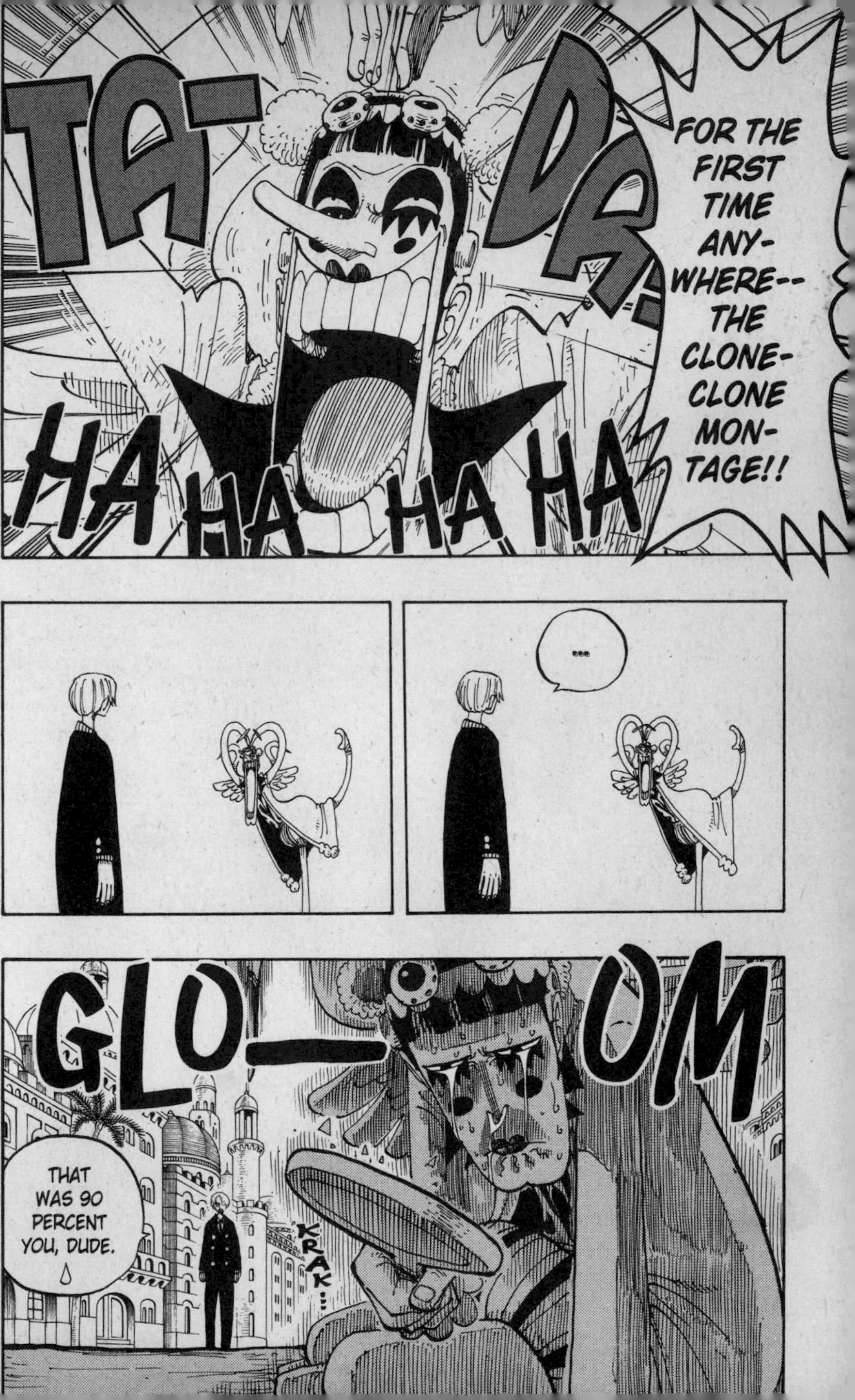
FOR THE FIRST TIME ANY-WHERE-- THE CLONE-CLONE MON-TAGE!!
TA-DA!
HA HA HA HA HA
...
GLO--OM
KRAK...
THAT WAS 90 PERCENT YOU, DUDE.

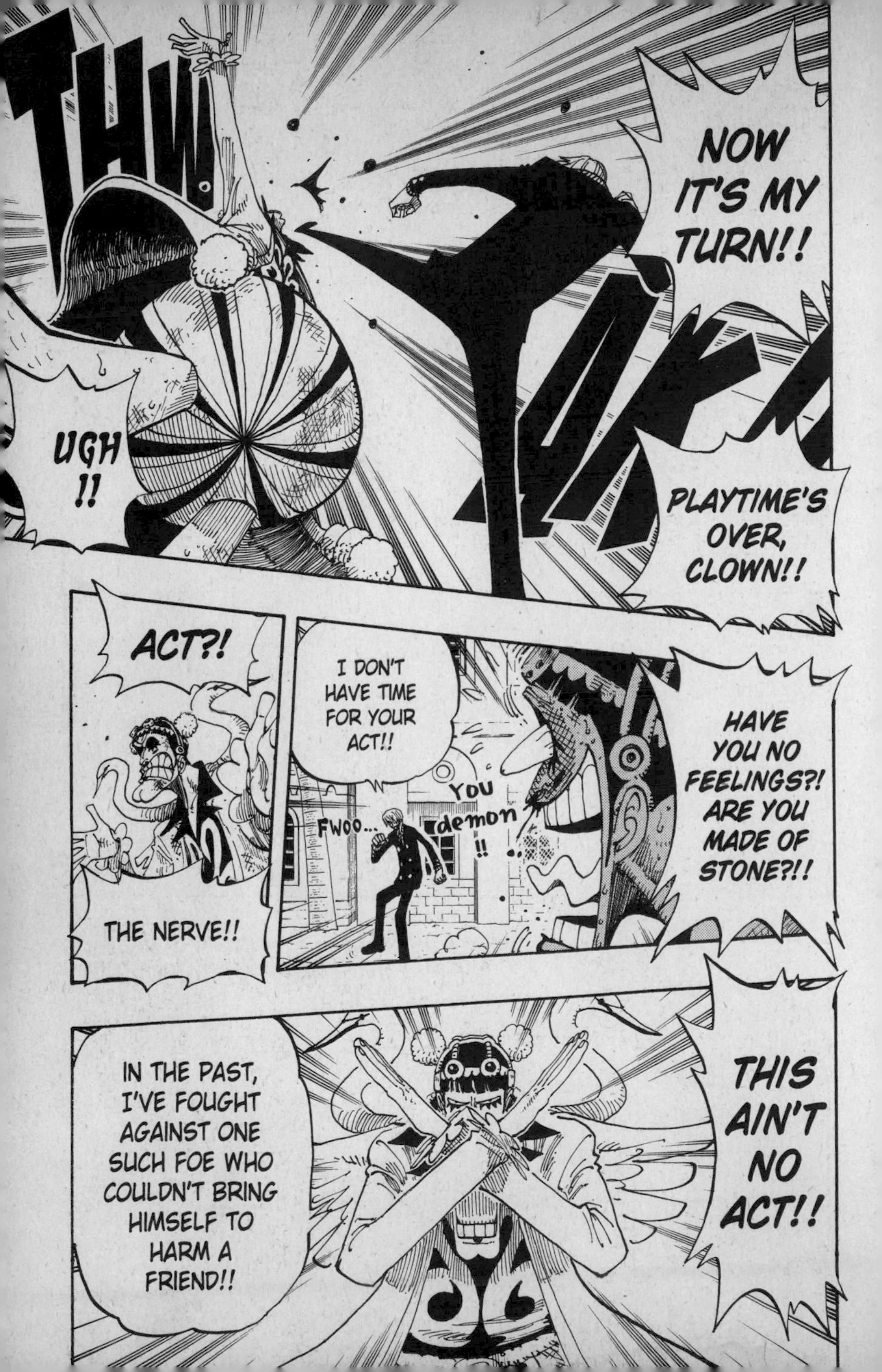
NOW IT'S MY TURN!!
THWAK
PLAYTIME'S OVER, CLOWN!!
UGH !!
HAVE YOU NO FEELINGS?! ARE YOU MADE OF STONE?!!
You demon !!
I DON'T HAVE TIME FOR YOUR ACT!!
FWOO...
ACT?!
THE NERVE!!
THIS AIN'T NO ACT!!
IN THE PAST, I'VE FOUGHT AGAINST ONE SUCH FOE WHO COULDN'T BRING HIMSELF TO HARM A FRIEND!!

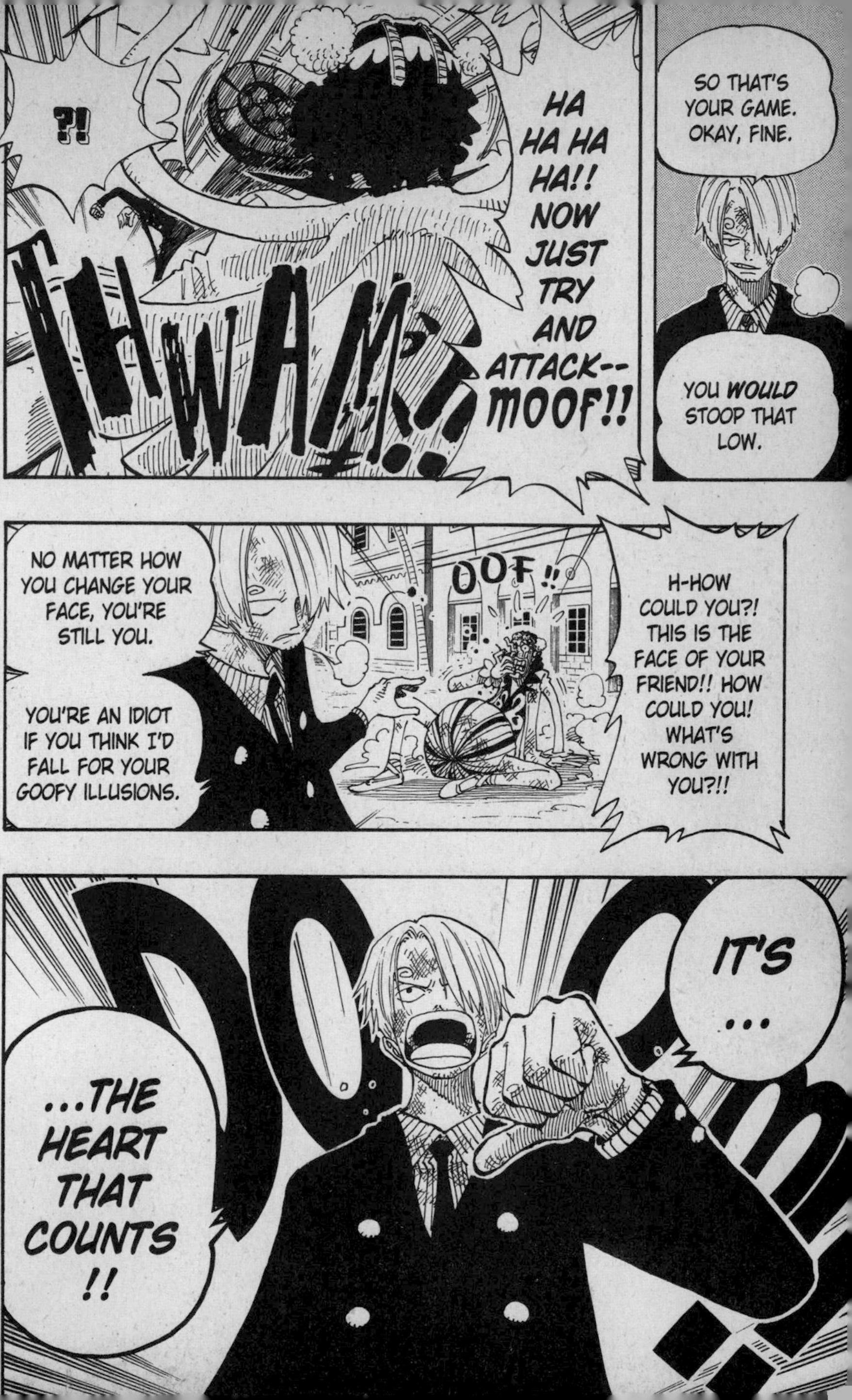
SO THAT'S YOUR GAME. OKAY, FINE.
YOU WOULD STOOP THAT LOW.
HA HA HA HA!! NOW JUST TRY AND ATTACK-- MOOF!!
?!
THWAM!!
H-HOW COULD YOU?! THIS IS THE FACE OF YOUR FRIEND!! HOW COULD YOU! WHAT'S WRONG WITH YOU?!!
OOF!!
NO MATTER HOW YOU CHANGE YOUR FACE, YOU'RE STILL YOU.
YOU'RE AN IDIOT IF YOU THINK I'D FALL FOR YOUR GOOFY ILLUSIONS.
IT'S ...
...THE HEART THAT COUNTS!!

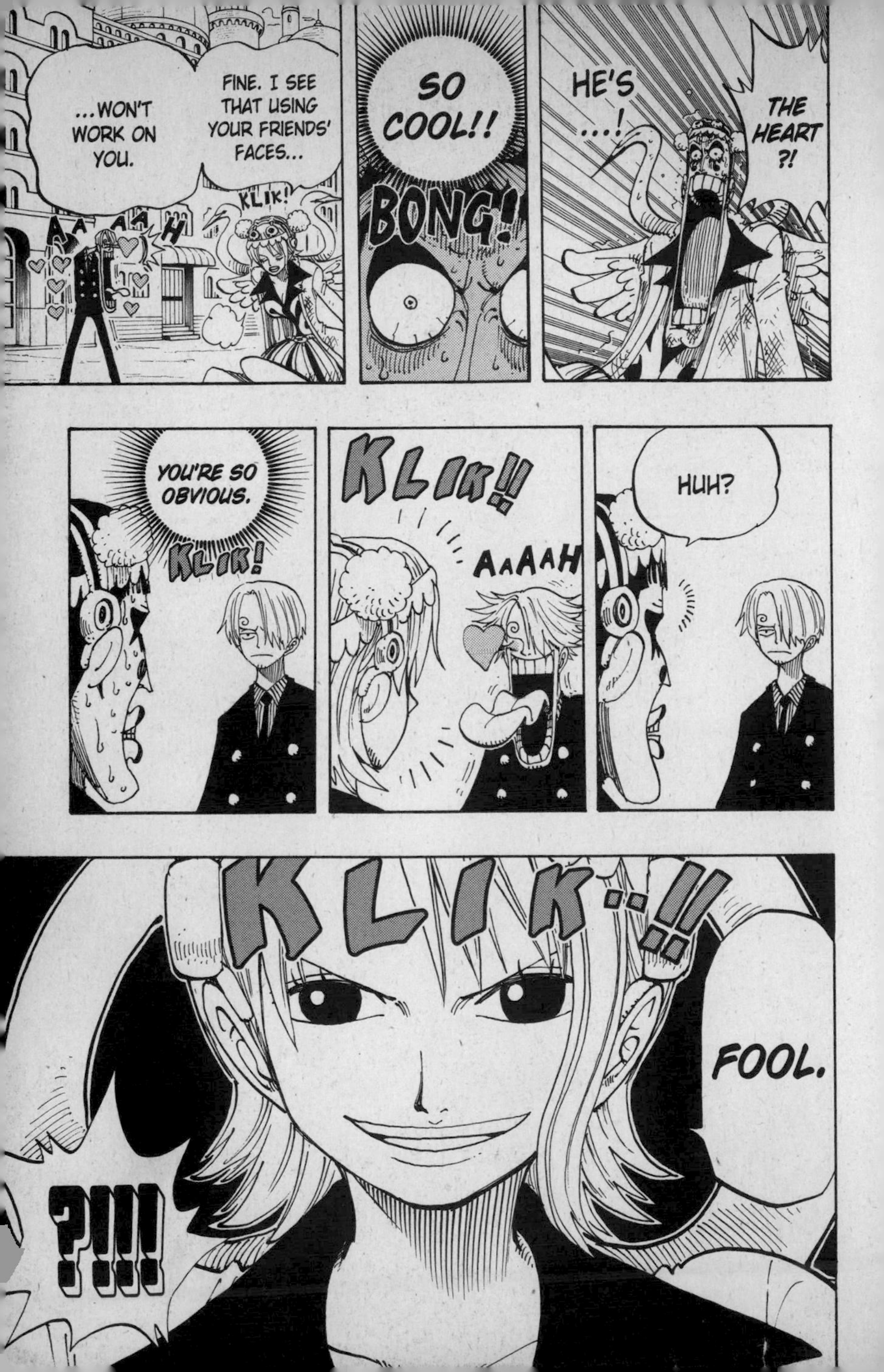
THE HEART ?!
HE'S ...!
SO COOL!!
BONG!!
FINE. I SEE THAT USING YOUR FRIENDS' FACES...
...WON'T WORK ON YOU.
KLIK!
AAAAH
HUH?
KLIK!!
AAAAH
YOU'RE SO OBVIOUS.
KLIK!
KLIK..!!
FOOL.
?!!!

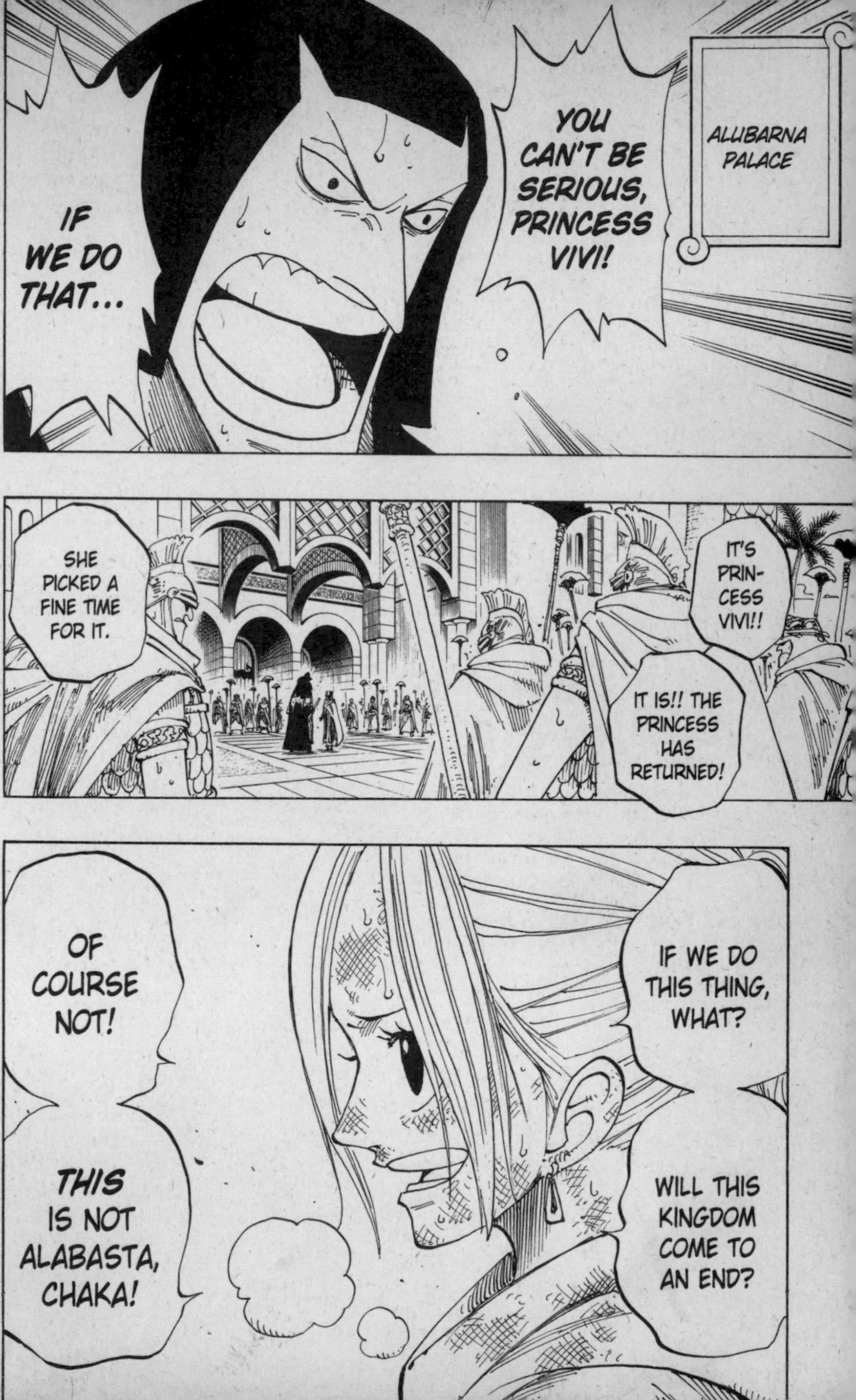
ALUBARNA PALACE
YOU CAN'T BE SERIOUS, PRINCESS VIVI!
IF WE DO THAT...
IT'S PRIN-CESS VIVI!!
IT IS!! THE PRINCESS HAS RETURNED!
SHE PICKED A FINE TIME FOR IT.
IF WE DO THIS THING, WHAT?
WILL THIS KINGDOM COME TO AN END?
OF COURSE NOT!
THIS IS NOT ALABASTA, CHAKA!

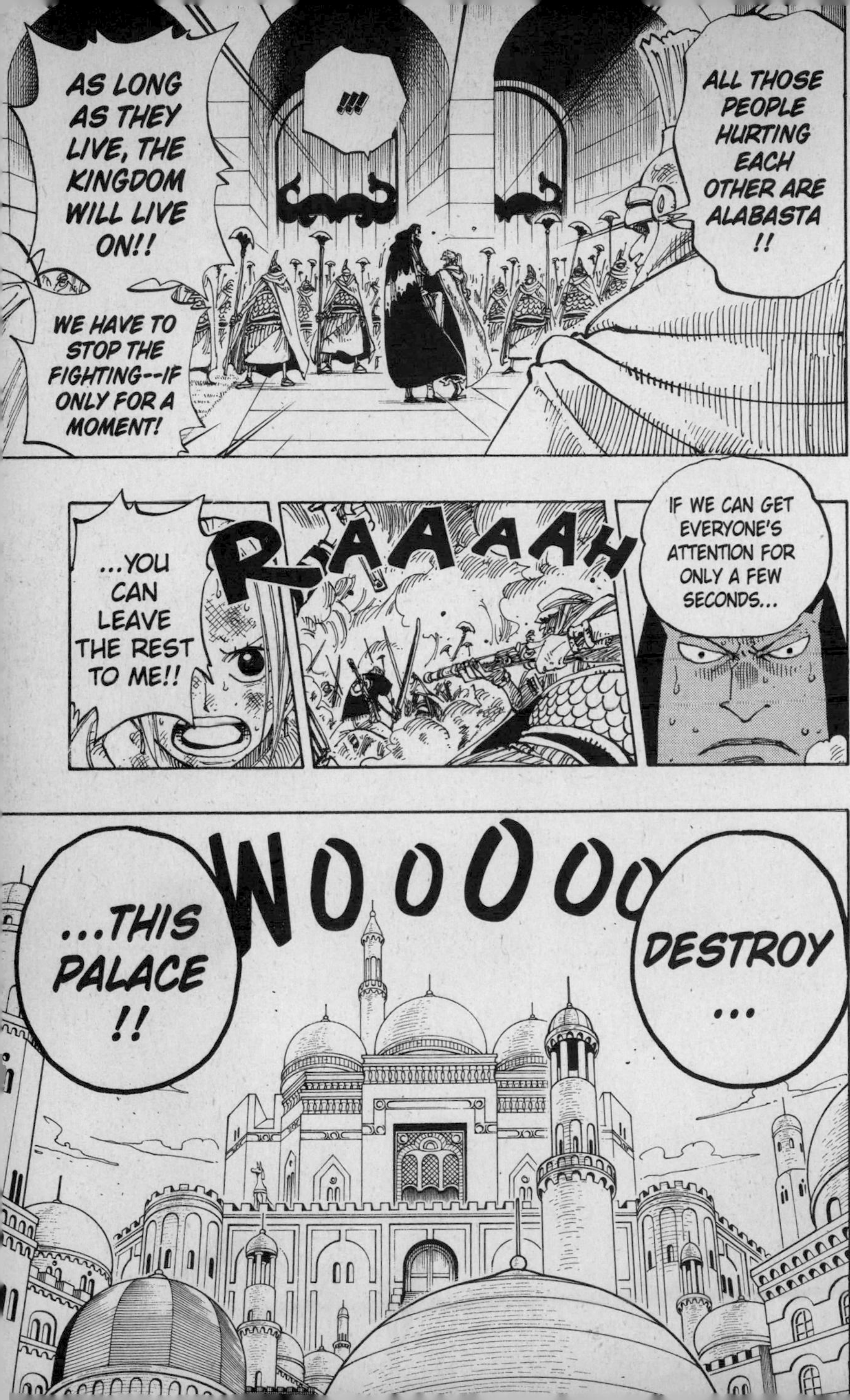
ALL THOSE PEOPLE HURTING EACH OTHER ARE ALABASTA !!
!!!
AS LONG AS THEY LIVE, THE KINGDOM WILL LIVE ON!!
WE HAVE TO STOP THE FIGHTING--IF ONLY FOR A MOMENT!
IF WE CAN GET EVERYONE'S ATTENTION FOR ONLY A FEW SECONDS...
RAAAAH
...YOU CAN LEAVE THE REST TO ME!!
DESTROY ...
WOOOOO
...THIS PALACE !!

Reader: Hello. In Volume 19, someone began the Question Corner in the style of Ms. Merry Christmas. So why not do it in the style of Mr. 4?
--Vice-President of the Black Transponder Snail Fan Club.

S.............(To be continued in the next volume.)

Oda: I can't allow it. It would take too long.

Q: Hello, I've been wondering about something lately. You always begin the Question Corner with "Let's begin the Question Corner," right? Well, that's sooo boring, so I came up with this! "S!" How's that? ♪ It's a takeoff on the popular greeting, "Oha!" ♪ Let's say that from now on!

A: Hey, hey! We can't do that! That's a total rip-off. Show a little more originality, okay, people? "S!" (broad smile)

Q: In a Question Corner in Volume 19, someone requested that you draw the six main characters with your left hand, but you only drew Luffy, Zolo and Nami! Can you please draw the other three?

A: H-Here you go. Now gimme a break.

Chapter 188:

OH COME MY WAY KARATE

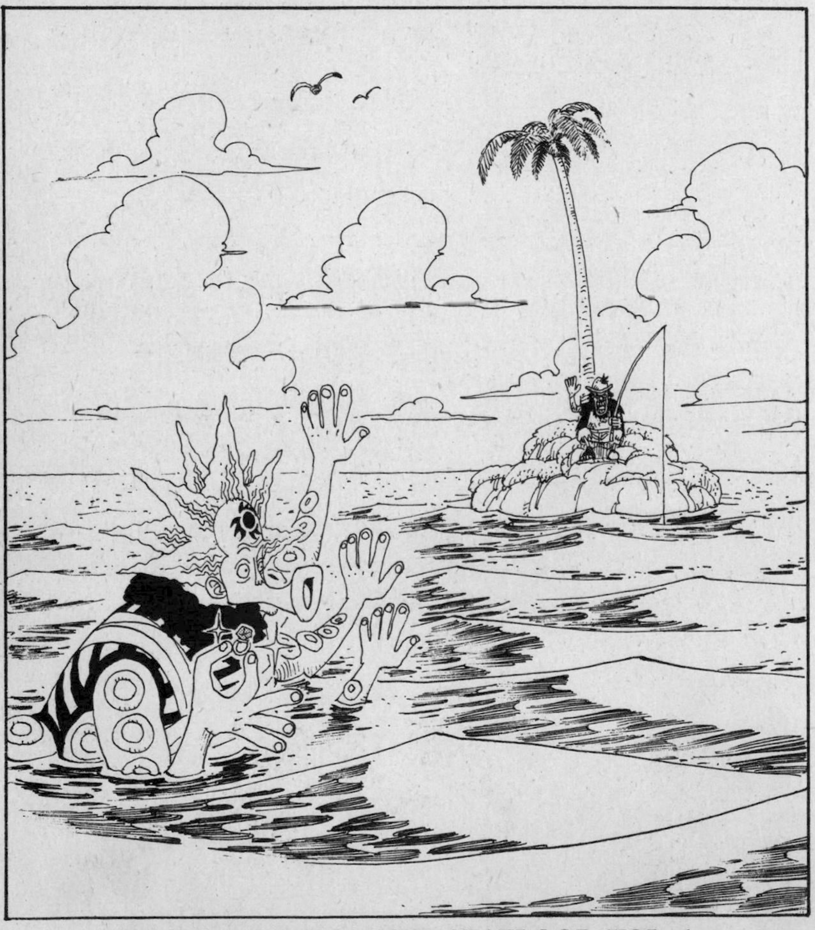

HACHI'S WALK ON THE SEAFLOOR, VOL. 6:
"HACHI RECEIVES A RING IN GRATITUDE"

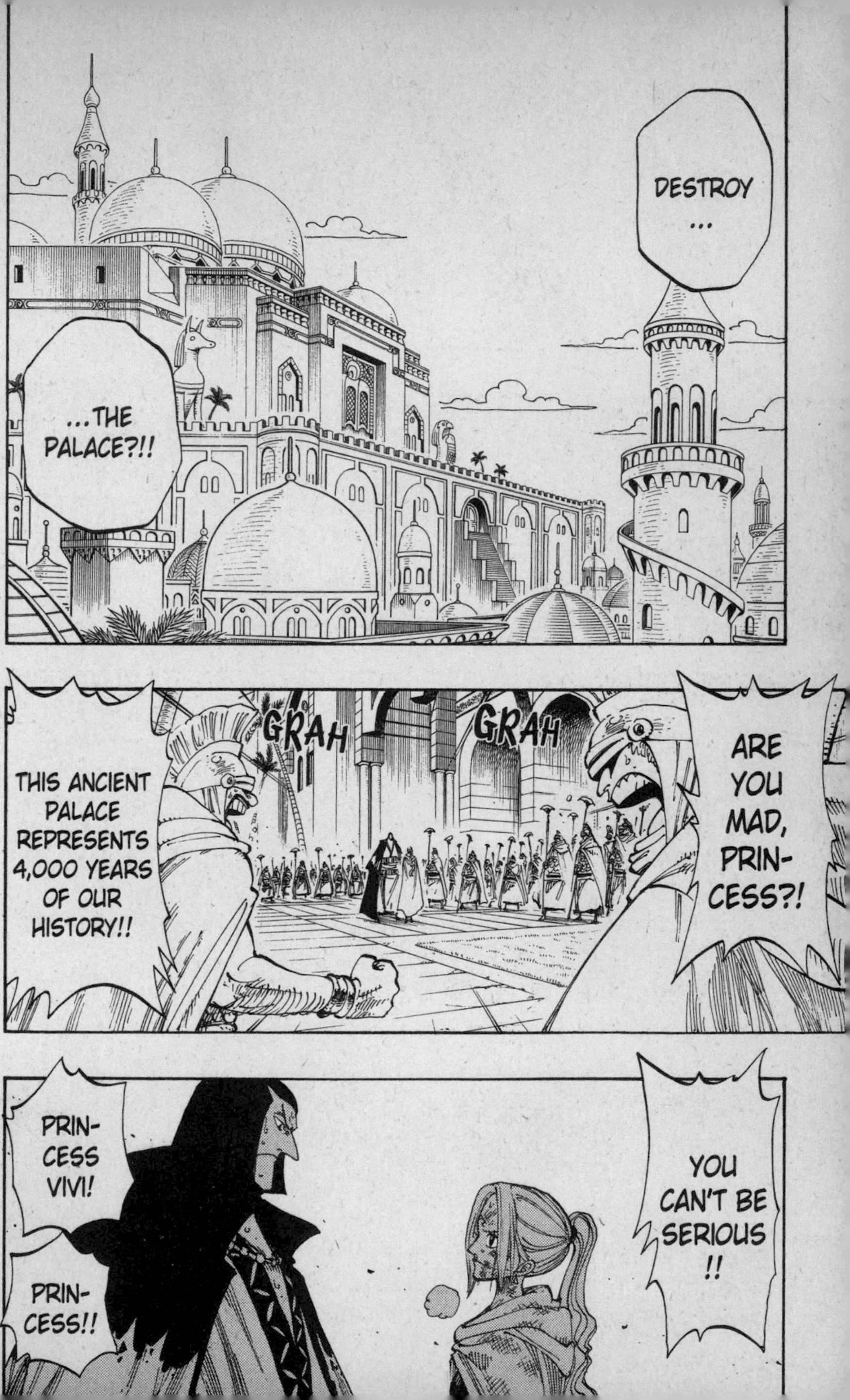
DESTROY ...
...THE PALACE?!!
ARE YOU MAD, PRINCESS?!
GRAH
GRAH
THIS ANCIENT PALACE REPRESENTS 4,000 YEARS OF OUR HISTORY!!
YOU CAN'T BE SERIOUS!!
PRINCESS VIVI!
PRINCESS!!

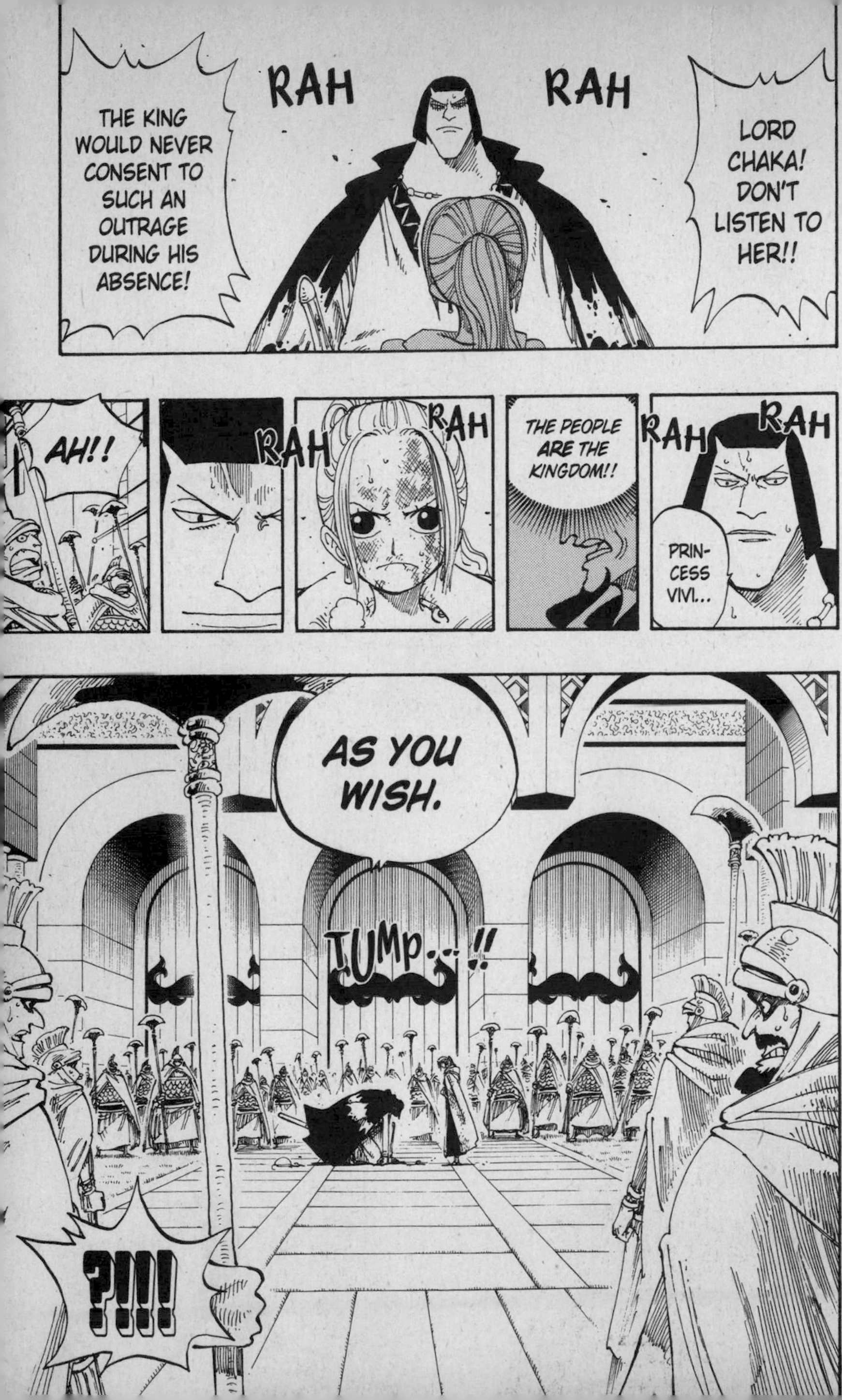
LORD CHAKA! DON'T LISTEN TO HER!!
RAH
RAH
THE KING WOULD NEVER CONSENT TO SUCH AN OUTRAGE DURING HIS ABSENCE!
RAH
RAH
PRIN-CESS VIVI...
RAH
THE PEOPLE ARE THE KINGDOM!!
RAH
RAH
AH!!
AS YOU WISH.
TUMP...!!
?!!!

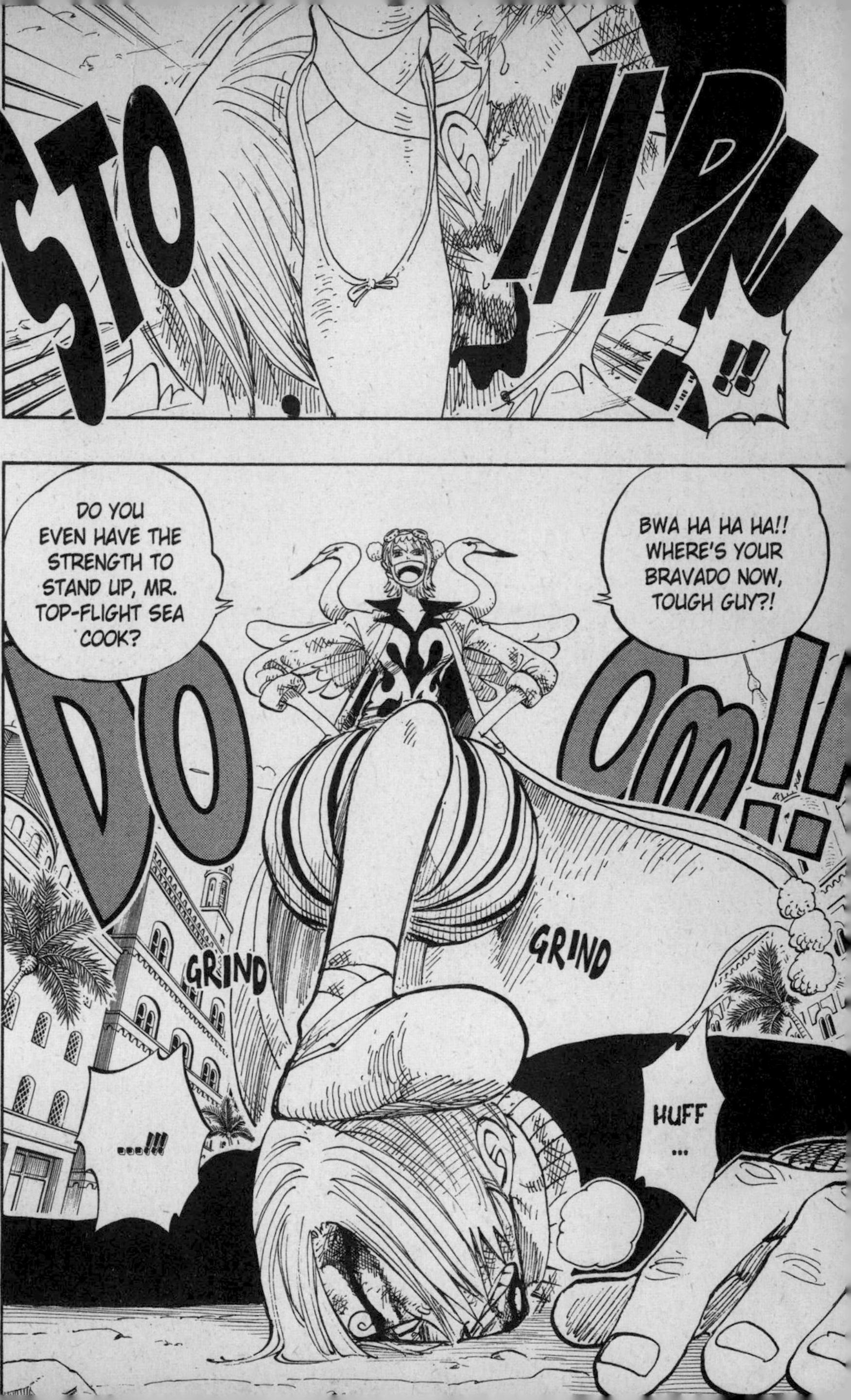
STOMP..!!
BWA HA HA HA!! WHERE'S YOUR BRAVADO NOW, TOUGH GUY?!
DO YOU EVEN HAVE THE STRENGTH TO STAND UP, MR. TOP-FLIGHT SEA COOK?
DOOM!!
GRIND
GRIND
HUFF ...
...!!!

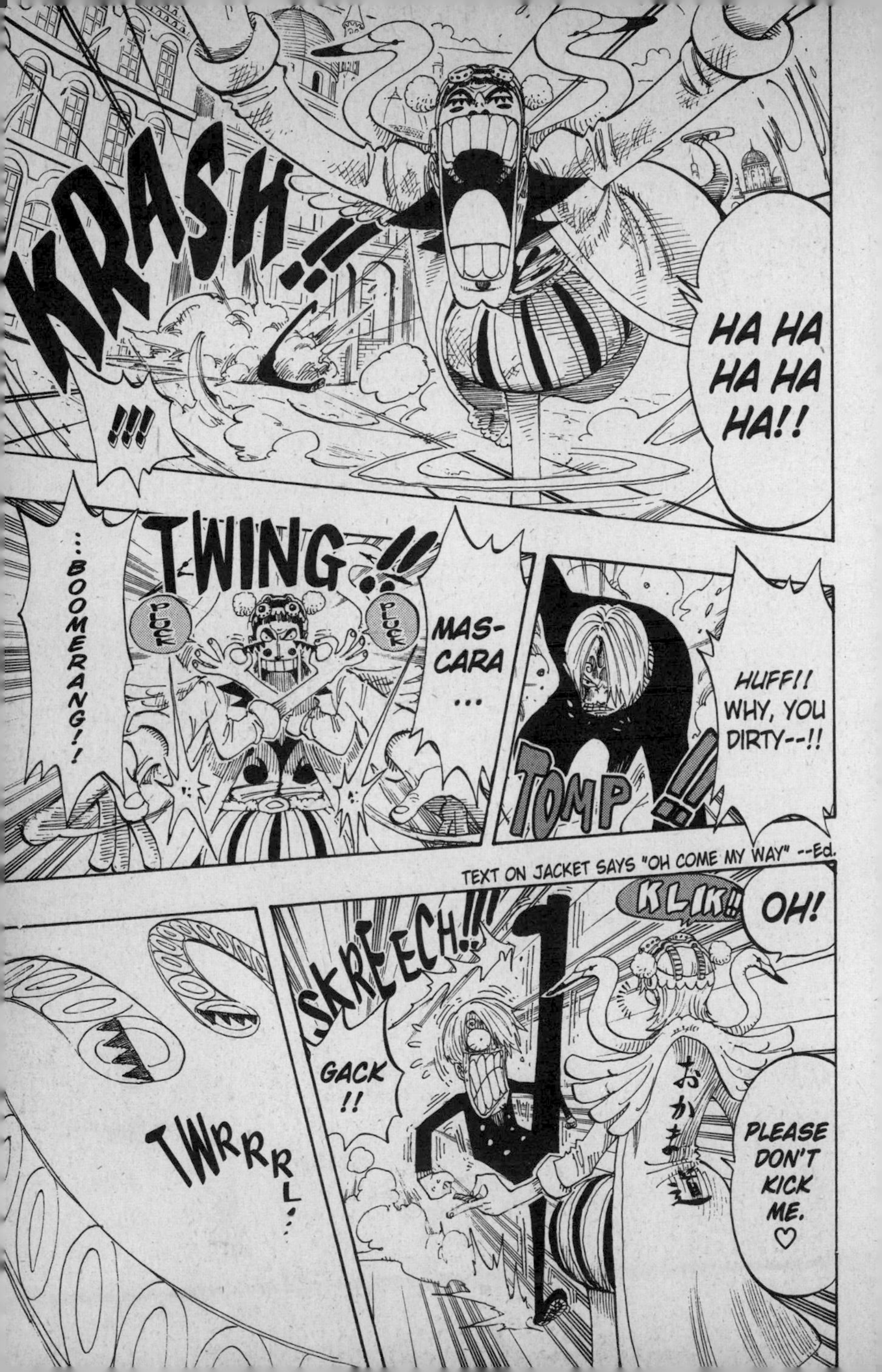
HA HA HA HA HA!!
KRASH!!
!!!
HUFF!! WHY, YOU DIRTY--!!
TOMP!!
MAS-CARA...
TWING!!
PLUCK
PLUCK
...BOOMERANG!!
TEXT ON JACKET SAYS "OH COME MY WAY" --Ed.
OH!
KLIK!!
SKREECH!!
おかま道
PLEASE DON'T KICK ME. ♡
GACK!!
TWRRRL

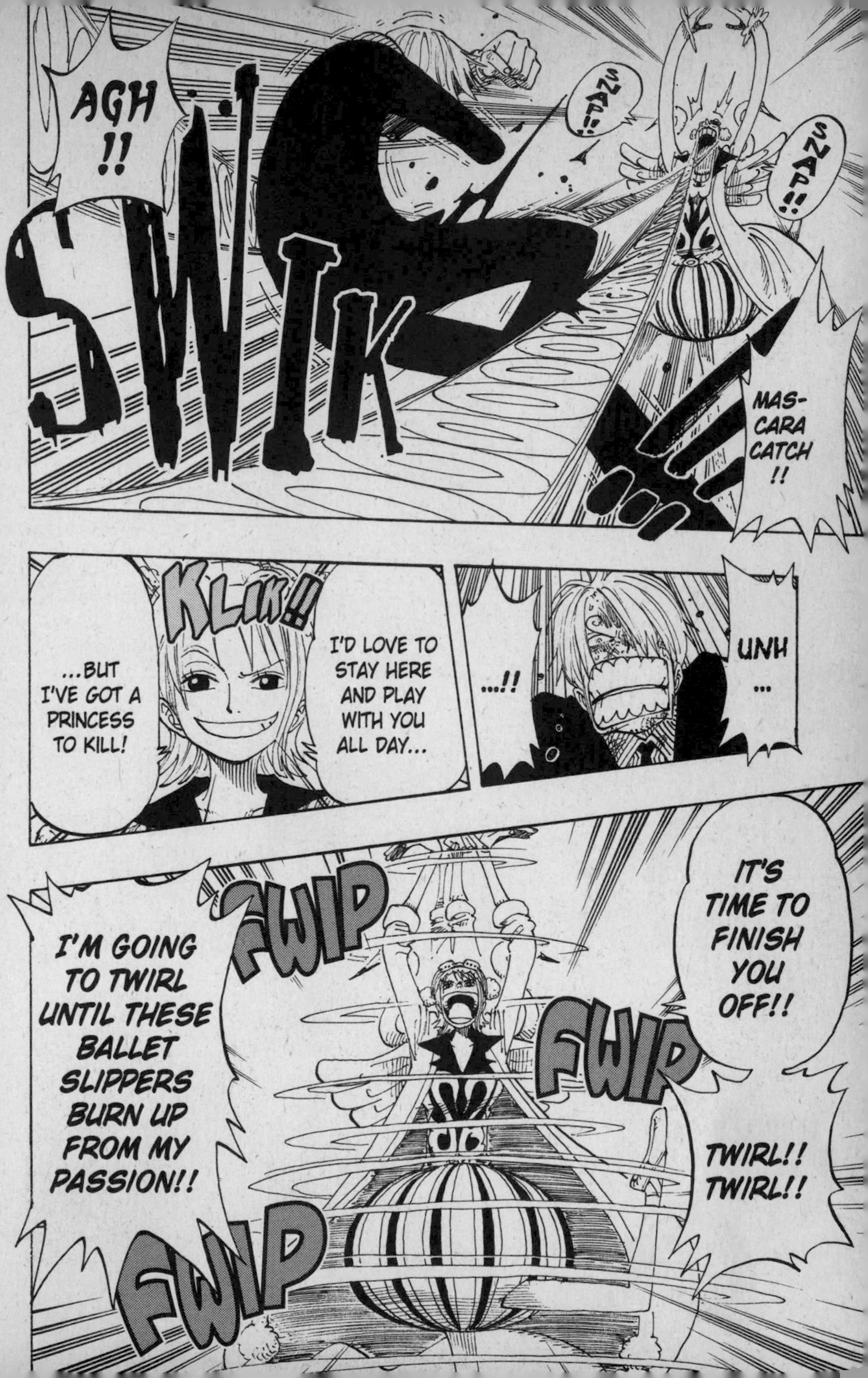
SNAP!!
SNAP!!
MAS-CARA CATCH!!
AGH!!
SWIK
UNH...
...!!
I'D LOVE TO STAY HERE AND PLAY WITH YOU ALL DAY...
KLIK!!
...BUT I'VE GOT A PRINCESS TO KILL!
IT'S TIME TO FINISH YOU OFF!!
FWIP
TWIRL!! TWIRL!!
FWIP
I'M GOING TO TWIRL UNTIL THESE BALLET SLIPPERS BURN UP FROM MY PASSION!!
FWIP

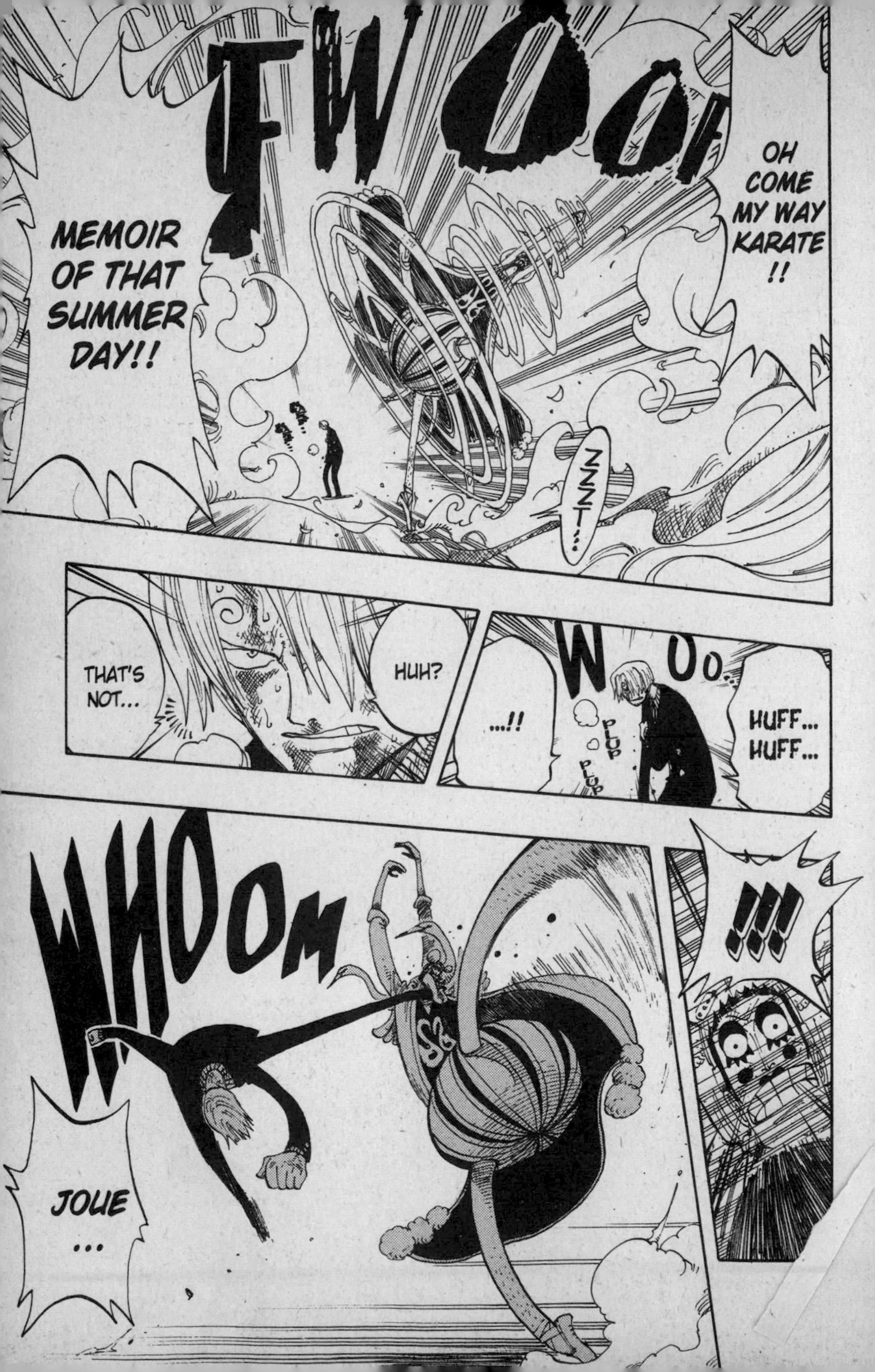

FWOOF
OH COME MY WAY KARATE !!
MEMOIR OF THAT SUMMER DAY!!
ZZZT!!
HUFF... HUFF...
WOO..
PLUP
PLUP
...!!
HUH?
THAT'S NOT...
!!!
WHOOM
JOUE ...

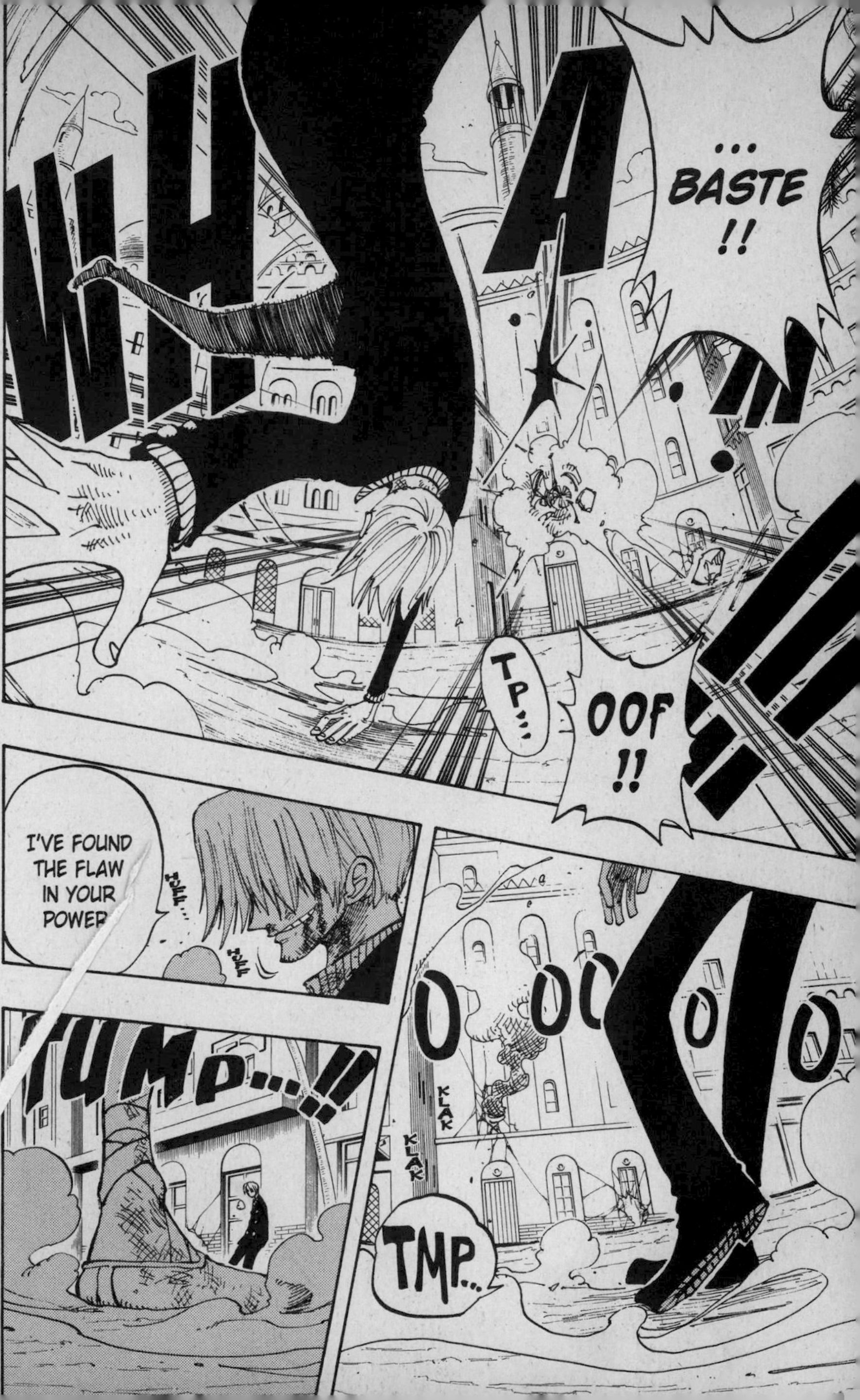

...BASTE !!
WHA
TP...
OOF !!
OOOOO
KLAK
KLAK
TMP...
I'VE FOUND THE FLAW IN YOUR POWER
HUFF...
HUFF
UMP...!!

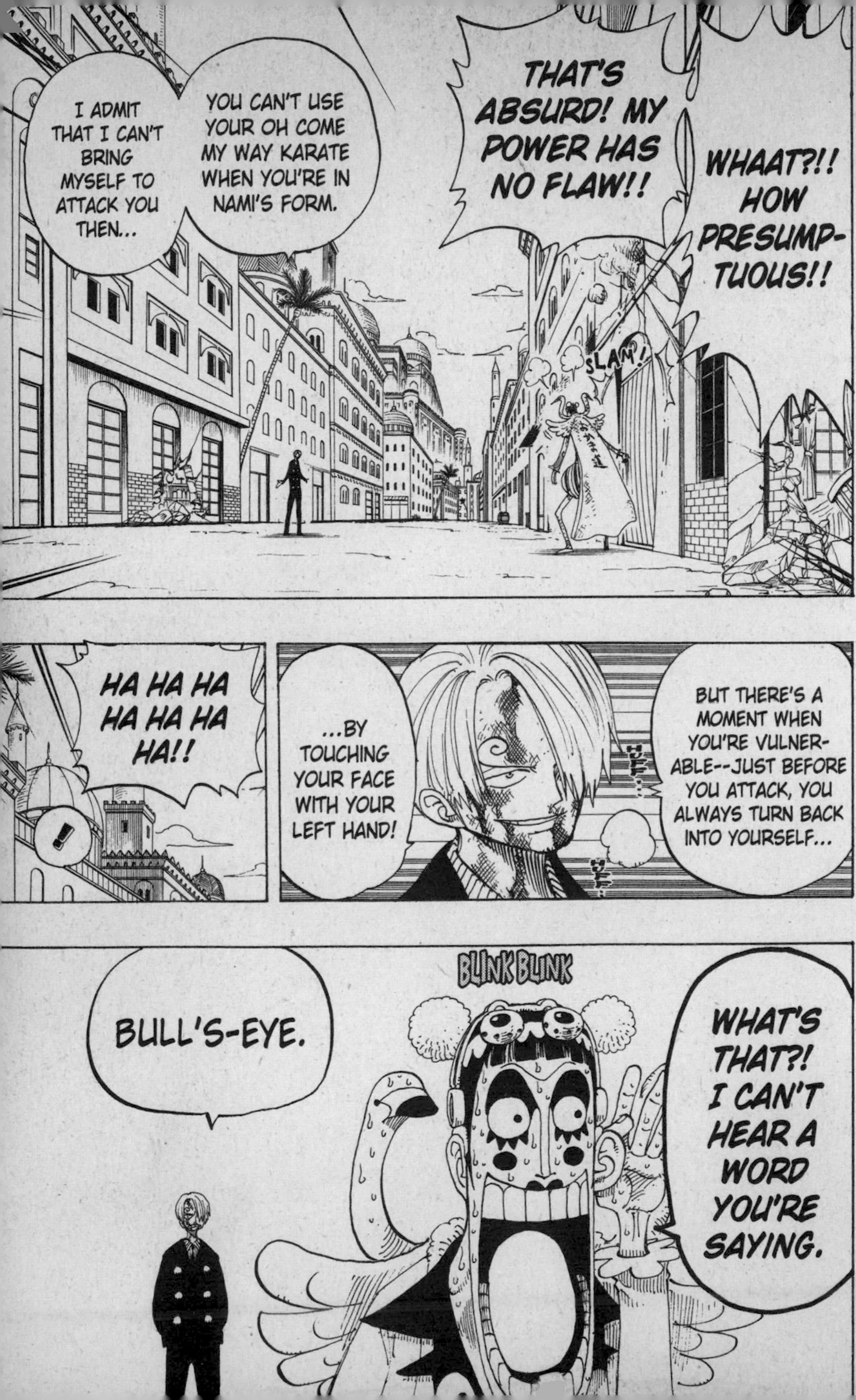
THAT'S ABSURD! MY POWER HAS NO FLAW!!
WHAAT?!! HOW PRESUMP-TUOUS!!
SLAM!
YOU CAN'T USE YOUR OH COME MY WAY KARATE WHEN YOU'RE IN NAMI'S FORM.
I ADMIT THAT I CAN'T BRING MYSELF TO ATTACK YOU THEN...
BUT THERE'S A MOMENT WHEN YOU'RE VULNER-ABLE--JUST BEFORE YOU ATTACK, YOU ALWAYS TURN BACK INTO YOURSELF...
...BY TOUCHING YOUR FACE WITH YOUR LEFT HAND!
HA HA HA HA HA HA HA!!
!
WHAT'S THAT?! I CAN'T HEAR A WORD YOU'RE SAYING.
BLINK BLINK
BULL'S-EYE.

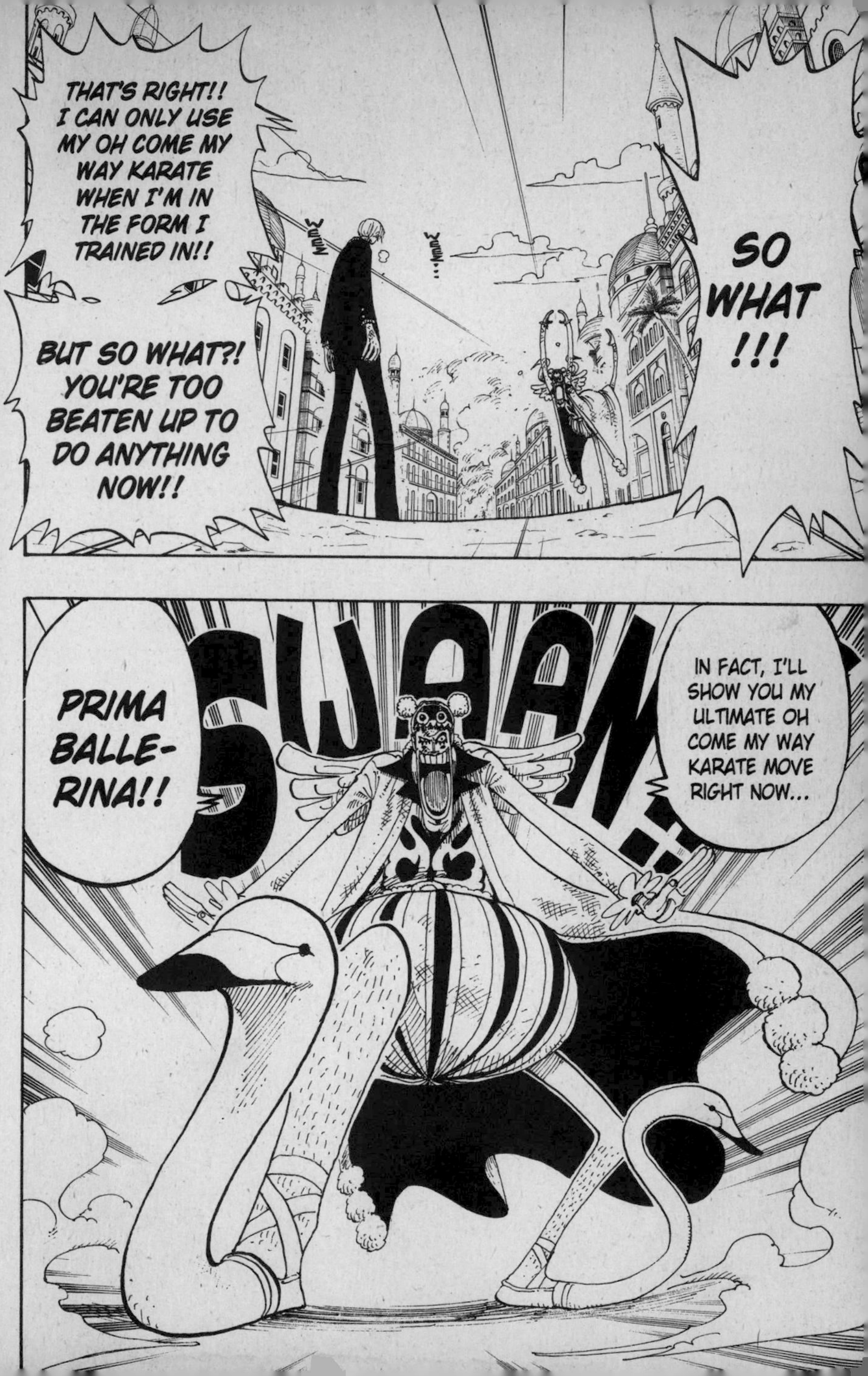
SO WHAT!!!
THAT'S RIGHT!! I CAN ONLY USE MY OH COME MY WAY KARATE WHEN I'M IN THE FORM I TRAINED IN!!
BUT SO WHAT?! YOU'RE TOO BEATEN UP TO DO ANYTHING NOW!!
IN FACT, I'LL SHOW YOU MY ULTIMATE OH COME MY WAY KARATE MOVE RIGHT NOW...
PRIMA BALLE-RINA!!

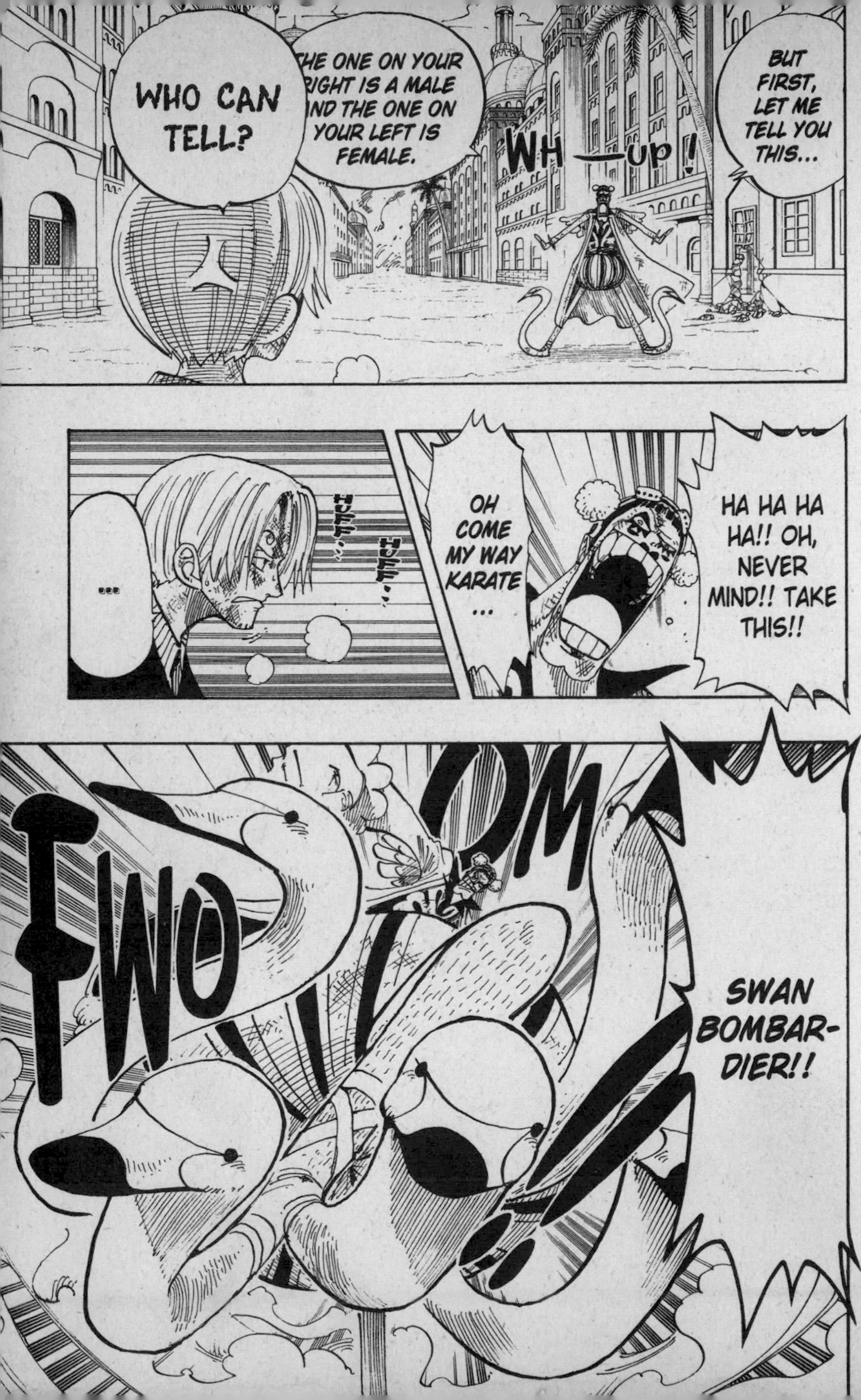
BUT FIRST, LET ME TELL YOU THIS...
WH—up!
THE ONE ON YOUR RIGHT IS A MALE AND THE ONE ON YOUR LEFT IS FEMALE.
WHO CAN TELL?
HA HA HA HA!! OH, NEVER MIND!! TAKE THIS!!
OH COME MY WAY KARATE ...
HUFF... HUFF...
...
SWAN BOMBARDIER!!
FWOOM

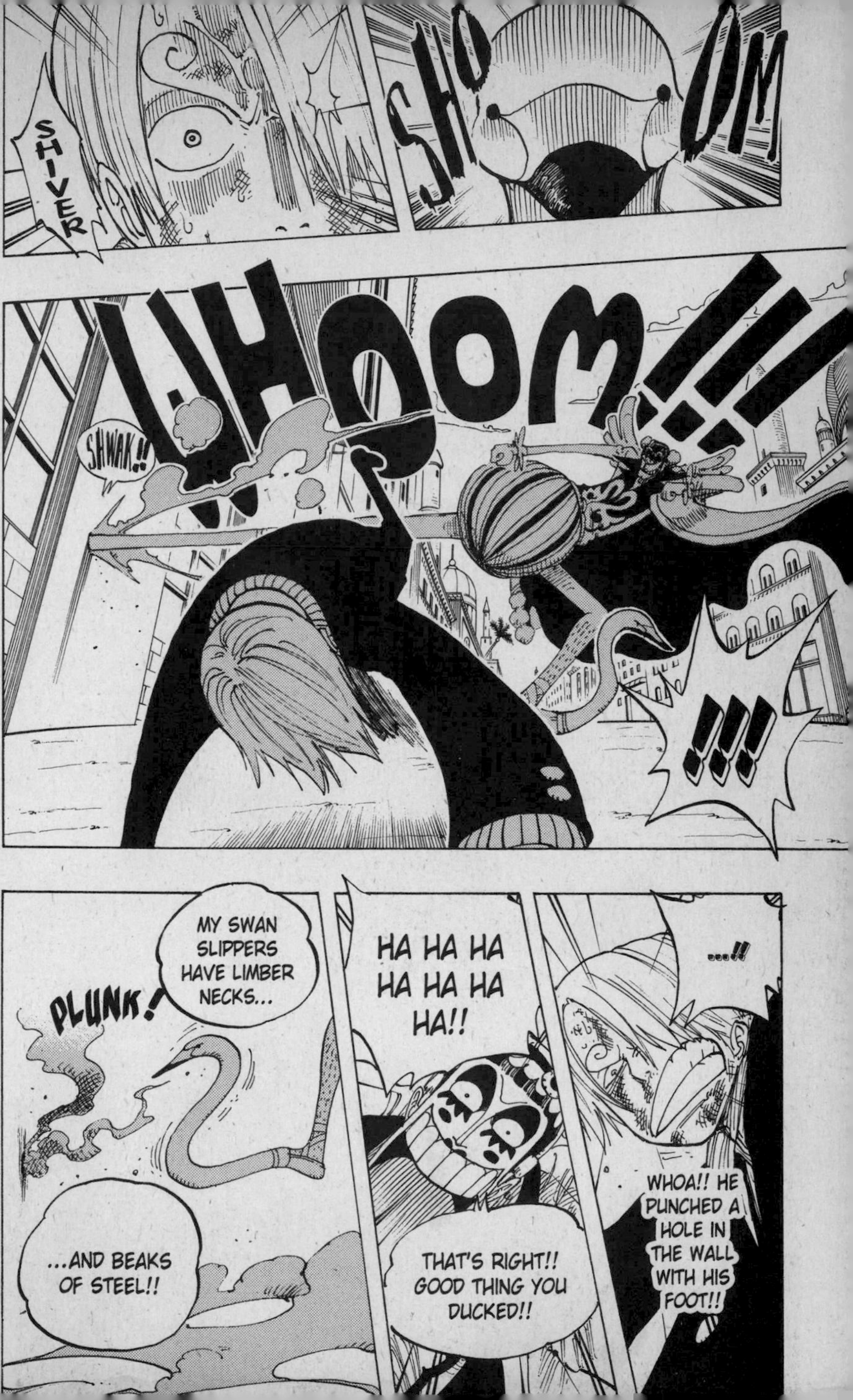
SHOOM
SHIVER
WHOOM!!!
!!!
SHWAK!!
...!!
WHOA!! HE PUNCHED A HOLE IN THE WALL WITH HIS FOOT!!
HA HA HA HA HA HA HA!!
THAT'S RIGHT!! GOOD THING YOU DUCKED!!
MY SWAN SLIPPERS HAVE LIMBER NECKS...
PLUNK!
...AND BEAKS OF STEEL!!

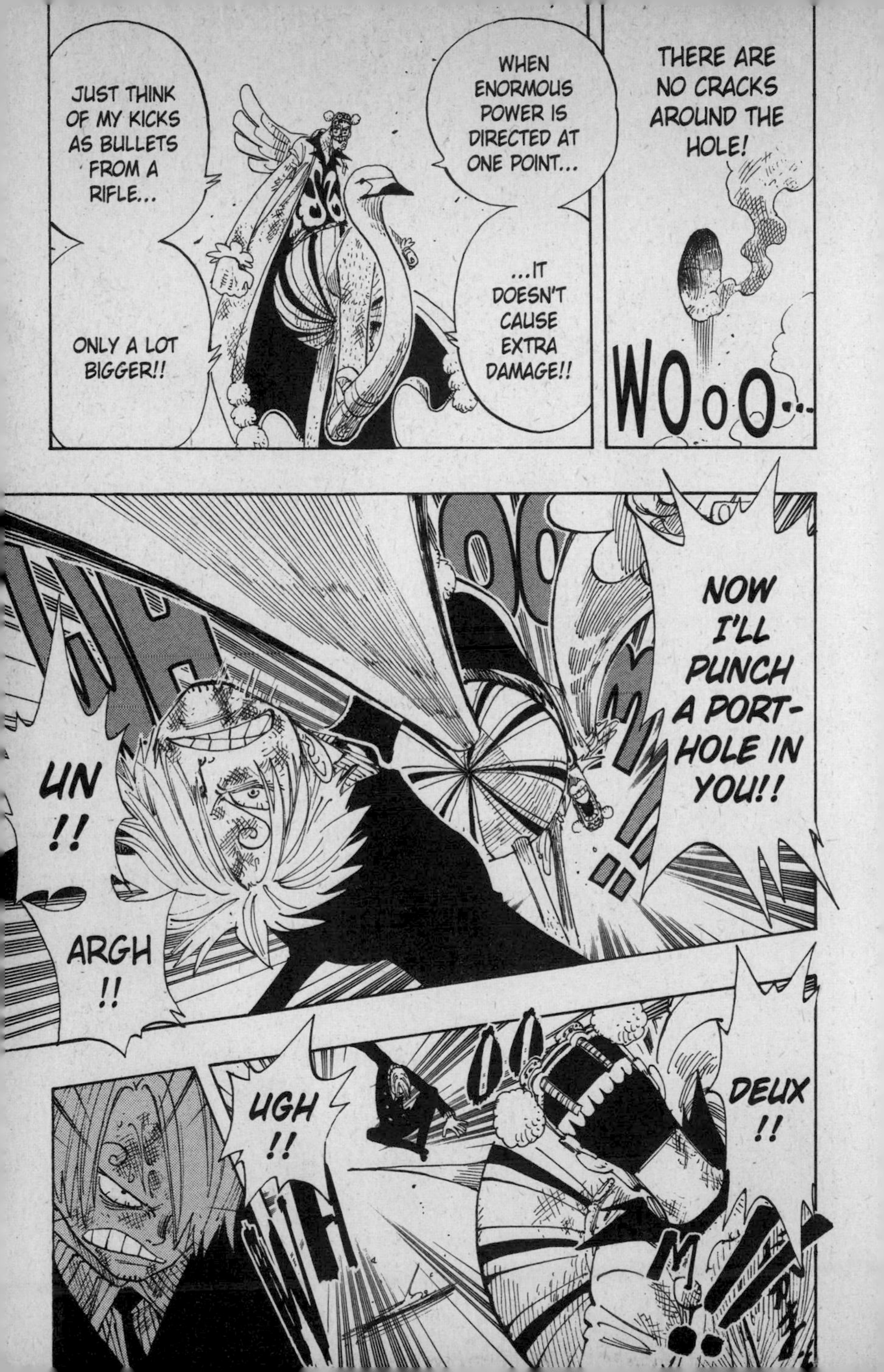
THERE ARE NO CRACKS AROUND THE HOLE!
WOoO...
WHEN ENORMOUS POWER IS DIRECTED AT ONE POINT...
...IT DOESN'T CAUSE EXTRA DAMAGE!!
JUST THINK OF MY KICKS AS BULLETS FROM A RIFLE...
ONLY A LOT BIGGER!!
NOW I'LL PUNCH A PORT-HOLE IN YOU!!
UN !!
ARGH !!
DEUX !!
UGH !!

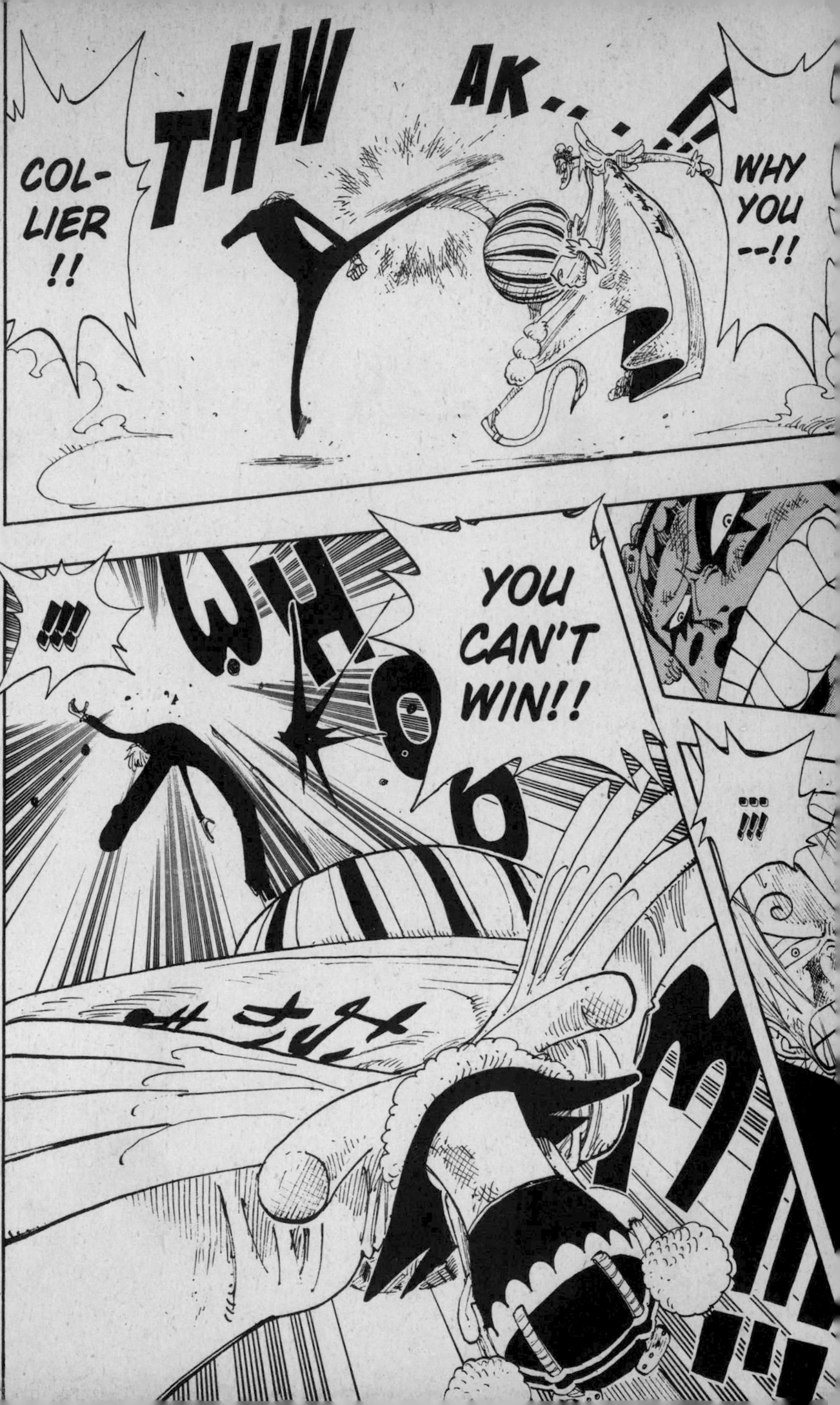
WHY YOU --!!
THWAK...!!
COL-LIER!!
...!!!
YOU CAN'T WIN!!
!!!

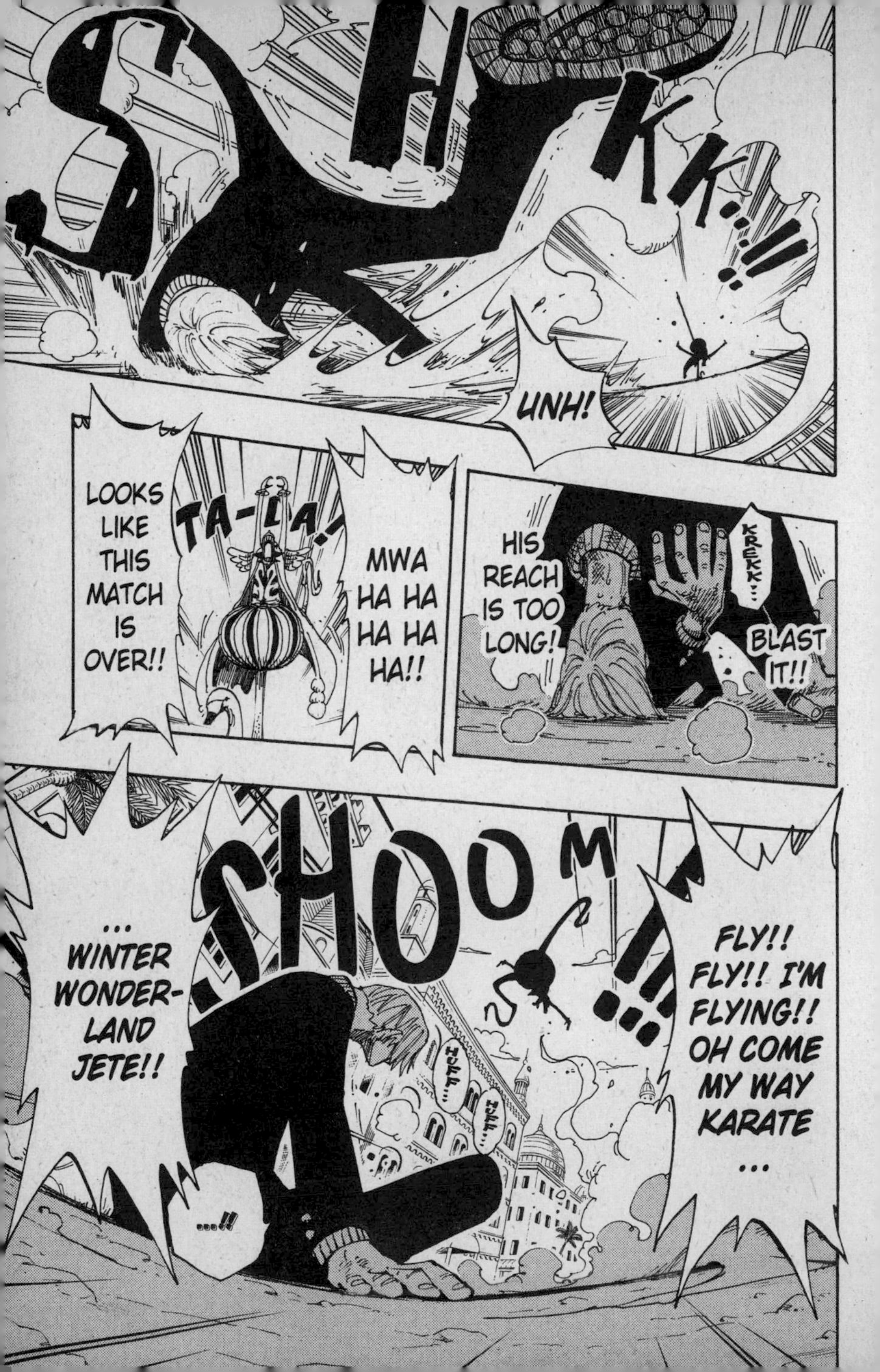
SHKK...!!
UNH!
KREKK...
HIS REACH IS TOO LONG!
BLAST IT!!
MWA HA HA HA HA HA!!
TA-LA!
LOOKS LIKE THIS MATCH IS OVER!!
FLY!! FLY!! I'M FLYING!! OH COME MY WAY KARATE ...
SHOOM...!!
HUFF...
HUFF...
... WINTER WONDER-LAND JETE!!
...!!

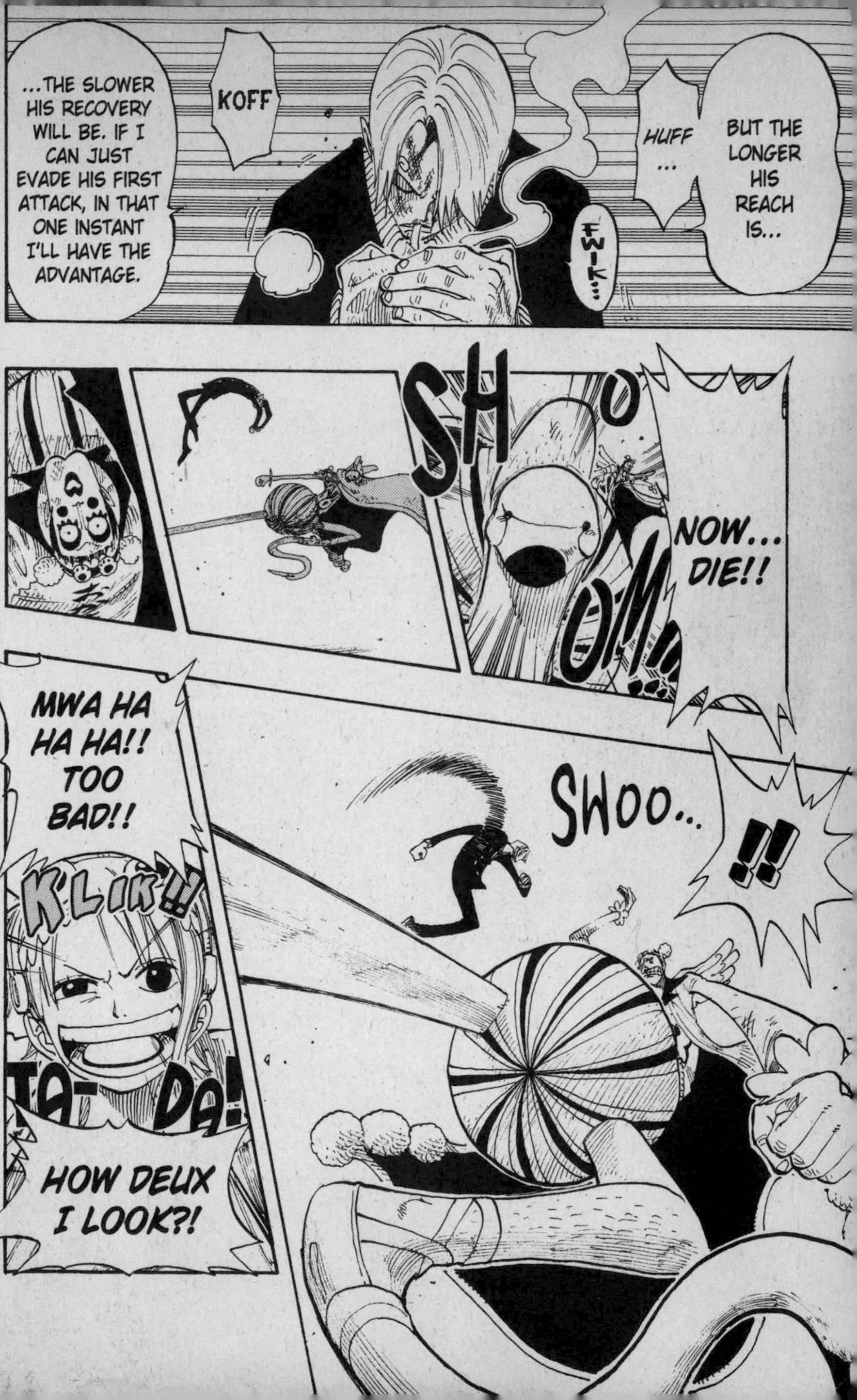
BUT THE LONGER HIS REACH IS...
HUFF ...
FWIK...
KOFF
...THE SLOWER HIS RECOVERY WILL BE. IF I CAN JUST EVADE HIS FIRST ATTACK, IN THAT ONE INSTANT I'LL HAVE THE ADVANTAGE.
SHOOM
NOW... DIE!!
!!
SWOO...
MWA HA HA HA!! TOO BAD!!
K'LIK!!
TA-DA!
HOW DEUX I LOOK?!

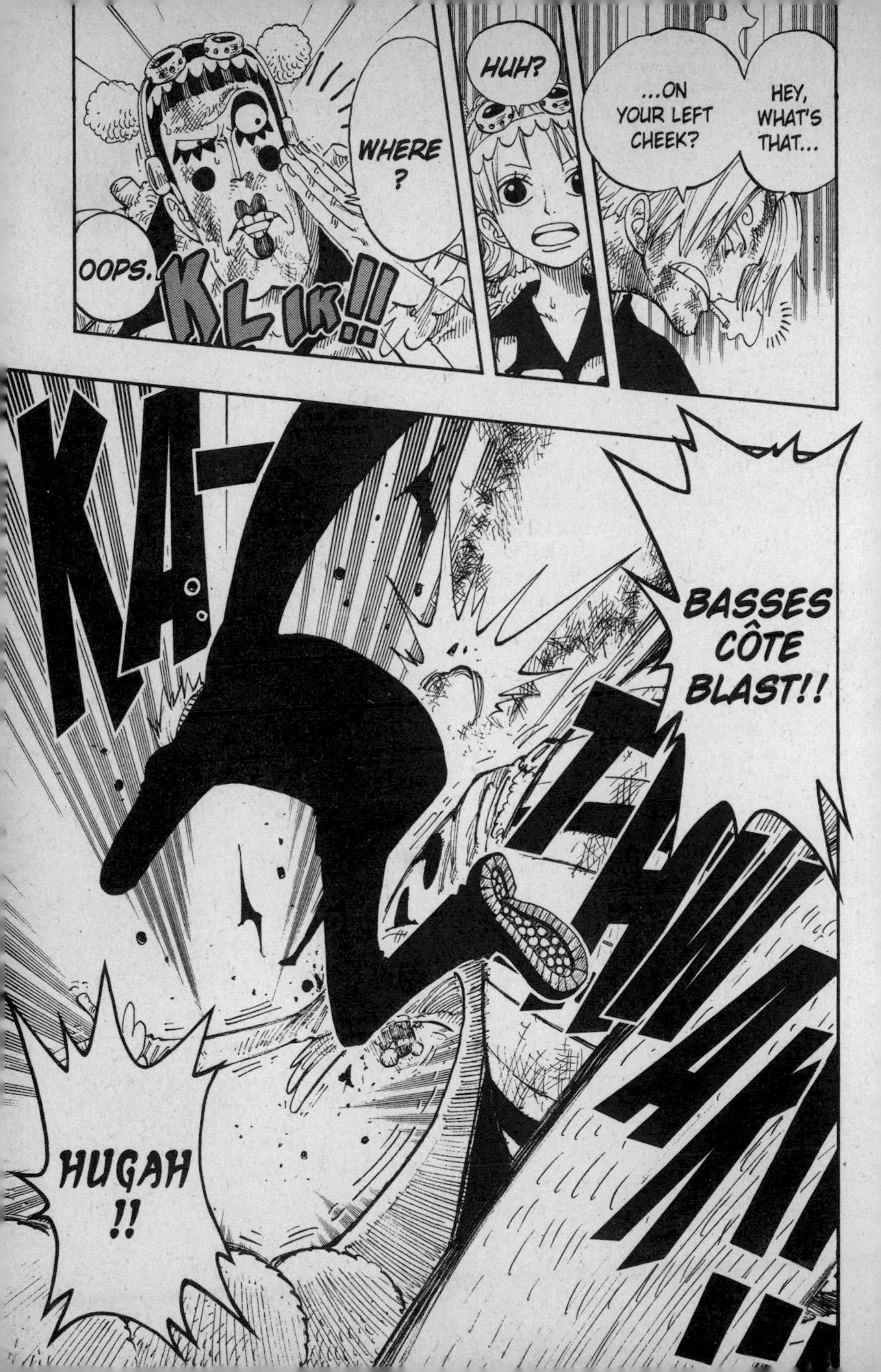
HEY, WHAT'S THAT...
...ON YOUR LEFT CHEEK?
HUH?
WHERE ?
OOPS.
KLIK!!
BASSES CÔTE BLAST!!
KA-
HUGAH !!

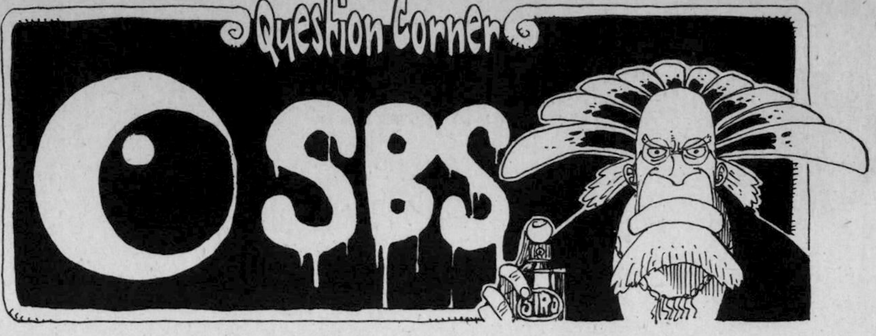
Question Corner
SBS

Reader: The *One Piece* anime isn't shown where I live! How can this be? Please, even if it's a rerun, let it air where I live! I know, it's probably impossible...

Oda: It shouldn't be impossible. I've been getting letters like yours for a while now, but there's not much I can do about it personally. The One Piece anime (as of today, December 4, 2001) is currently carried by 27 stations, and recently began airing even in Taiwan. Three Japanese prefectures--Aomori, Yamaguchi, and Oita--can't get it, though I think there are a few people even in those places who can pick up the signal from neighboring prefectures. So let's make some waves here. One Piece is a production of Fuji TV, so send a letter to your local affiliate and tell them you want it! If all your voices reach the grown-ups at the television stations, I'm sure they will give the matter serious consideration. There are quite a few anime shows that can only be seen by people who live in the Tokyo area. I grew up in Kyushu, so there were a lot of anime I couldn't get. I understand your plight. Tokyo gets all the breaks!

Reader: Eiichiro Oda Sensei,

Let's cut to the chase.

Sincerely,

Meguko

Oda: Yes, well... I suppose I should answer your question right away. Er...um... Yes. Err...yes. Um...

Chapter 189:
2

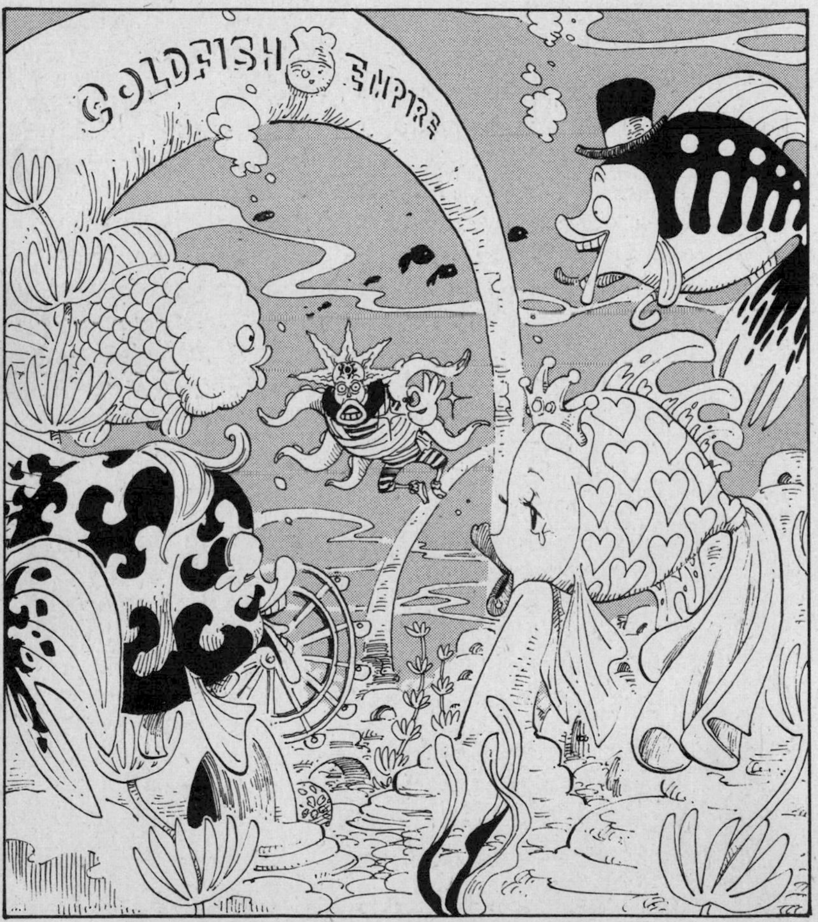
GOLDFISH EMPIRE

HACHI'S WALK ON THE SEAFLOOR, VOL. 7:
"THE GOLDFISH PRINCESS WHO LOST HER RING"

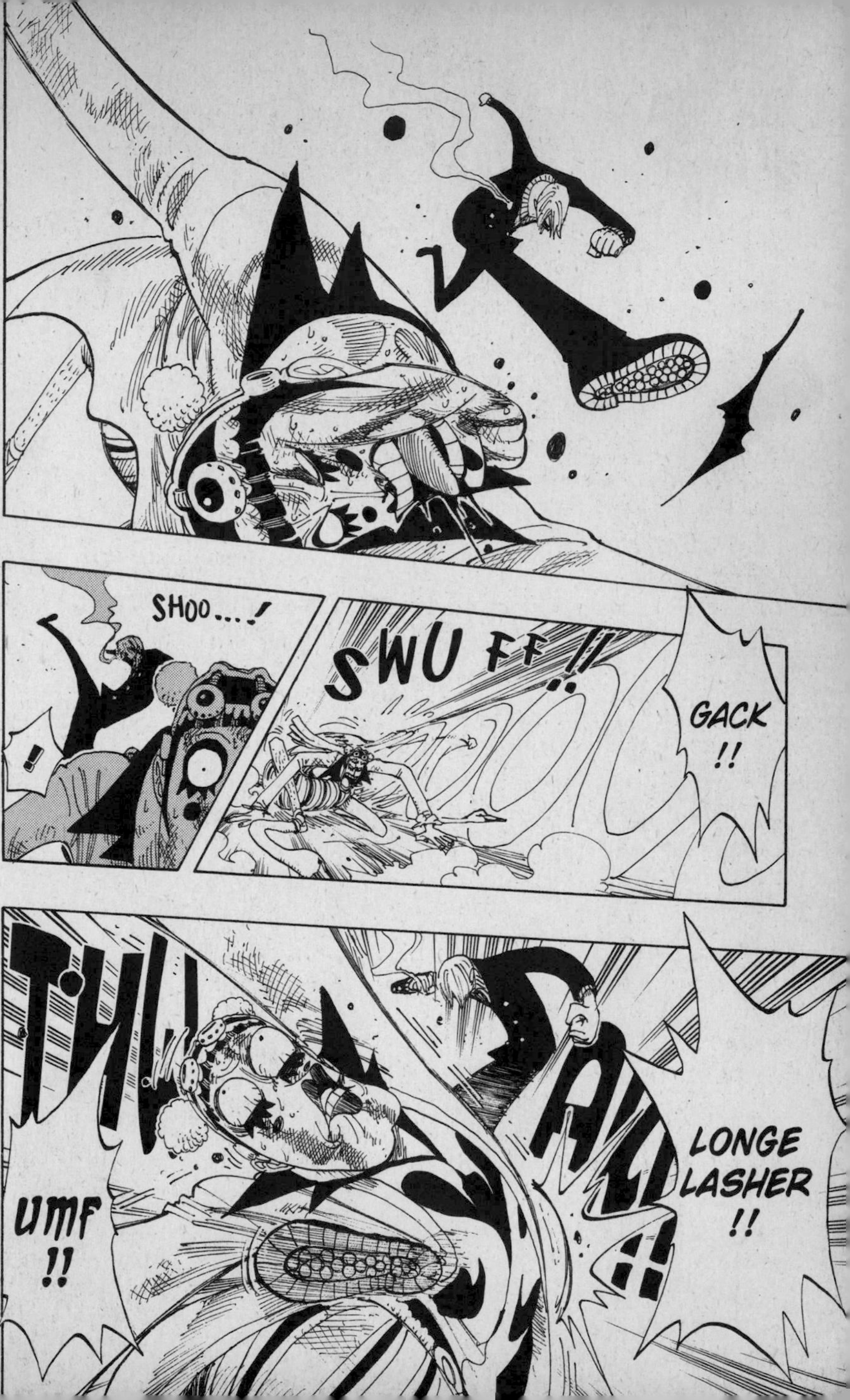
GACK !!
SWU FF !!
SHOO...!
!
LONGE LASHER !!
UMF !!

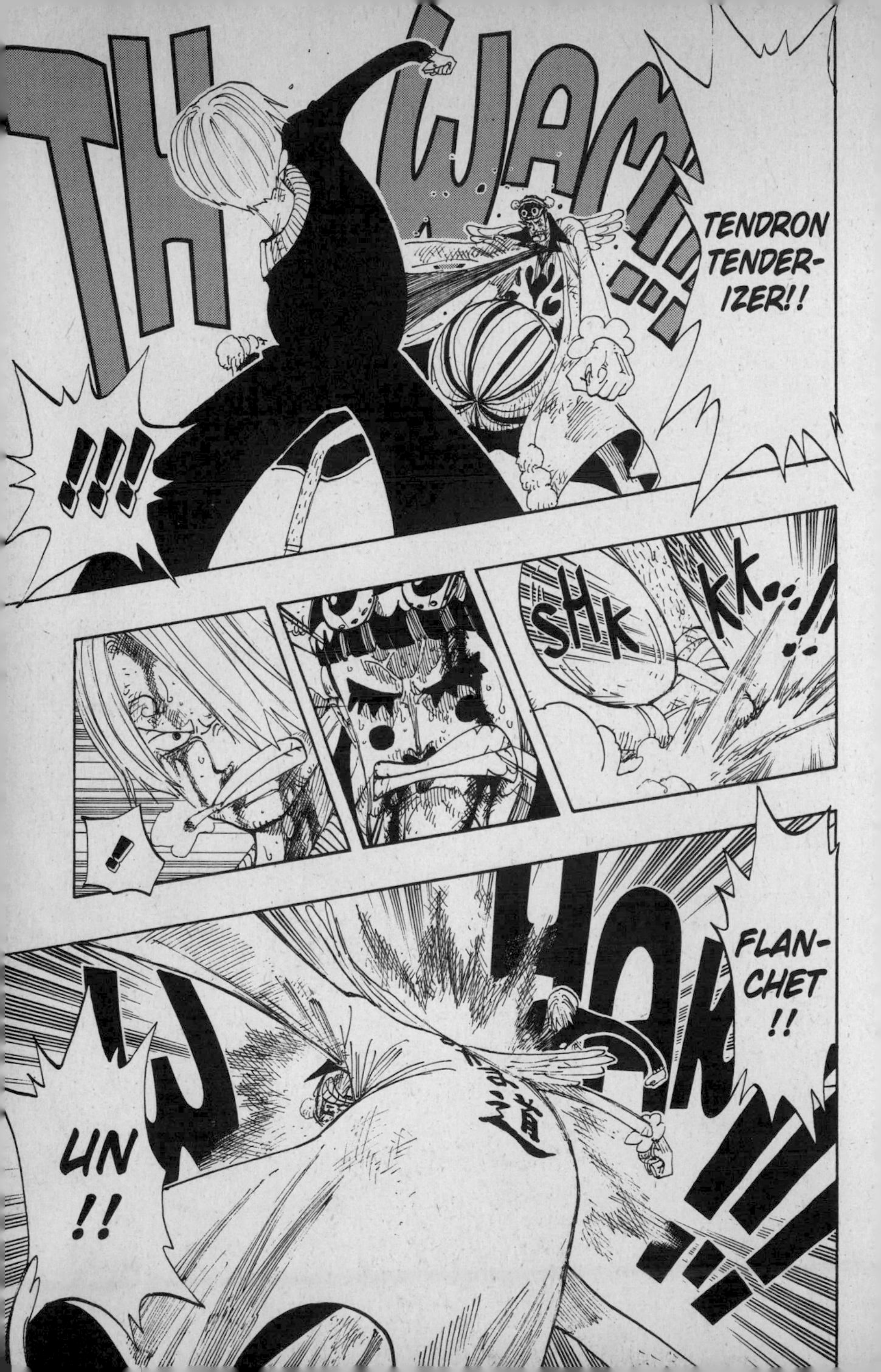
TENDRON TENDER-IZER!!
THWAM
!!!
SHKK...!!
!
FLAN-CHET!!
WHAK!!!
UN!!

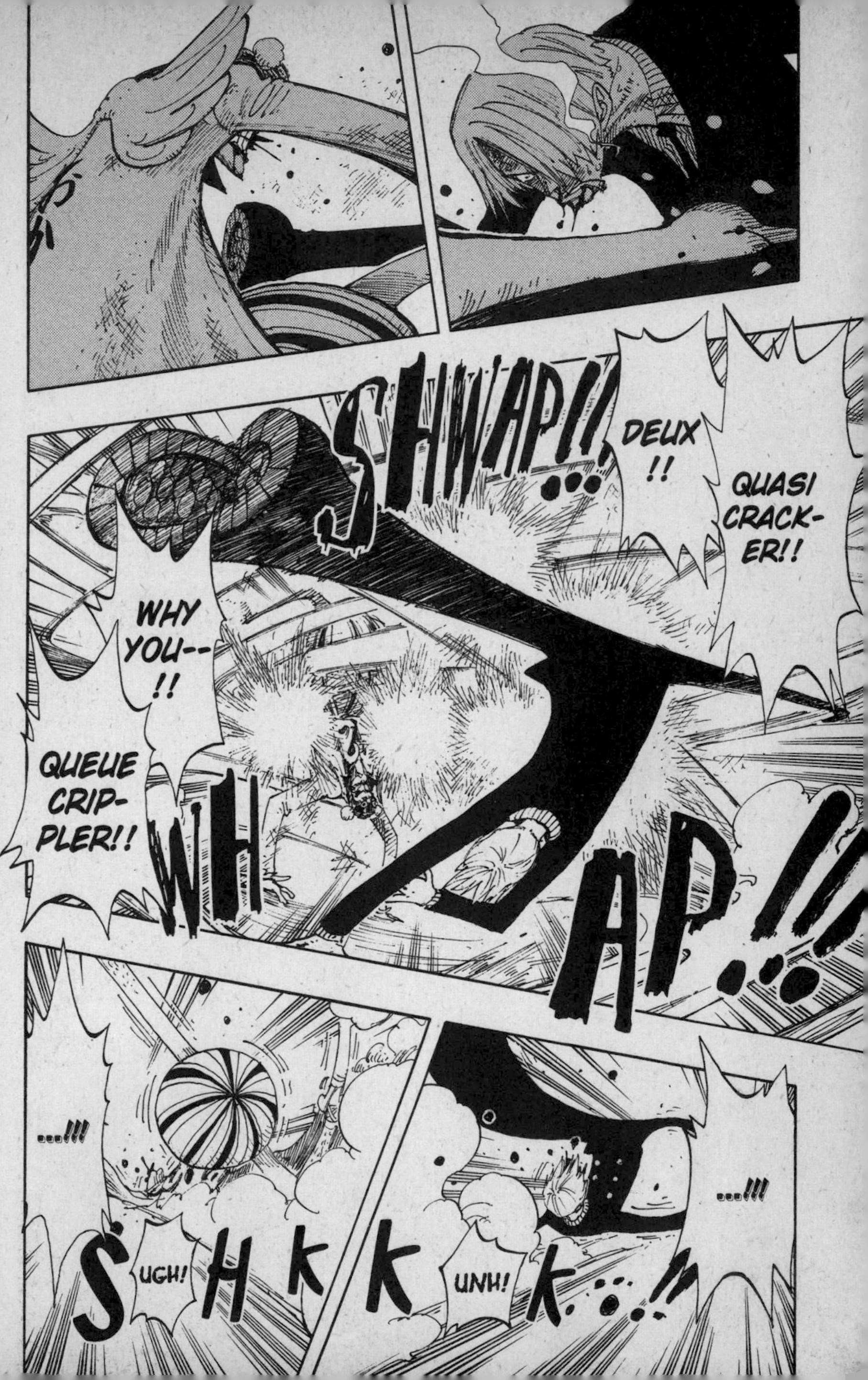

QUASI CRACK-ER!!
DEUX!!
SHWAP!!
WHY YOU--!!
AP!!
WH
QUEUE CRIP-PLER!!
...!!!
UNH!
K...!!
...!!!
UGH!
SHKK

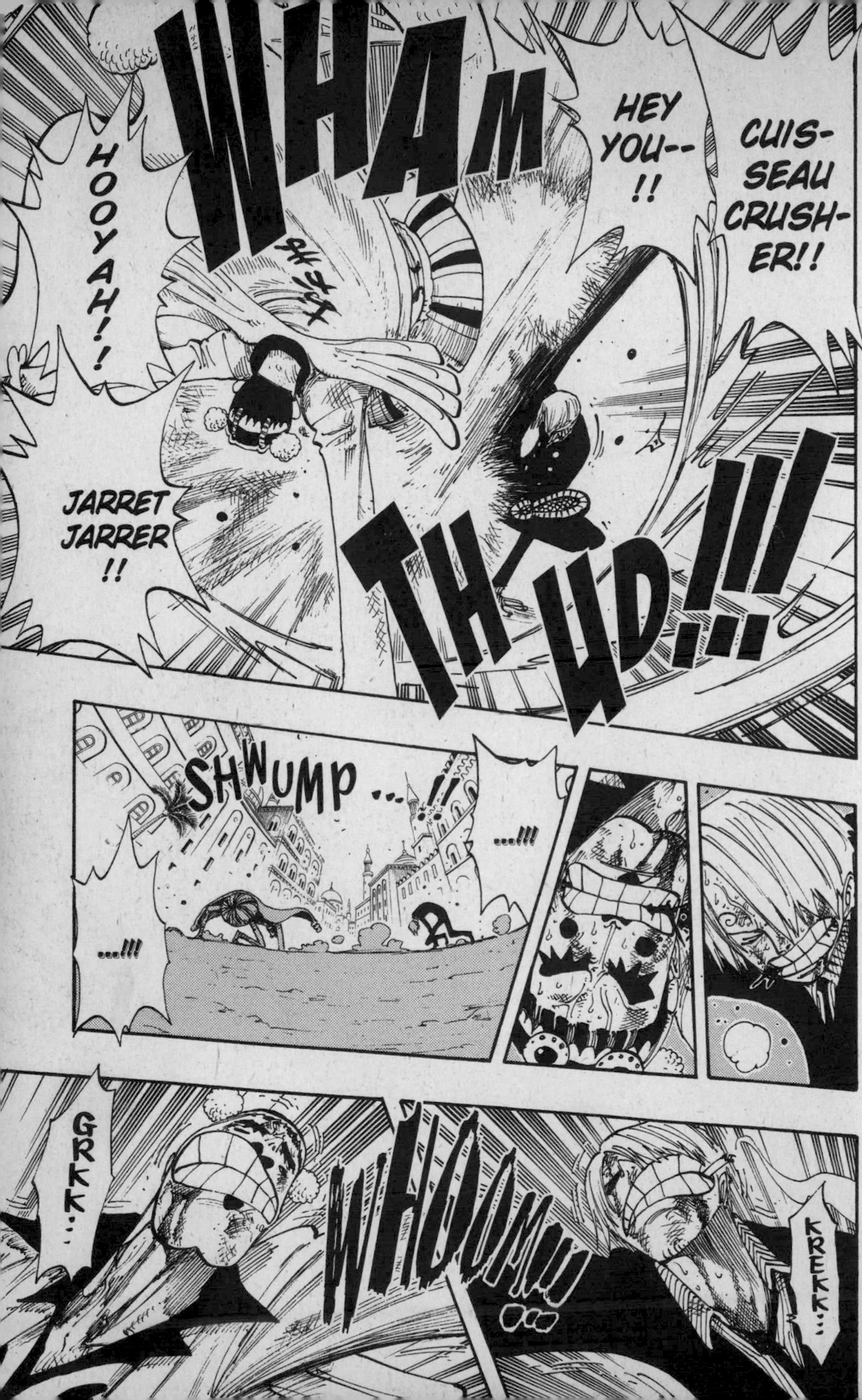
CUIS-
SEAU
CRUSH-
ER!!
HEY YOU-- !!
WHAM
HOOYAH!!
THUD!!!
JARRET JARRER !!
SHWUMP ...!!
...!!!
...!!!
KREKK...
WHOOM...
GRKK...

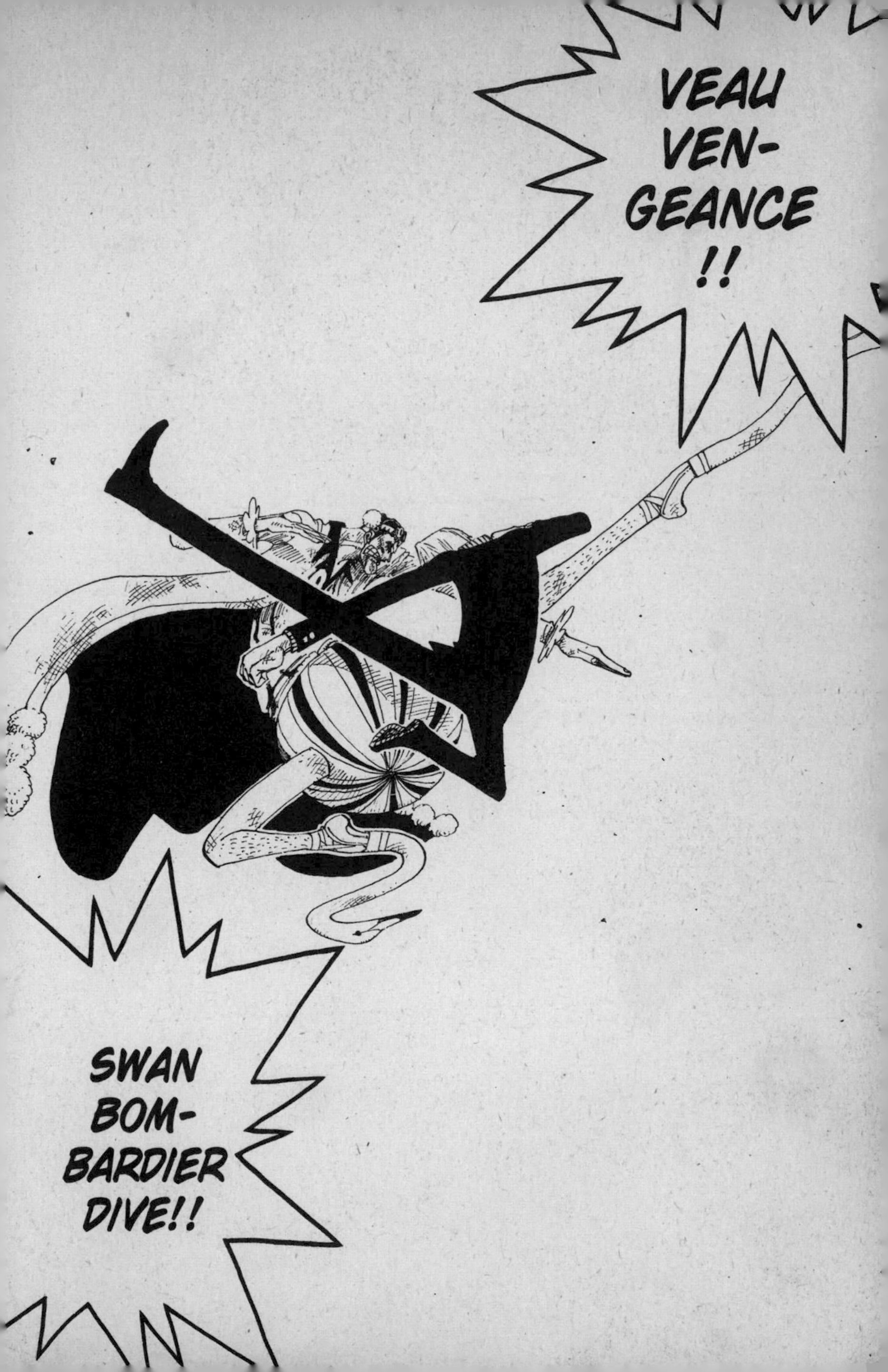
VEAU VEN-GEANCE !!
SWAN BOM-BARDIER DIVE!!

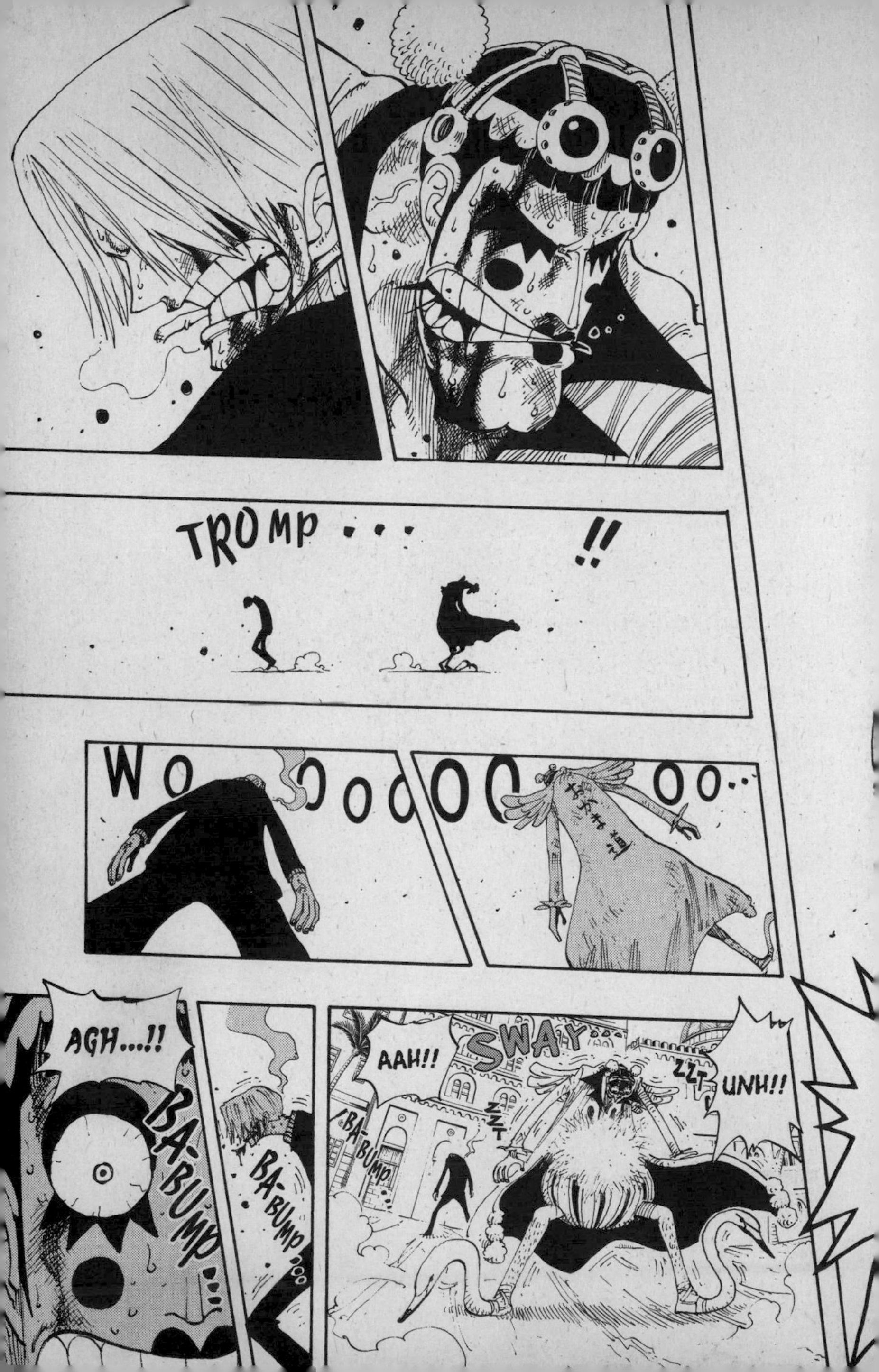
TROMP...
!!
WO oooOO oo..
UNH!!
ZZT
SWAY
AAH!!
ZZT
BA-BUMP...
BA-BUMP...
AGH...!!
BA-BUMP...!!

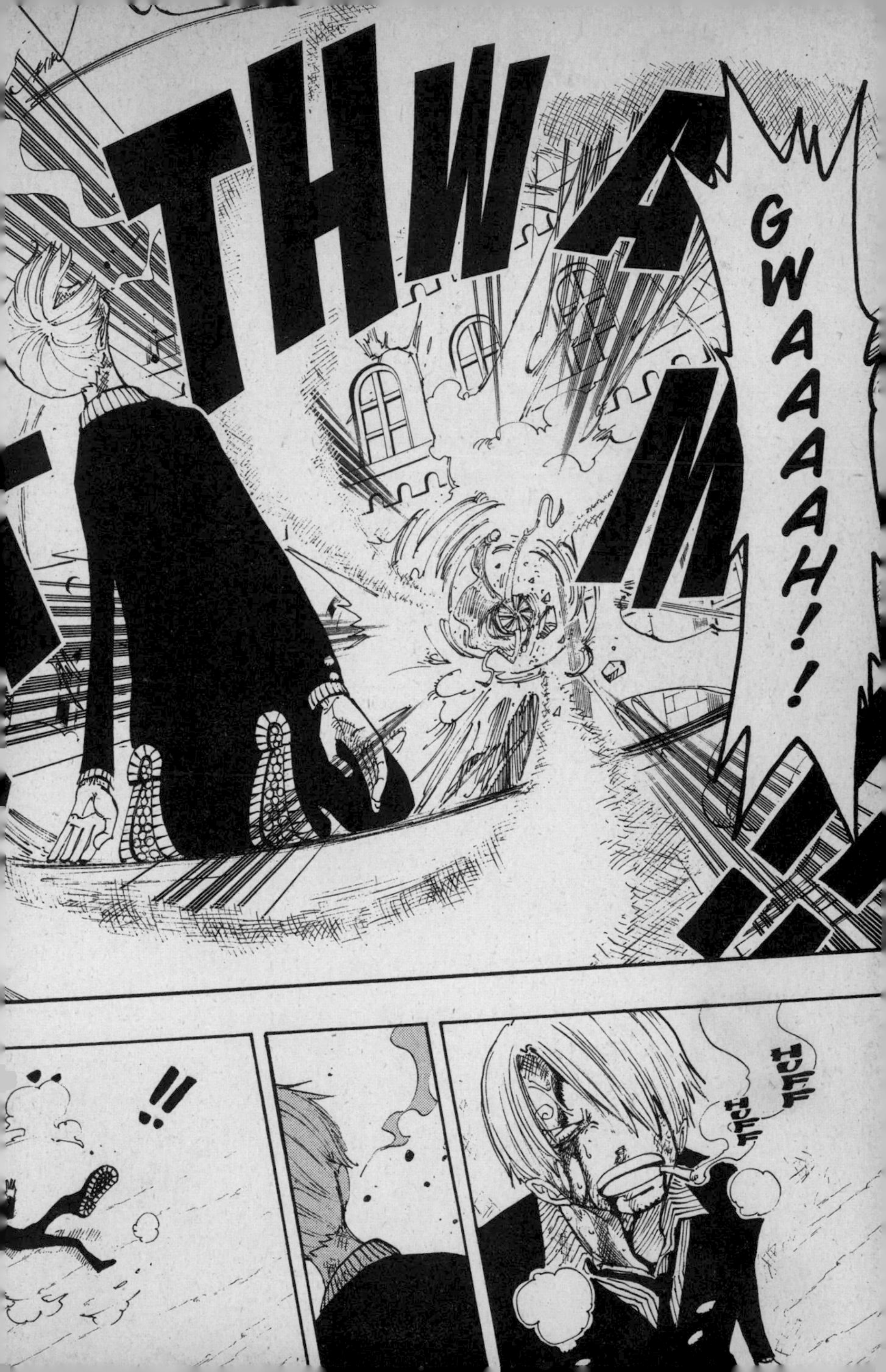
GWAAAAAH!!!
THWAM!!
!!
HUFF
HUFF

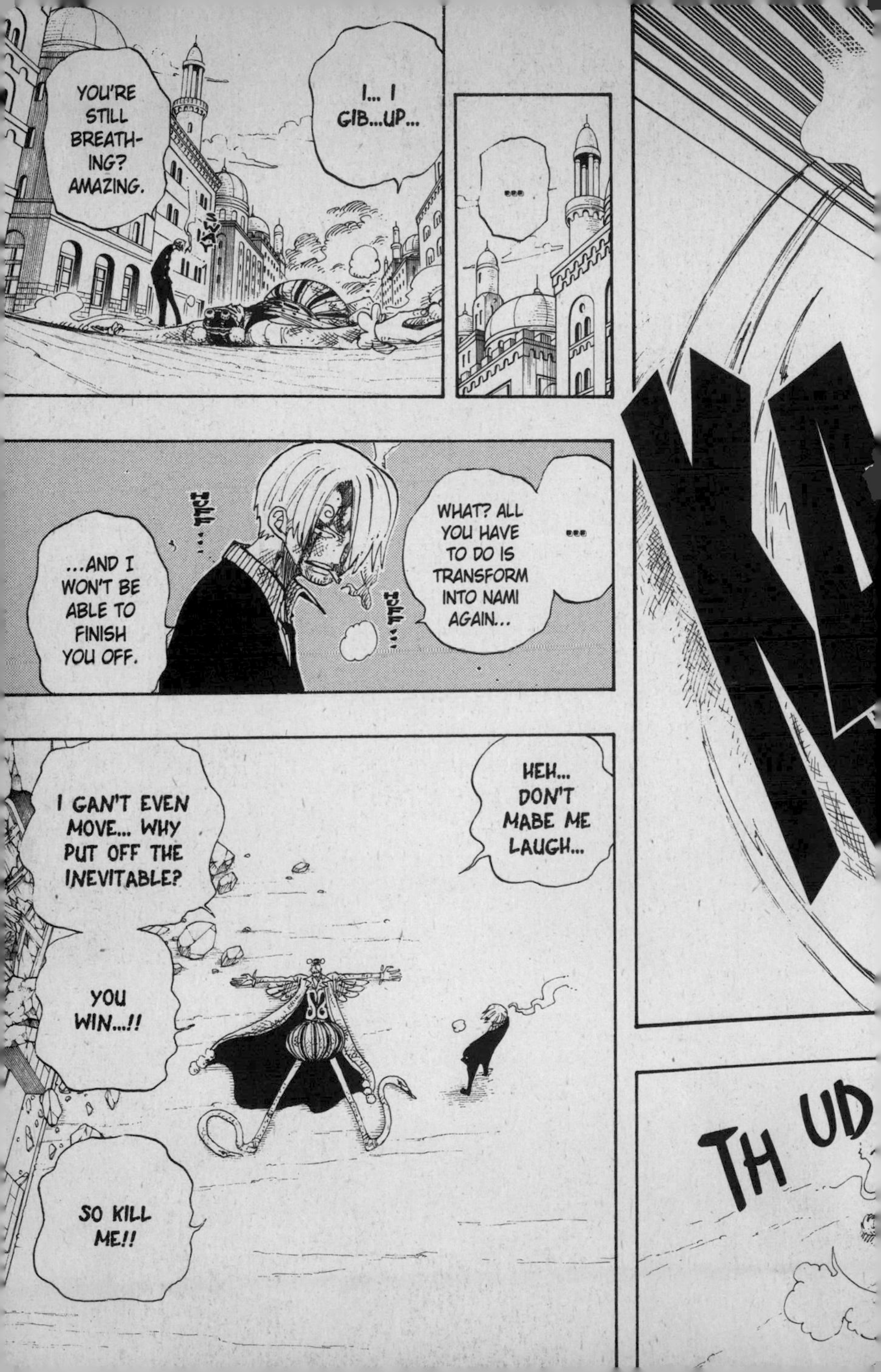
...
I... I GIB...UP...
YOU'RE STILL BREATHING? AMAZING.
SWAY
...
WHAT? ALL YOU HAVE TO DO IS TRANSFORM INTO NAMI AGAIN...
HUFF...
HUFF...
...AND I WON'T BE ABLE TO FINISH YOU OFF.
HEH... DON'T MABE ME LAUGH...
I GAN'T EVEN MOVE... WHY PUT OFF THE INEVITABLE?
YOU WIN...!!
SO KILL ME!!
TH UD

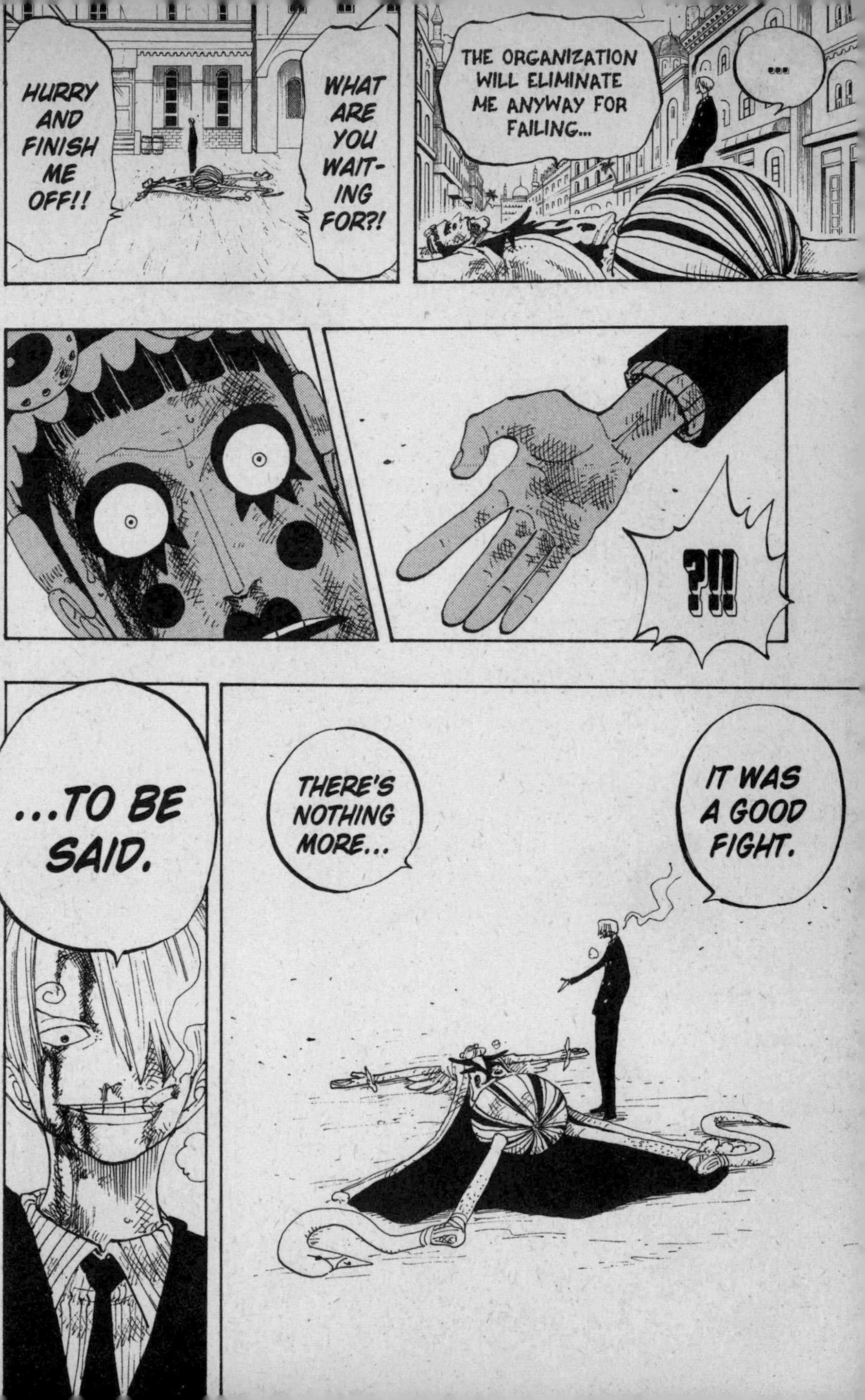
...
THE ORGANIZATION WILL ELIMINATE ME ANYWAY FOR FAILING...
WHAT ARE YOU WAIT-ING FOR?!
HURRY AND FINISH ME OFF!!
?!!
IT WAS A GOOD FIGHT.
THERE'S NOTHING MORE...
...TO BE SAID.

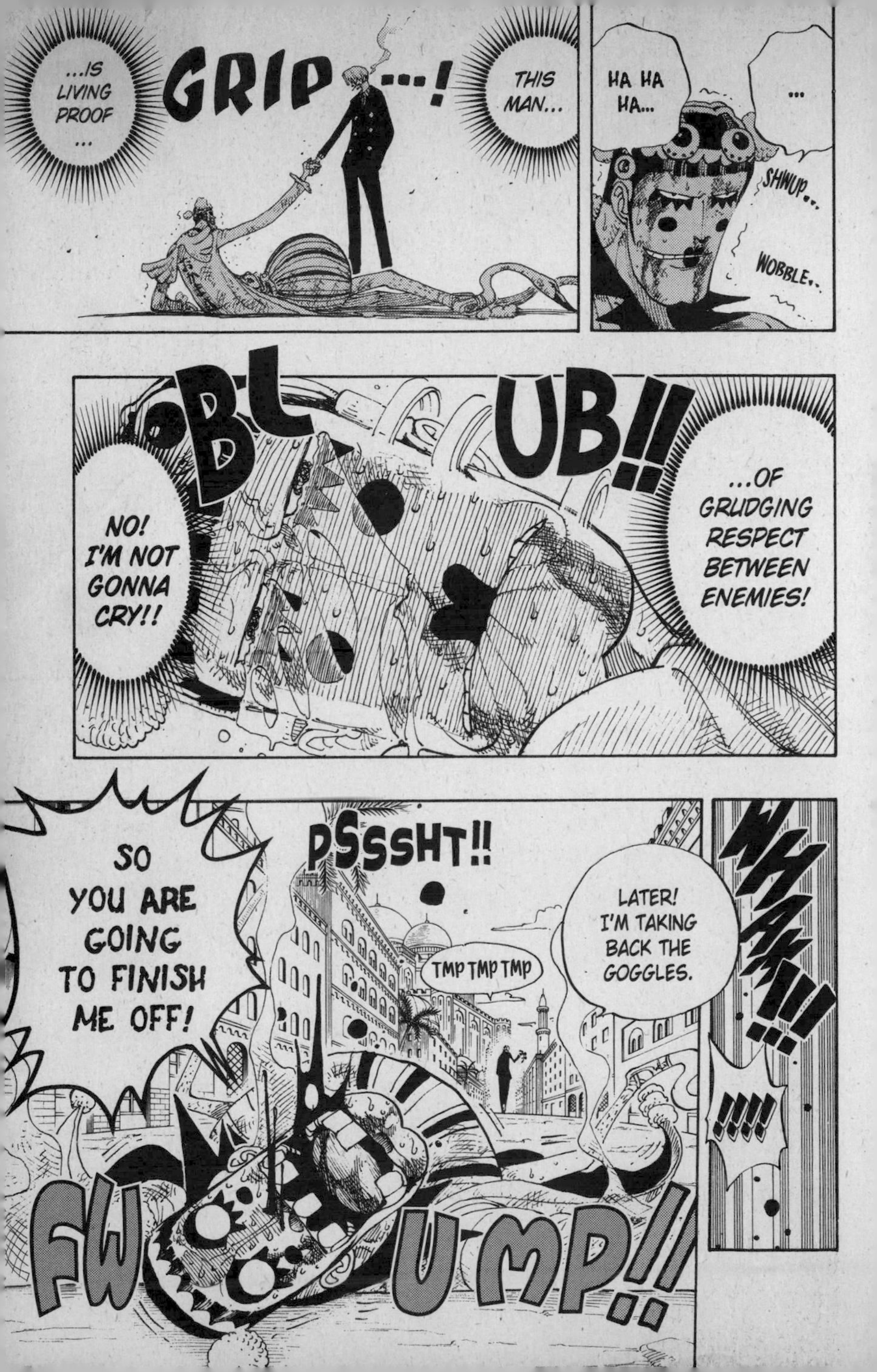
HA HA HA...
...
SHWUP...
WOBBLE...
THIS MAN...
GRIP...!
...IS LIVING PROOF...
...OF GRUDGING RESPECT BETWEEN ENEMIES!
BLUB!!
NO! I'M NOT GONNA CRY!!
WHAAAH!!!
!!!!
LATER! I'M TAKING BACK THE GOGGLES.
TMP TMP TMP
PSSSHT!!
SO YOU ARE GOING TO FINISH ME OFF!
FWUMP!!

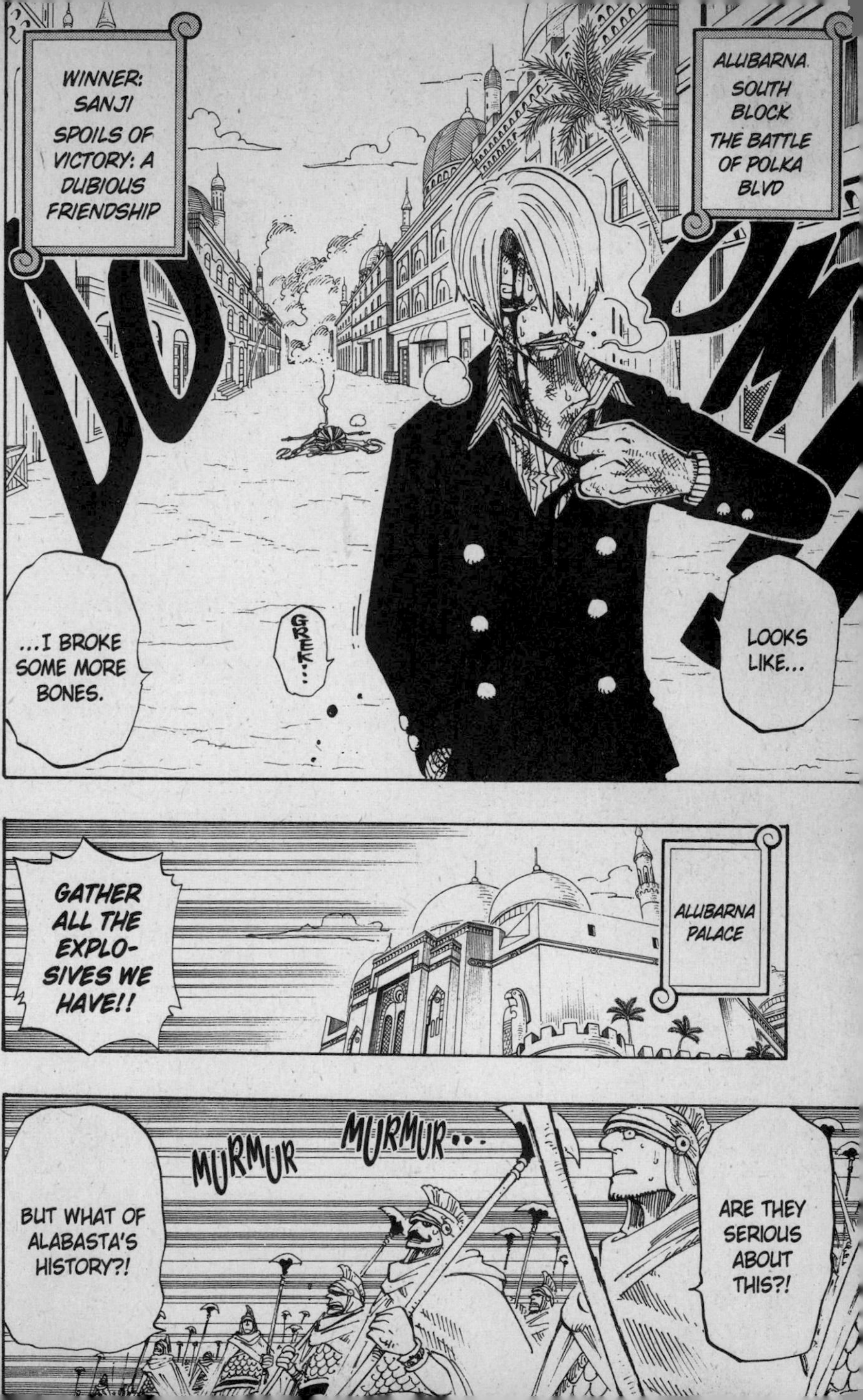
ALUBARNA SOUTH BLOCK THE BATTLE OF POLKA BLVD
WINNER: SANJI SPOILS OF VICTORY: A DUBIOUS FRIENDSHIP
LOOKS LIKE...
GREK...
...I BROKE SOME MORE BONES.
ALUBARNA PALACE
GATHER ALL THE EXPLO-SIVES WE HAVE!!
ARE THEY SERIOUS ABOUT THIS?!
MURMUR...
MURMUR
BUT WHAT OF ALABASTA'S HISTORY?!

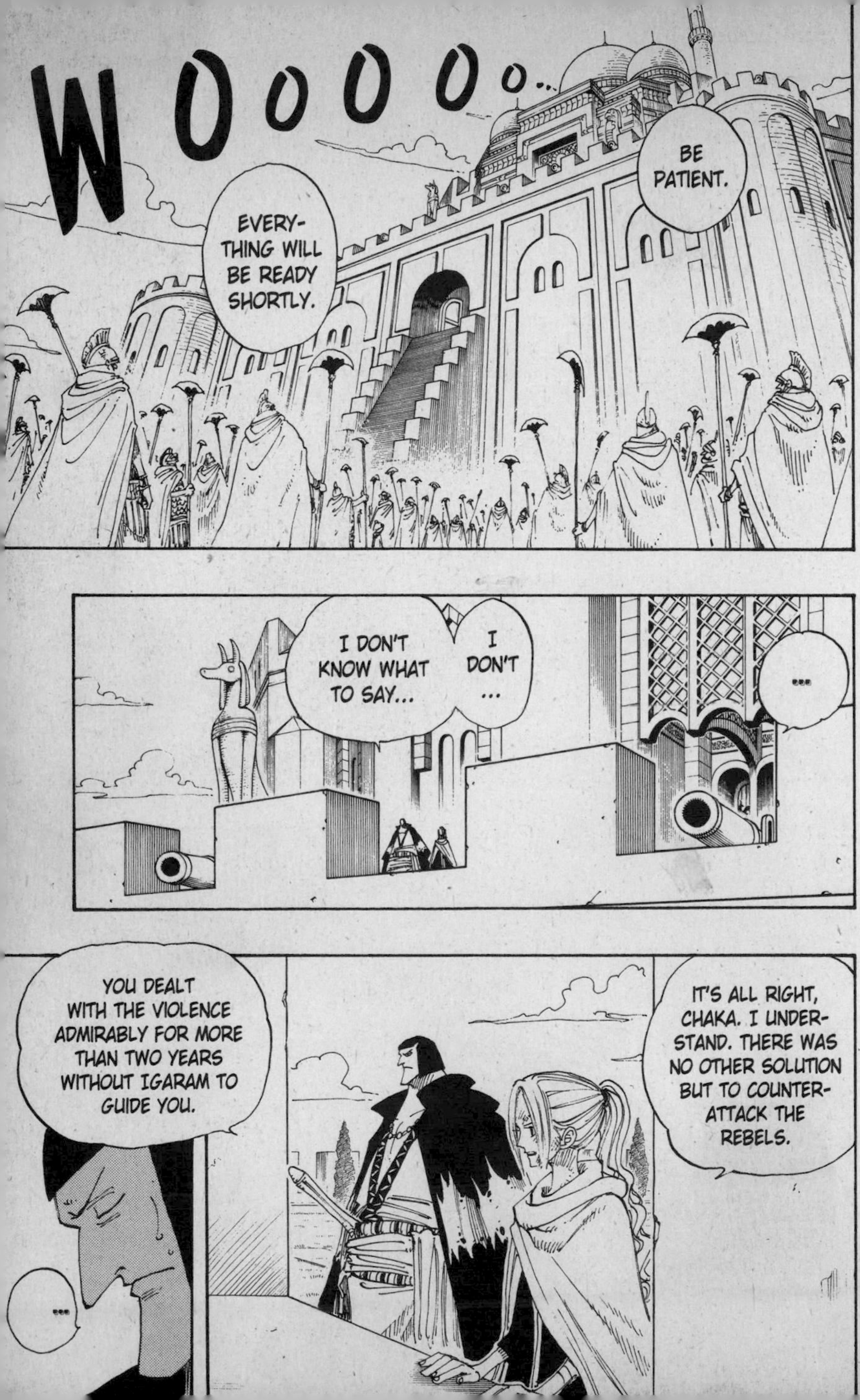
WOOOOO...
BE PATIENT.
EVERYTHING WILL BE READY SHORTLY.
...
I DON'T ...
I DON'T KNOW WHAT TO SAY...
IT'S ALL RIGHT, CHAKA. I UNDERSTAND. THERE WAS NO OTHER SOLUTION BUT TO COUNTERATTACK THE REBELS.
YOU DEALT WITH THE VIOLENCE ADMIRABLY FOR MORE THAN TWO YEARS WITHOUT IGARAM TO GUIDE YOU.
...

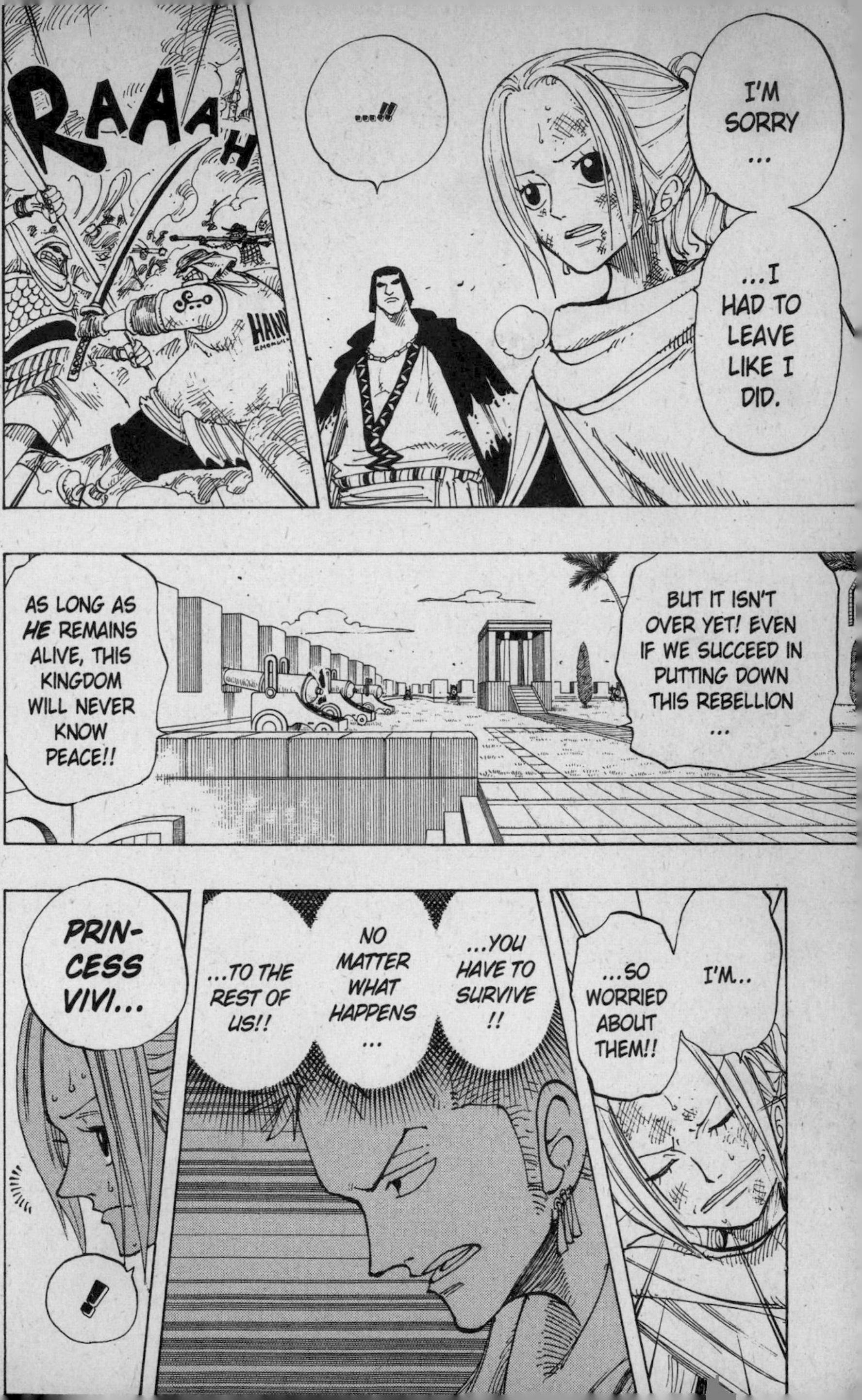
I'M SORRY ...
...I HAD TO LEAVE LIKE I DID.
...!!
RAAAH
BUT IT ISN'T OVER YET! EVEN IF WE SUCCEED IN PUTTING DOWN THIS REBELLION ...
AS LONG AS *HE* REMAINS ALIVE, THIS KINGDOM WILL NEVER KNOW PEACE!!
I'M..
...SO WORRIED ABOUT THEM!!
...YOU HAVE TO SURVIVE !!
NO MATTER WHAT HAPPENS ...
...TO THE REST OF US!!
PRIN-CESS VIVI...
!

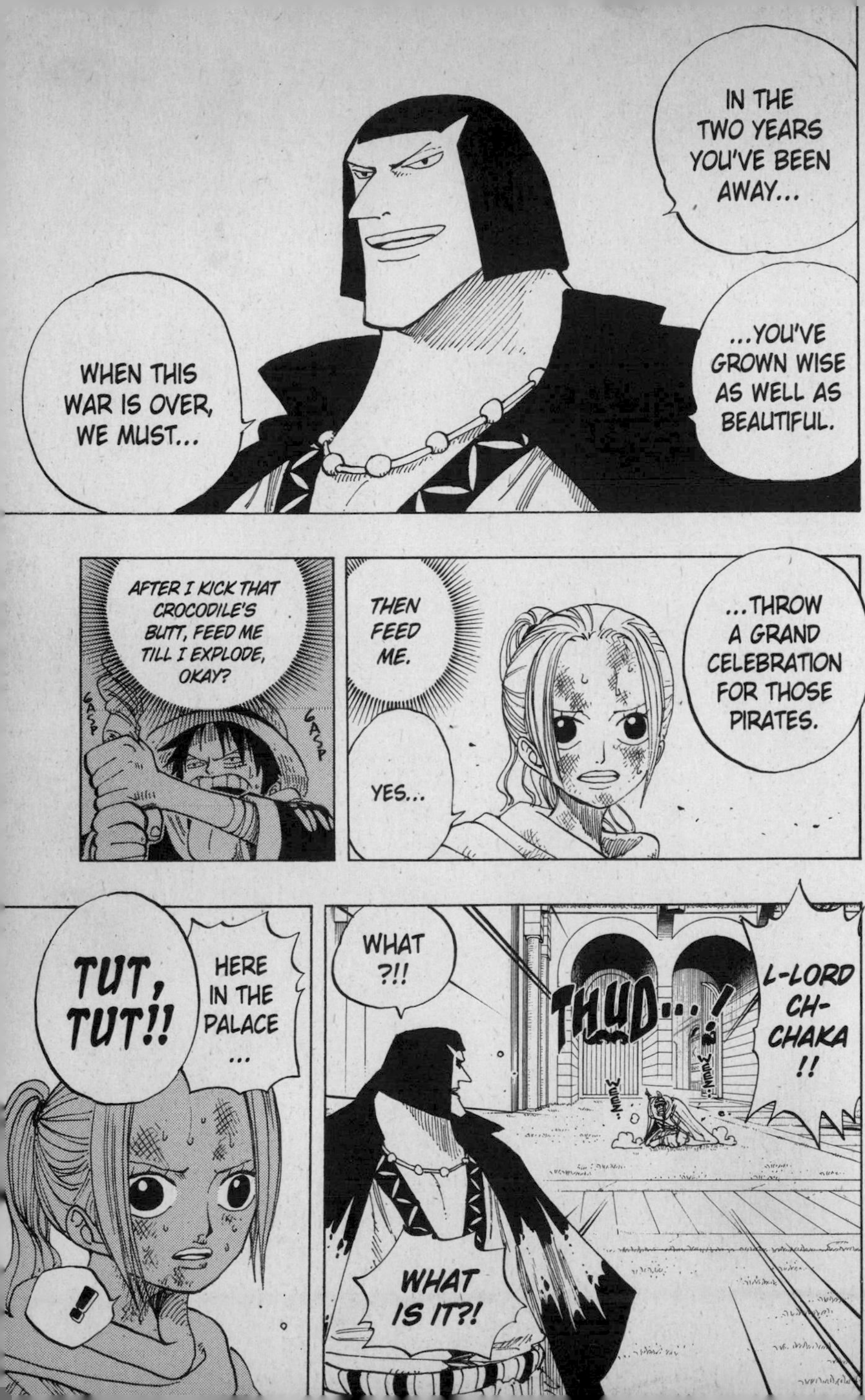
IN THE TWO YEARS YOU'VE BEEN AWAY...
...YOU'VE GROWN WISE AS WELL AS BEAUTIFUL.
WHEN THIS WAR IS OVER, WE MUST...
...THROW A GRAND CELEBRATION FOR THOSE PIRATES.
THEN FEED ME.
YES...
AFTER I KICK THAT CROCODILE'S BUTT, FEED ME TILL I EXPLODE, OKAY?
GASP
GASP
L-LORD CH-CHAKA !!
THUD...!
WHAT ?!!
WHAT IS IT?!
HERE IN THE PALACE ...
TUT, TUT!!
!

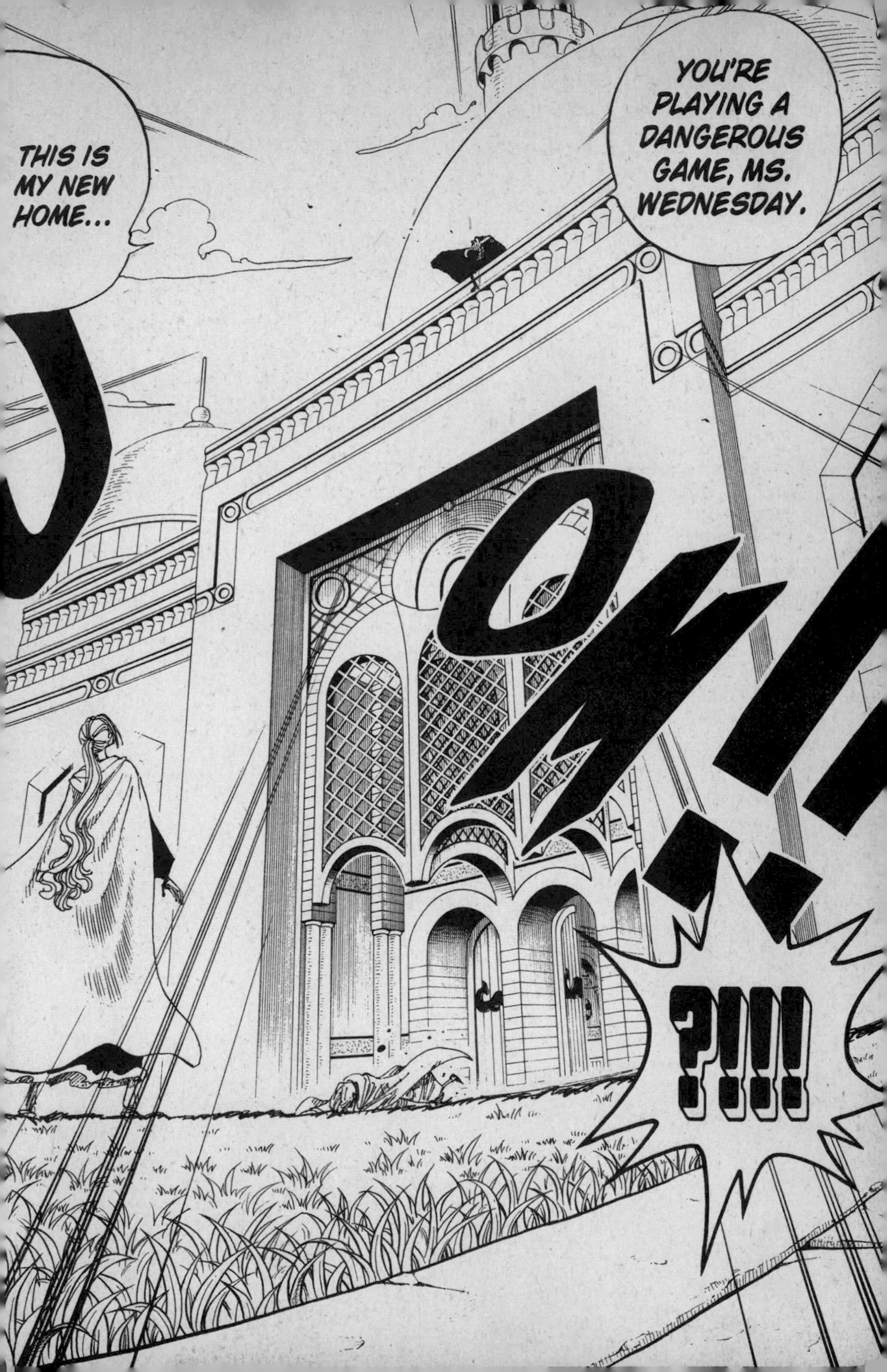
YOU'RE PLAYING A DANGEROUS GAME, MS. WEDNESDAY.
THIS IS MY NEW HOME...
?!!!

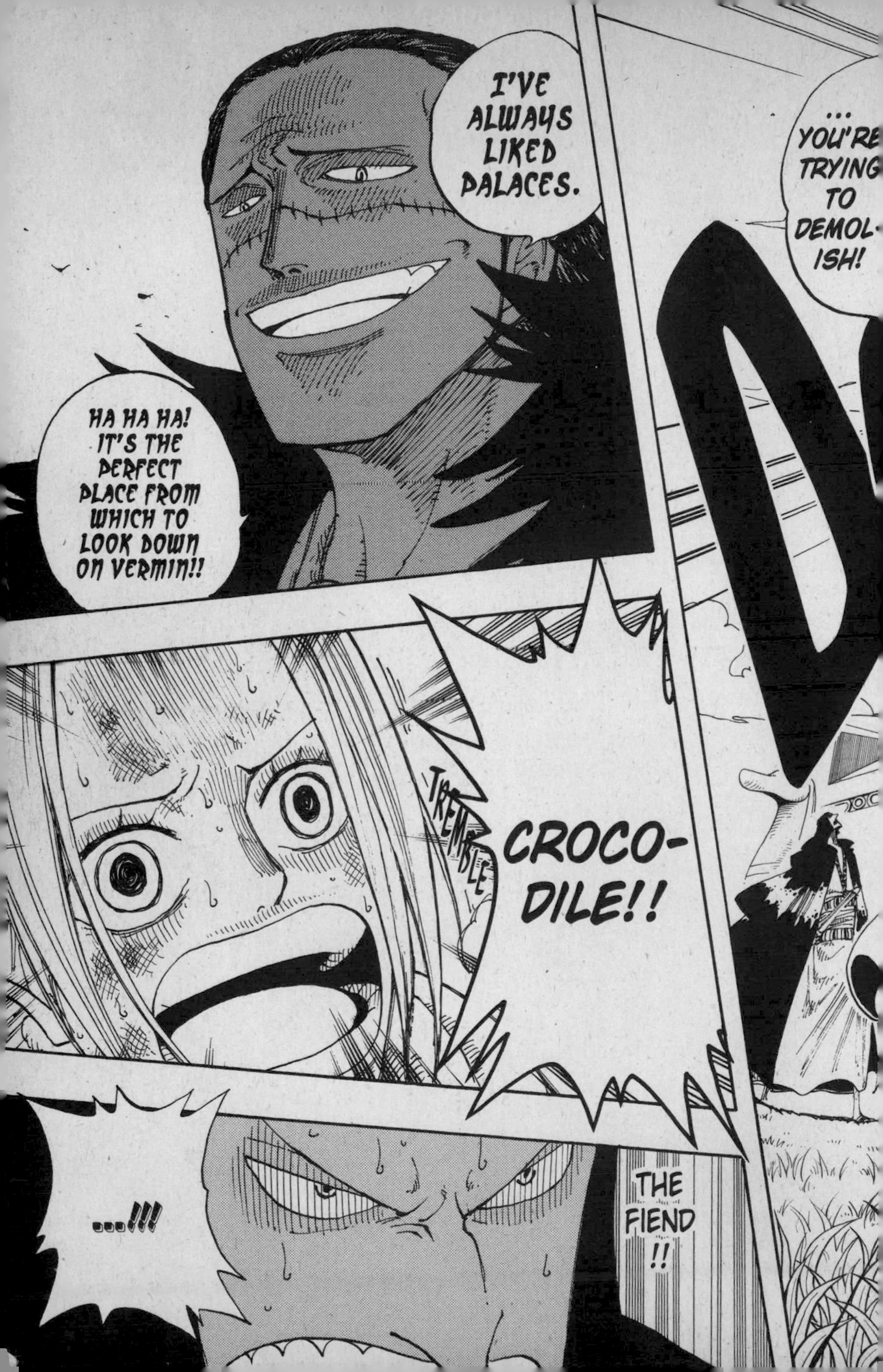
... YOU'RE TRYING TO DEMOL-ISH!
I'VE ALWAYS LIKED PALACES.
HA HA HA! IT'S THE PERFECT PLACE FROM WHICH TO LOOK DOWN ON VERMIN!!
TREMBLE
CROCO-DILE!!
THE FIEND!!
...!!!

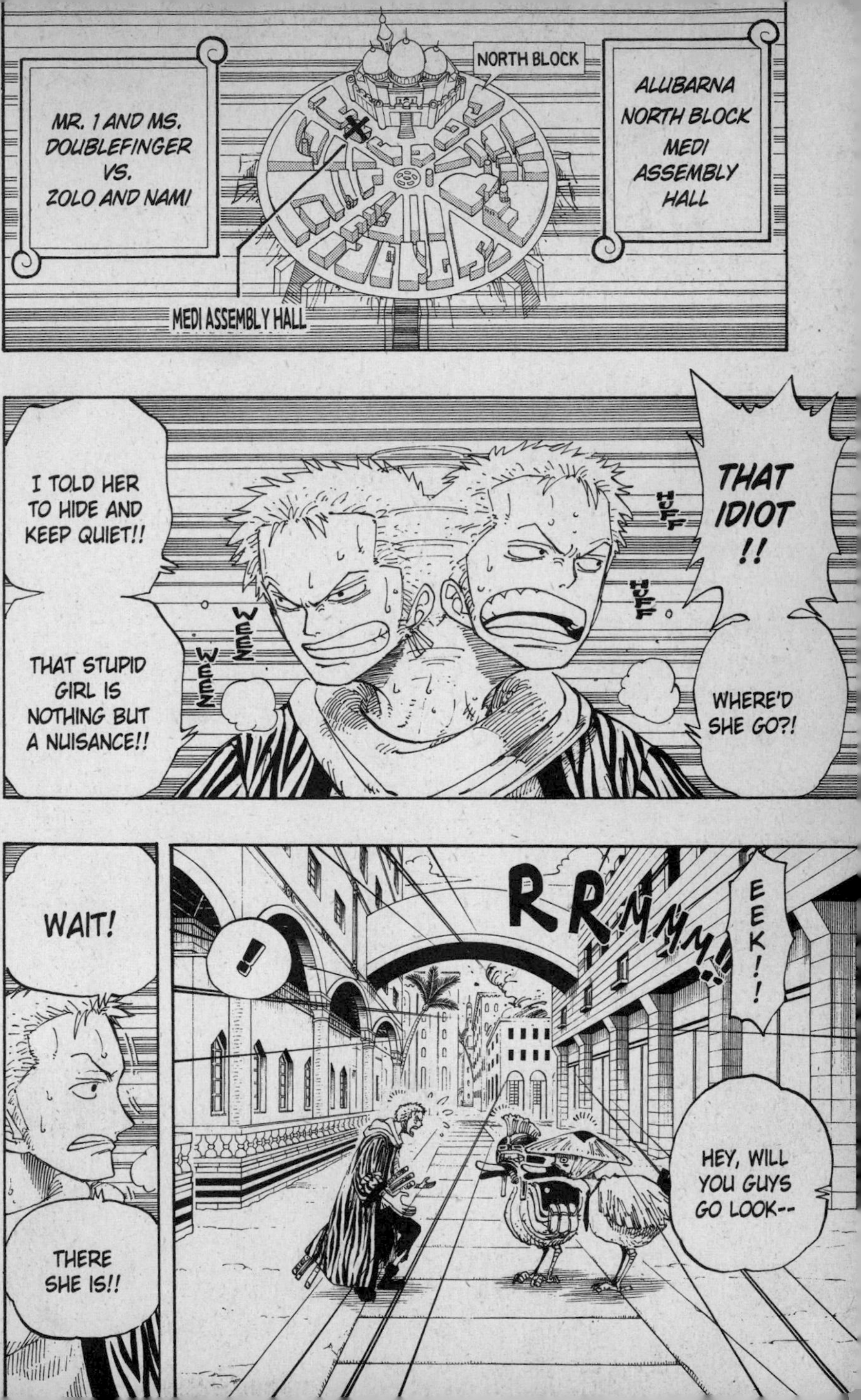
ALUBARNA NORTH BLOCK MEDI ASSEMBLY HALL
NORTH BLOCK
MR. 1 AND MS. DOUBLEFINGER VS. ZOLO AND NAMI
MEDI ASSEMBLY HALL
THAT IDIOT!!
HUFF
HUFF
WHERE'D SHE GO?!
I TOLD HER TO HIDE AND KEEP QUIET!!
WEEZ
WEEZ
THAT STUPID GIRL IS NOTHING BUT A NUISANCE!!
EEK!!
RRMMMM!!
HEY, WILL YOU GUYS GO LOOK--
!
WAIT!
THERE SHE IS!!

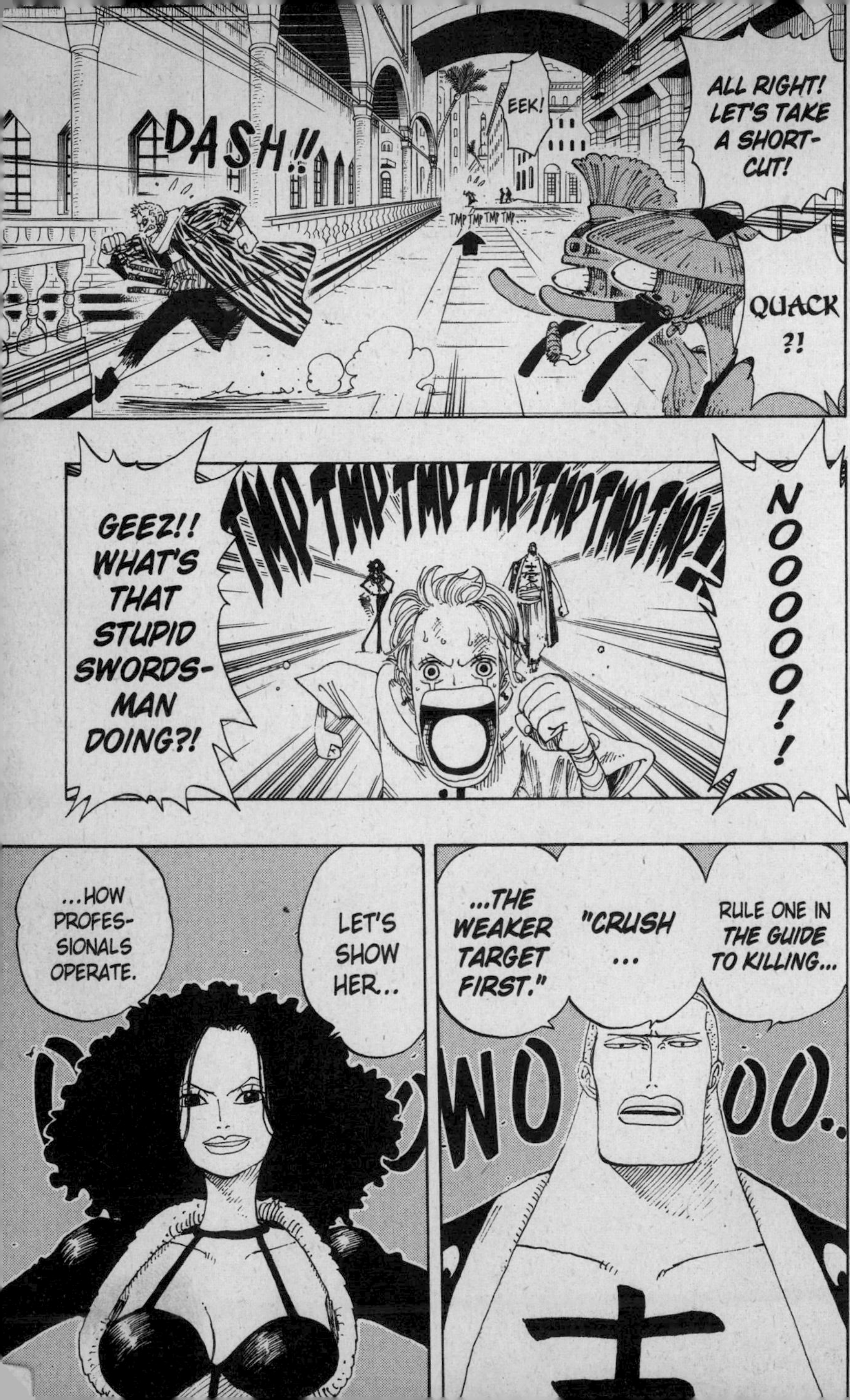
ALL RIGHT! LET'S TAKE A SHORT-CUT!
QUACK ?!
EEK!
TMP TMP TMP TMP...
DASH!!
NOOOOOO!!
TMP TMP TMP TMP TMP TMP TMP!!
GEEZ!! WHAT'S THAT STUPID SWORDS-MAN DOING?!
RULE ONE IN THE GUIDE TO KILLING...
"CRUSH ...
...THE WEAKER TARGET FIRST."
LET'S SHOW HER...
...HOW PROFES-SIONALS OPERATE.

Chapter 190:
CLIMATE BATON

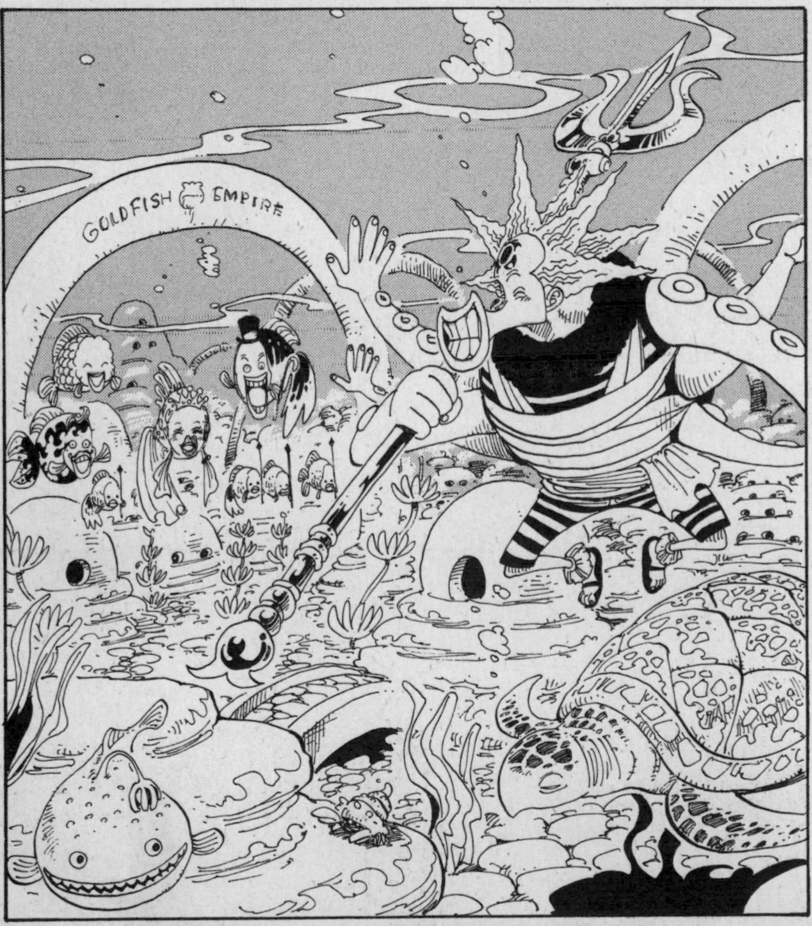
GOLDFISH EMPIRE

HACHI'S WALK ON THE SEAFLOOR, VOL. 8:
"A GOLDEN TRIDENT GIVEN IN GRATITUDE"

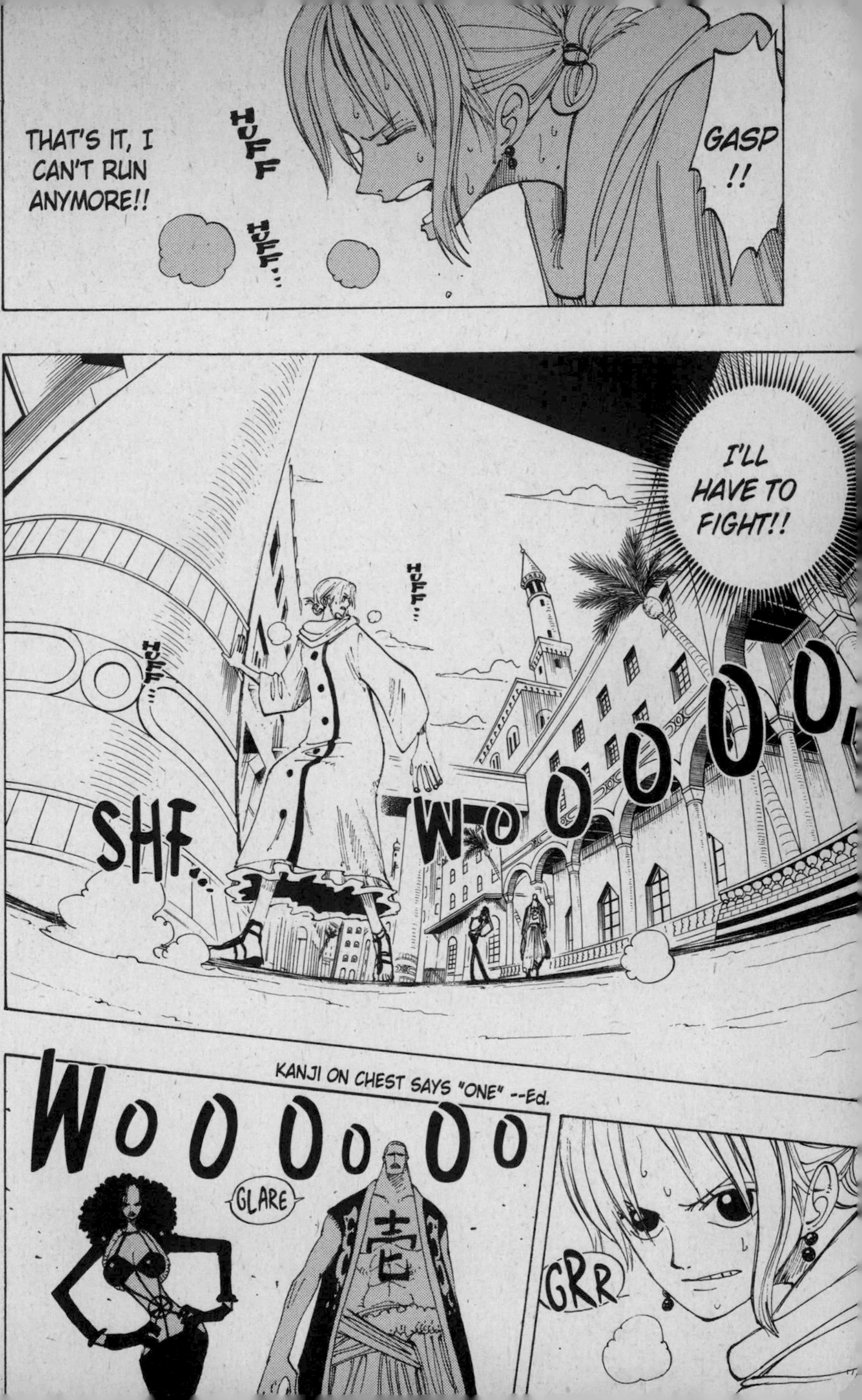
GASP!!
HUFF
HUFF...
THAT'S IT, I CAN'T RUN ANYMORE!!
I'LL HAVE TO FIGHT!!
WOOOOOOO
HUFF...
HUFF...
SHF...
KANJI ON CHEST SAYS "ONE" --Ed.
GRR
WOOOOOO
GLARE

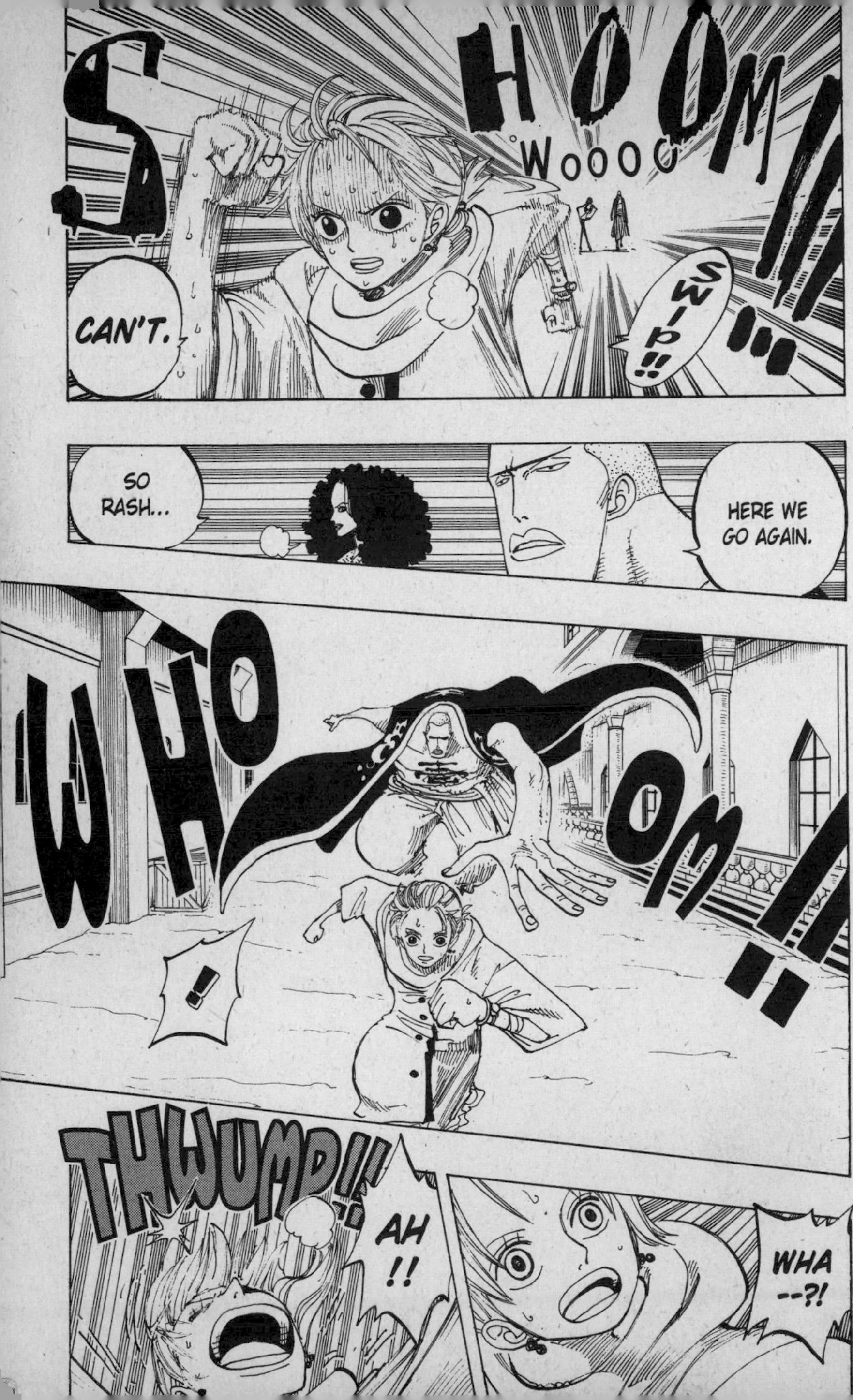
SWIP!!
SHOOM!!...
WOOOO
CAN'T.
HERE WE GO AGAIN.
SO RASH...
WHOOM!!
!
WHA--?!
AH!!
THWUMP!!

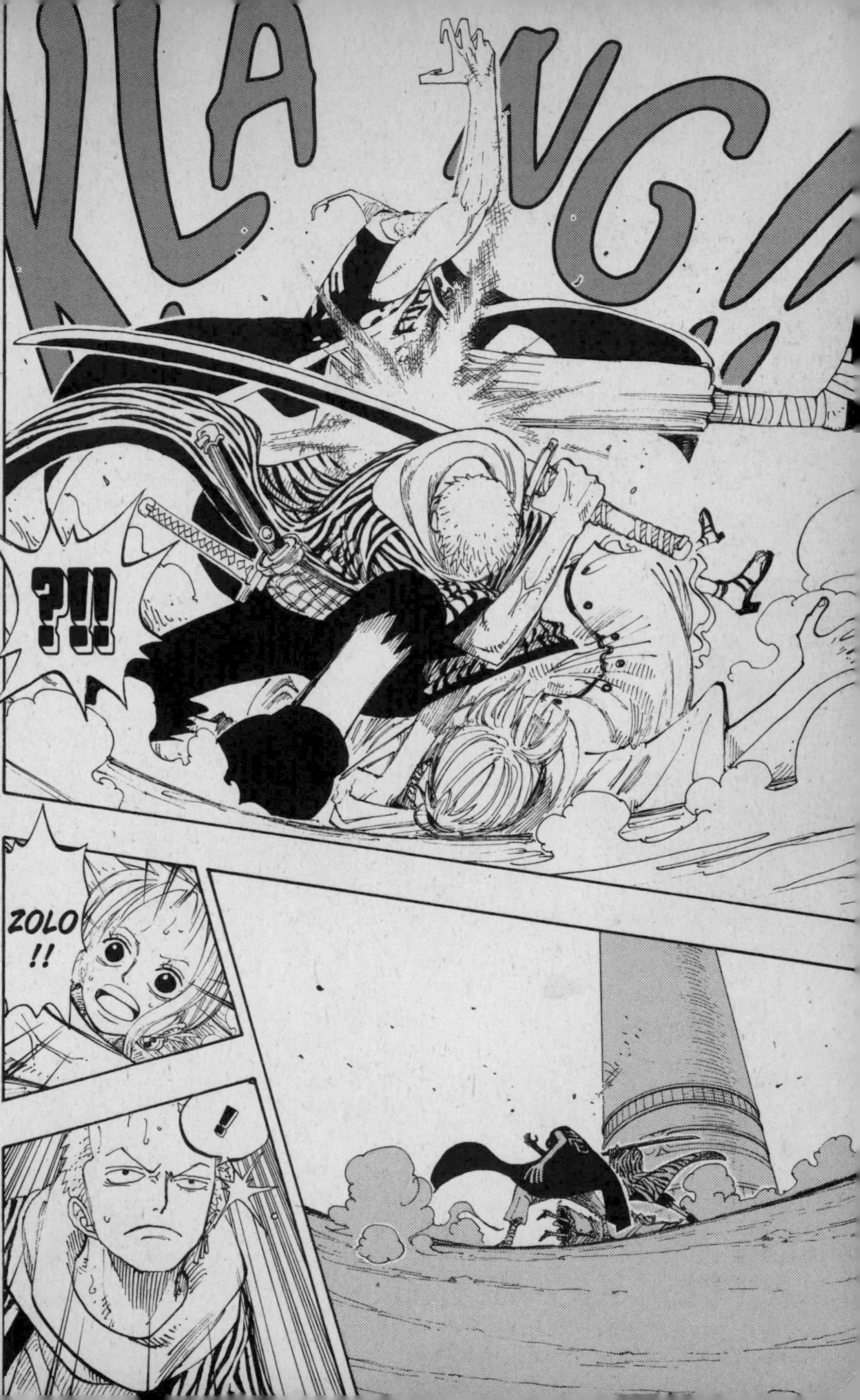
KLANG!!
?!!
ZOLO !!
!

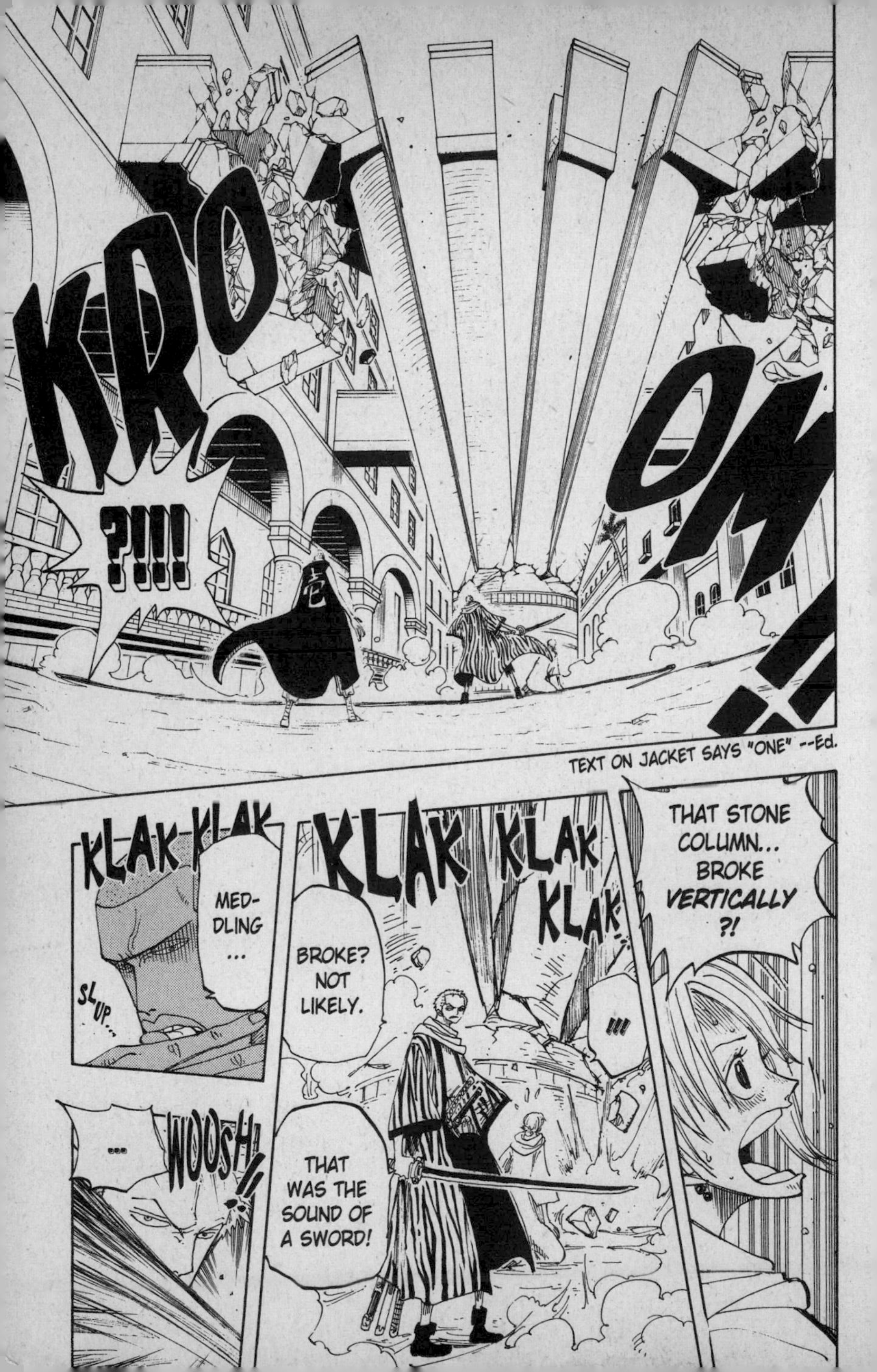
KROOOM!!
?!!!
TEXT ON JACKET SAYS "ONE" --Ed.
THAT STONE COLUMN... BROKE VERTICALLY?!
!!!
KLAK KLAK KLAK KLAK
BROKE? NOT LIKELY.
THAT WAS THE SOUND OF A SWORD!
KLAK KLAK
MED-DLING...
SLUP...
...
WOOSH!!

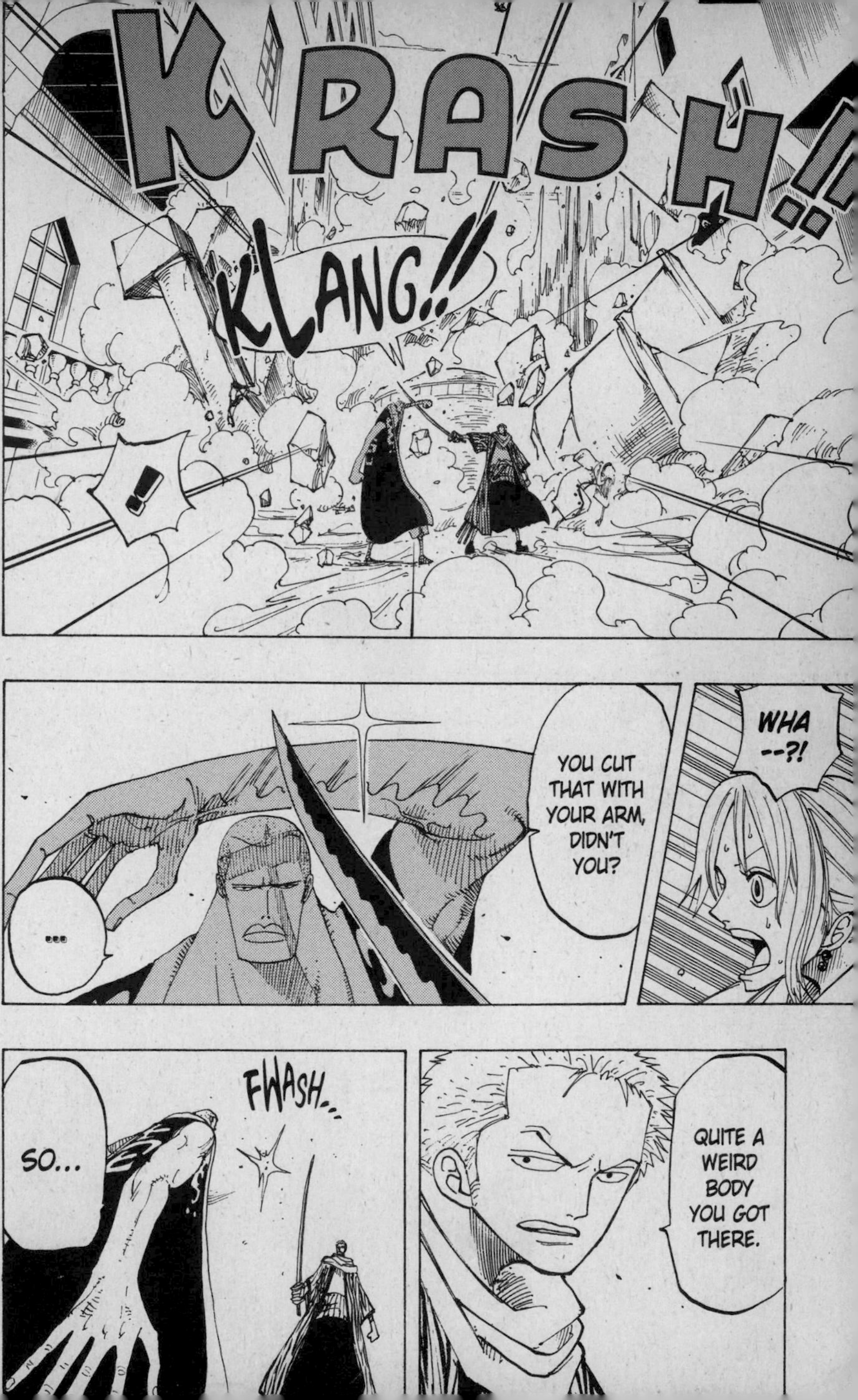
KRASH!!
KLANG!!
!
WHA--?!
YOU CUT THAT WITH YOUR ARM, DIDN'T YOU?
...
QUITE A WEIRD BODY YOU GOT THERE.
FWASH...
SO...

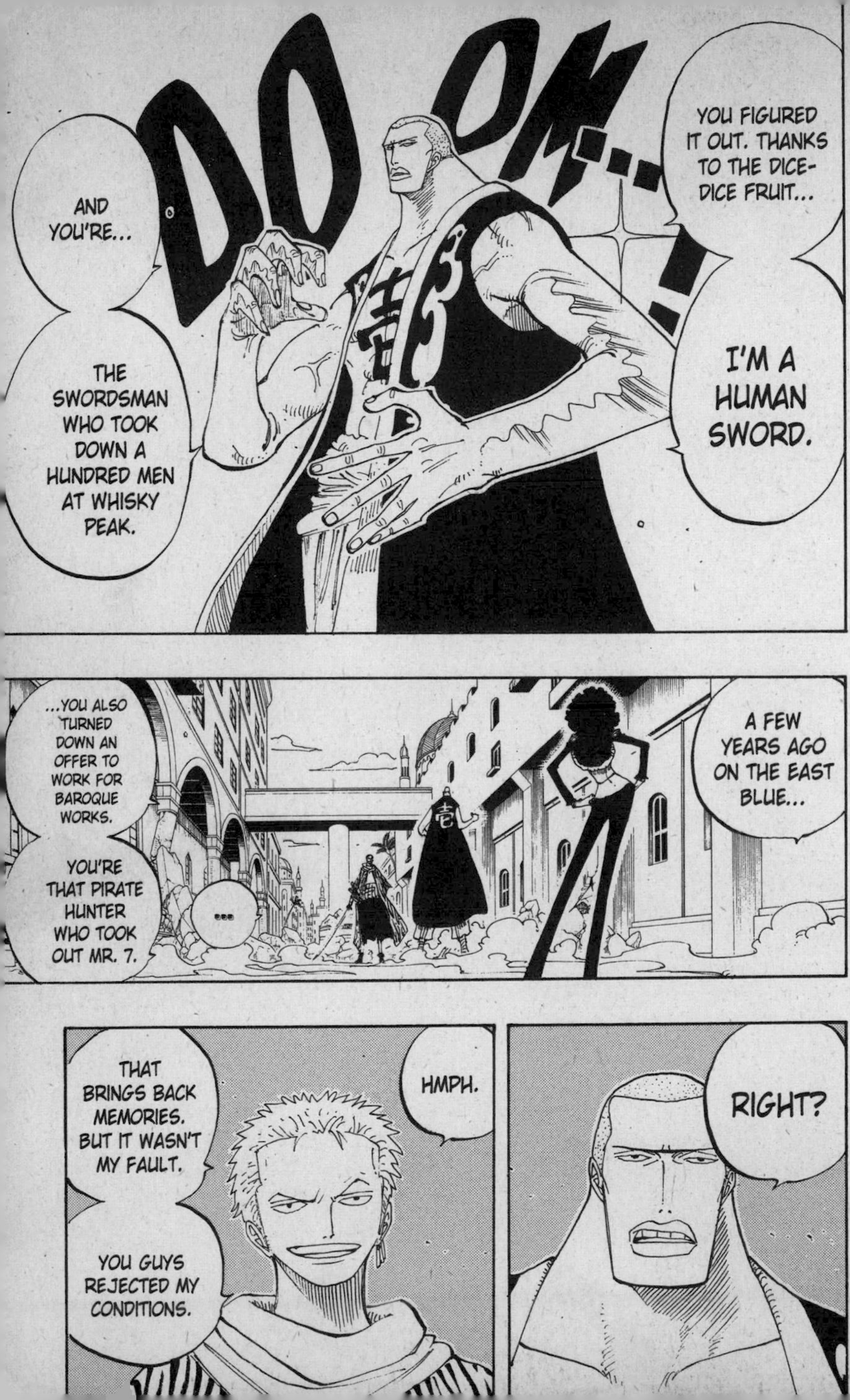
YOU FIGURED IT OUT. THANKS TO THE DICE-DICE FRUIT...
I'M A HUMAN SWORD.
DOOM...!
AND YOU'RE...
THE SWORDSMAN WHO TOOK DOWN A HUNDRED MEN AT WHISKY PEAK.
A FEW YEARS AGO ON THE EAST BLUE...
...YOU ALSO TURNED DOWN AN OFFER TO WORK FOR BAROQUE WORKS.
YOU'RE THAT PIRATE HUNTER WHO TOOK OUT MR. 7.
...
RIGHT?
HMPH.
THAT BRINGS BACK MEMORIES. BUT IT WASN'T MY FAULT.
YOU GUYS REJECTED MY CONDITIONS.

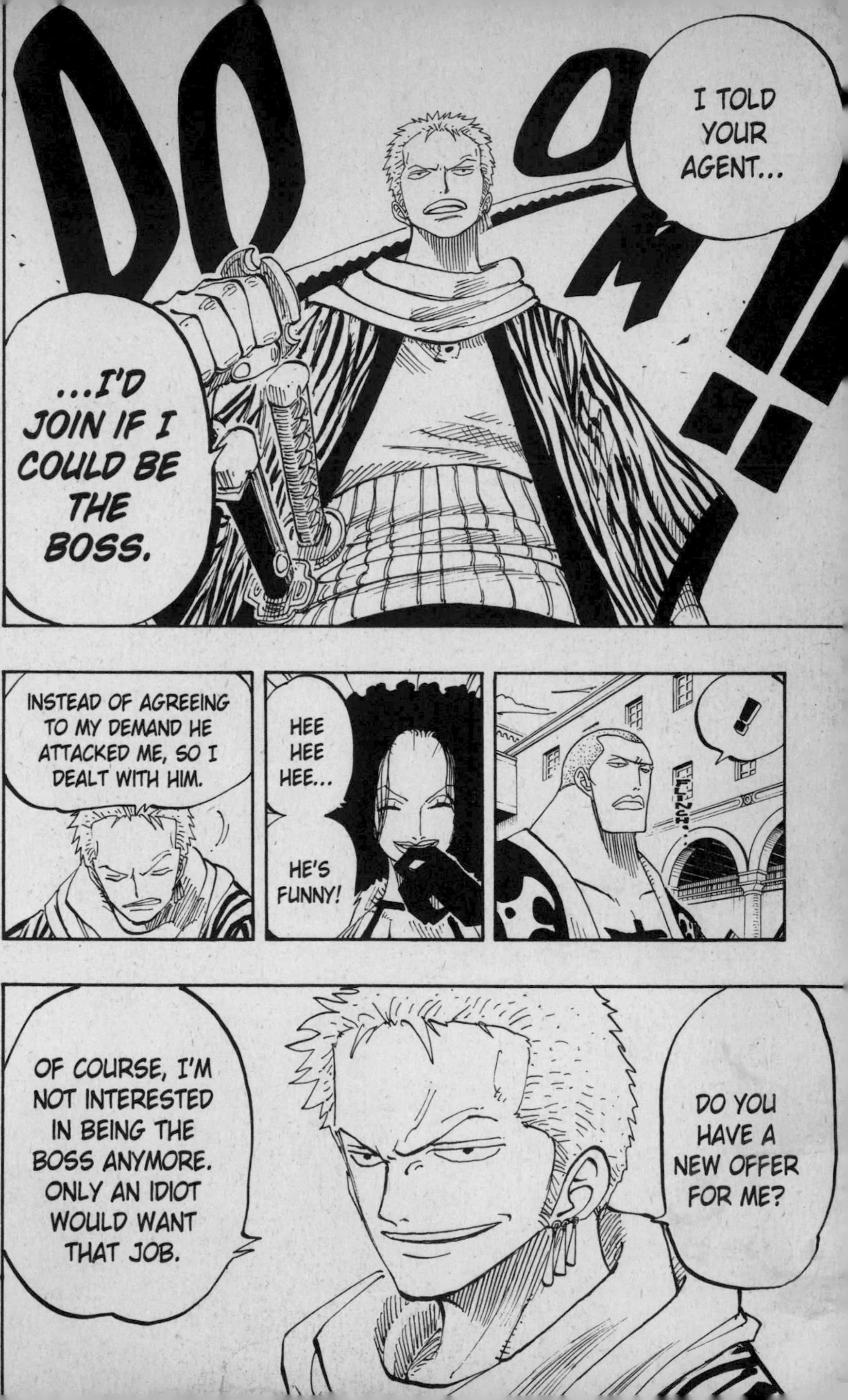
I TOLD YOUR AGENT...
DOOM!!!
...I'D JOIN IF I COULD BE THE BOSS.
!
FLINCH
HEE HEE HEE...
HE'S FUNNY!
INSTEAD OF AGREEING TO MY DEMAND HE ATTACKED ME, SO I DEALT WITH HIM.
DO YOU HAVE A NEW OFFER FOR ME?
OF COURSE, I'M NOT INTERESTED IN BEING THE BOSS ANYMORE. ONLY AN IDIOT WOULD WANT THAT JOB.

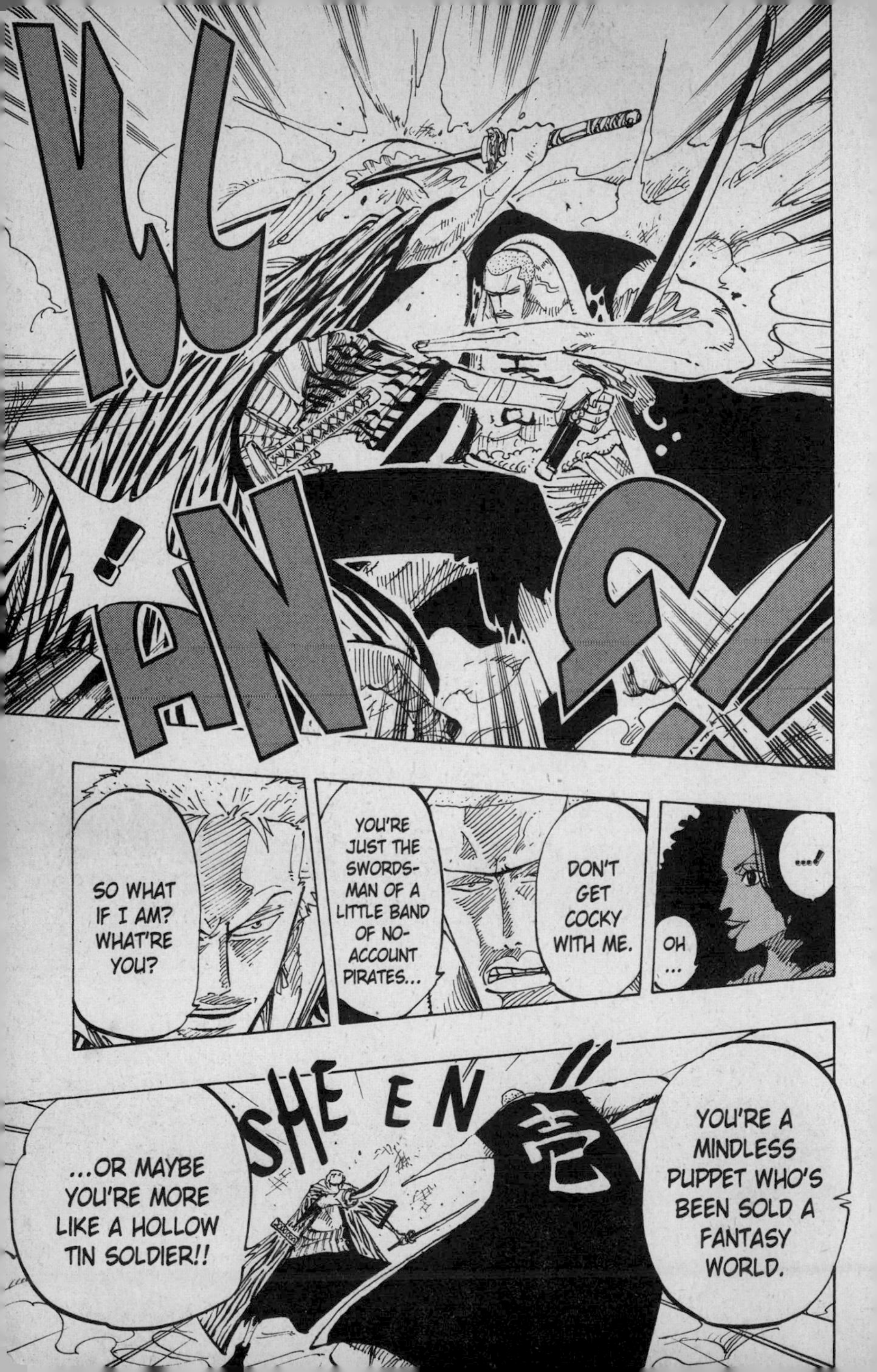
WHANG!!
...!
OH ...
DON'T GET COCKY WITH ME.
YOU'RE JUST THE SWORDS-MAN OF A LITTLE BAND OF NO-ACCOUNT PIRATES...
SO WHAT IF I AM? WHAT'RE YOU?
YOU'RE A MINDLESS PUPPET WHO'S BEEN SOLD A FANTASY WORLD.
SHEEN
壱
...OR MAYBE YOU'RE MORE LIKE A HOLLOW TIN SOLDIER!!

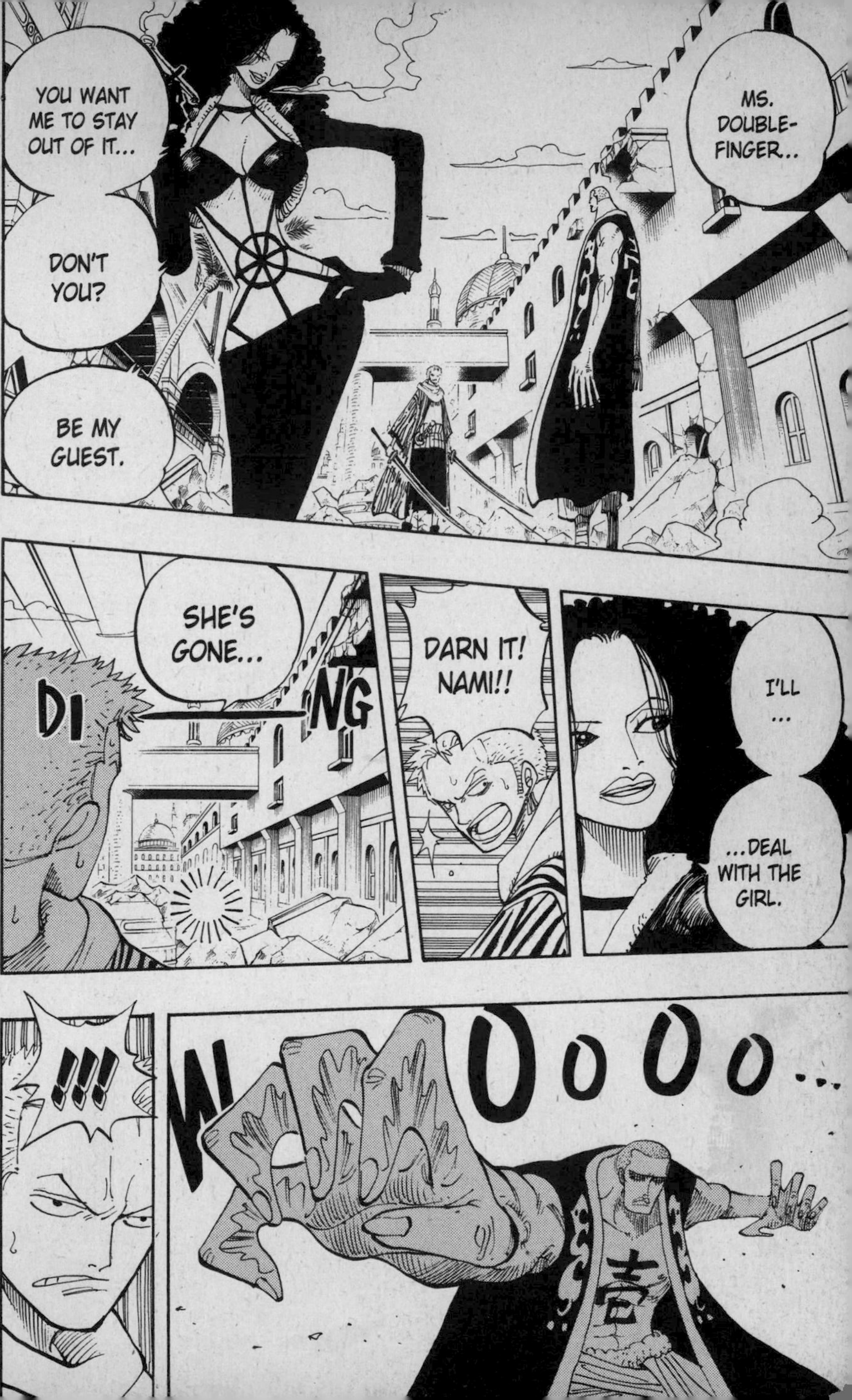
MS. DOUBLE-FINGER...
YOU WANT ME TO STAY OUT OF IT...
DON'T YOU?
BE MY GUEST.
I'LL ...
...DEAL WITH THE GIRL.
DARN IT! NAMI!!
SHE'S GONE...
DI
NG
WOOOO...
!!!

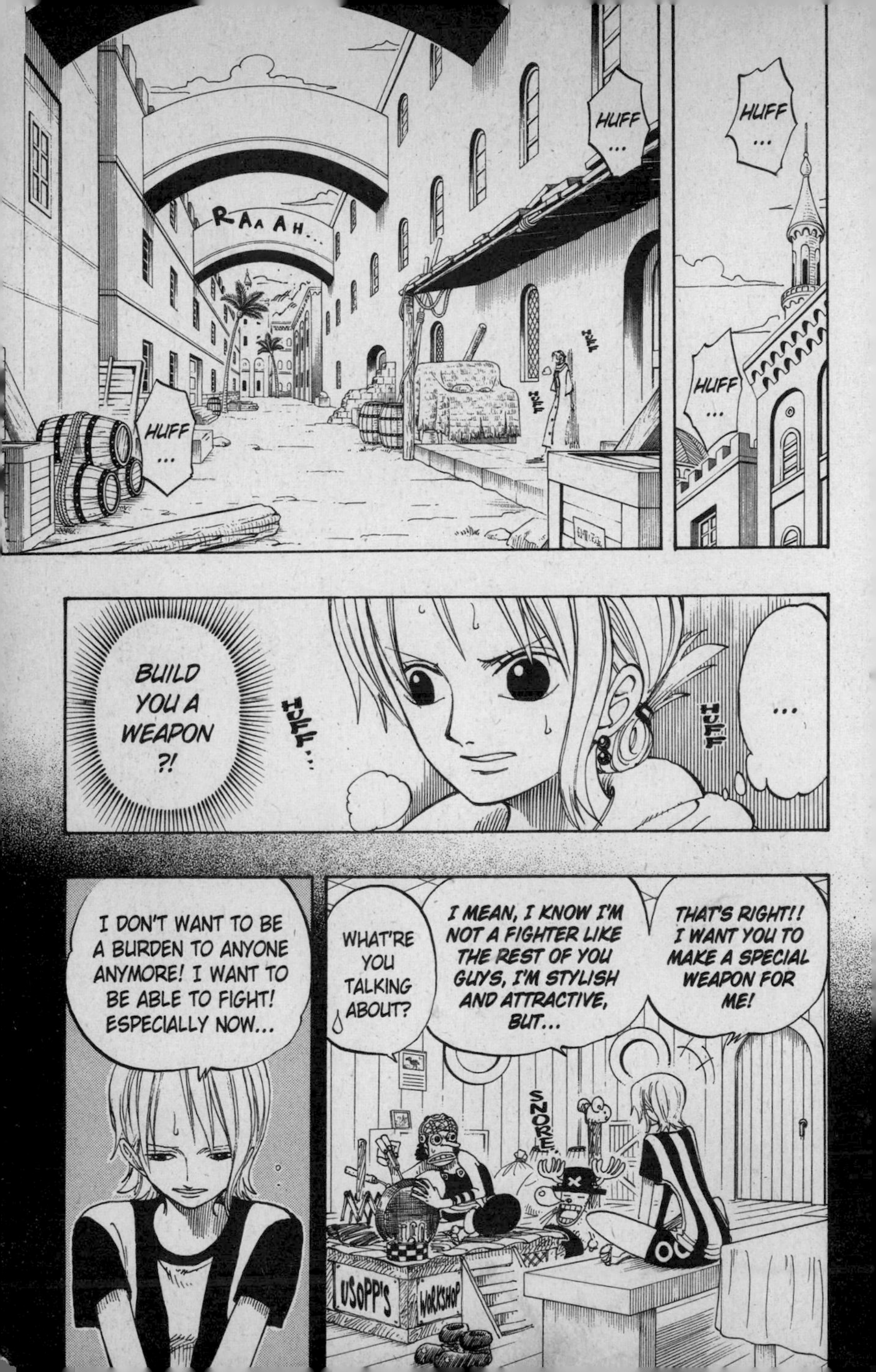
HUFF...
HUFF...
RAAAH...
HUFF...
HUFF...
...
HUFF
BUILD YOU A WEAPON?!
HUFF...
THAT'S RIGHT!! I WANT YOU TO MAKE A SPECIAL WEAPON FOR ME!
I MEAN, I KNOW I'M NOT A FIGHTER LIKE THE REST OF YOU GUYS, I'M STYLISH AND ATTRACTIVE, BUT...
WHAT'RE YOU TALKING ABOUT?
SNORE
USOPP'S
WORKSHOP
I DON'T WANT TO BE A BURDEN TO ANYONE ANYMORE! I WANT TO BE ABLE TO FIGHT! ESPECIALLY NOW...

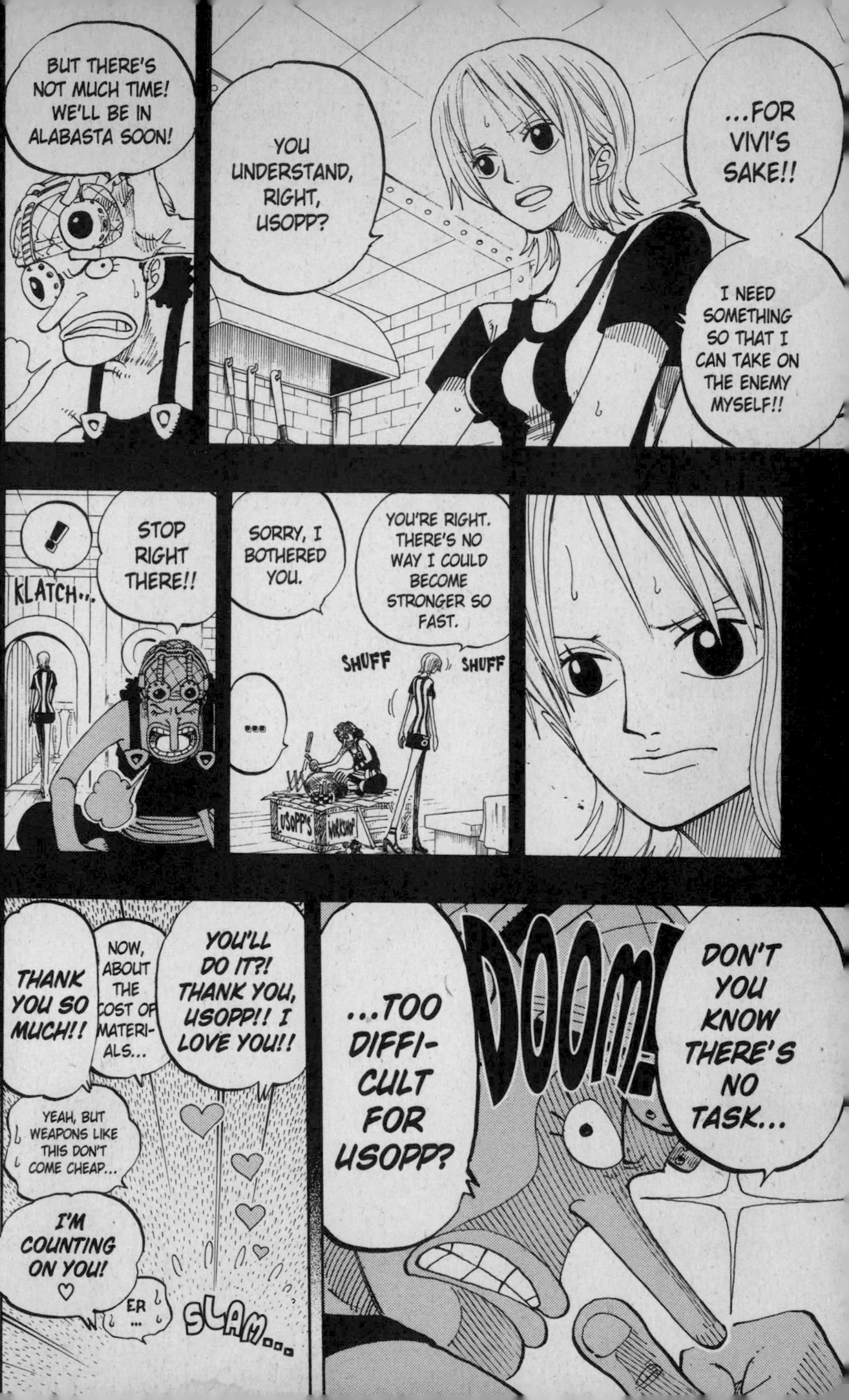
...FOR VIVI'S SAKE!!
I NEED SOMETHING SO THAT I CAN TAKE ON THE ENEMY MYSELF!!
YOU UNDERSTAND, RIGHT, USOPP?
BUT THERE'S NOT MUCH TIME! WE'LL BE IN ALABASTA SOON!
YOU'RE RIGHT. THERE'S NO WAY I COULD BECOME STRONGER SO FAST.
SORRY, I BOTHERED YOU.
SHUFF
SHUFF
...
USOPP'S WORKSHOP
STOP RIGHT THERE!!
!
KLATCH...
DON'T YOU KNOW THERE'S NO TASK...
DOOM!
...TOO DIFFI-CULT FOR USOPP?
YOU'LL DO IT?! THANK YOU, USOPP!! I LOVE YOU!!
NOW, ABOUT THE COST OF MATERI-ALS...
THANK YOU SO MUCH!!
YEAH, BUT WEAPONS LIKE THIS DON'T COME CHEAP...
I'M COUNTING ON YOU! ♡
ER...
SLAM...

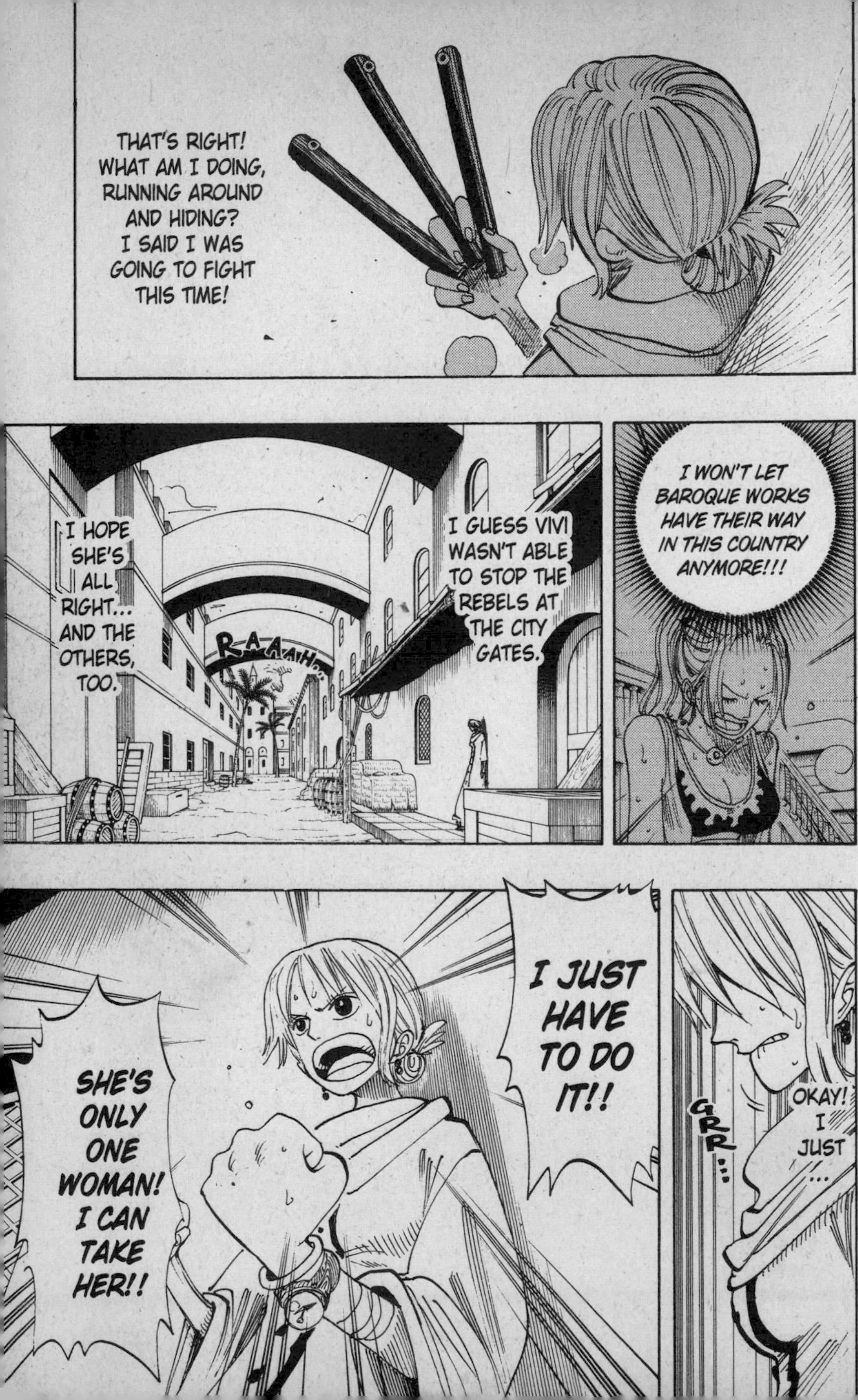
THAT'S RIGHT! WHAT AM I DOING, RUNNING AROUND AND HIDING? I SAID I WAS GOING TO FIGHT THIS TIME!
I WON'T LET BAROQUE WORKS HAVE THEIR WAY IN THIS COUNTRY ANYMORE!!!
I GUESS VIVI WASN'T ABLE TO STOP THE REBELS AT THE CITY GATES.
I HOPE SHE'S ALL RIGHT... AND THE OTHERS, TOO.
OKAY! I JUST...
GRR...
I JUST HAVE TO DO IT!!
SHE'S ONLY ONE WOMAN! I CAN TAKE HER!!

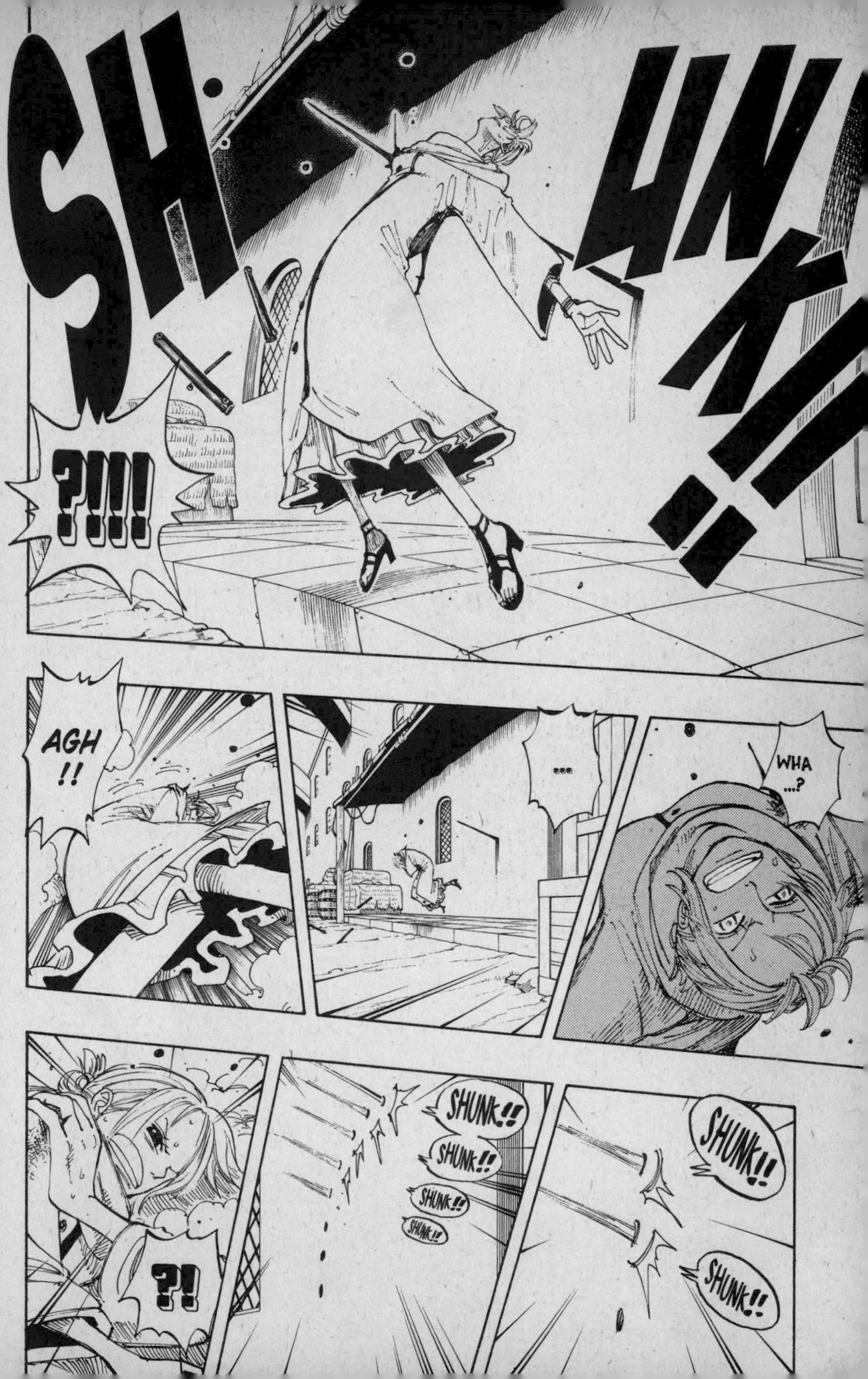
SHUNK!!
?!!!
WHA ...?
...
AGH !!
SHUNK!!
SHUNK!!
SHUNK!!
SHUNK!!
SHUNK!!
SHUNK!!
?!

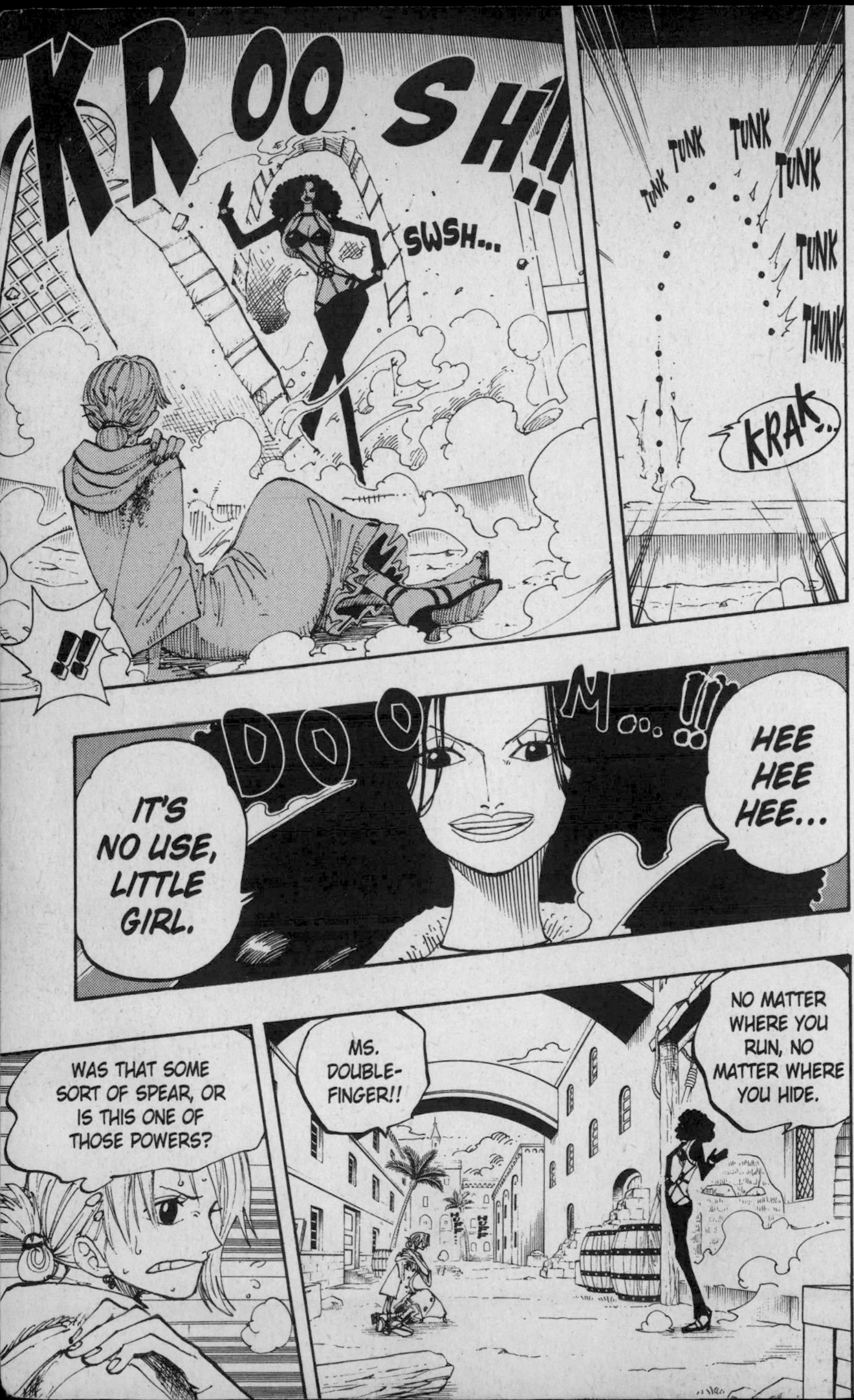
TUNK TUNK TUNK TUNK TUNK THUNK
KRAK...
KR OO SH!!
SWSH...
!!
DOOOM..!!
HEE HEE HEE...
IT'S NO USE, LITTLE GIRL.
NO MATTER WHERE YOU RUN, NO MATTER WHERE YOU HIDE.
MS. DOUBLE-FINGER!!
WAS THAT SOME SORT OF SPEAR, OR IS THIS ONE OF THOSE POWERS?

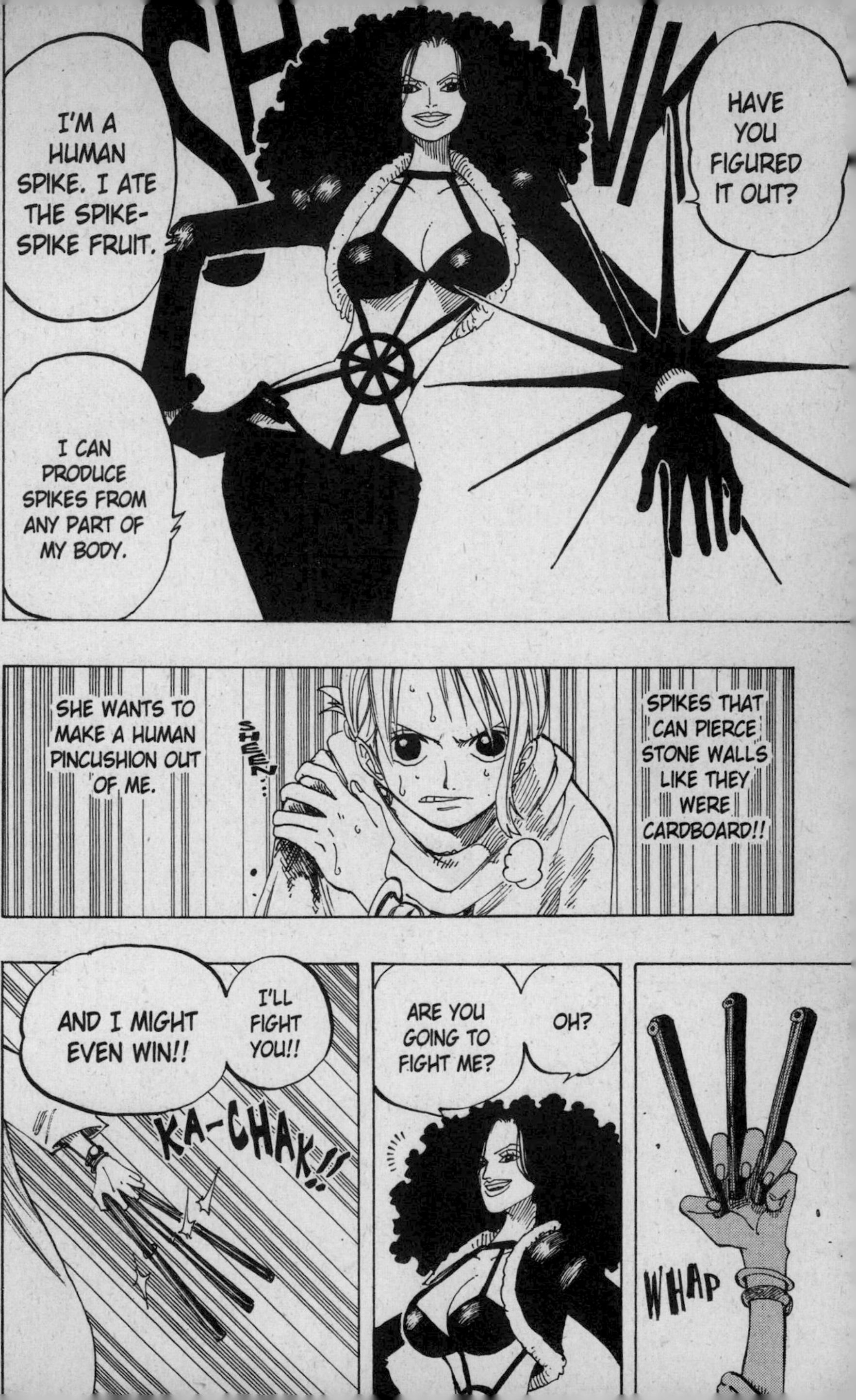
HAVE YOU FIGURED IT OUT?
I'M A HUMAN SPIKE. I ATE THE SPIKE-SPIKE FRUIT.
I CAN PRODUCE SPIKES FROM ANY PART OF MY BODY.
SPIKES THAT CAN PIERCE STONE WALLS LIKE THEY WERE CARDBOARD!!
SHEEN...
SHE WANTS TO MAKE A HUMAN PINCUSHION OUT OF ME.
WHAP
OH?
ARE YOU GOING TO FIGHT ME?
I'LL FIGHT YOU!!
AND I MIGHT EVEN WIN!!
KA-CHAK!!

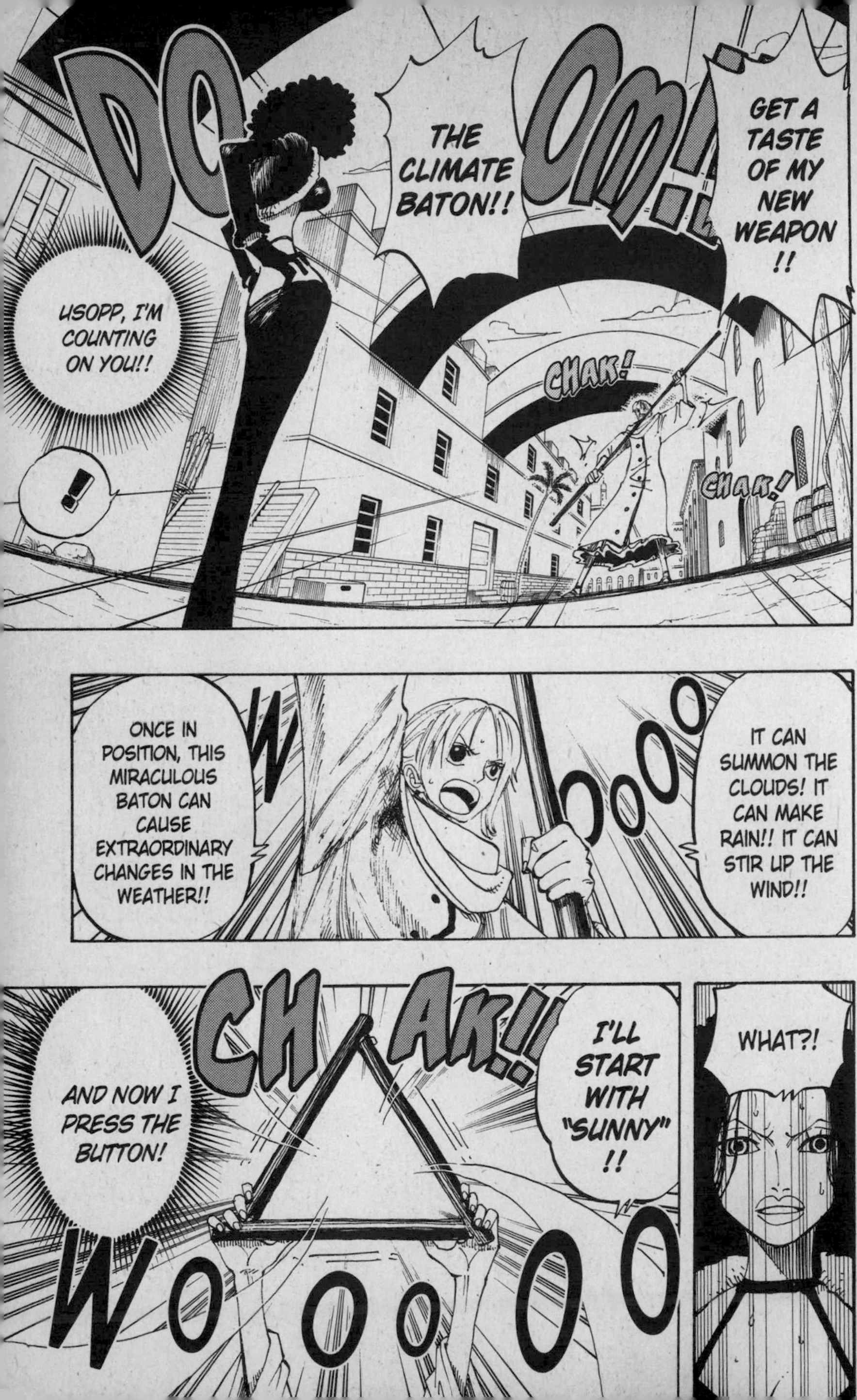
GET A TASTE OF MY NEW WEAPON!!
DOOM!!
THE CLIMATE BATON!!
USOPP, I'M COUNTING ON YOU!!
CHAK!
CHAK!
!
IT CAN SUMMON THE CLOUDS! IT CAN MAKE RAIN!! IT CAN STIR UP THE WIND!!
WOOOOO
ONCE IN POSITION, THIS MIRACULOUS BATON CAN CAUSE EXTRAORDINARY CHANGES IN THE WEATHER!!
WHAT?!
I'LL START WITH "SUNNY"!!
CHAK!!
AND NOW I PRESS THE BUTTON!
WOOOOO

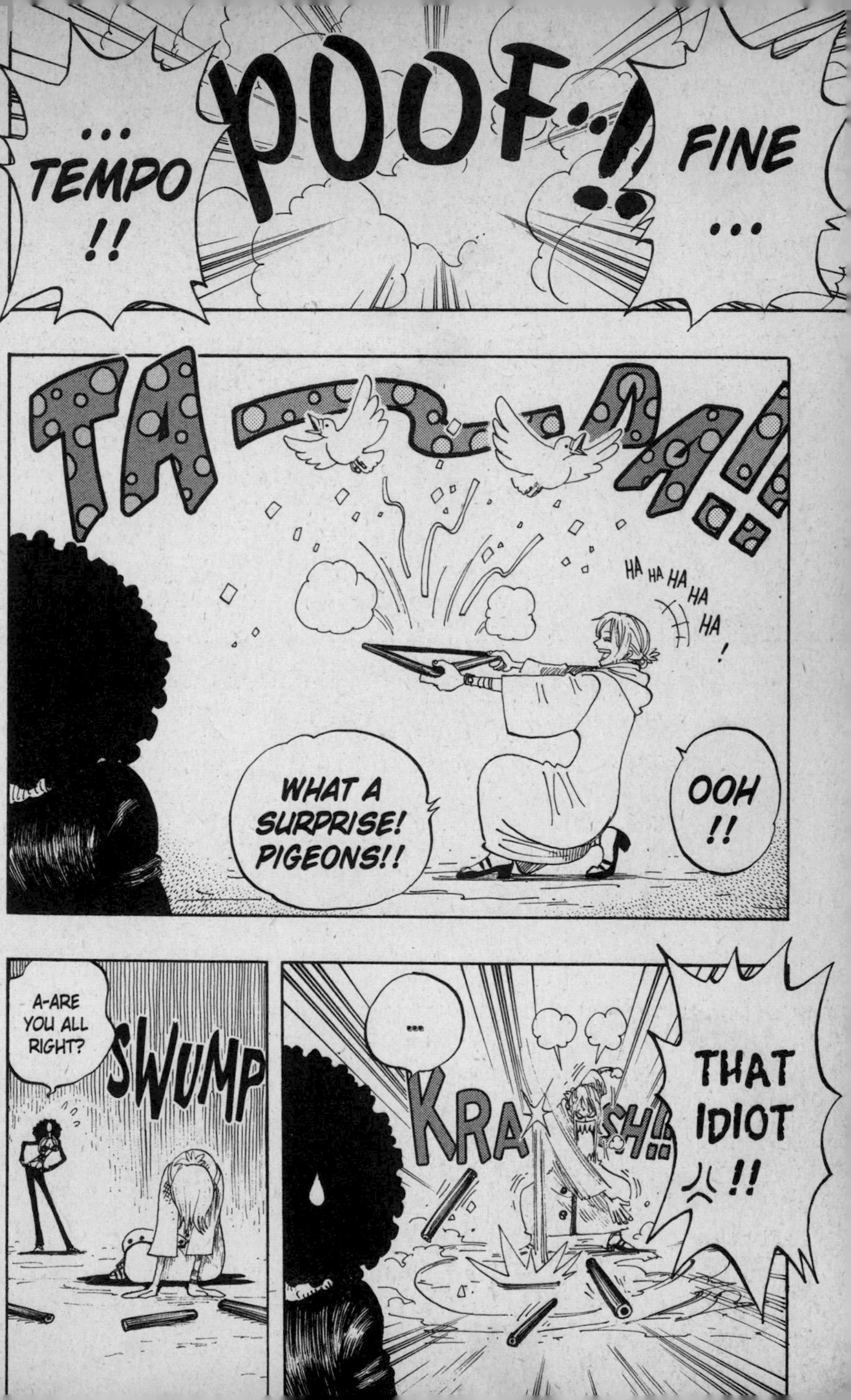
FINE ...
POOF!!
... TEMPO !!
TA~A!!
HA HA HA HA HA!
OOH !!
WHAT A SURPRISE! PIGEONS!!
THAT IDIOT !!
KRASH!!
...
SWUMP
A-ARE YOU ALL RIGHT?

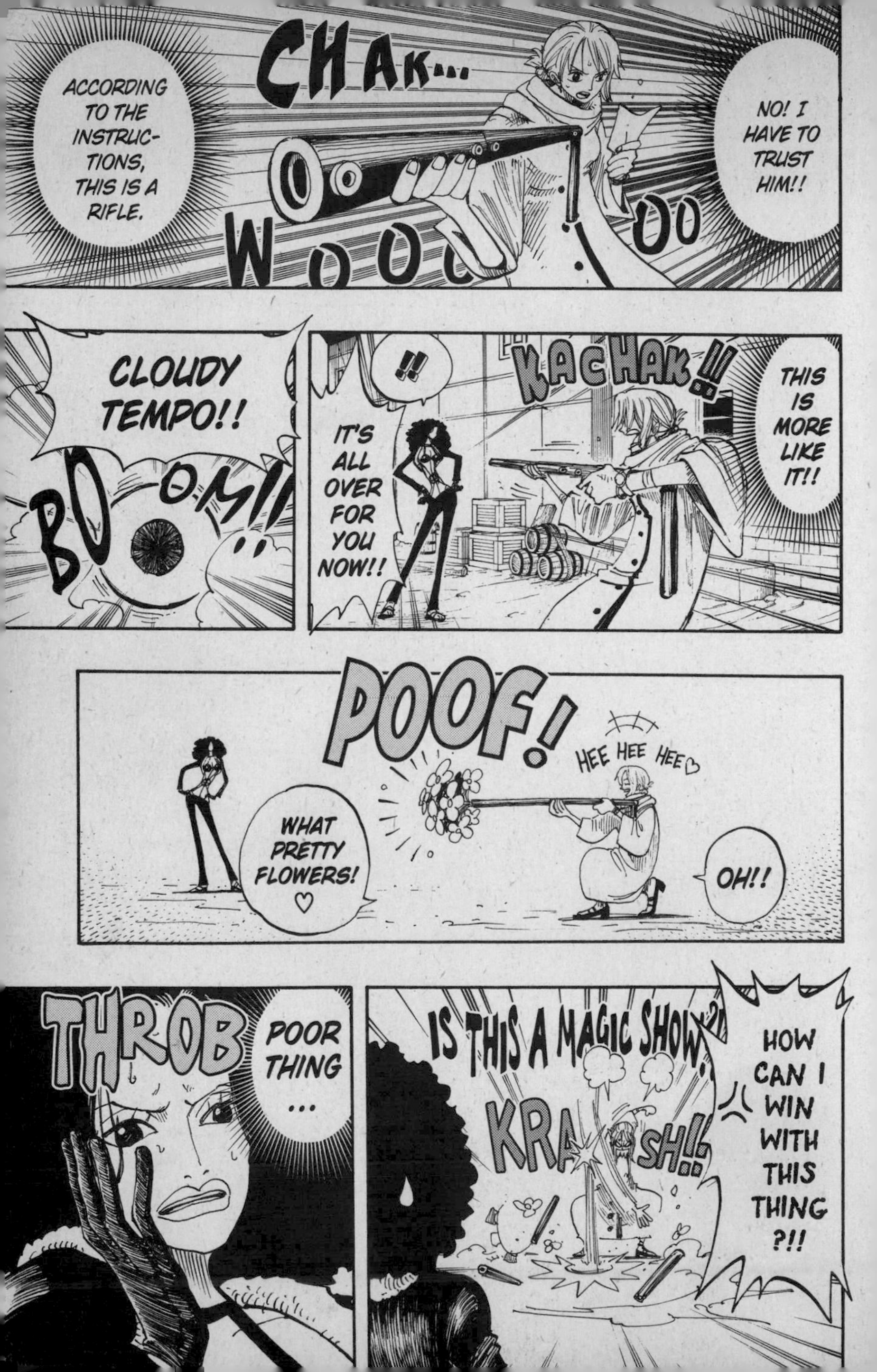
NO! I HAVE TO TRUST HIM!!
CHAK...
ACCORDING TO THE INSTRUCTIONS, THIS IS A RIFLE.
WOOOOOO
THIS IS MORE LIKE IT!!
KACHAK!!
!!
IT'S ALL OVER FOR YOU NOW!!
CLOUDY TEMPO!!
BOOM!!
HEE HEE HEE♡
POOF!
OH!!
WHAT PRETTY FLOWERS! ♡
HOW CAN I WIN WITH THIS THING?!!
IS THIS A MAGIC SHOW?!
KRASH!!
POOR THING...
THROB

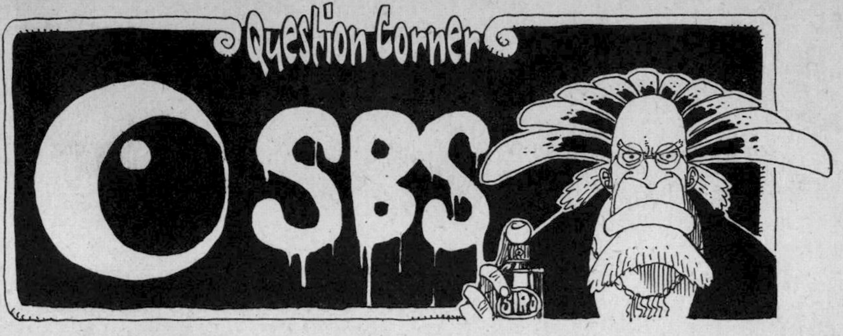
Question Corner
SBS

Reader: What are *orenji peko* and *appuru tee*?

Oda: Surely, you know what apple tea is? It's tea. Orange pekoe is a variety of tea as well. The agents of Baroque Works all have their own favorite teas. For example, Mr. 3 likes Earl Grey, Ms. Golden Week likes green tea, Mr. 5 prefers gunpowder tea, and Ms. Valentine likes lemon tea. They're always drinking tea in various situations. However, Mr. 2 prefers octopars.

Reader: Hello, Oda Sensei. As I was rereading the books, I noticed that in Vol. 18, page 162, panel 2, there's a person like this (←left). Then in Vol. 19, page 15, panel 5, there's a person like this (→right). Are these two the same person?

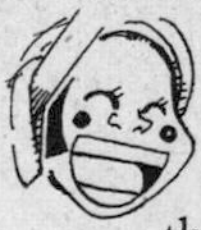

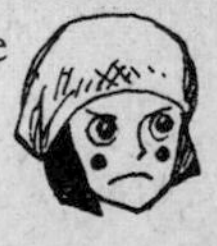

Oda: Yes, they're the same person. If you look closely at the rebel forces, you'll find a number of members of the old Sand-Sand Band. Very perceptive of you to notice.

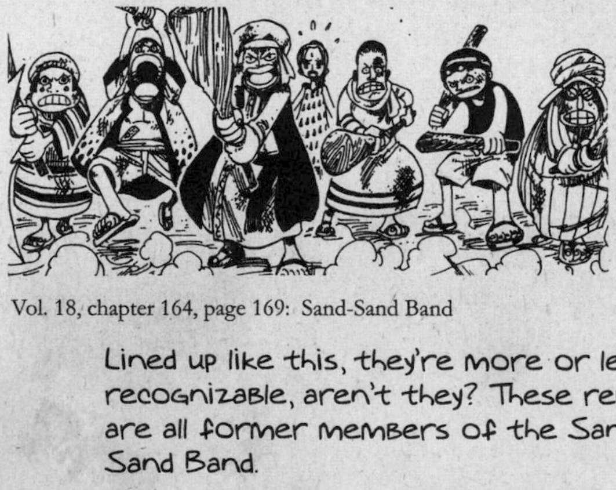

Vol. 18, chapter 164, page 169: Sand-Sand Band

11 years later

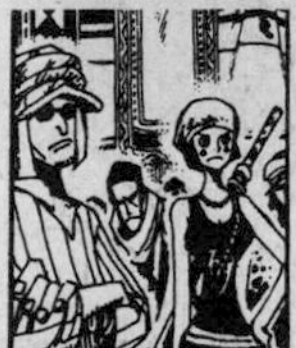

Vol. 19, chapter 167, page 15

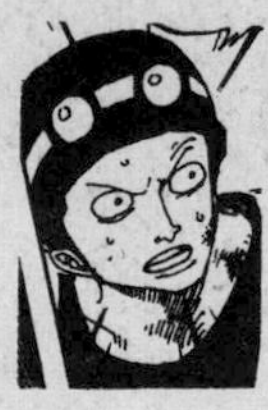

Vol. 19, chapter 172, page 114

Lined up like this, they're more or less recognizable, aren't they? These rebels are all former members of the Sand-Sand Band.

Chapter 191:
SHE WHO CONTROLS THE WEATHER

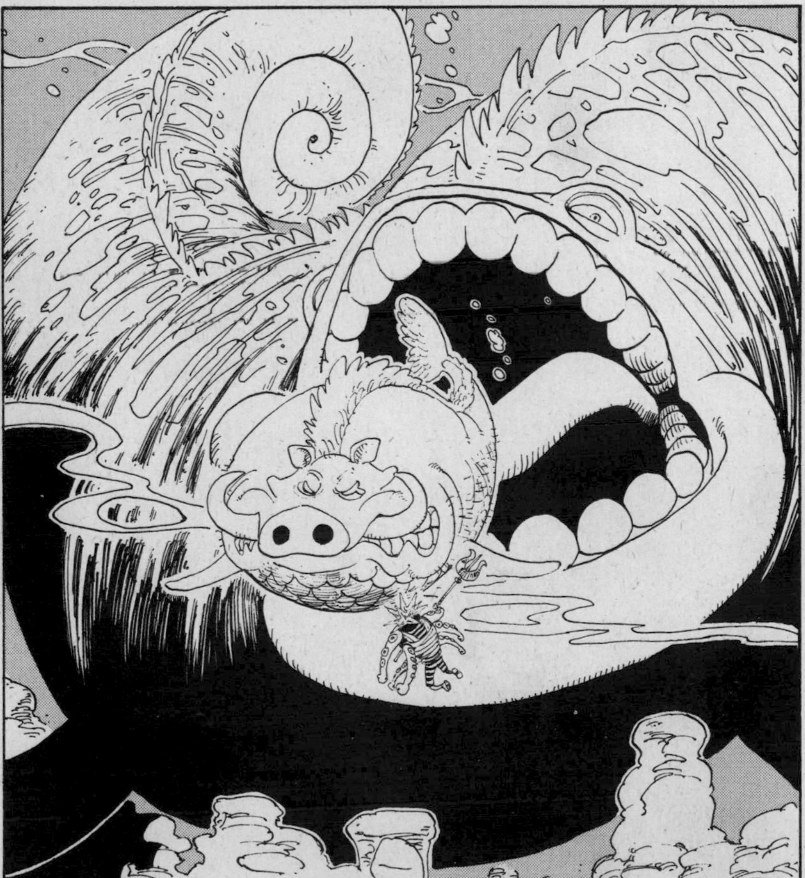

HACHI'S WALK ON THE SEAFLOOR, VOL. 9:
"A SEA BOAR HUNTED BY A SEA MONSTER"

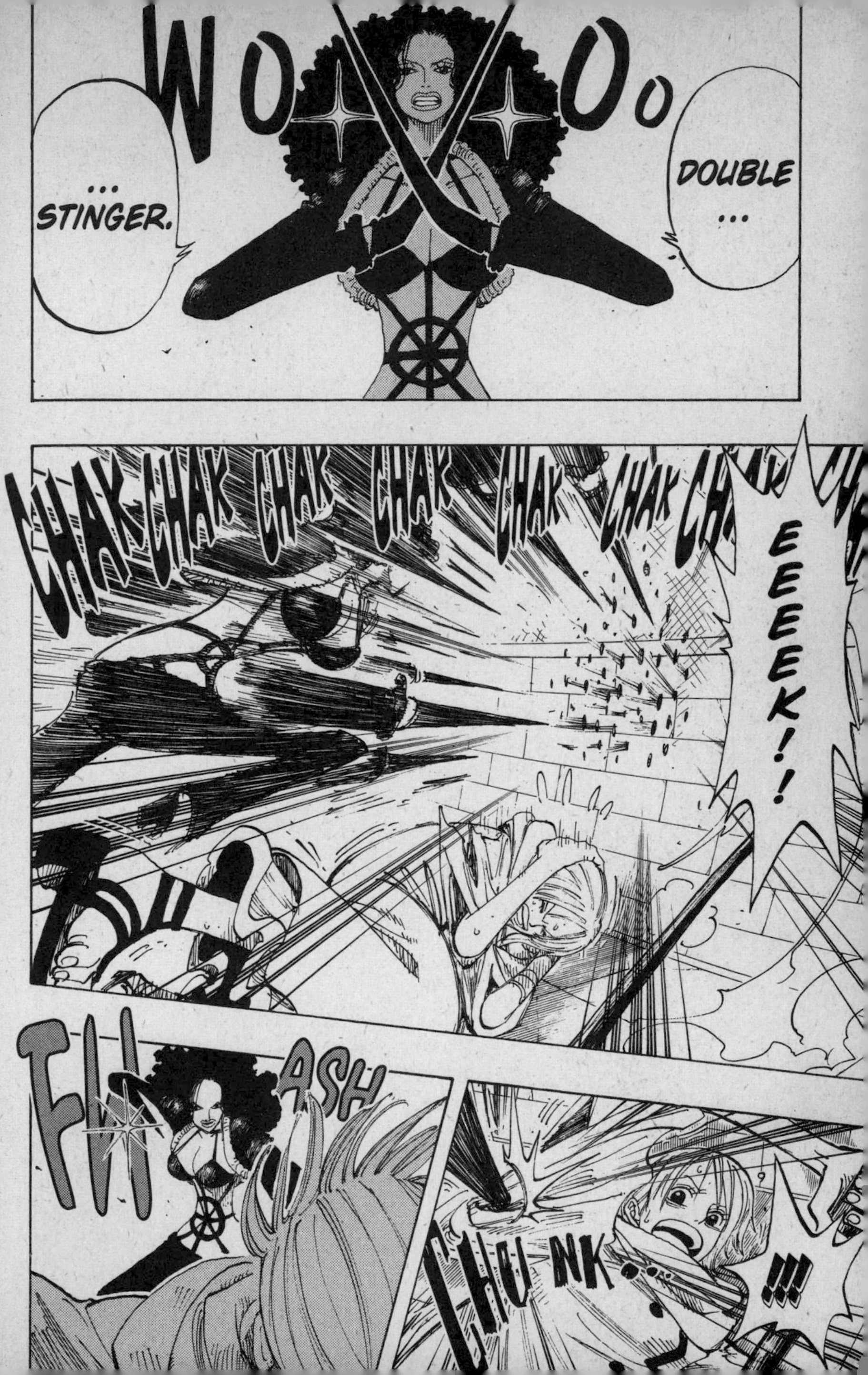
DOUBLE ...
WOOo
... STINGER.
CHAK CHAK CHAK CHAK CHAK CHAK CHA
EEEEEK!!
THUNK!!!
FLASH

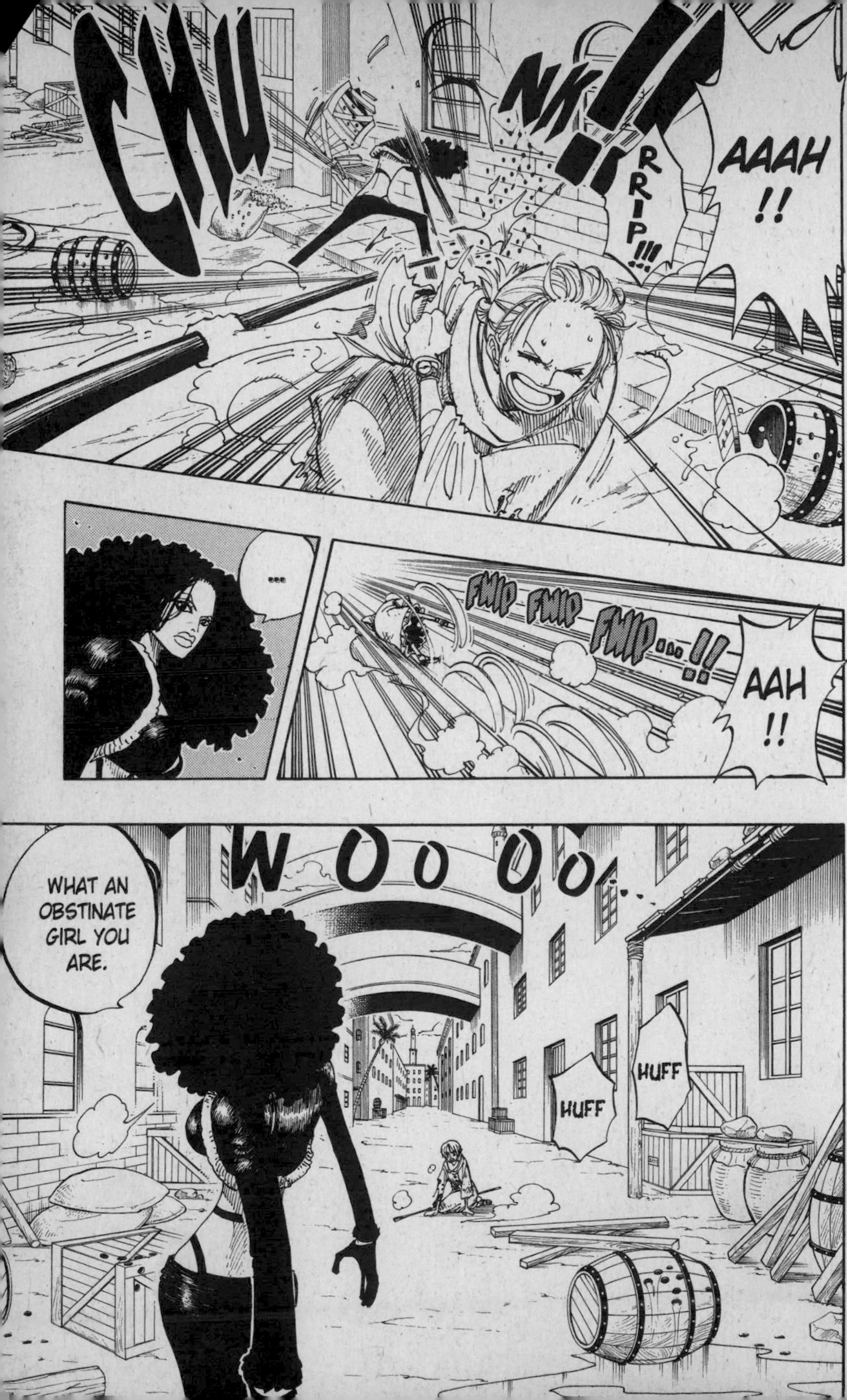
AAAH!!
RRIP!!!
CHUNK!!
AAH!!
FWIP FWIP FWIP...!!
...
WOOOO...
HUFF
HUFF
WHAT AN OBSTINATE GIRL YOU ARE.

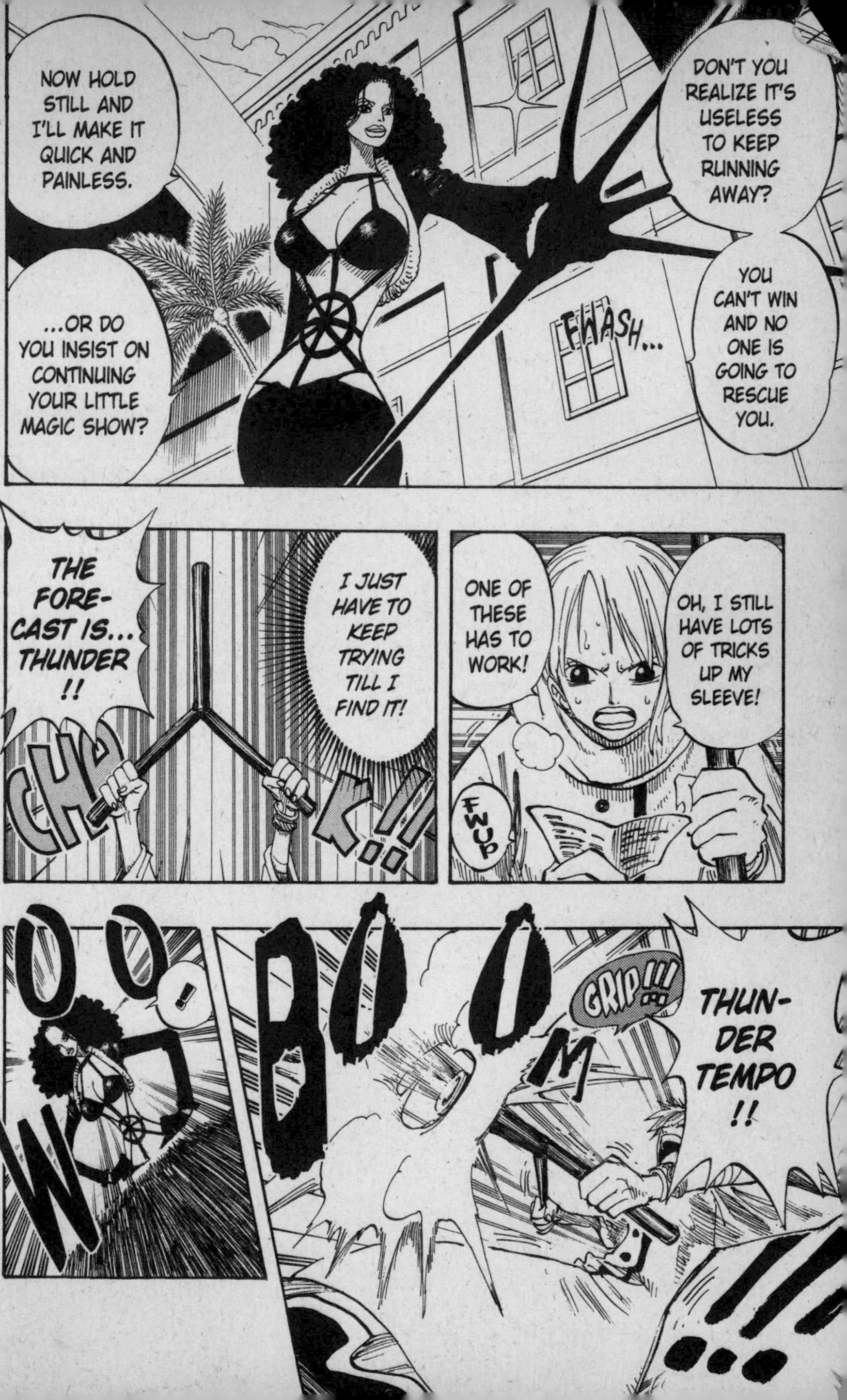
DON'T YOU REALIZE IT'S USELESS TO KEEP RUNNING AWAY?
NOW HOLD STILL AND I'LL MAKE IT QUICK AND PAINLESS.
FWASH...
YOU CAN'T WIN AND NO ONE IS GOING TO RESCUE YOU.
...OR DO YOU INSIST ON CONTINUING YOUR LITTLE MAGIC SHOW?
OH, I STILL HAVE LOTS OF TRICKS UP MY SLEEVE!
ONE OF THESE HAS TO WORK!
FWUP
I JUST HAVE TO KEEP TRYING TILL I FIND IT!
THE FORE-CAST IS... THUNDER!!
CHK!!
THUN-DER TEMPO!!
GRIP!!!
BOOM
!!
!
WOO

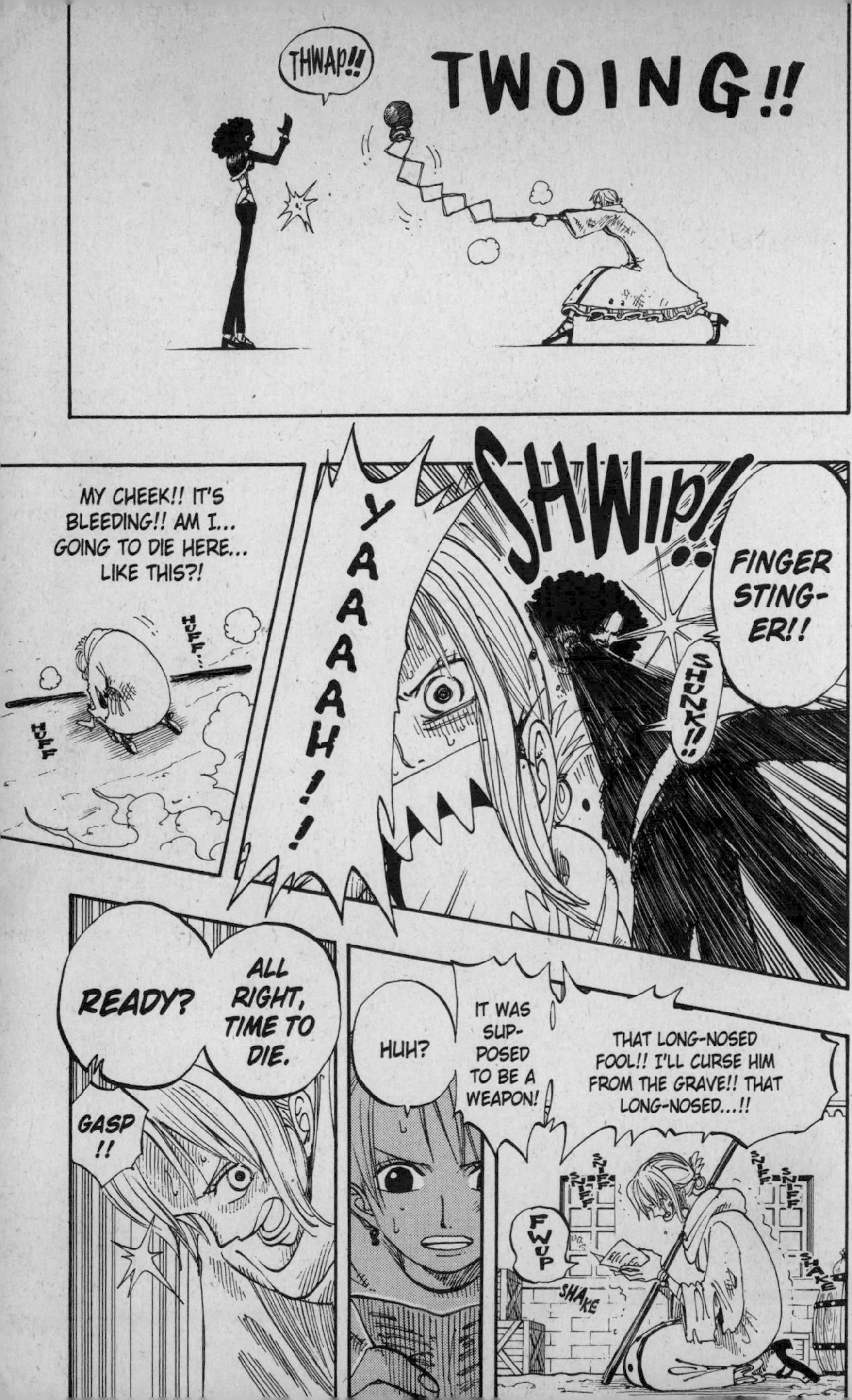

TWOING!!
THWAP!!
SHWIP!
FINGER STINGER!!
SHUNK!!
YAAAAAH!!!
MY CHEEK!! IT'S BLEEDING!! AM I... GOING TO DIE HERE... LIKE THIS?!
HUFF...
HUFF
THAT LONG-NOSED FOOL!! I'LL CURSE HIM FROM THE GRAVE!! THAT LONG-NOSED...!!
SNIFF
SNIFF
SNIFF
SNIFF
FWUP
SHAKE
SHAKE
IT WAS SUPPOSED TO BE A WEAPON!
HUH?
ALL RIGHT, TIME TO DIE.
READY?
GASP!!

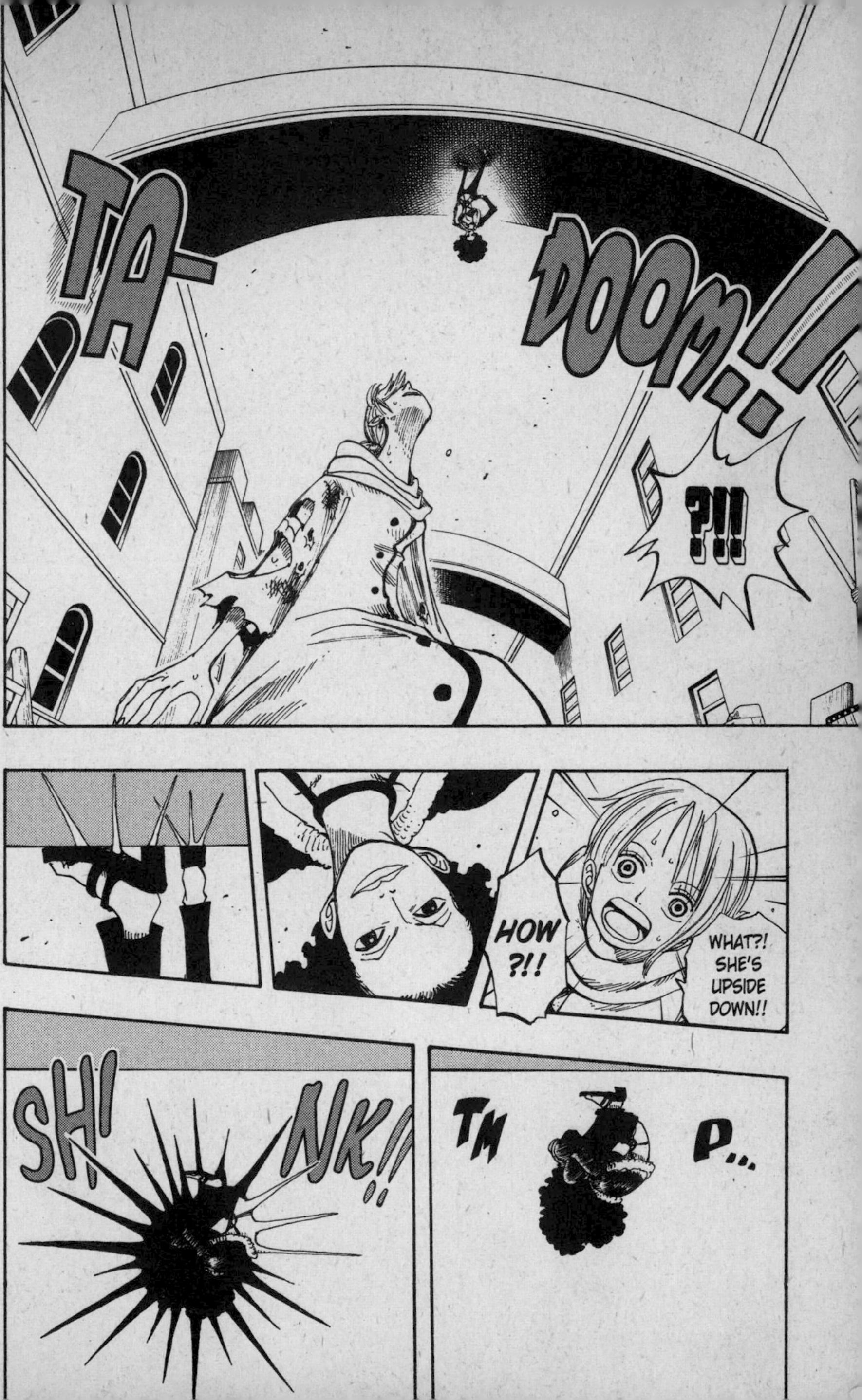
TA-DOOM!!
?!!
WHAT?! SHE'S UPSIDE DOWN!!
HOW ?!!
TMP...
SHINK!!

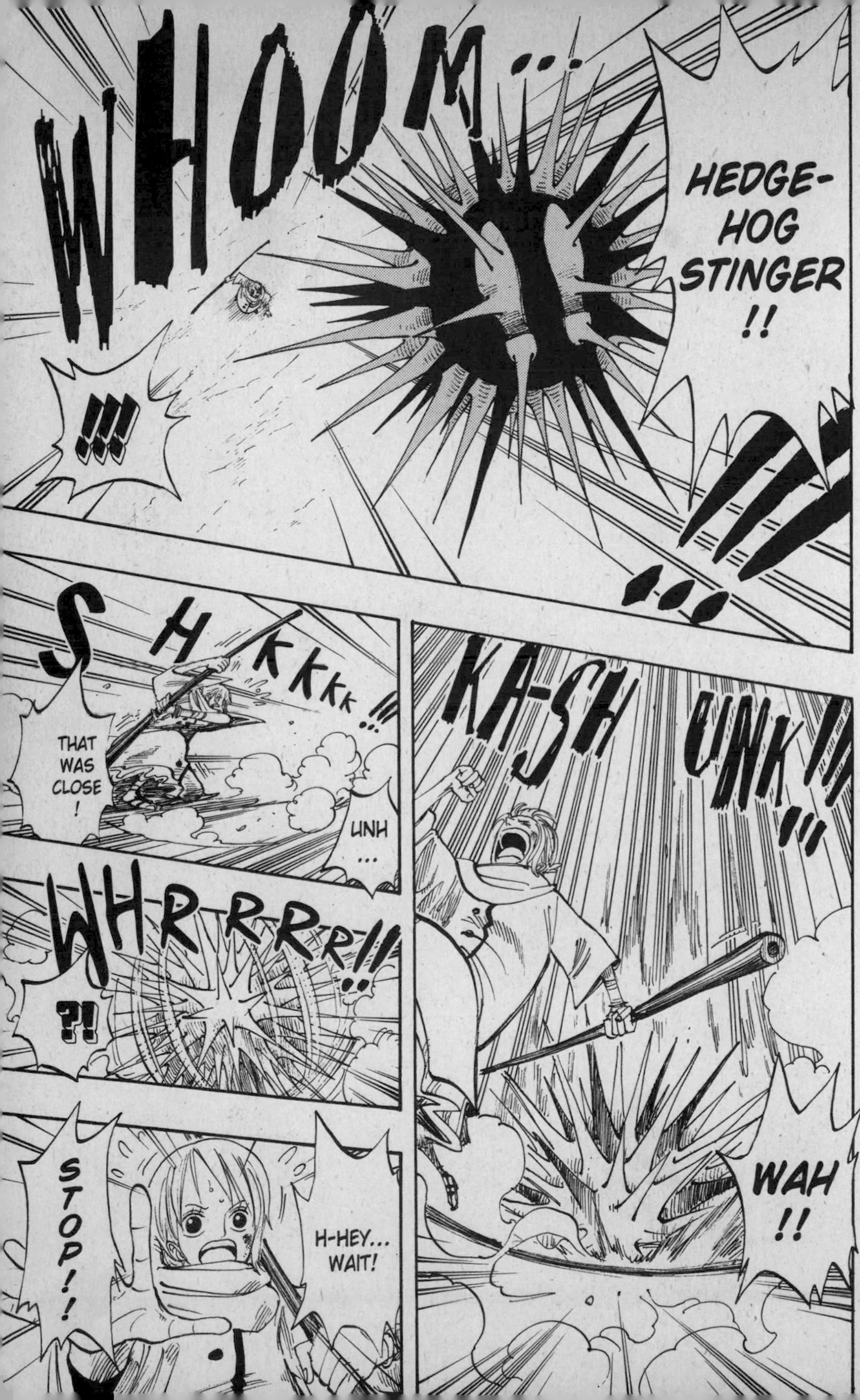
HEDGE-HOG STINGER!!
!!...
WHOOM..!
!!!
KA-SHUNK!!!
WAH!!
SHKKKK!!!
UNH...
THAT WAS CLOSE!
WHRRRRR!!
?!
H-HEY... WAIT!
STOP!!

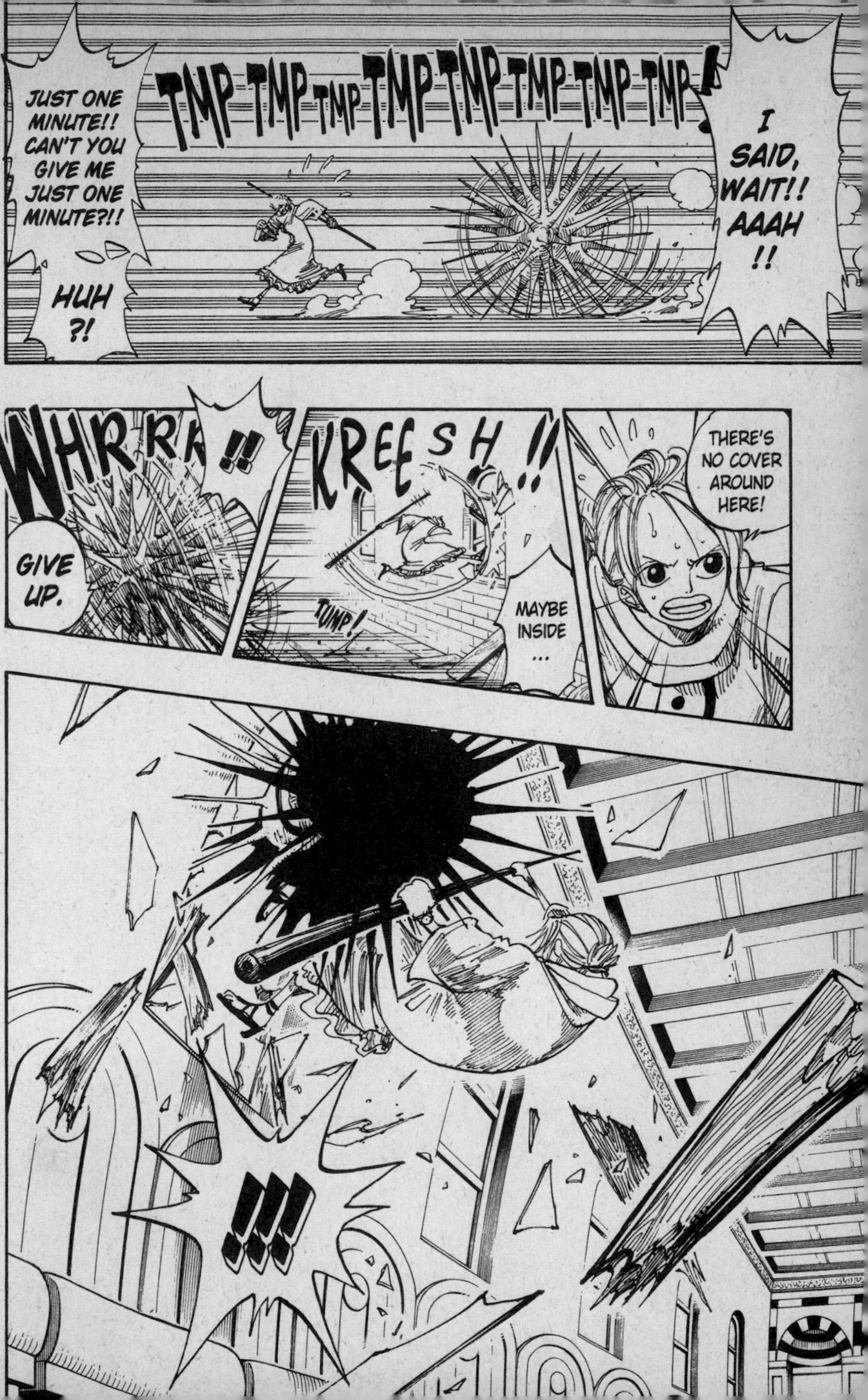
I SAID, WAIT!! AAAH !!
TMP TMP TMP TMP TMP TMP TMP TMP!
JUST ONE MINUTE!! CAN'T YOU GIVE ME JUST ONE MINUTE?!!
HUH ?!
THERE'S NO COVER AROUND HERE!
MAYBE INSIDE ...
KREESH!!
TUMP!
WHRRRK!!
GIVE UP.
!!!

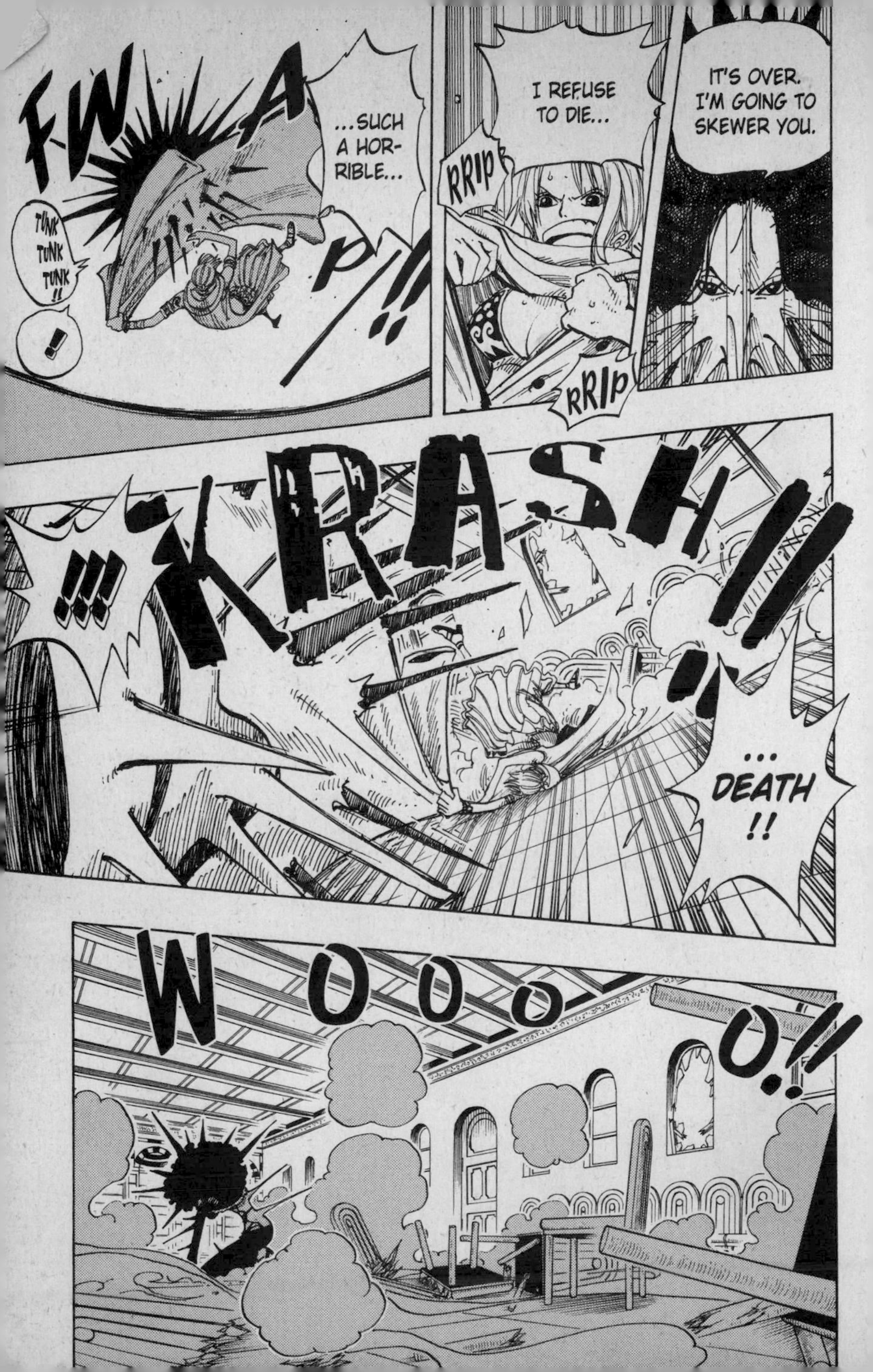
IT'S OVER. I'M GOING TO SKEWER YOU.
I REFUSE TO DIE...
RRIP
RRIP
...SUCH A HOR-RIBLE...
FWAP!!
TUNK TUNK TUNK!!
!
KRASH!!
... DEATH!!
!!!
WOOOOO!!

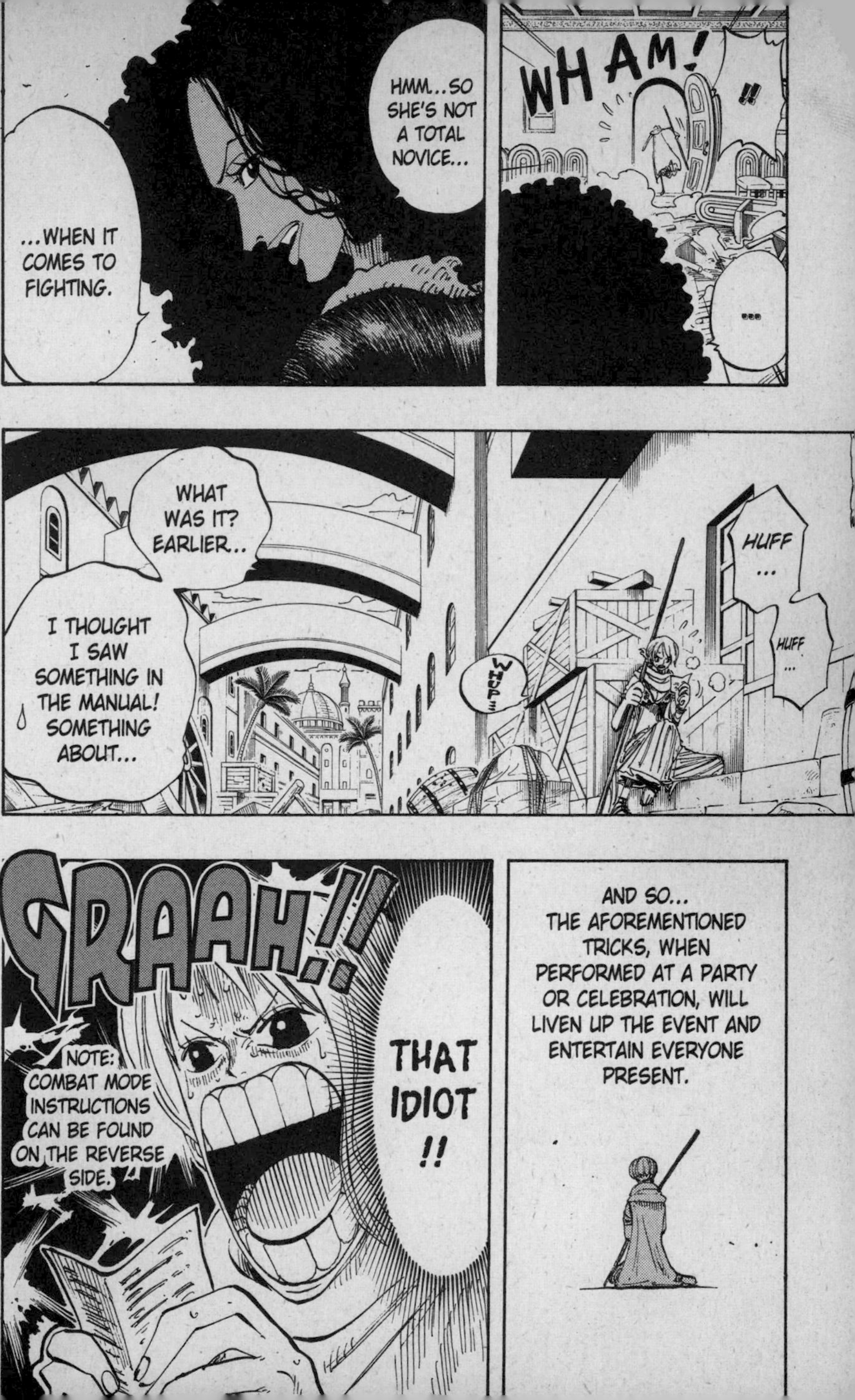
WHAM!!
...
HMM...SO SHE'S NOT A TOTAL NOVICE...
...WHEN IT COMES TO FIGHTING.
HUFF...
HUFF...
WHUP!!
WHAT WAS IT? EARLIER...
I THOUGHT I SAW SOMETHING IN THE MANUAL! SOMETHING ABOUT...
AND SO... THE AFOREMENTIONED TRICKS, WHEN PERFORMED AT A PARTY OR CELEBRATION, WILL LIVEN UP THE EVENT AND ENTERTAIN EVERYONE PRESENT.
GRAAH!!
THAT IDIOT!!
NOTE: COMBAT MODE INSTRUCTIONS CAN BE FOUND ON THE REVERSE SIDE.

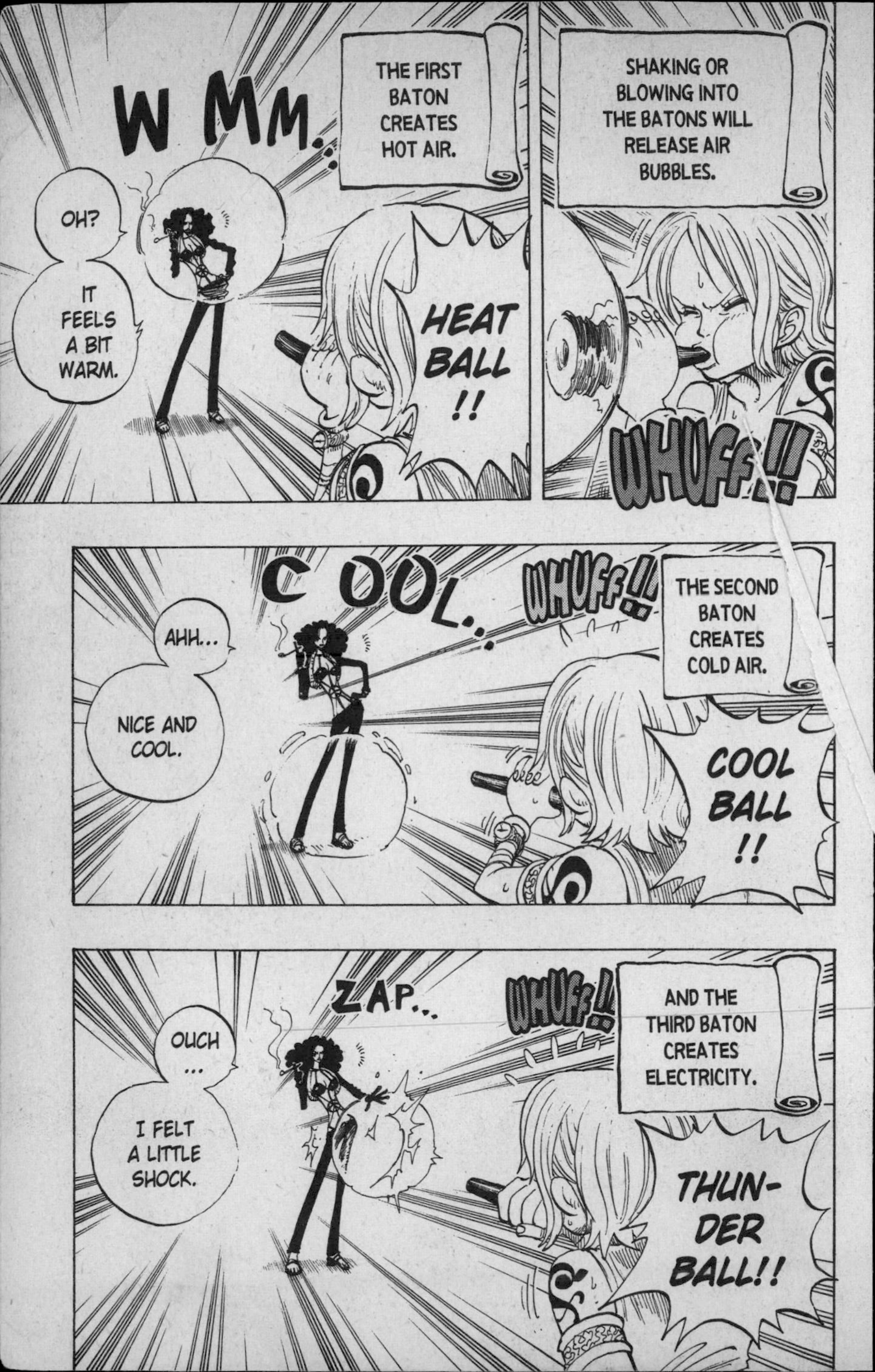
SHAKING OR BLOWING INTO THE BATONS WILL RELEASE AIR BUBBLES.
WHUFF!!
THE FIRST BATON CREATES HOT AIR.
HEAT BALL!!
W MM..
OH?
IT FEELS A BIT WARM.
THE SECOND BATON CREATES COLD AIR.
COOL BALL!!
WHUFF!!
C OOL..
AHH...
NICE AND COOL.
AND THE THIRD BATON CREATES ELECTRICITY.
THUN-DER BALL!!
WHUFF!!
ZAP...
OUCH...
I FELT A LITTLE SHOCK.

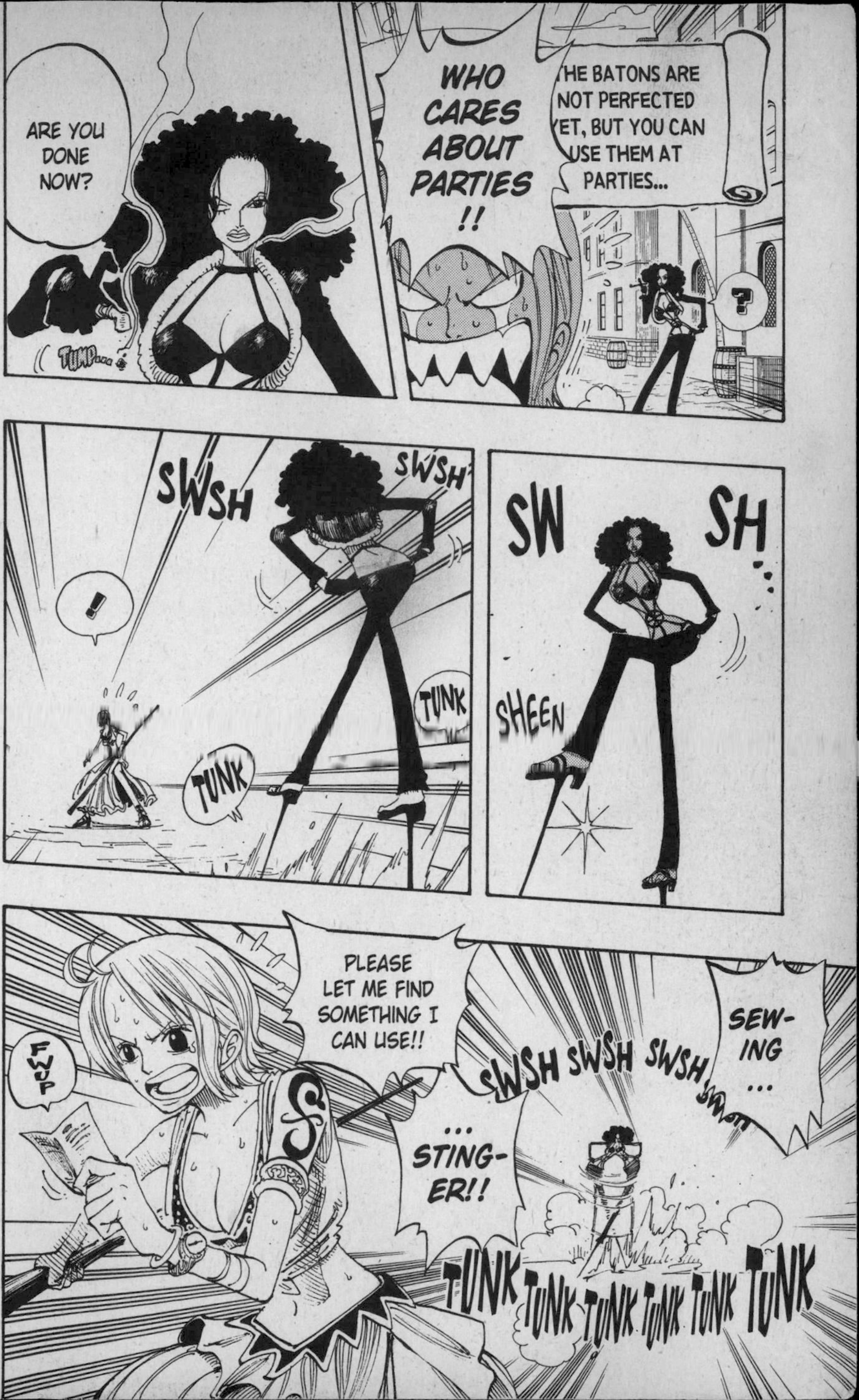
HE BATONS ARE NOT PERFECTED ET, BUT YOU CAN USE THEM AT PARTIES...
WHO CARES ABOUT PARTIES!!
?
ARE YOU DONE NOW?
TUMP...
SW SH
SHEEN
SWSH
SWSH
!
TUNK
TUNK
SEW-ING...
SWSH SWSH SWSH SWSH
...STING-ER!!
PLEASE LET ME FIND SOMETHING I CAN USE!!
FWUP
TUNK TUNK TUNK TUNK TUNK TUNK

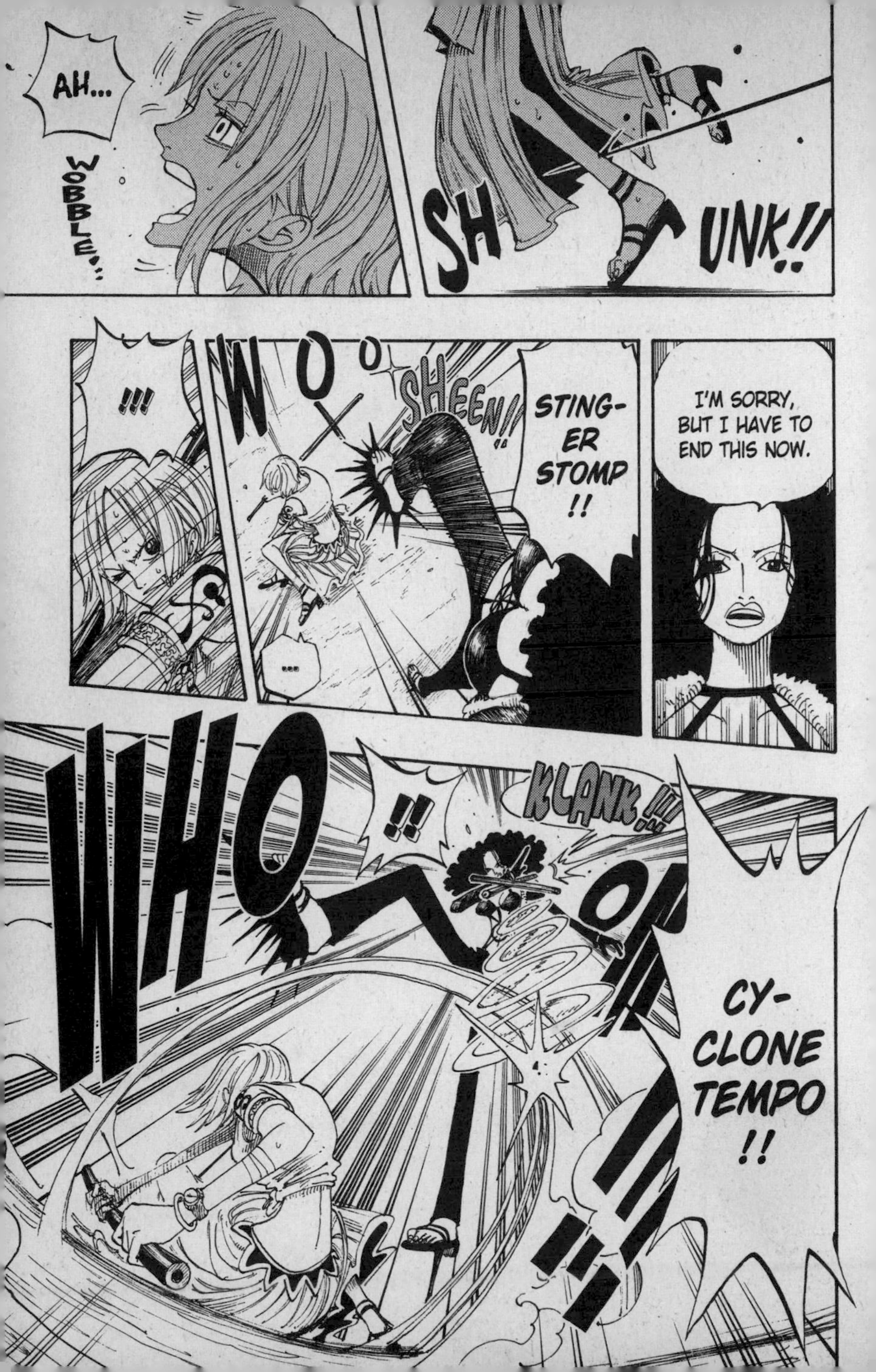
SH
UNK!!
AH...
WOBBLE...
I'M SORRY, BUT I HAVE TO END THIS NOW.
STING-ER STOMP!!
SHEEN!!
WOO
...
!!!
CY-CLONE TEMPO!!
KLANK!!!
!!
WHO
O

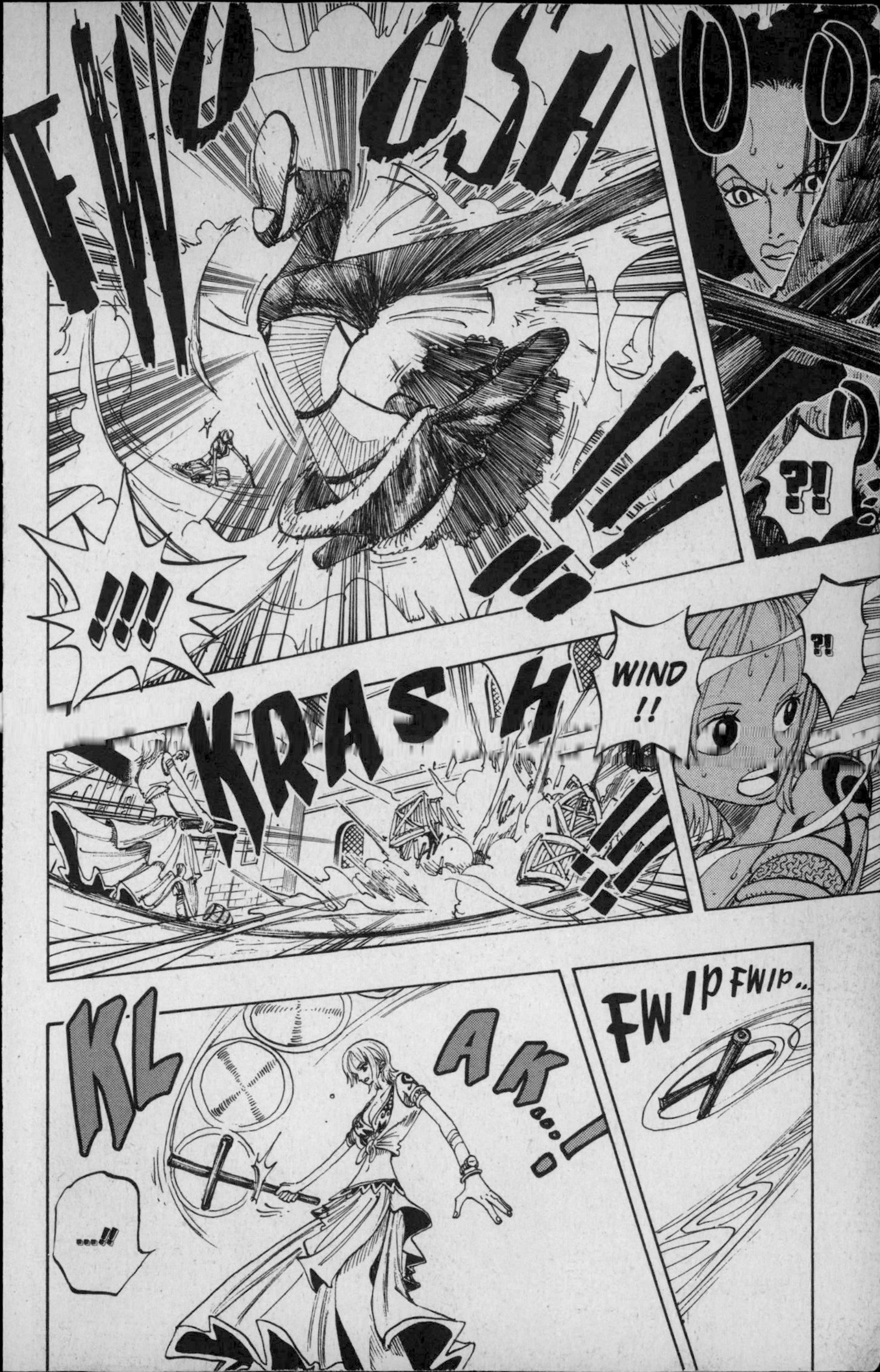
?!
FWOOSH
!!!
?!
WIND !!
KRASH
FWIP FWIP...
KLAK...!
...!!

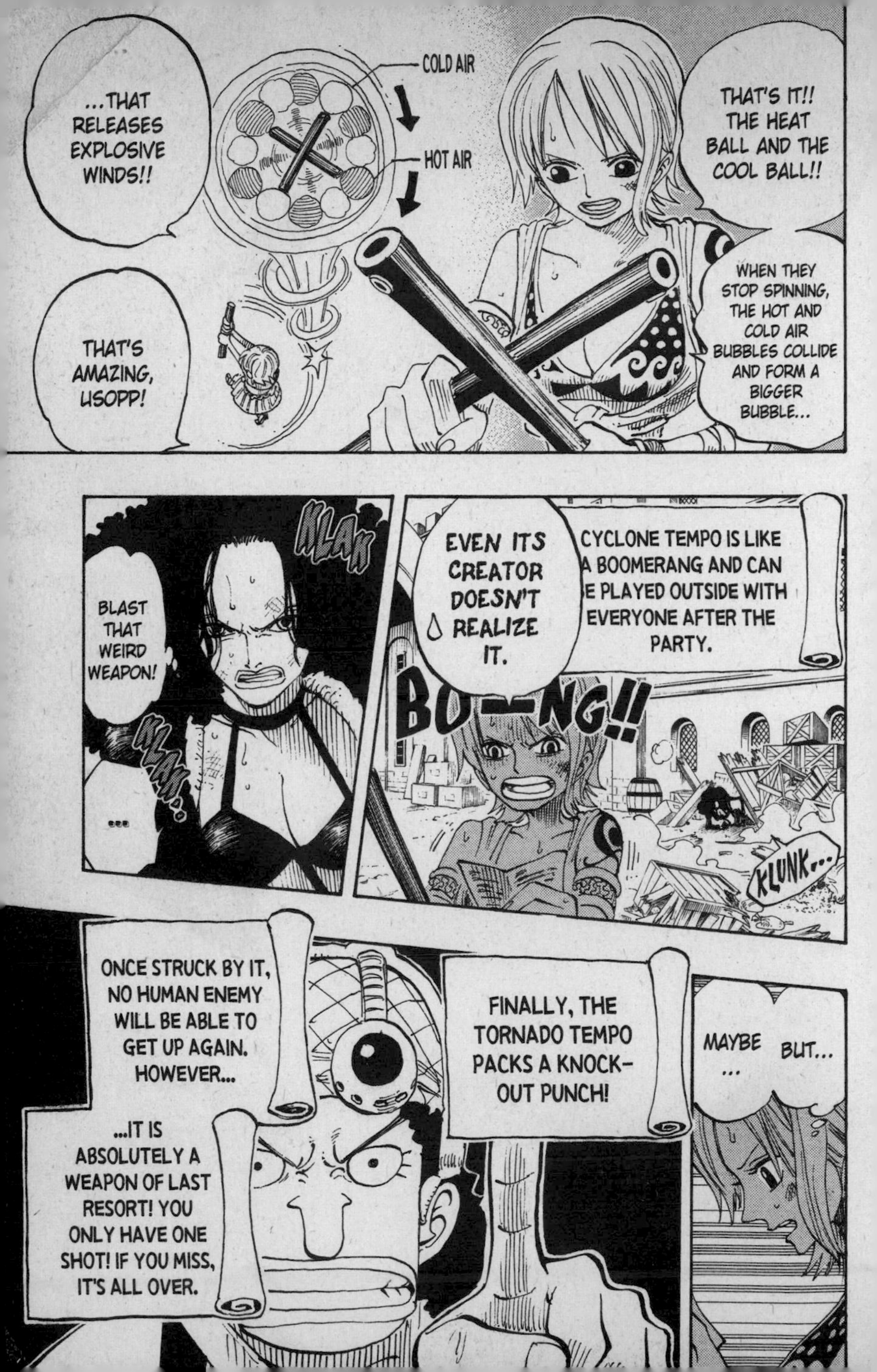
THAT'S IT!! THE HEAT BALL AND THE COOL BALL!!
WHEN THEY STOP SPINNING, THE HOT AND COLD AIR BUBBLES COLLIDE AND FORM A BIGGER BUBBLE...
COLD AIR
HOT AIR
...THAT RELEASES EXPLOSIVE WINDS!!
THAT'S AMAZING, USOPP!
CYCLONE TEMPO IS LIKE A BOOMERANG AND CAN E PLAYED OUTSIDE WITH EVERYONE AFTER THE PARTY.
EVEN ITS CREATOR DOESN'T REALIZE IT.
BO—NG!!
KLUNK...
KLAK
BLAST THAT WEIRD WEAPON!
KLAK..
...
MAYBE... BUT...
FINALLY, THE TORNADO TEMPO PACKS A KNOCK-OUT PUNCH!
ONCE STRUCK BY IT, NO HUMAN ENEMY WILL BE ABLE TO GET UP AGAIN. HOWEVER...
...IT IS ABSOLUTELY A WEAPON OF LAST RESORT! YOU ONLY HAVE ONE SHOT! IF YOU MISS, IT'S ALL OVER.

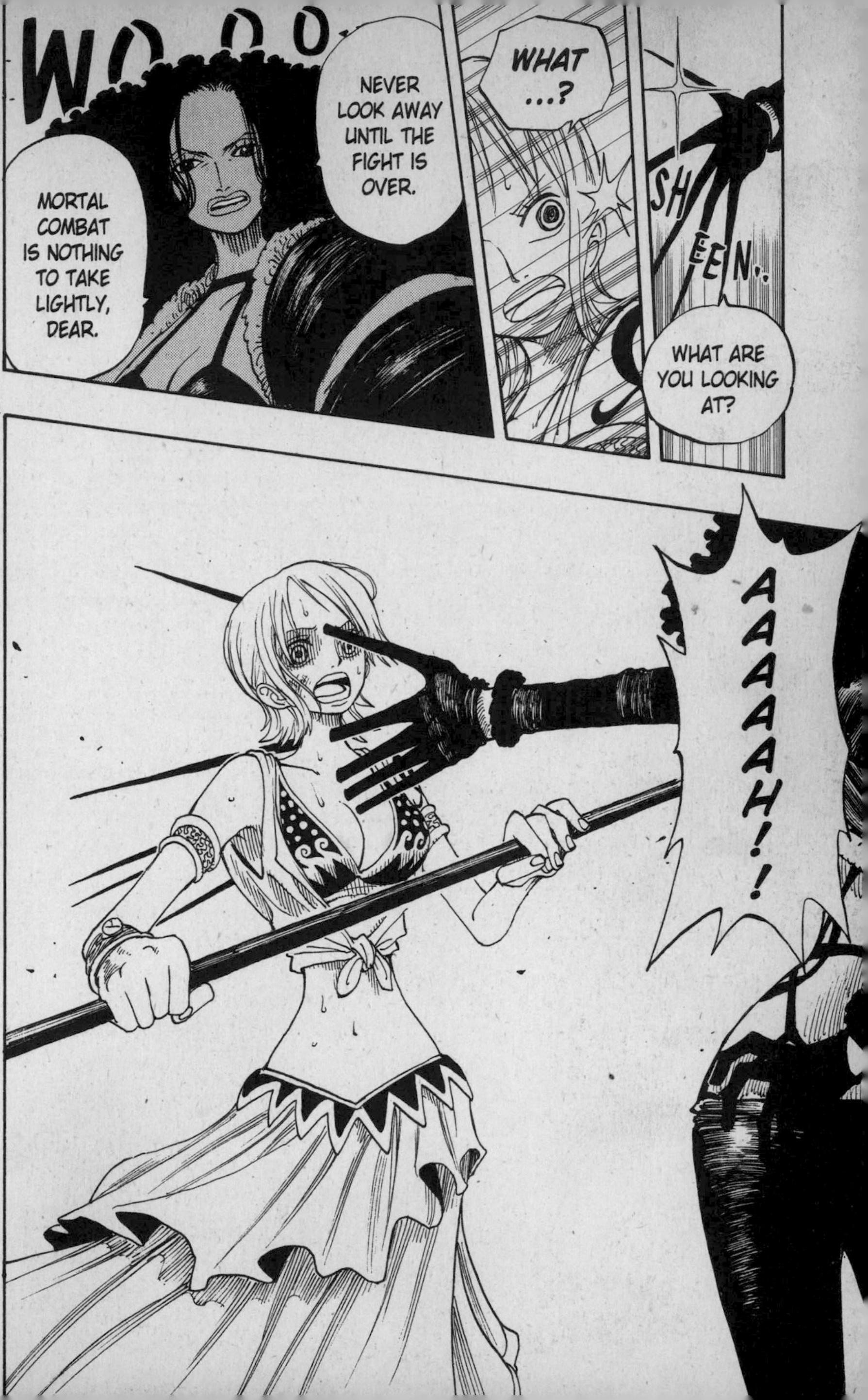
SHEEN..
WHAT ARE YOU LOOKING AT?
WHAT ...?
NEVER LOOK AWAY UNTIL THE FIGHT IS OVER.
WOOO
MORTAL COMBAT IS NOTHING TO TAKE LIGHTLY, DEAR.
AAAAAH!!

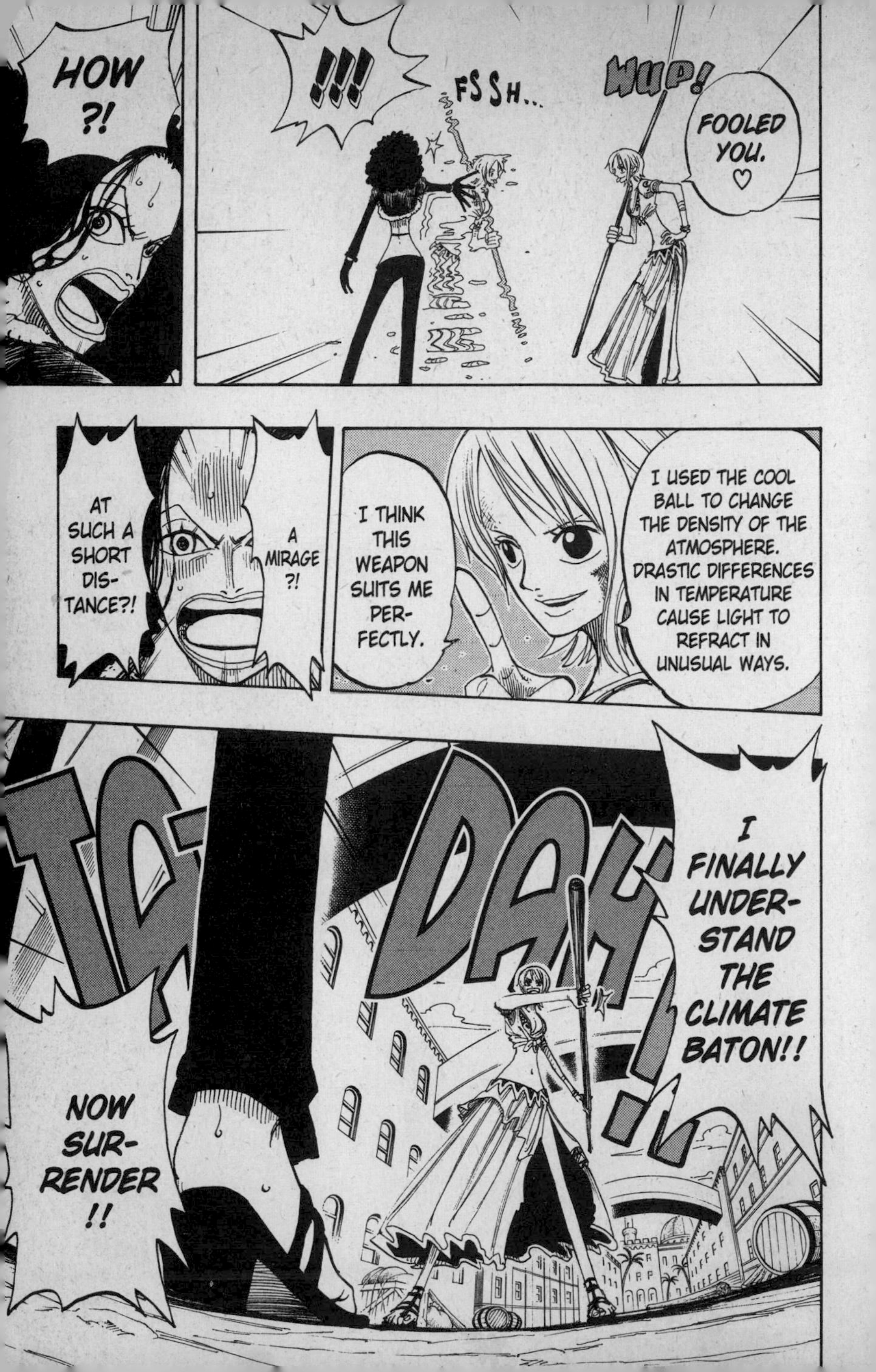
WUP!
FOOLED YOU. ♡
!!!
FSSH...
HOW ?!
I USED THE COOL BALL TO CHANGE THE DENSITY OF THE ATMOSPHERE. DRASTIC DIFFERENCES IN TEMPERATURE CAUSE LIGHT TO REFRACT IN UNUSUAL WAYS.
I THINK THIS WEAPON SUITS ME PERFECTLY.
A MIRAGE ?!
AT SUCH A SHORT DISTANCE?!
TA DAH!!
I FINALLY UNDERSTAND THE CLIMATE BATON!!
NOW SURRENDER!!

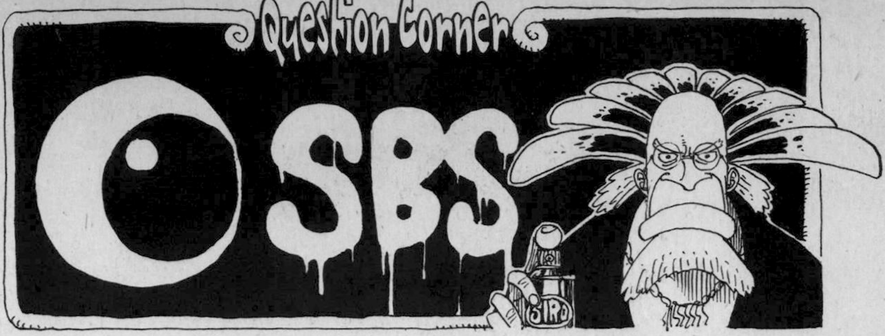
Question Corner
SBS

Reader: Oda Sensei, I read Vol. 19 and was shocked! In the first panel on page 104, Sam is amongst the crowd that is running away! What's he doing in Alabasta? And why is he drunk again? Please tell me!!

--Takashima 192

Oda: Yes, that surprised me too. I completely forgot I'd drawn that. But he **is** there, that's for sure. So how did he get there? Just hear me out... That was Sam's second daughter's wedding day. When his older daughter was eight years old, Sam's wife left him and Sam had to raise his daughters by himself. The second daughter grew up to be a delinquent and caused him a lot of headaches. She got into fights and even ran away from home. Now that daughter was getting married. He used to tell his daughter, "I can't wait till you leave home!" But actually, he felt sad. And happy, too. Sam said, "How can I **not** drink tonight?" and he drank and drank and wandered and wandered until he found himself in Alabasta. The people around him were in an uproar, so Sam joined in--although Sam's reason and that of the crowd's differed slightly.

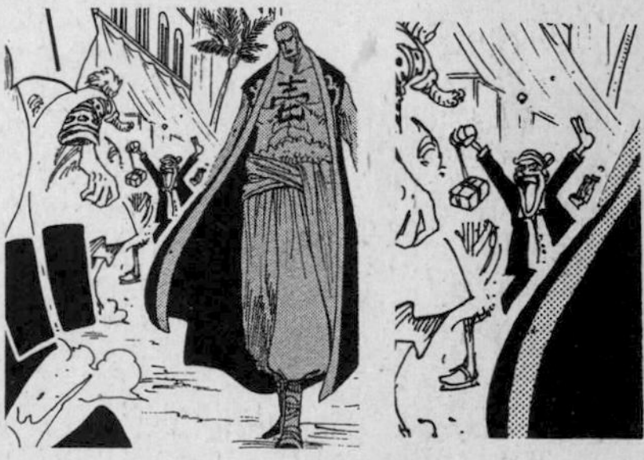

Reader: Sensei, I was watching TV the other day and somebody said that "Buggy pants are going to be the new rage." Will you buy some Buggy pants?

Oda: I won't buy them.

Chapter 192:
TORNADO WARNING

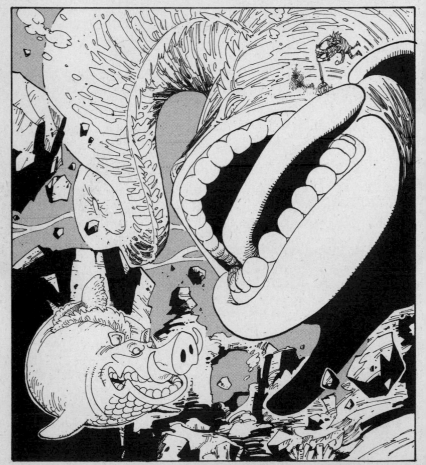

**HACHI'S WALK ON THE SEAFLOOR, VOL. 10:
"HACHI SAVES THE SEA BOAR"**

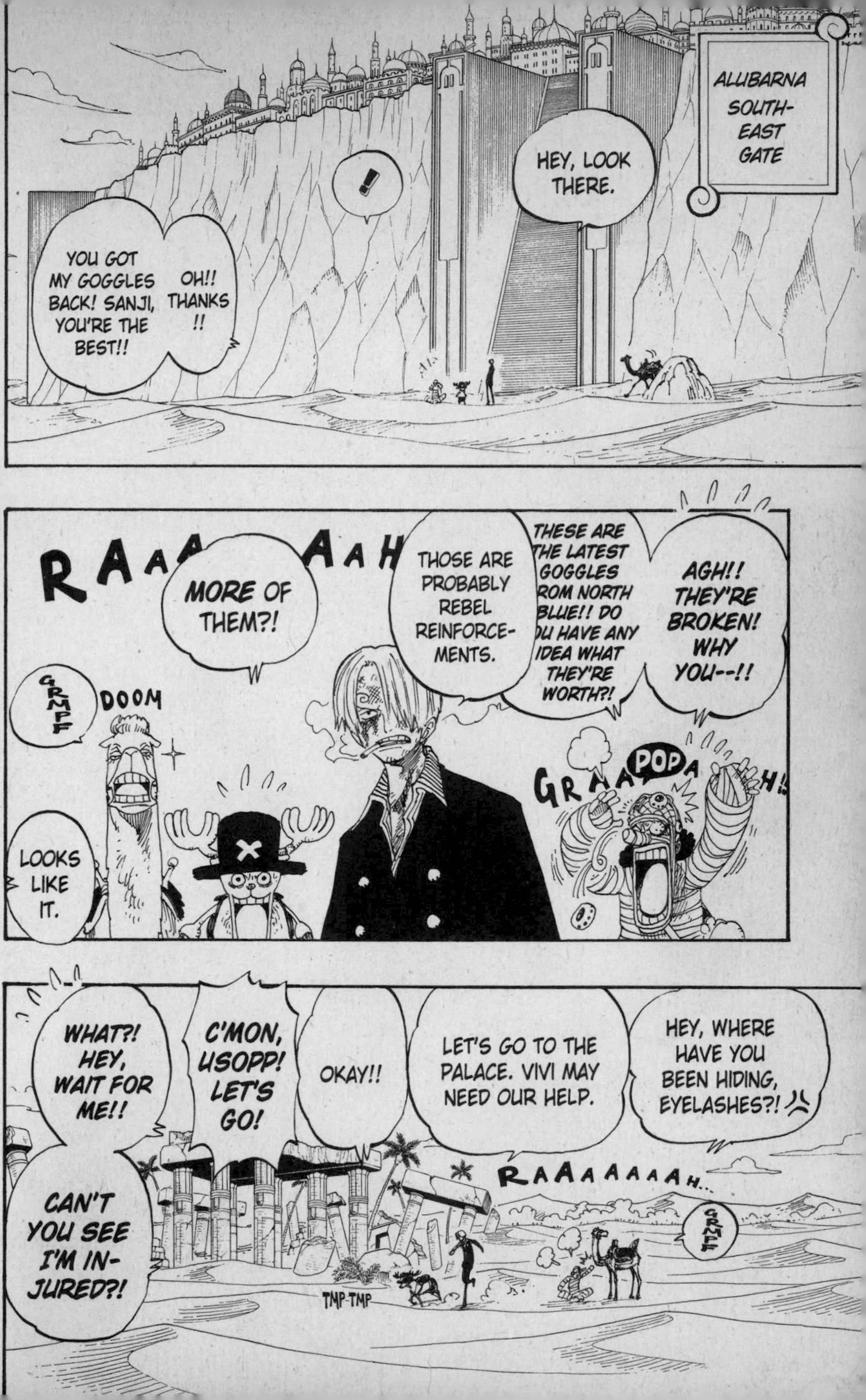

ALUBARNA SOUTH-EAST GATE
HEY, LOOK THERE.
!
OH!! THANKS !!
YOU GOT MY GOGGLES BACK! SANJI, YOU'RE THE BEST!!
AGH!! THEY'RE BROKEN! WHY YOU--!!
THESE ARE THE LATEST GOGGLES ROM NORTH BLUE!! DO U HAVE ANY IDEA WHAT THEY'RE WORTH?!
GRAA POP AAH!!
THOSE ARE PROBABLY REBEL REINFORCEMENTS.
RAAAAAH
MORE OF THEM?!
DOOM
GRMPF
LOOKS LIKE IT.
HEY, WHERE HAVE YOU BEEN HIDING, EYELASHES?!
LET'S GO TO THE PALACE. VIVI MAY NEED OUR HELP.
OKAY!!
C'MON, USOPP! LET'S GO!
WHAT?! HEY, WAIT FOR ME!!
CAN'T YOU SEE I'M IN-JURED?!
RAAAAAAAH..
GRMPF
TMP-TMP

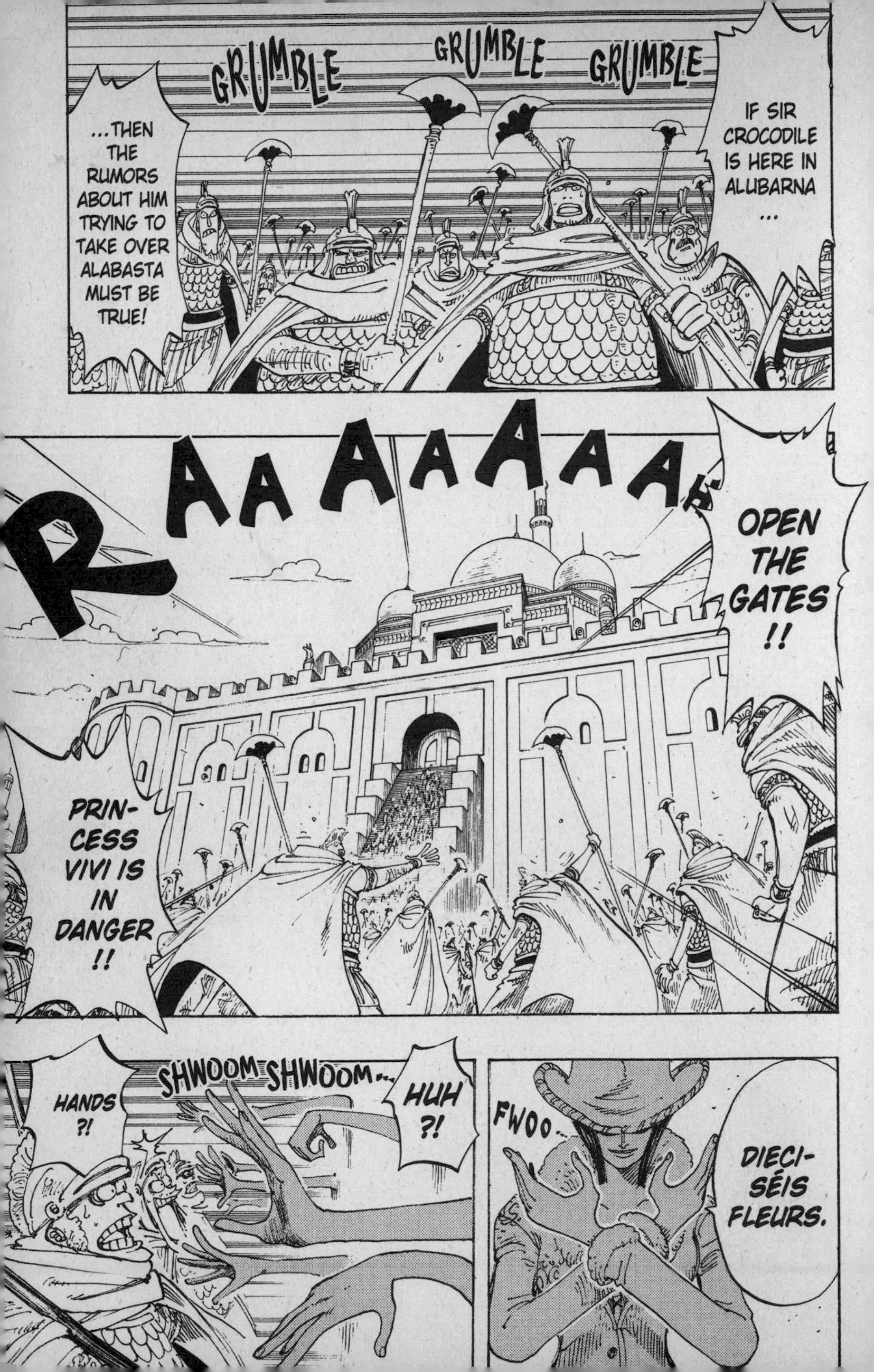
GRUMBLE GRUMBLE GRUMBLE
IF SIR CROCODILE IS HERE IN ALUBARNA...
...THEN THE RUMORS ABOUT HIM TRYING TO TAKE OVER ALABASTA MUST BE TRUE!
RAAAAAAAH
OPEN THE GATES!!
PRINCESS VIVI IS IN DANGER!!
DIECISÉIS FLEURS.
FWOO...
HUH?!
SHWOOM SHWOOM...
HANDS?!

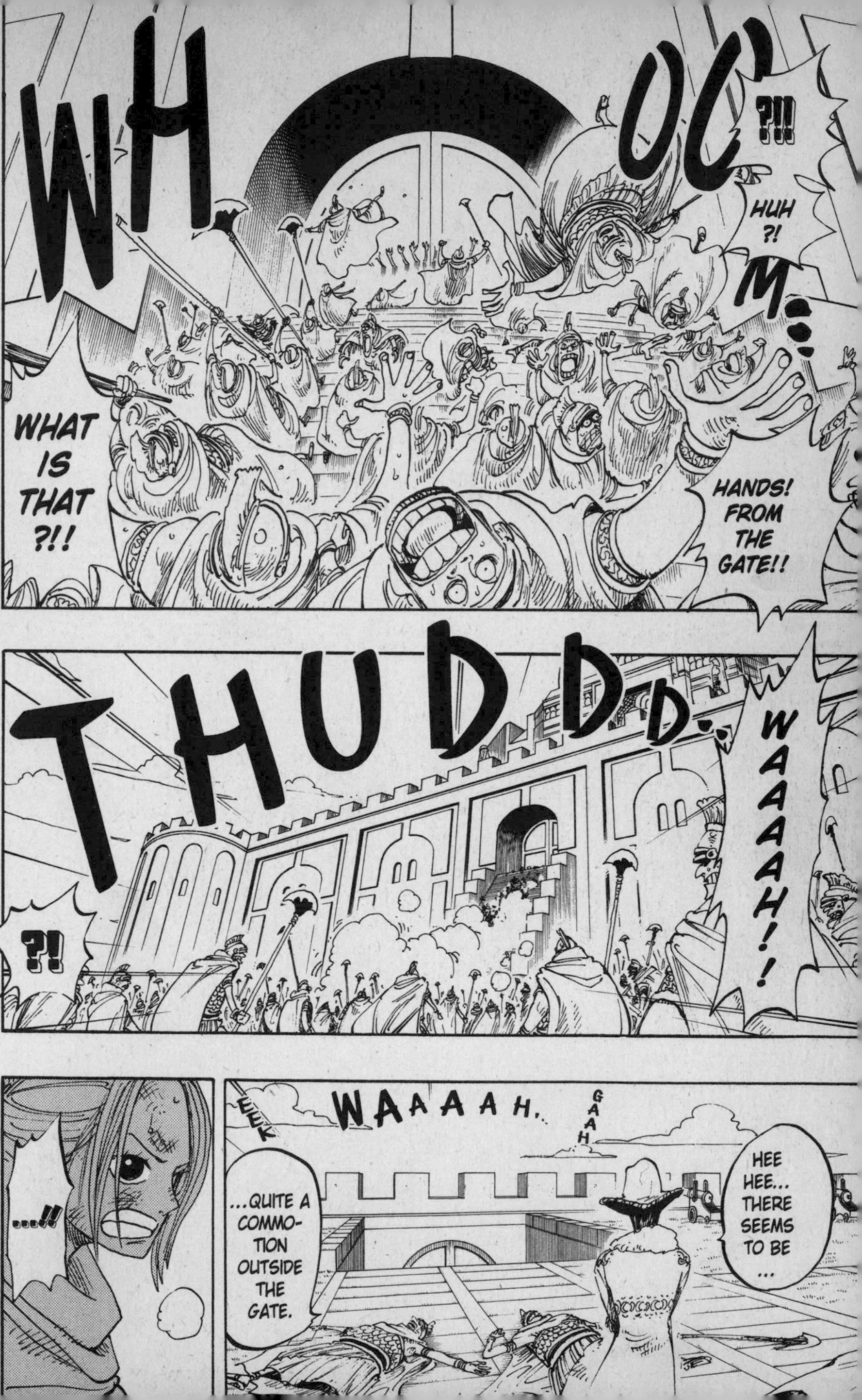
WHOOM..
?!!
HUH ?!
HANDS! FROM THE GATE!!
WHAT IS THAT ?!!
WAAAAAH!!
THUDD..
?!
HEE HEE... THERE SEEMS TO BE ...
...QUITE A COMMOTION OUTSIDE THE GATE.
GAAH
WAAAAH..
EEK
...!!

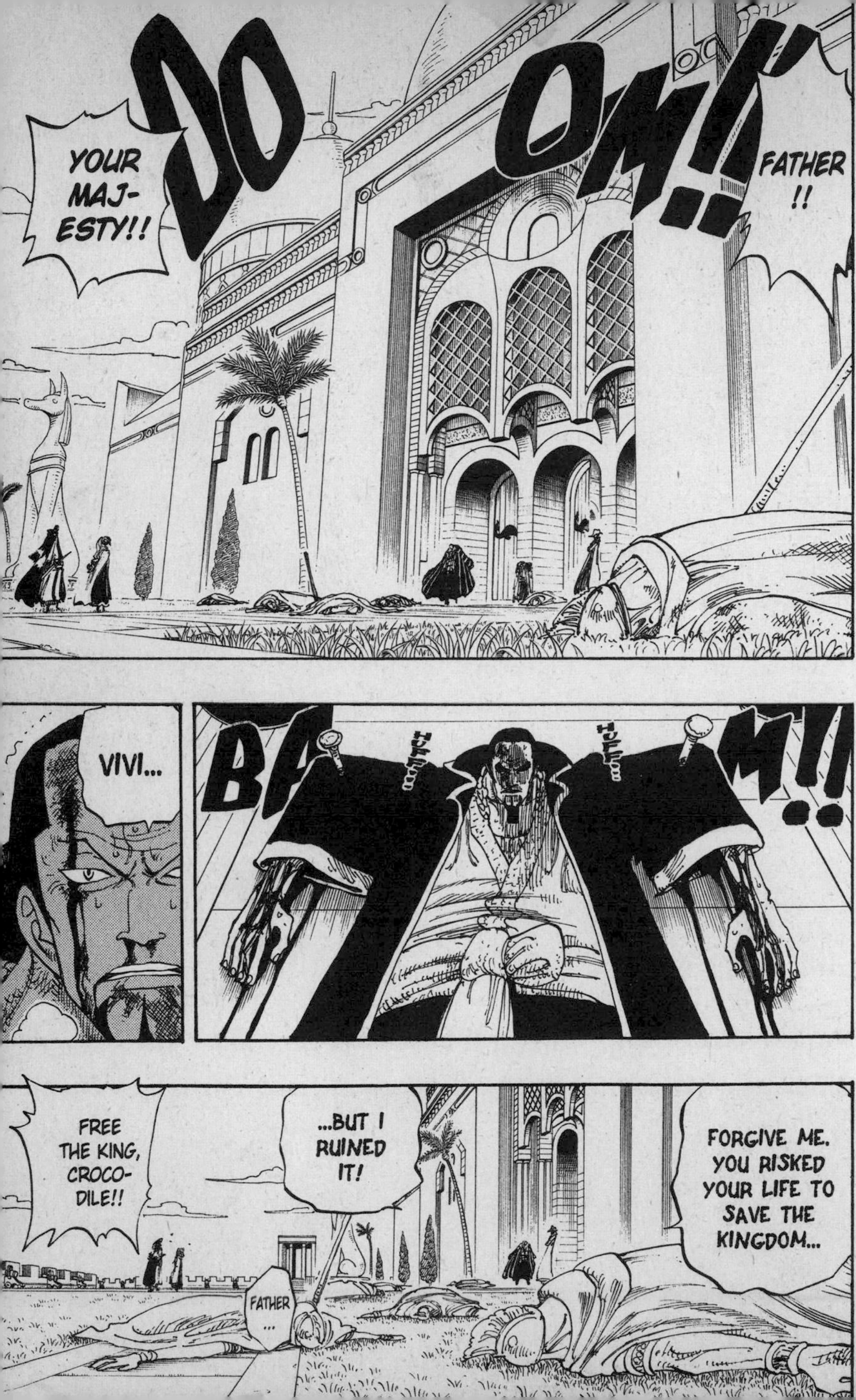
FATHER !!
DOOM!!
YOUR MAJ-ESTY!!
HUFF...
HUFF...
BAM!!
VIVI...
FORGIVE ME. YOU RISKED YOUR LIFE TO SAVE THE KINGDOM...
...BUT I RUINED IT!
FREE THE KING, CROCO-DILE!!
FATHER ...

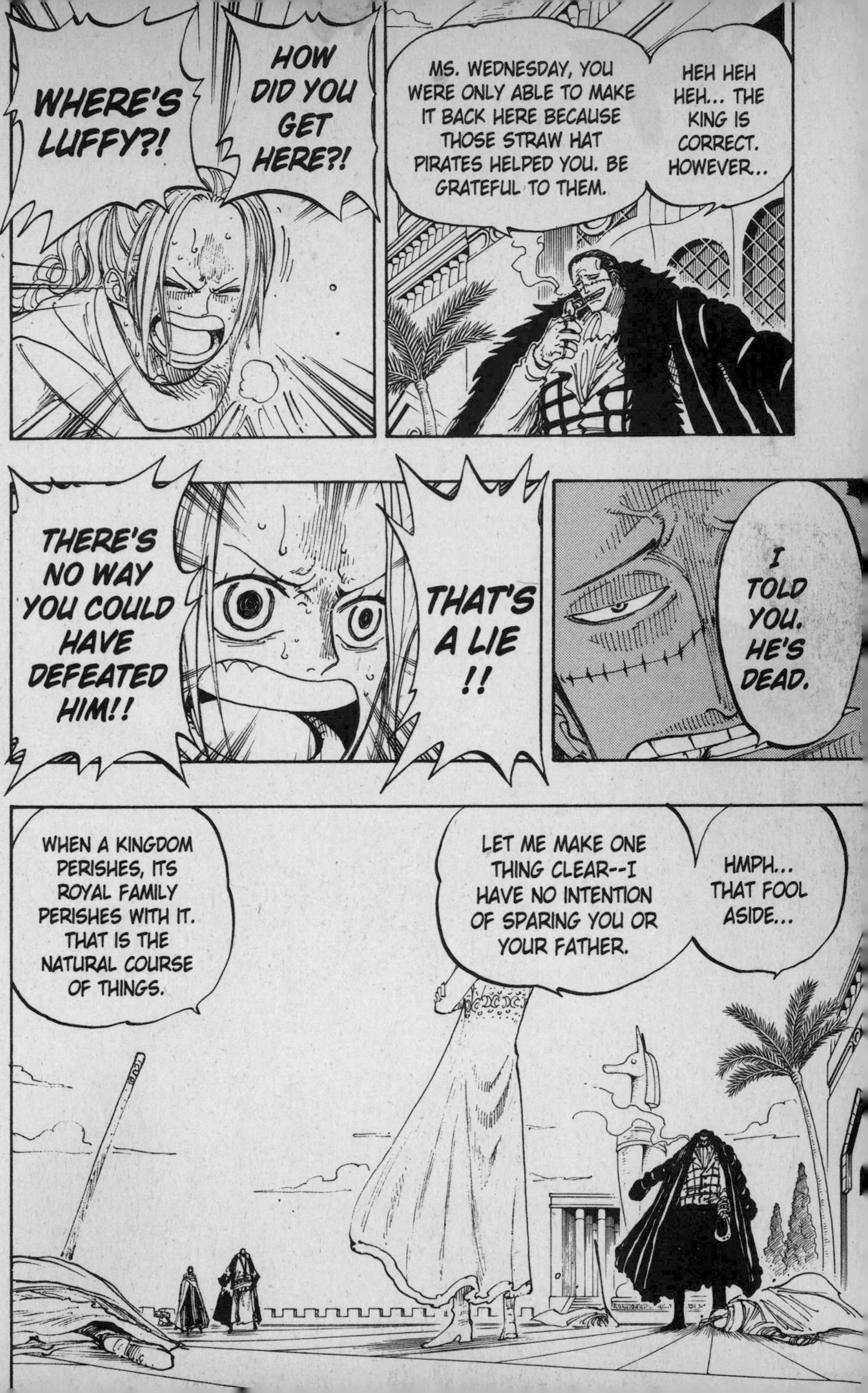
MS. WEDNESDAY, YOU WERE ONLY ABLE TO MAKE IT BACK HERE BECAUSE THOSE STRAW HAT PIRATES HELPED YOU. BE GRATEFUL TO THEM.
HEH HEH HEH... THE KING IS CORRECT. HOWEVER...
HOW DID YOU GET HERE?!
WHERE'S LUFFY?!
I TOLD YOU. HE'S DEAD.
THAT'S A LIE !!
THERE'S NO WAY YOU COULD HAVE DEFEATED HIM!!
HMPH... THAT FOOL ASIDE...
LET ME MAKE ONE THING CLEAR--I HAVE NO INTENTION OF SPARING YOU OR YOUR FATHER.
WHEN A KINGDOM PERISHES, ITS ROYAL FAMILY PERISHES WITH IT. THAT IS THE NATURAL COURSE OF THINGS.

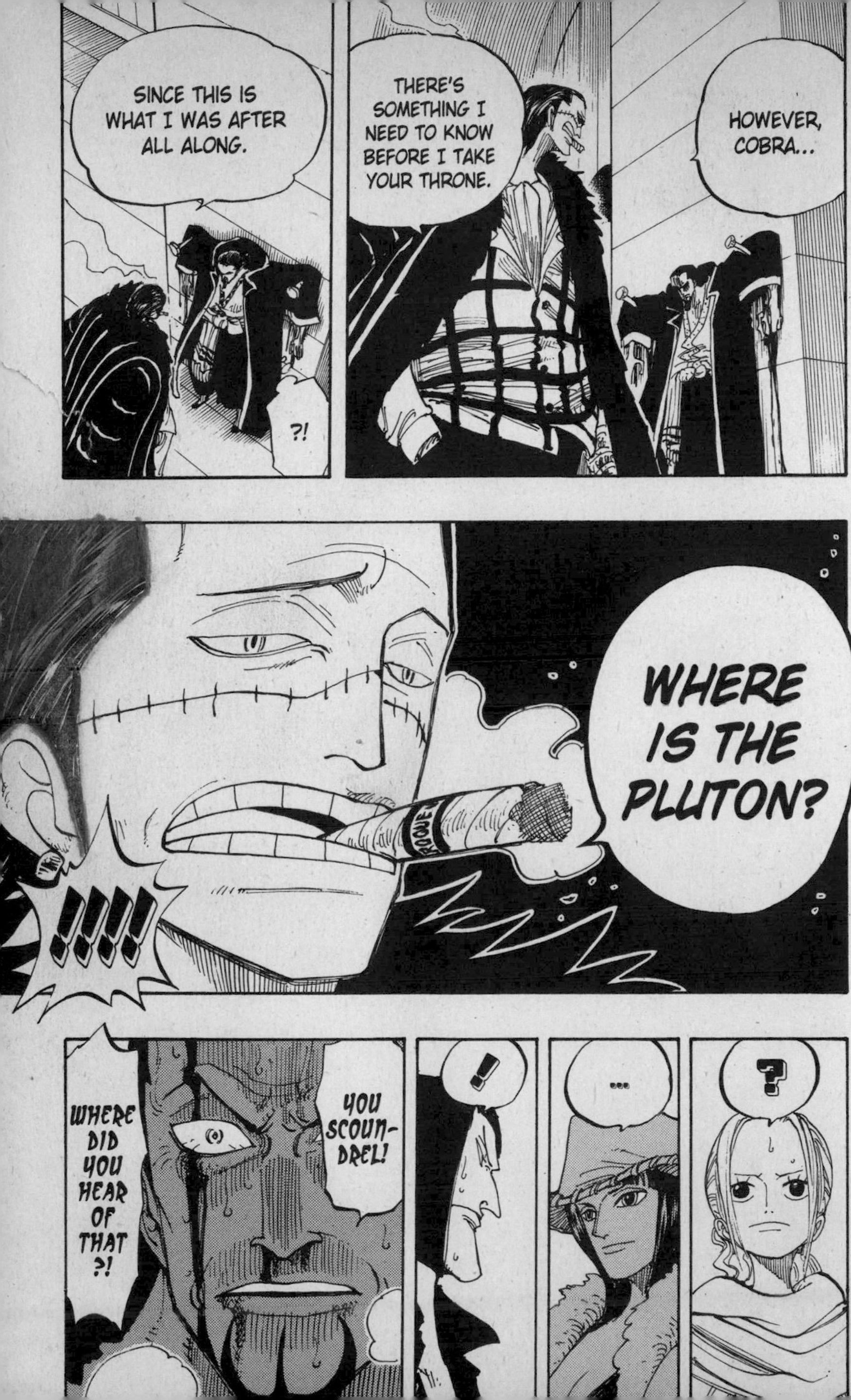
HOWEVER, COBRA...
THERE'S SOMETHING I NEED TO KNOW BEFORE I TAKE YOUR THRONE.
SINCE THIS IS WHAT I WAS AFTER ALL ALONG.
?!
WHERE IS THE PLUTON?
!!!!
?
...
!
YOU SCOUN-DREL!
WHERE DID YOU HEAR OF THAT?!

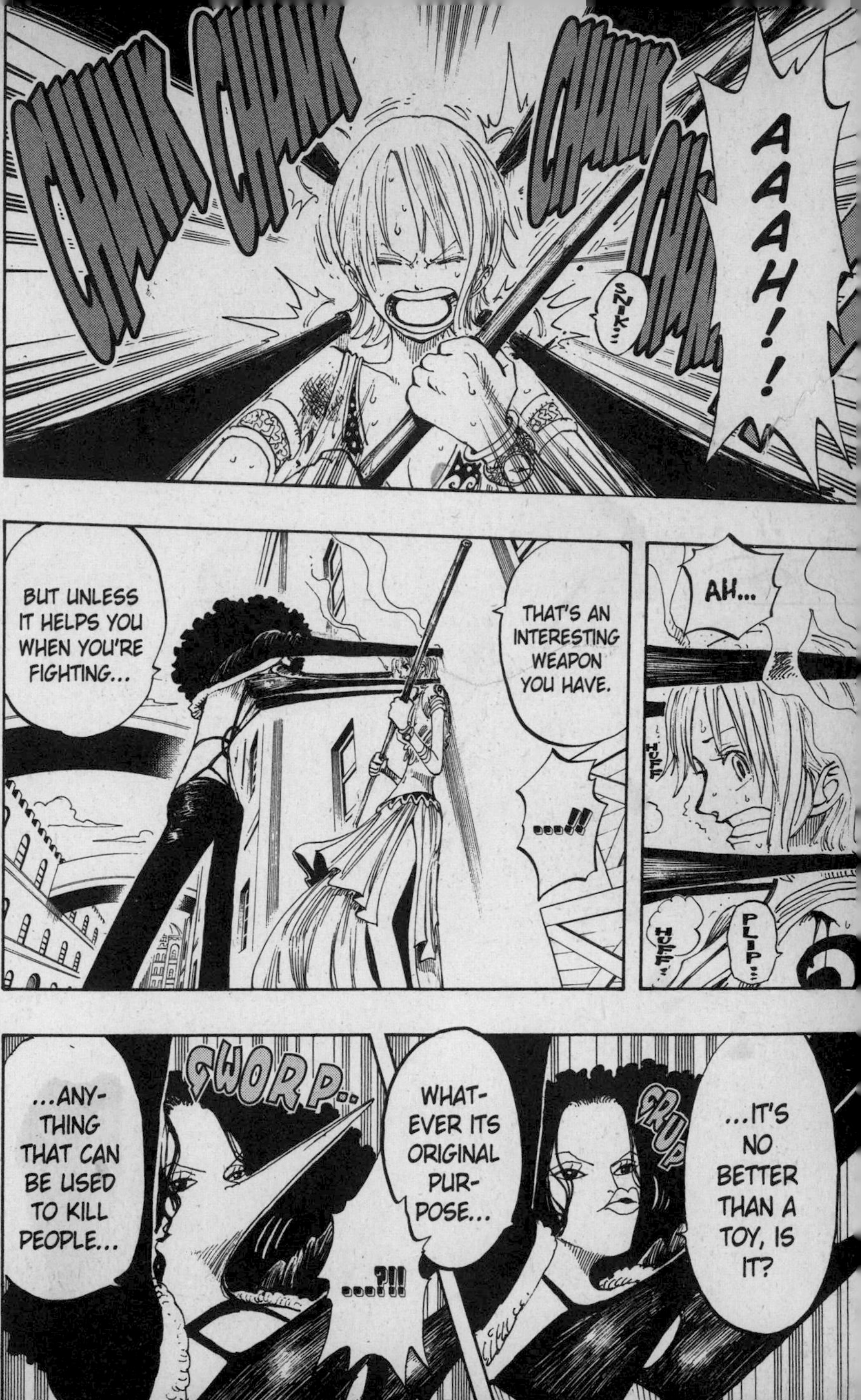
CHUNK CHUNK
CHUNK
AAAAH!!
SNIK...
AH...
THAT'S AN INTERESTING WEAPON YOU HAVE.
BUT UNLESS IT HELPS YOU WHEN YOU'RE FIGHTING...
...!!
HUFF
HUFF...
PLIP...
...IT'S NO BETTER THAN A TOY, IS IT?
GRUP
WHAT-EVER ITS ORIGINAL PUR-POSE...
...?!!
GWORP...
...ANY-THING THAT CAN BE USED TO KILL PEOPLE...

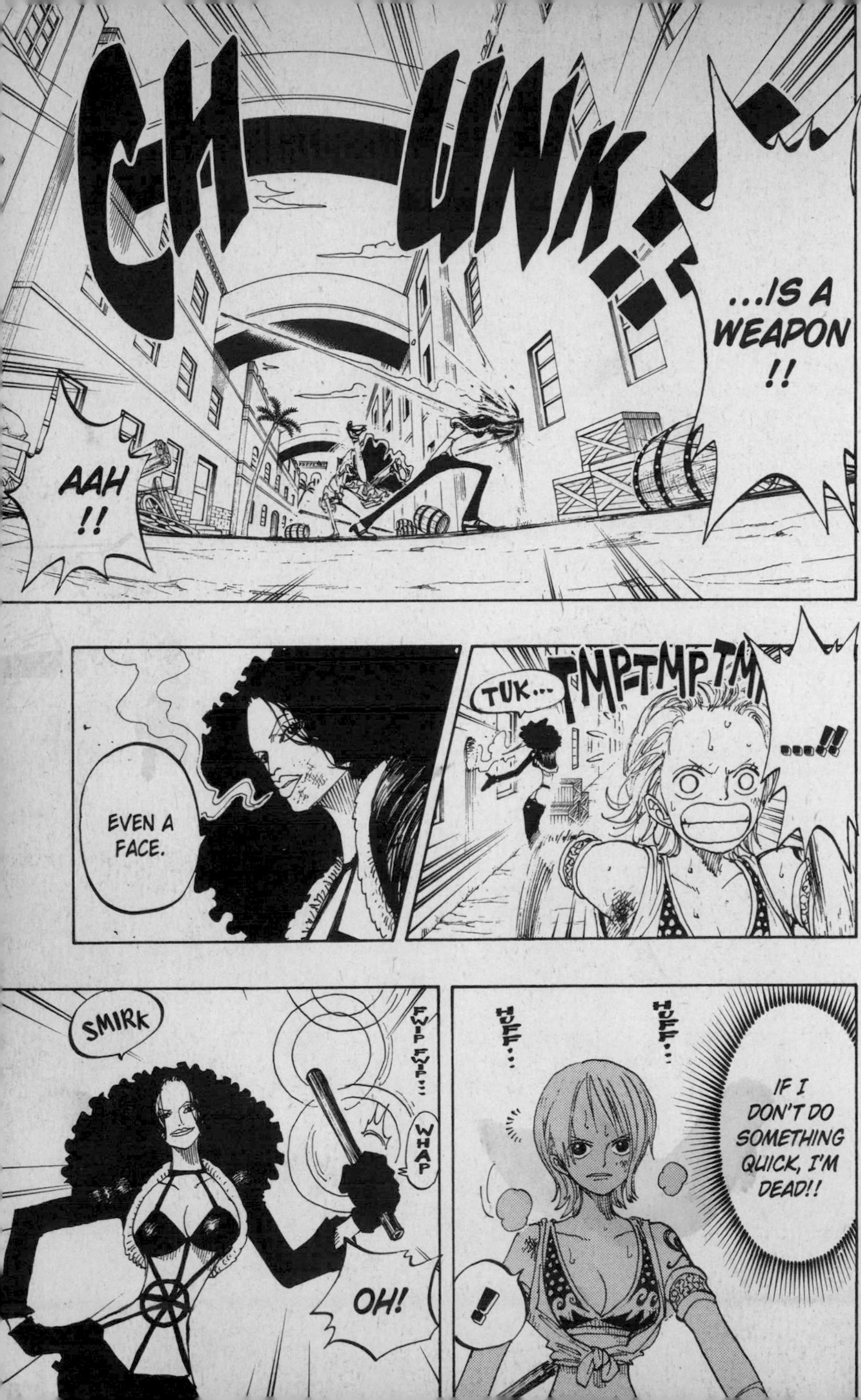
CH-UNK!!
...IS A WEAPON !!
AAH !!
TMP-TMPTM
TUK...
...!!
EVEN A FACE.
HUFF...
HUFF...
IF I DON'T DO SOMETHING QUICK, I'M DEAD!!
!
SMIRK
FWIP FWIP!!
WHAP
OH!

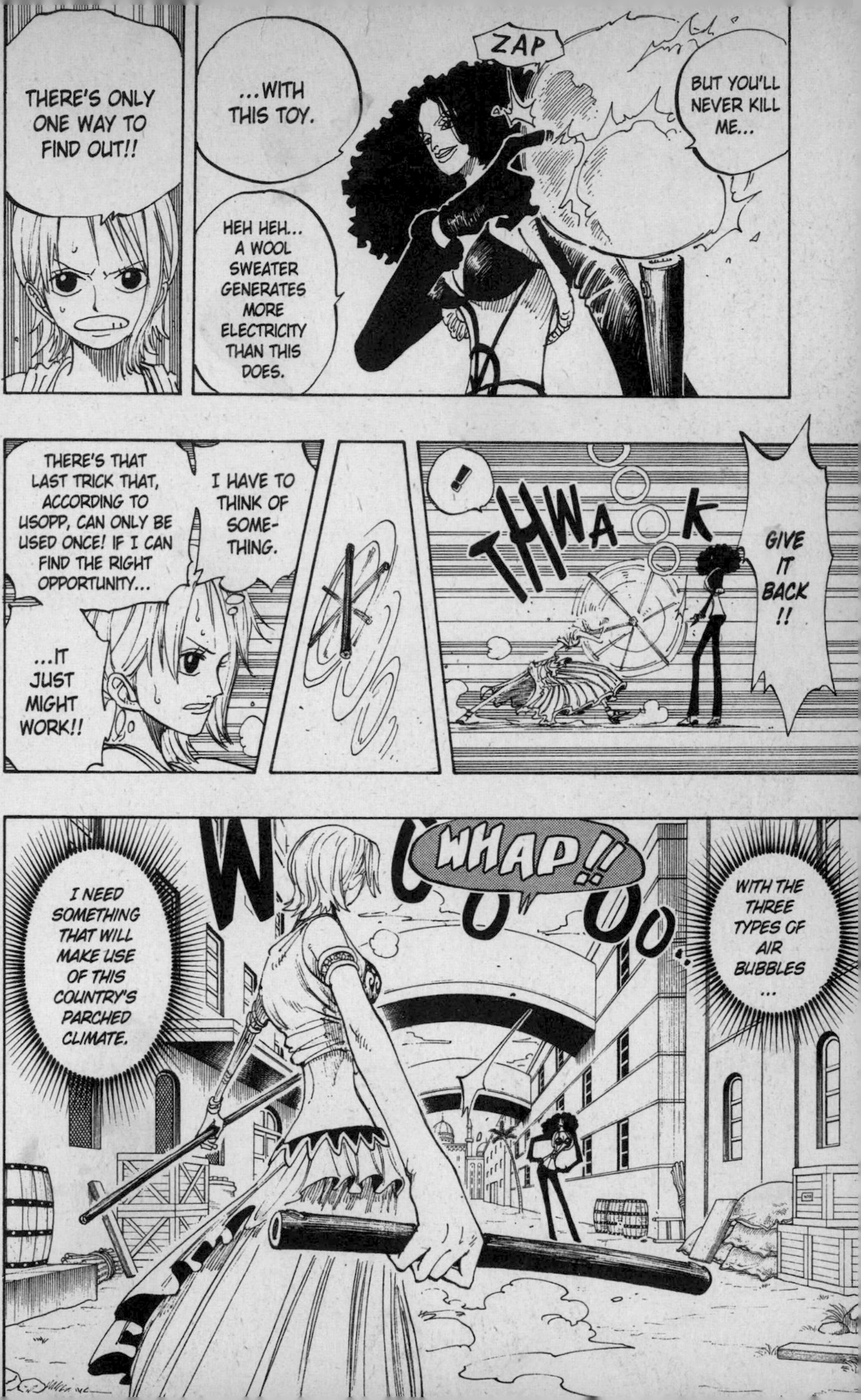
ZAP
BUT YOU'LL NEVER KILL ME...
...WITH THIS TOY.
HEH HEH... A WOOL SWEATER GENERATES MORE ELECTRICITY THAN THIS DOES.
THERE'S ONLY ONE WAY TO FIND OUT!!
!
THWAK
GIVE IT BACK!!
I HAVE TO THINK OF SOME-THING.
THERE'S THAT LAST TRICK THAT, ACCORDING TO USOPP, CAN ONLY BE USED ONCE! IF I CAN FIND THE RIGHT OPPORTUNITY...
...IT JUST MIGHT WORK!!
WITH THE THREE TYPES OF AIR BUBBLES...
WHAP!!
I NEED SOMETHING THAT WILL MAKE USE OF THIS COUNTRY'S PARCHED CLIMATE.

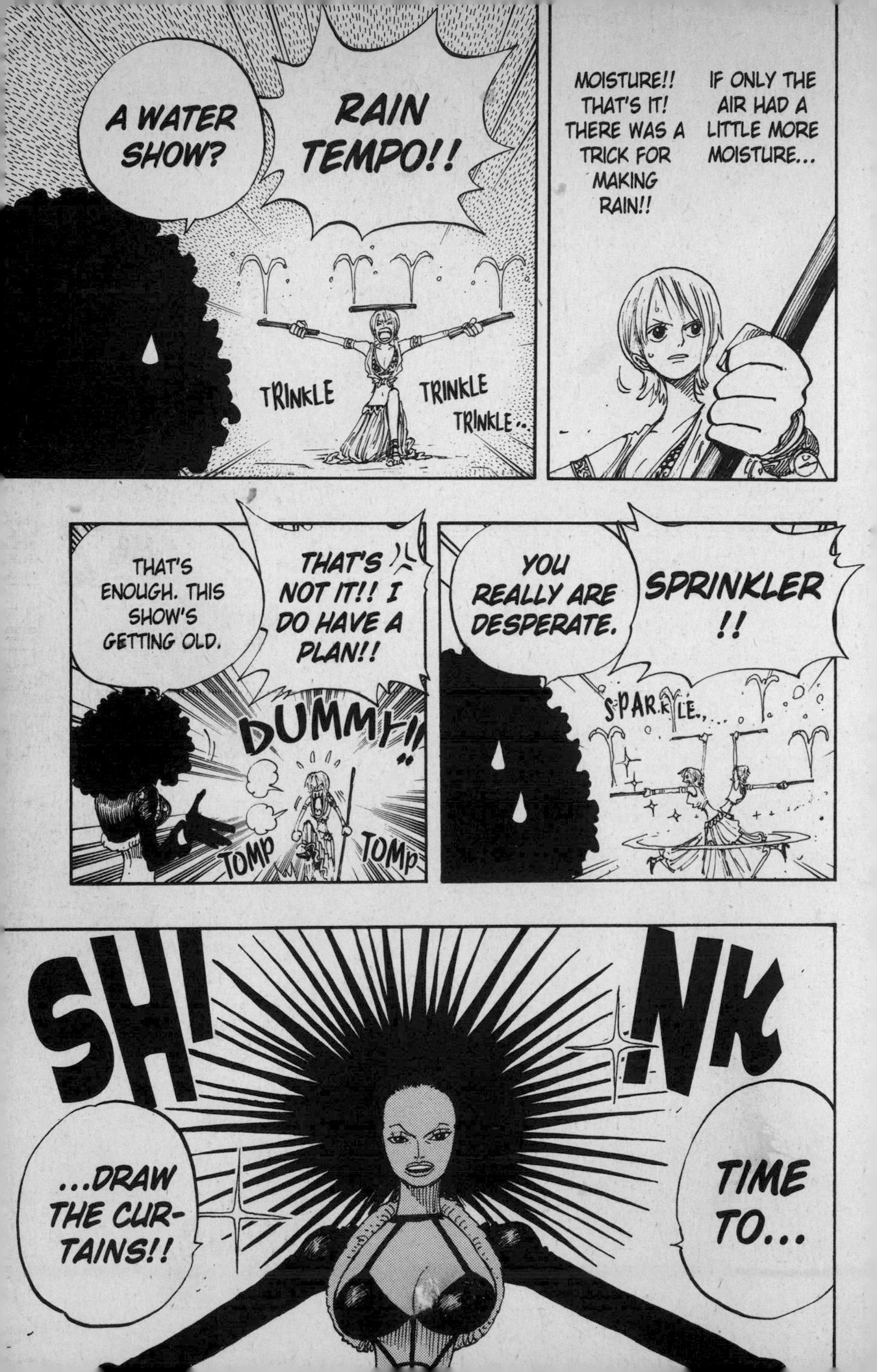
IF ONLY THE AIR HAD A LITTLE MORE MOISTURE...
MOISTURE!! THAT'S IT! THERE WAS A TRICK FOR MAKING RAIN!!
RAIN TEMPO!!
A WATER SHOW?
TRINKLE
TRINKLE
TRINKLE..
SPRINKLER!!
YOU REALLY ARE DESPERATE.
SPARKLE..
THAT'S NOT IT!! I DO HAVE A PLAN!!
THAT'S ENOUGH. THIS SHOW'S GETTING OLD.
DUMM!!
TOMP
TOMP
SHINK
TIME TO...
...DRAW THE CUR-TAINS!!

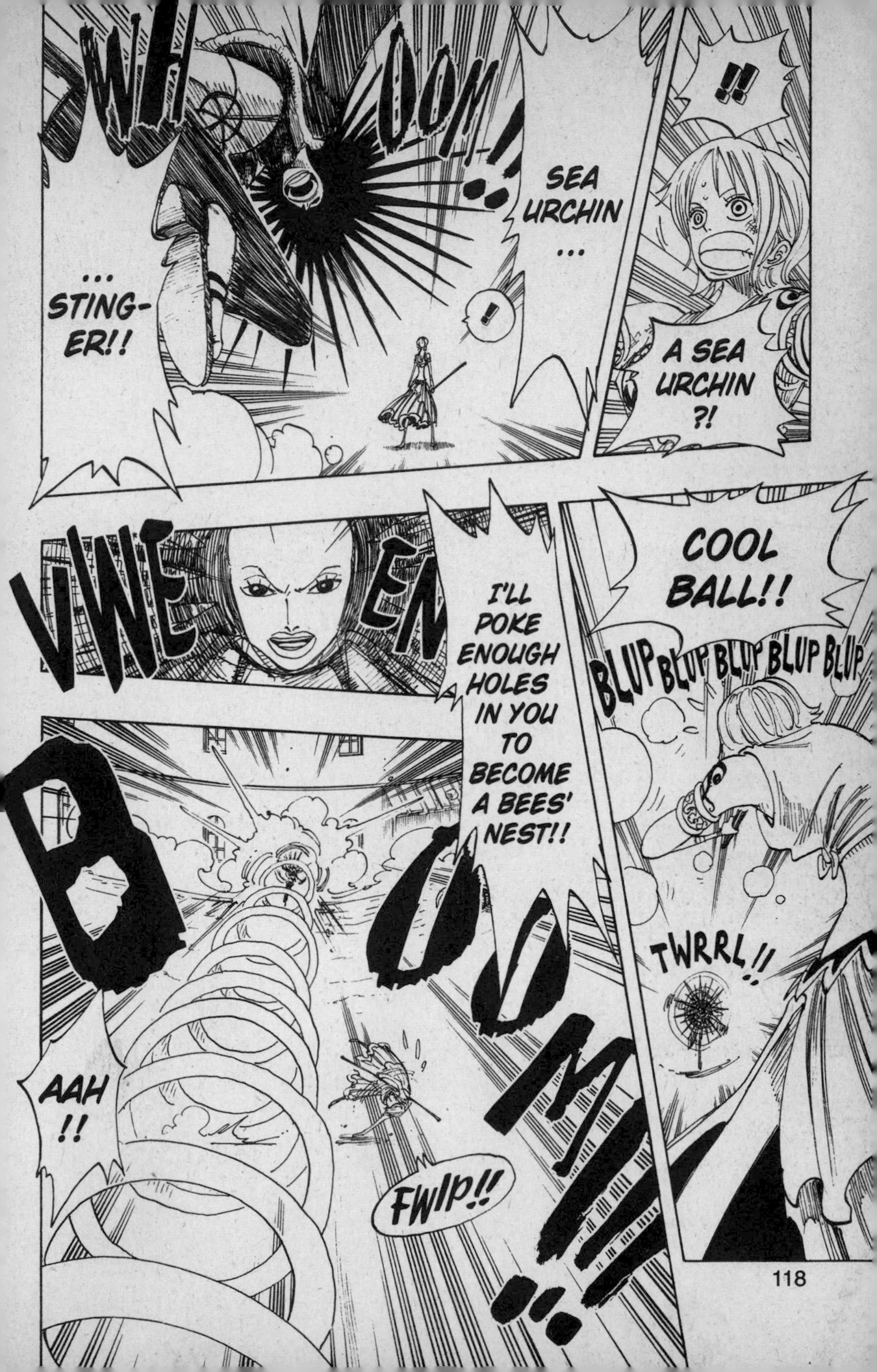
!!
A SEA URCHIN ?!
SEA URCHIN ...
WHOOM!!
!
... STING-ER!!
COOL BALL!!
BLUP BLUP BLUP BLUP BLUP
TWRRL!!
I'LL POKE ENOUGH HOLES IN YOU TO BECOME A BEES' NEST!!
VWEEN
BOOM!!
FWIP!!
AAH!!

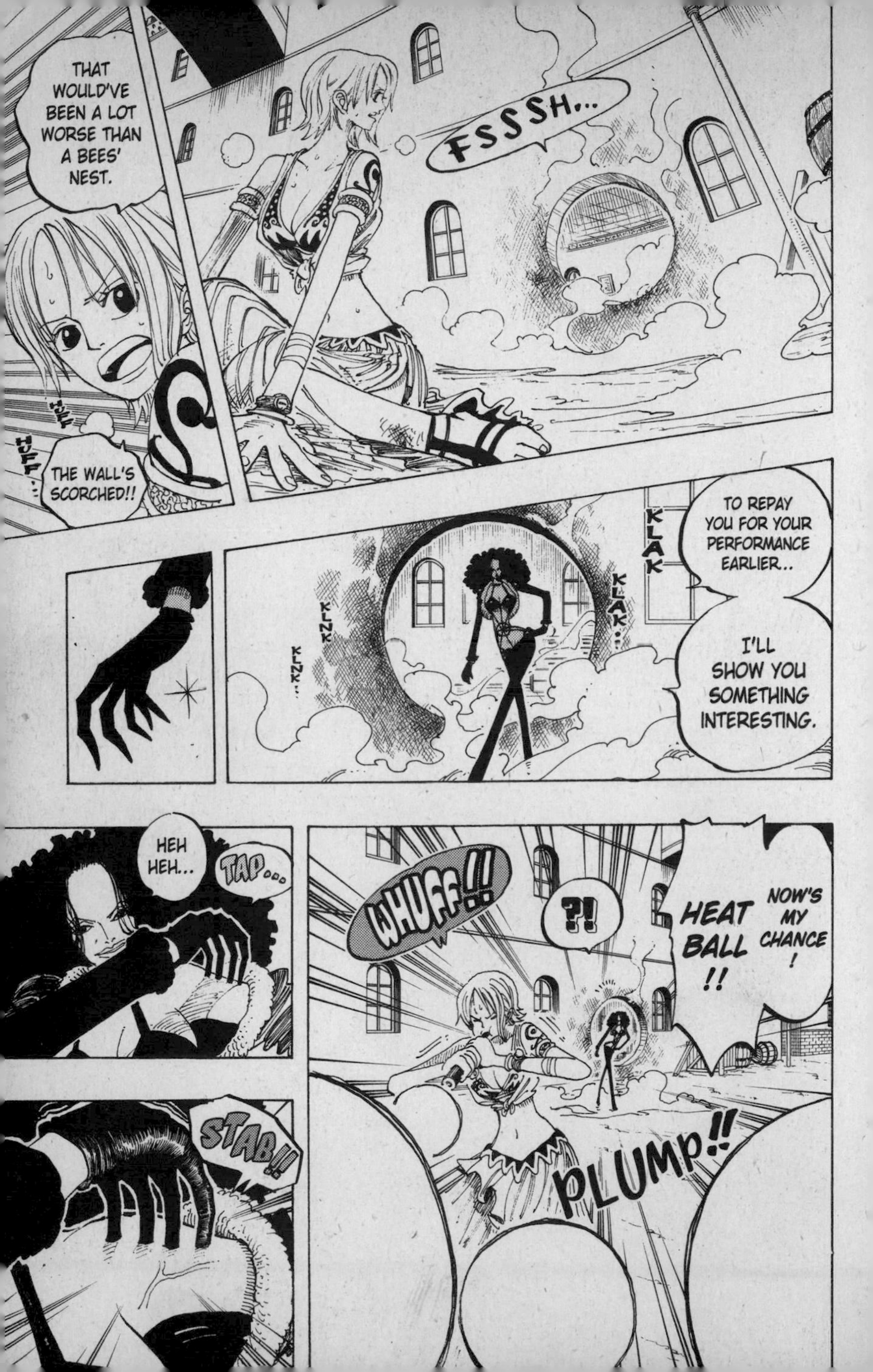
FSSSH...
THAT WOULD'VE BEEN A LOT WORSE THAN A BEES' NEST.
HUFF
HUFF...
THE WALL'S SCORCHED!!
KLAK
KLAK...
TO REPAY YOU FOR YOUR PERFORMANCE EARLIER..
I'LL SHOW YOU SOMETHING INTERESTING.
KLNK
KLNK...
NOW'S MY CHANCE!
HEAT BALL!!
?!
WHUFF!!
PLUMP!!
HEH HEH...
TAP...
STAB!!

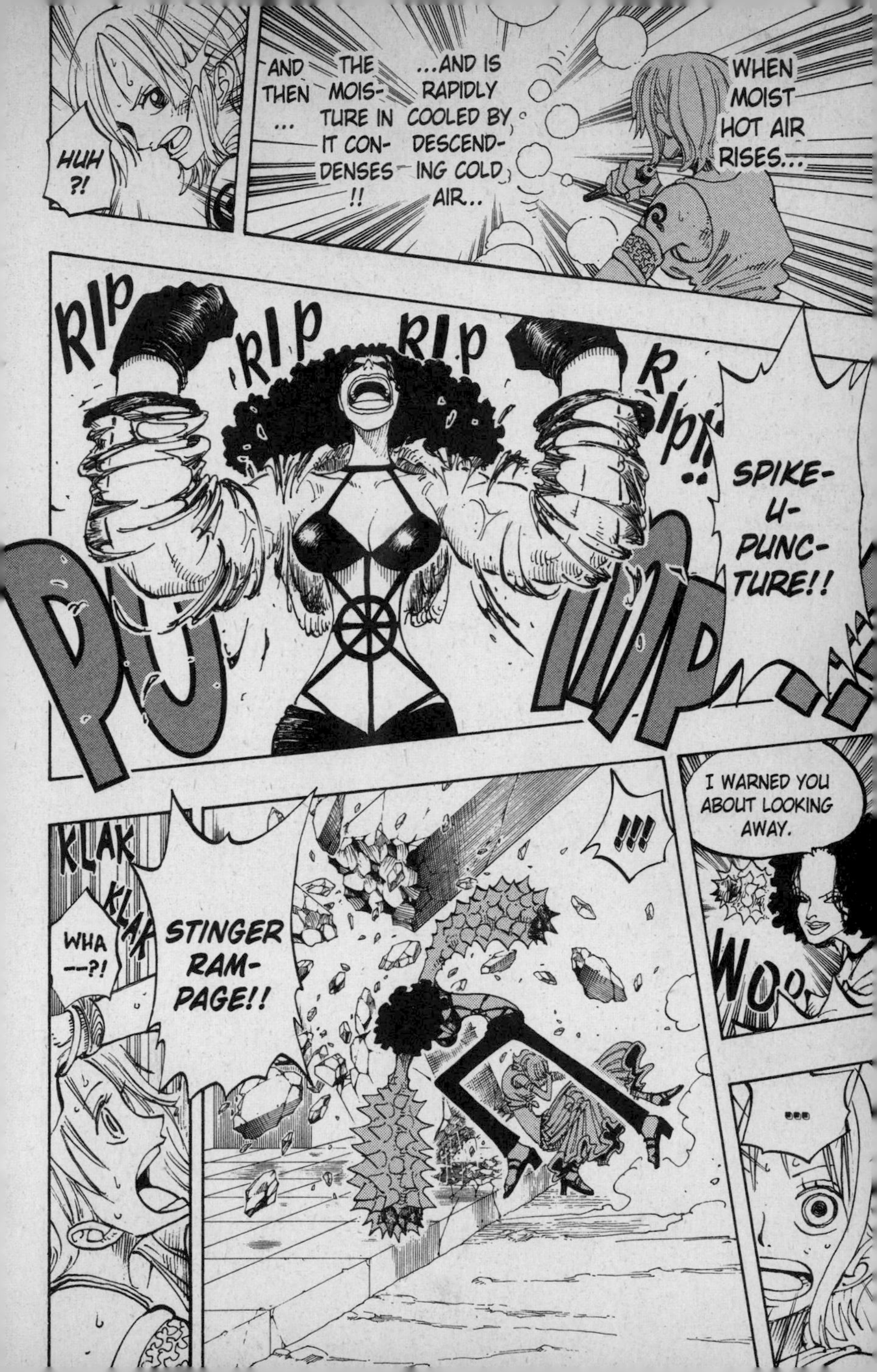
WHEN MOIST HOT AIR RISES...
...AND IS RAPIDLY COOLED BY DESCENDING COLD AIR...
THE MOISTURE IN IT CONDENSES!!
AND THEN ...
HUH ?!
SPIKE-U-PUNCTURE!!
RIP
RIP
RIP
RIP!!
PUMP...
I WARNED YOU ABOUT LOOKING AWAY.
WOO
...
!!!
STINGER RAMPAGE!!
KLAK KLAK KLAK
WHA--?!

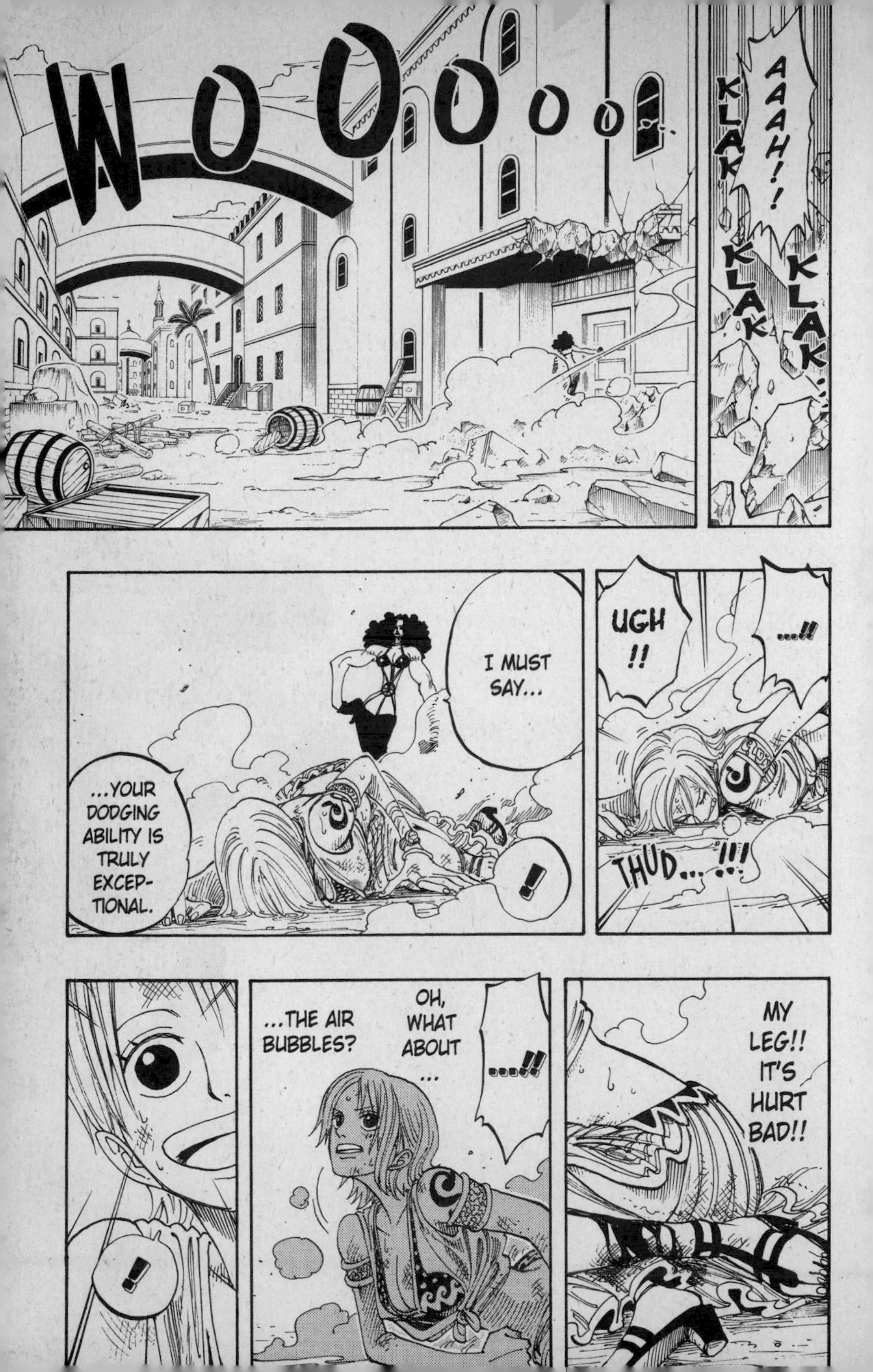
AAAH!!
KLAK KLAK...
KLAK KLAK
WOOOOoo..
UGH!!
...!!
THUD...!!!
I MUST SAY...
...YOUR DODGING ABILITY IS TRULY EXCEPTIONAL.
!
MY LEG!! IT'S HURT BAD!!
...!!
OH, WHAT ABOUT...
...THE AIR BUBBLES?
!

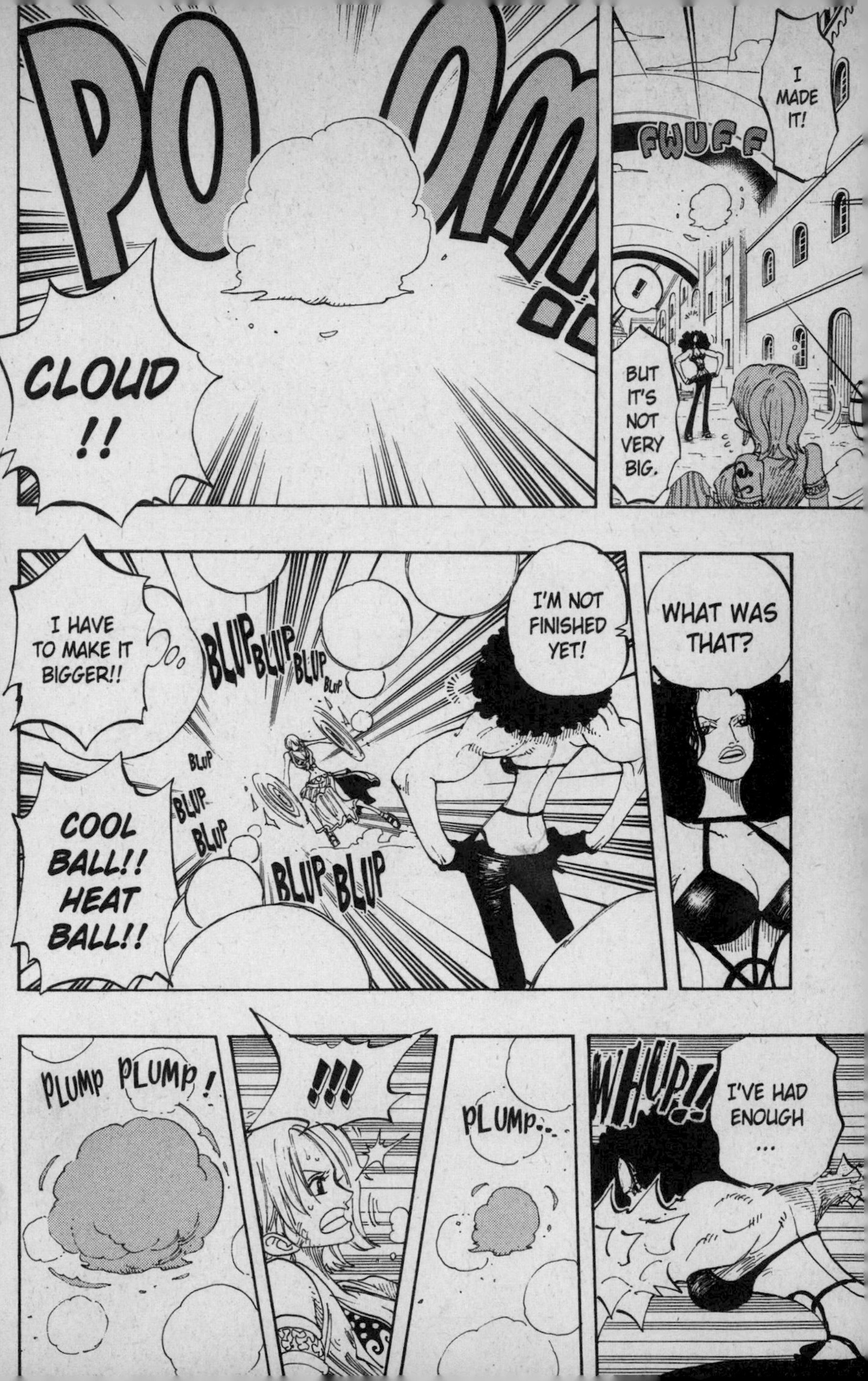
I MADE IT!
FWUFF
!
BUT IT'S NOT VERY BIG.
POOM
CLOUD!!
WHAT WAS THAT?
I'M NOT FINISHED YET!
I HAVE TO MAKE IT BIGGER!!
BLUP BLUP BLUP BLUP
BLUP BLUP BLUP
COOL BALL!! HEAT BALL!!
BLUP BLUP
WHUP!!
I'VE HAD ENOUGH...
PLUMP...
!!!
PLUMP PLUMP!

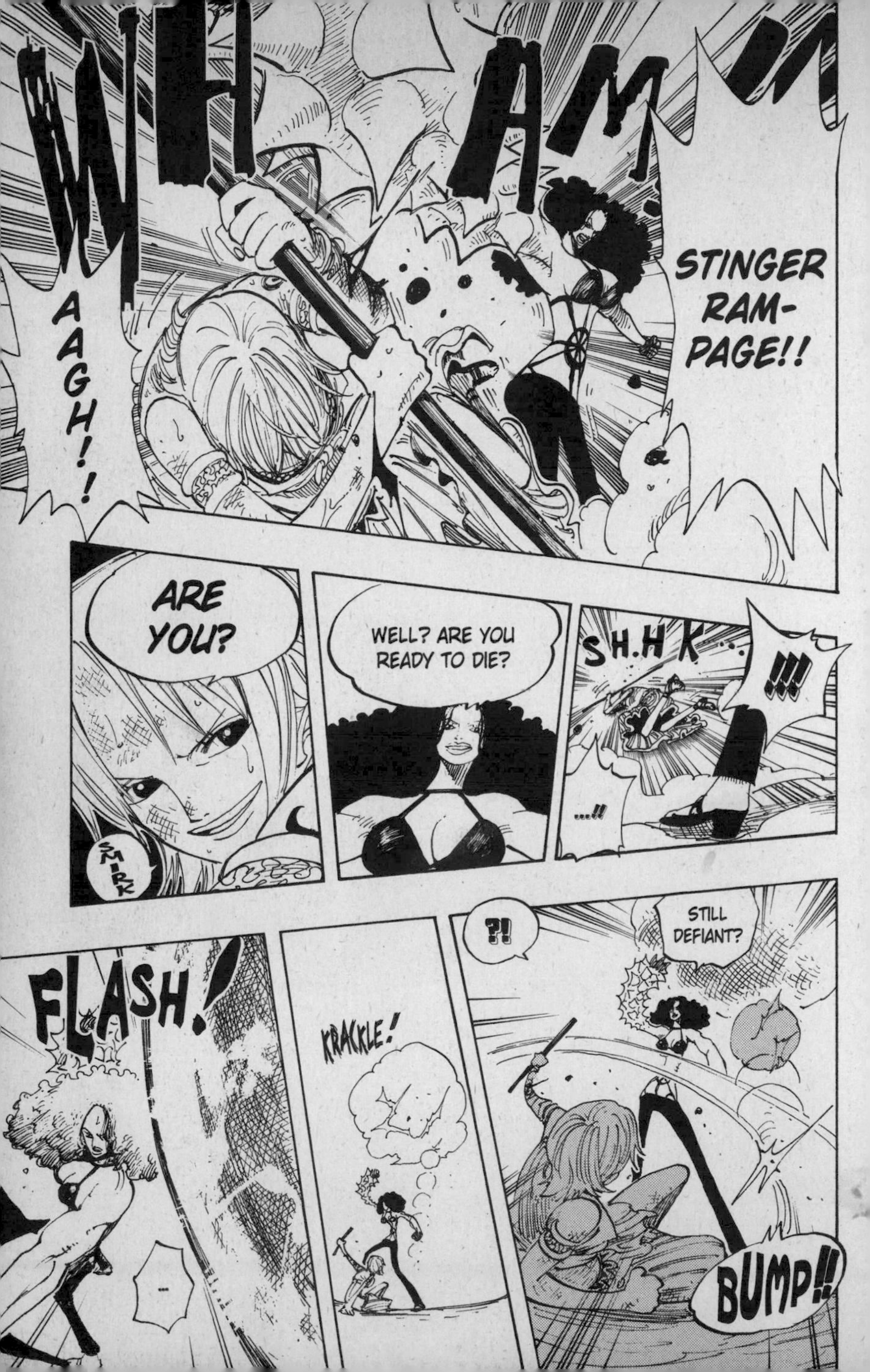
WHAM!
STINGER RAM-PAGE!!
AAGH!!
SH.HK...
!!!
...!!
WELL? ARE YOU READY TO DIE?
ARE YOU?
SMIRK
?!
STILL DEFIANT?
BUMP!!
KRACKLE!
FLASH!
...

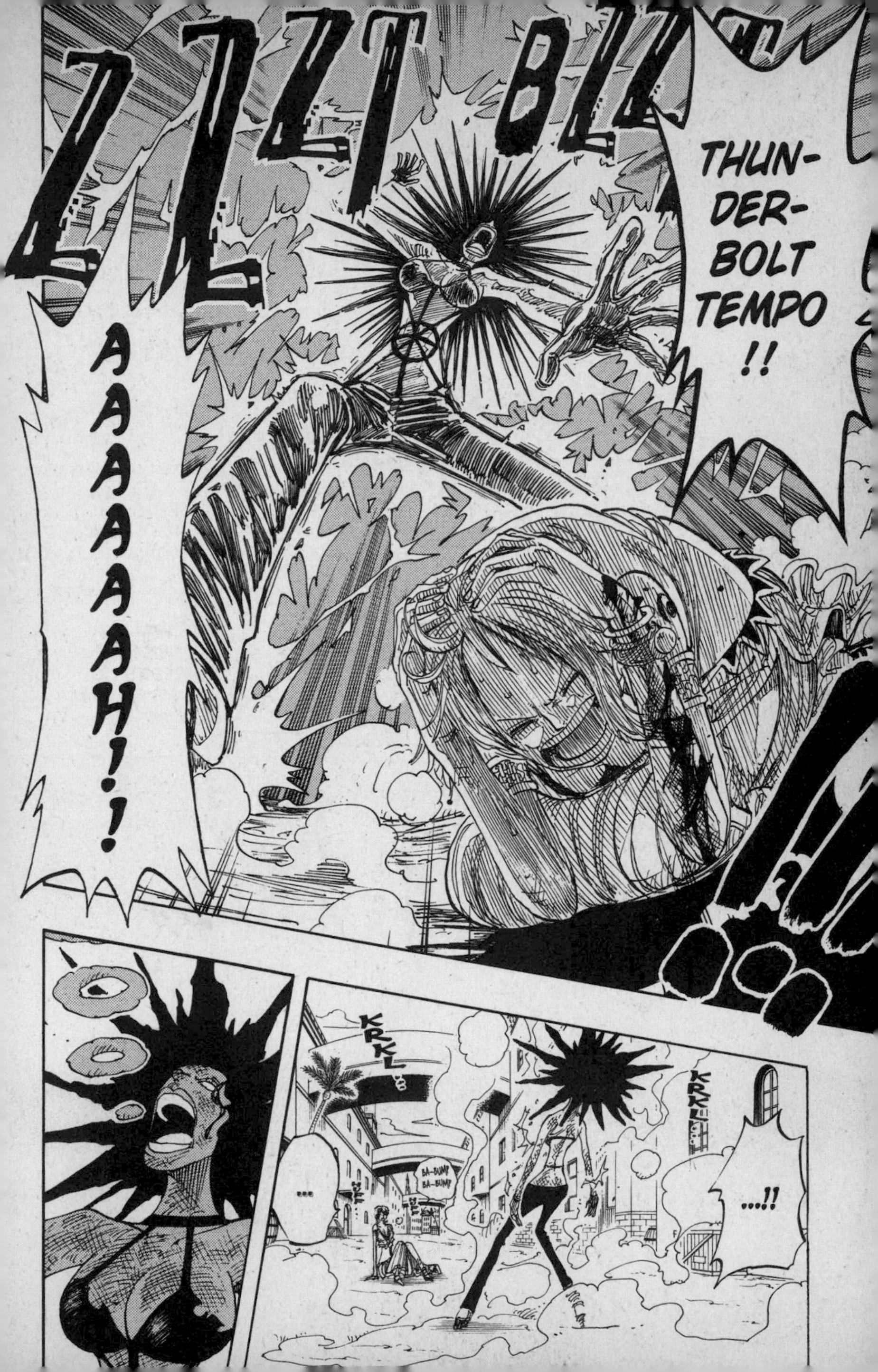
ZZZT BZZ
THUN-
DER-
BOLT
TEMPO
!!
AAAAAAAH!!!
...!!
KRKL
KRKL
...
BA-BUMP
BA-BUMP

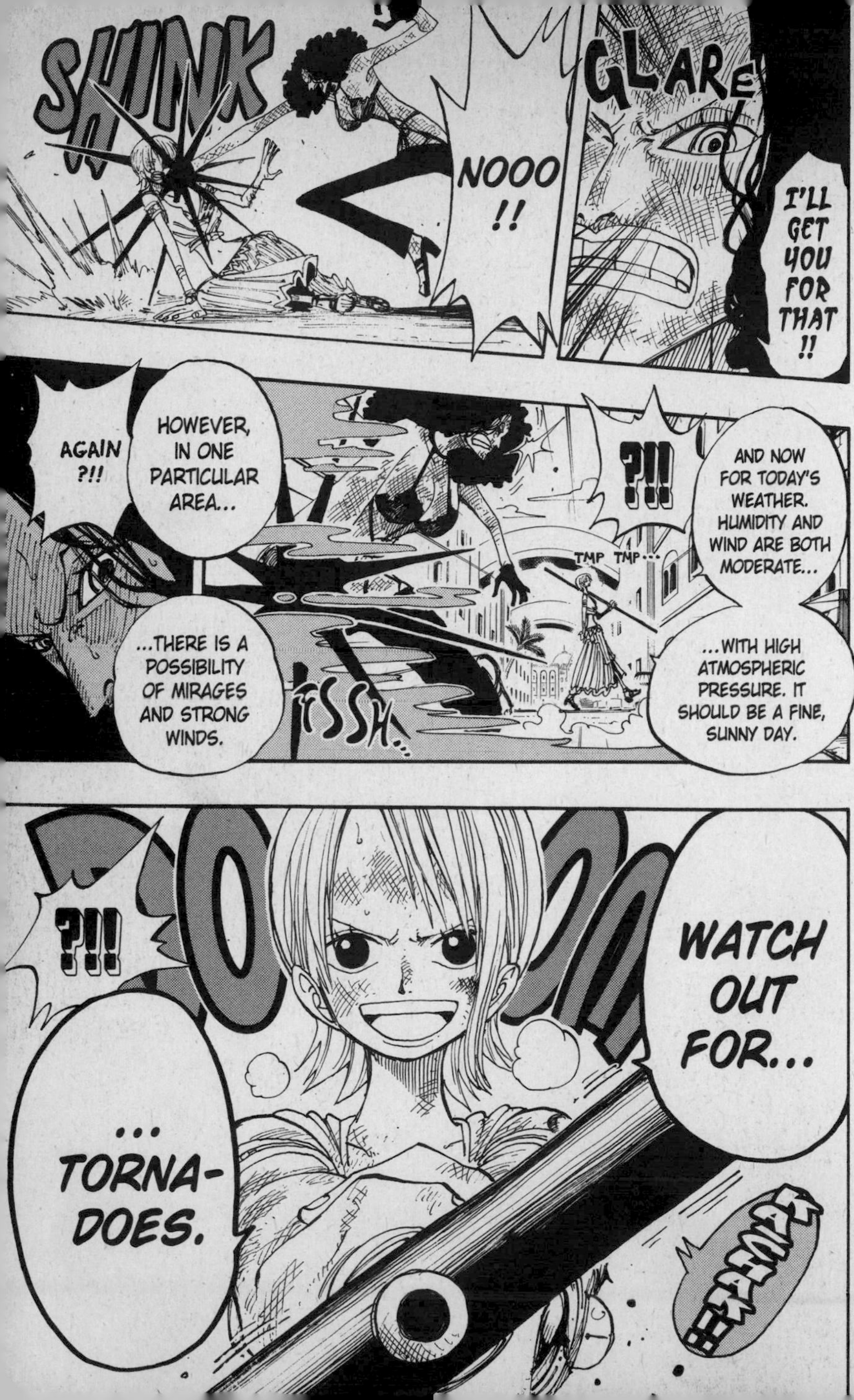
GLARE
I'LL GET YOU FOR THAT!!
NOOO!!
SHUNK
?!!
AND NOW FOR TODAY'S WEATHER. HUMIDITY AND WIND ARE BOTH MODERATE...
...WITH HIGH ATMOSPHERIC PRESSURE. IT SHOULD BE A FINE, SUNNY DAY.
TMP TMP...
HOWEVER, IN ONE PARTICULAR AREA...
...THERE IS A POSSIBILITY OF MIRAGES AND STRONG WINDS.
FSSH...
AGAIN ?!!
WATCH OUT FOR...
... TORNA-DOES.
?!!

Question Corner
SBS

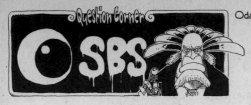

Oda: Time for an unusual stroll! Ms. Happy Birthday has sent us this maze game! I tried it, and it seems like the goal can be reached by various paths. So there's more than one solution! Have fun with those that you run into! Let's go for a walk!!

Reach the goal by passing every character in boy–girl order without passing any character twice.

*Mr. 2 can be counted as either gender. ('Cause he's iffy.)

Start
Luffy
Nami
Zolo
Vivi
Ms. Valentine
Igaram
Mr. 2
Mr. 1
Ms. Doublefinger
Sir Crocodile
Nojiko
Karoo
Kuina
Mr. 3
Ms. All Sunday
Toh-Toh
Tashigi
Ms. Merry Christmas
Sanji
Ms. Monday
Dr. Kureha
Koza
Chaka
Goal
Belle-Mère
King Cobra
Ms. Goldenweek

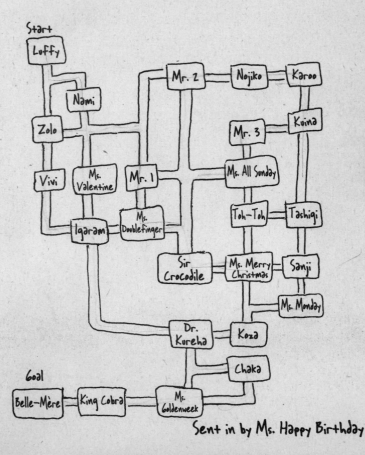

Sent in by Ms. Happy Birthday

Chapter 193:
UTOPIA

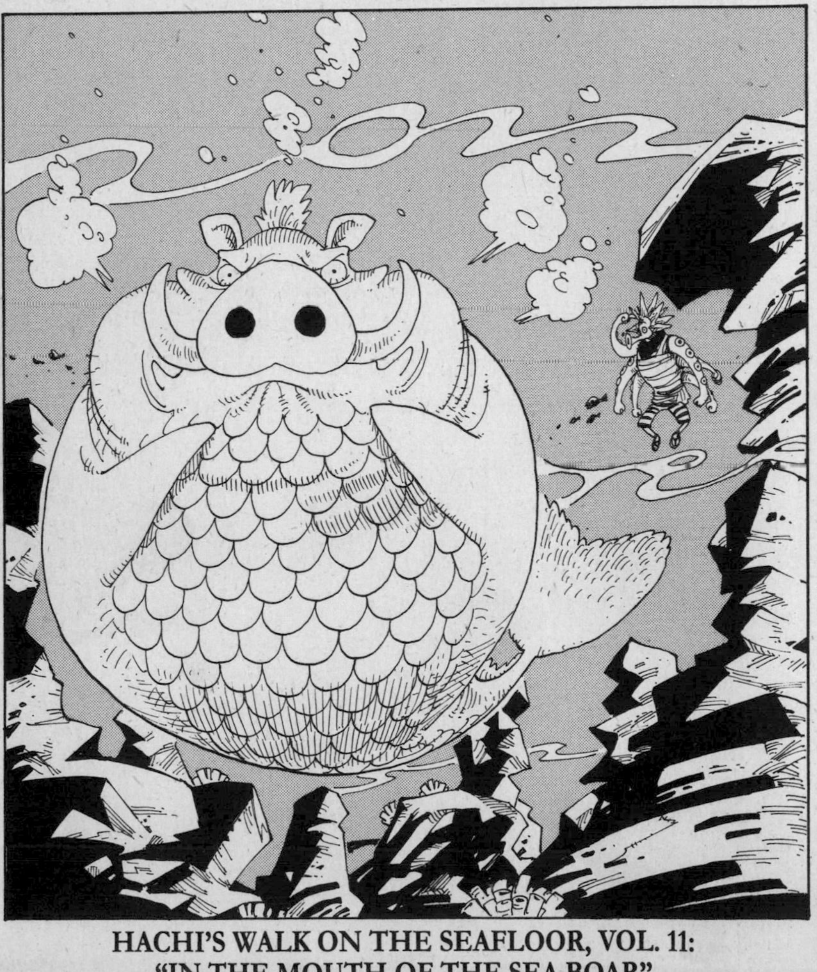

HACHI'S WALK ON THE SEAFLOOR, VOL. 11:
"IN THE MOUTH OF THE SEA BOAR"

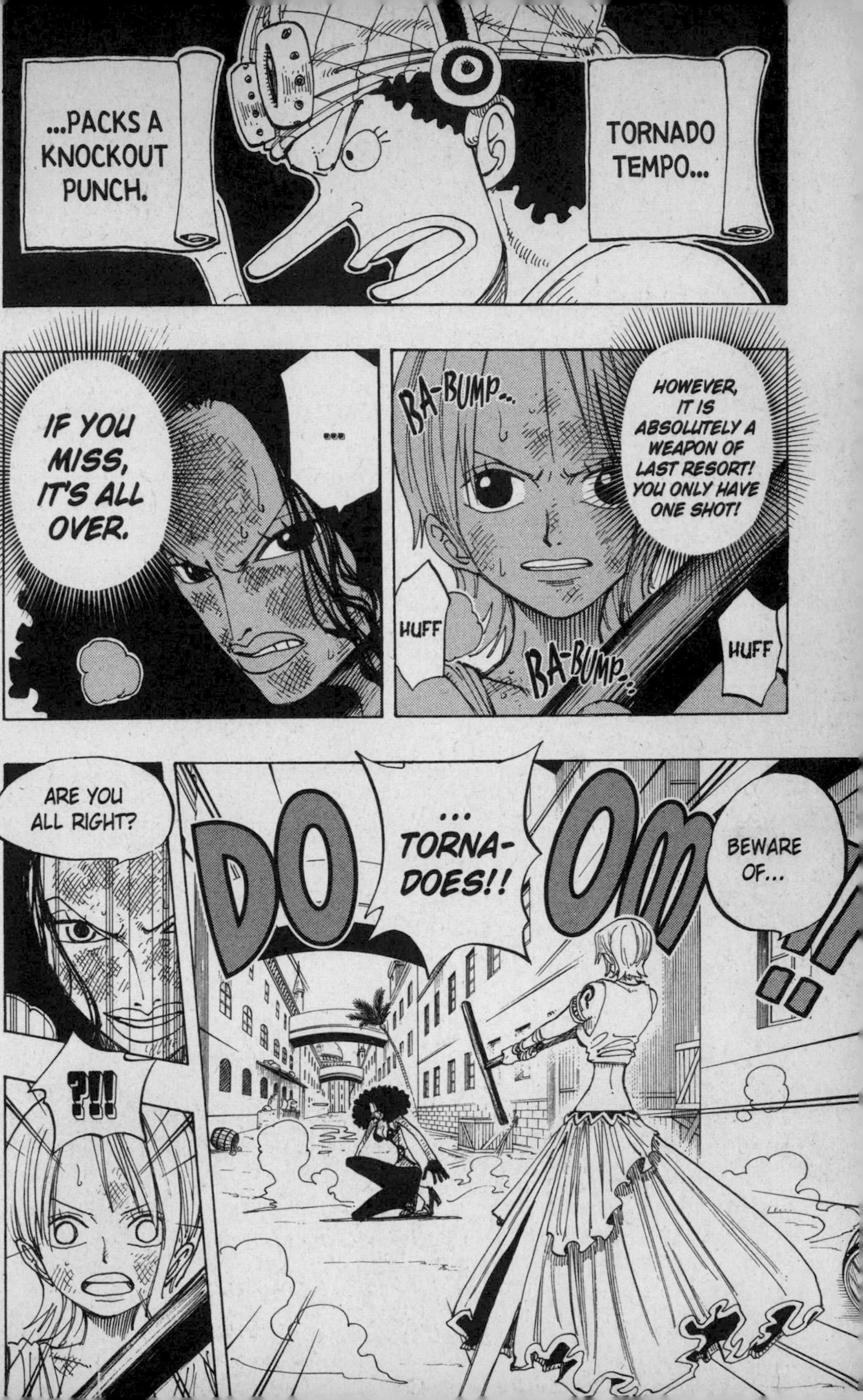
TORNADO TEMPO...
...PACKS A KNOCKOUT PUNCH.
BA-BUMP..
HOWEVER, IT IS ABSOLUTELY A WEAPON OF LAST RESORT! YOU ONLY HAVE ONE SHOT!
HUFF
BA-BUMP..
HUFF
...
IF YOU MISS, IT'S ALL OVER.
BEWARE OF...
...TORNA-DOES!!
DOOM!!
ARE YOU ALL RIGHT?
?!!

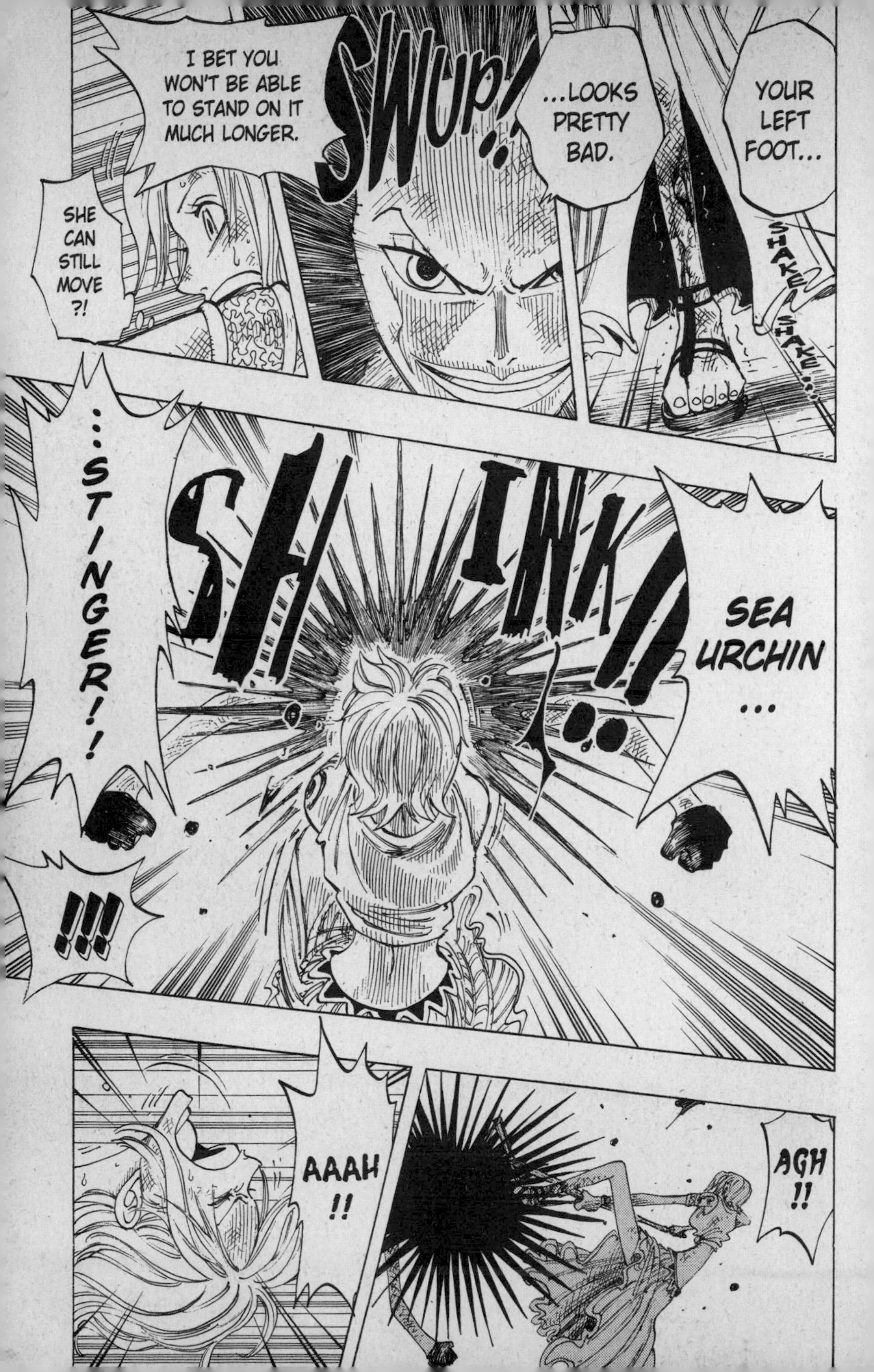
YOUR LEFT FOOT...
SHAKE SHAKE...
...LOOKS PRETTY BAD.
SWUP!!
I BET YOU WON'T BE ABLE TO STAND ON IT MUCH LONGER.
SHE CAN STILL MOVE ?!
SEA URCHIN...
SHINK!!
...STINGER!!
!!!
AGH!!
AAAH!!

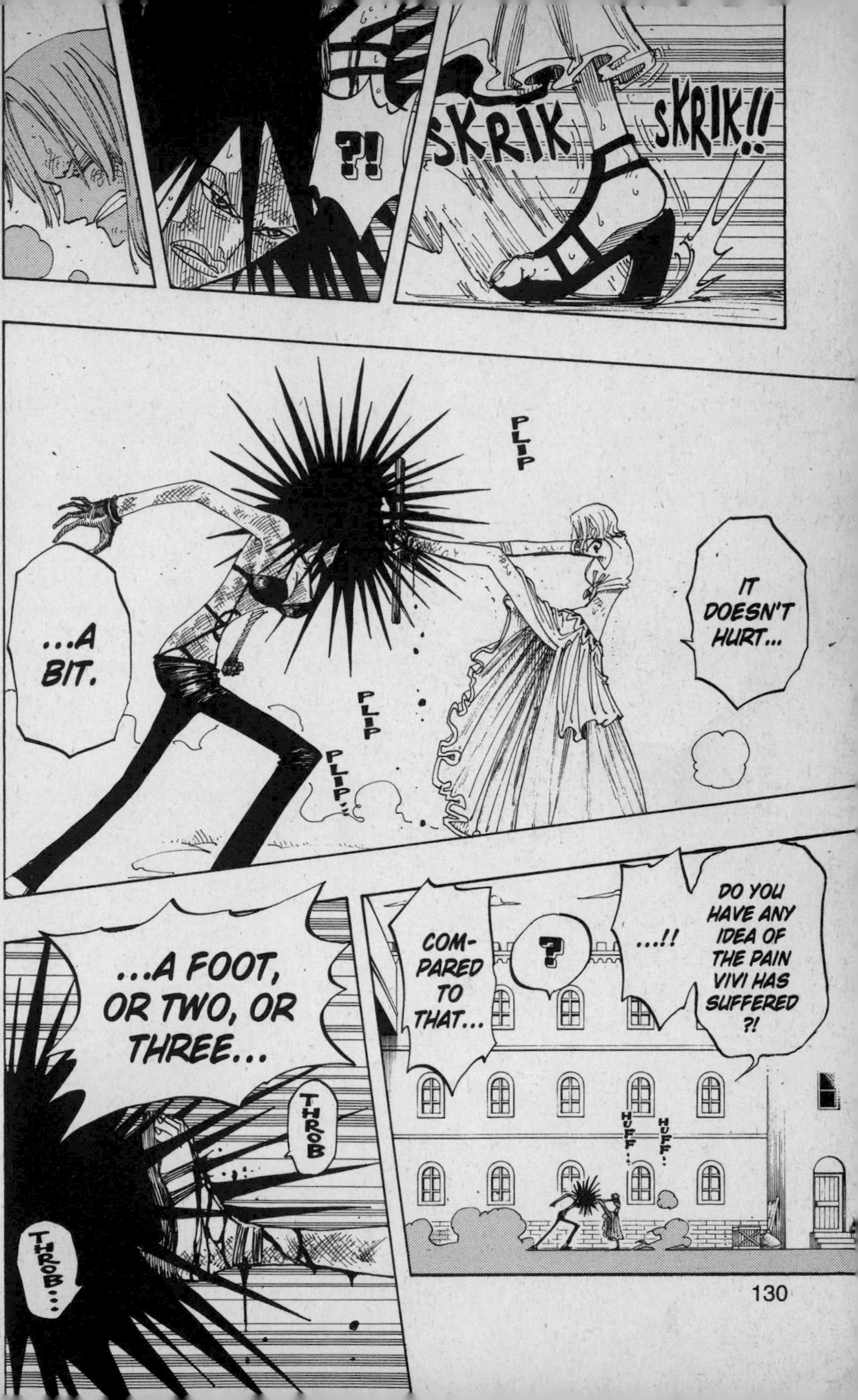
SKRIK!!
SKRIK
?!
PLIP
IT DOESN'T HURT...
...A BIT.
PLIP
PLIP...
DO YOU HAVE ANY IDEA OF THE PAIN VIVI HAS SUFFERED ?!
...!!
?
COM-PARED TO THAT...
HUFF...
HUFF...
...A FOOT, OR TWO, OR THREE...
THROB
THROB...

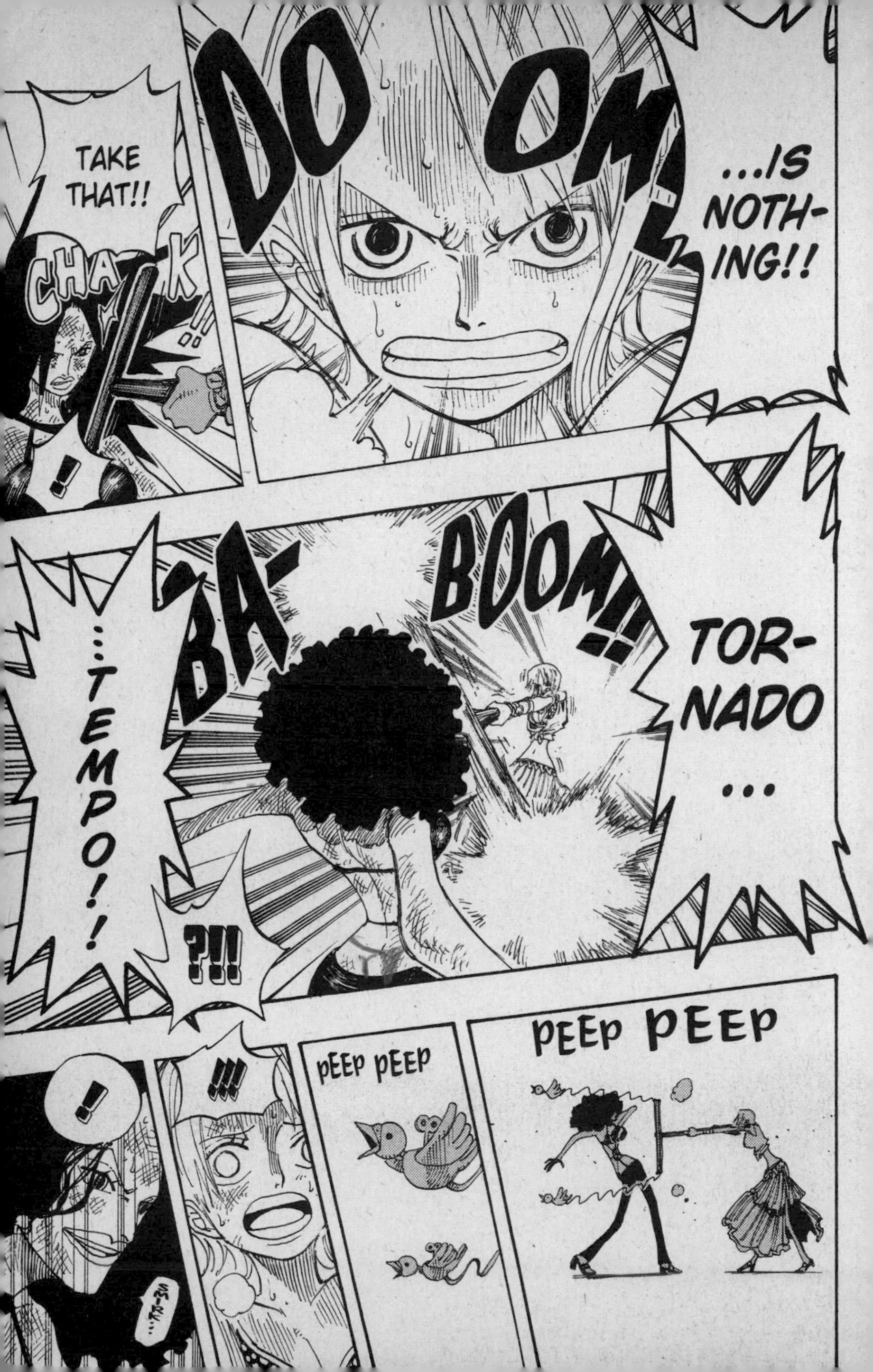

DOOM
...IS NOTHING!!
TAKE THAT!!
CHAK
!!
!
TORNADO...
BA-BOOM!!
...TEMPO!!
?!!
PEEP PEEP
PEEP PEEP
!!!
!
SMIRK...

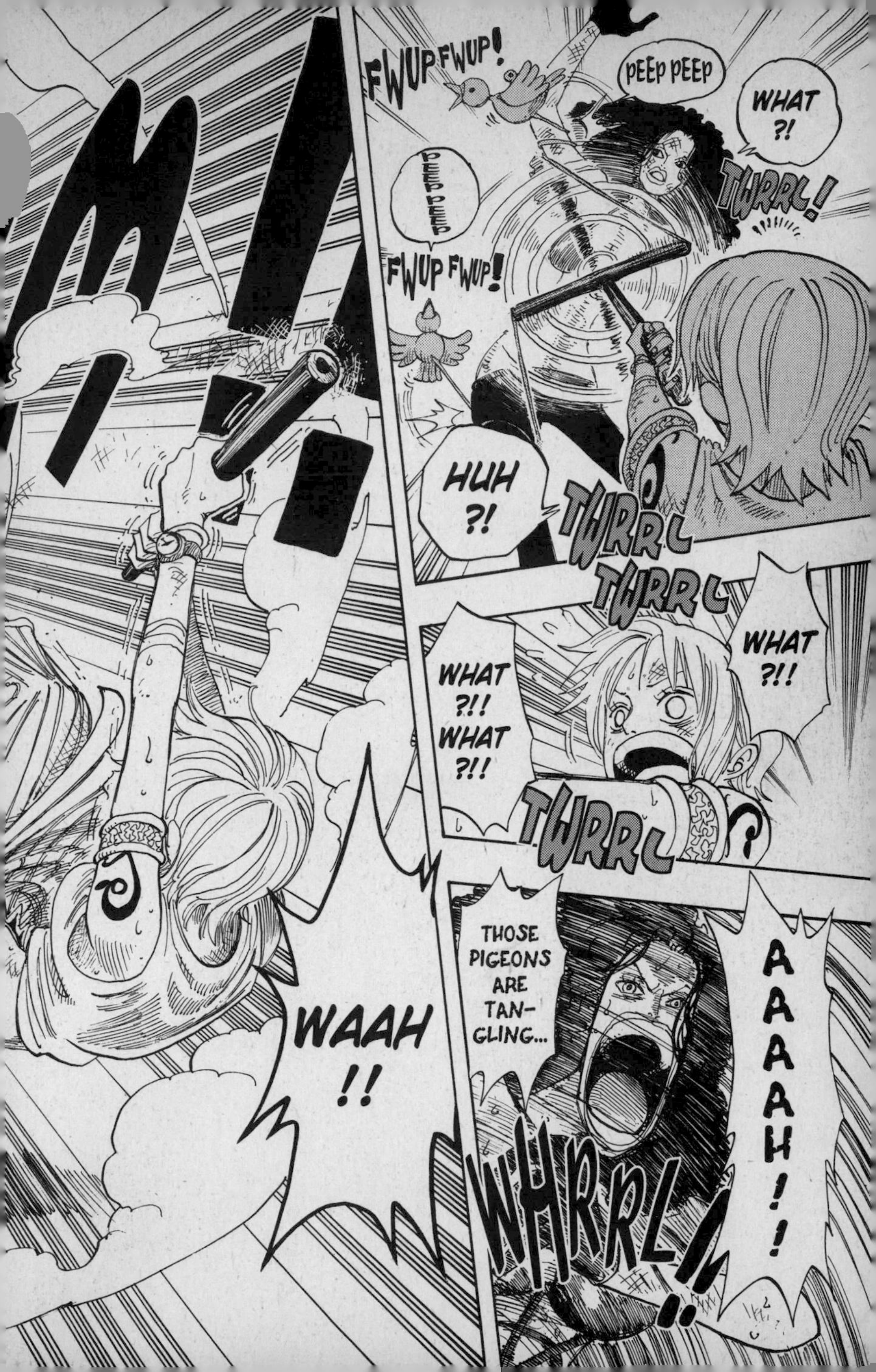

WHAT ?!
PEEP PEEP
FWUP FWUP!
TWRRL!
PEEP PEEP
FWUP FWUP!
HUH ?!
TWRRL
TWRRL
WHAT ?!!
WHAT ?!! WHAT ?!!
TWRRL
AAAAAH!!!
THOSE PIGEONS ARE TAN- GLING...
WHRRL!!
WAAH !!

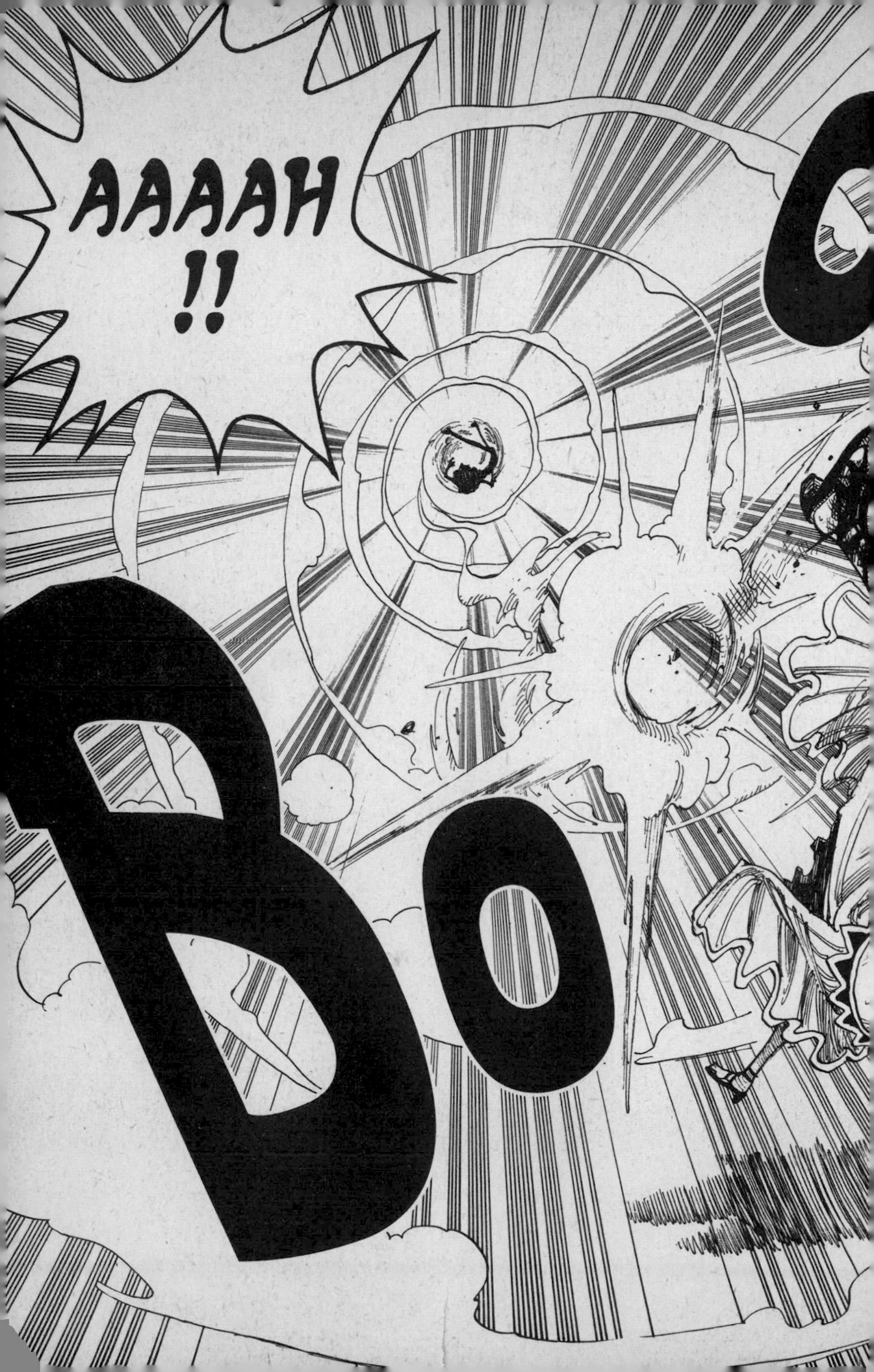
AAAAH
!!
BO

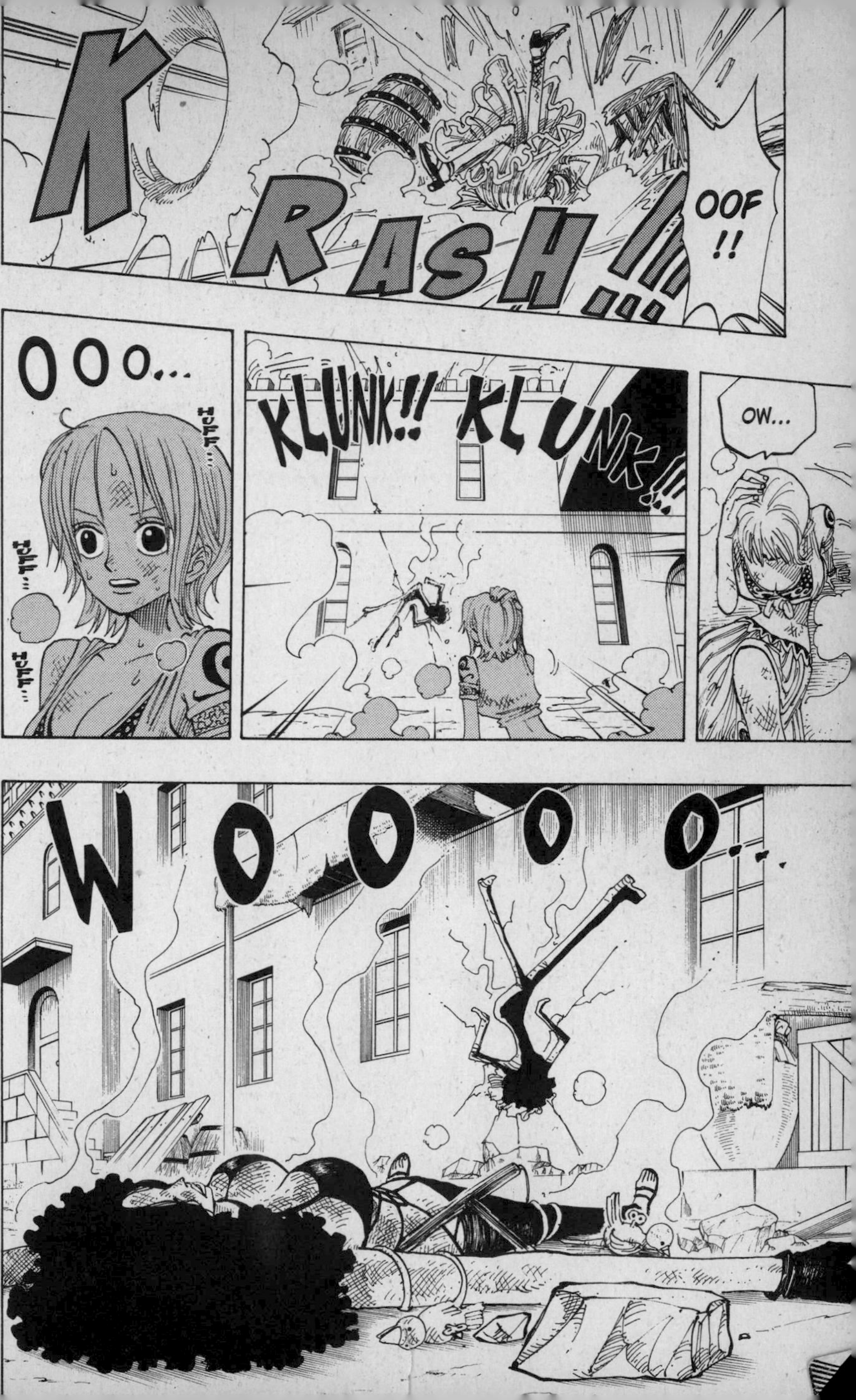
KRASH!!!
OOF!!
OW...
KLUNK!! KLUNK!!!
OOO...
HUFF...
HUFF...
HUFF...
WOOOO...

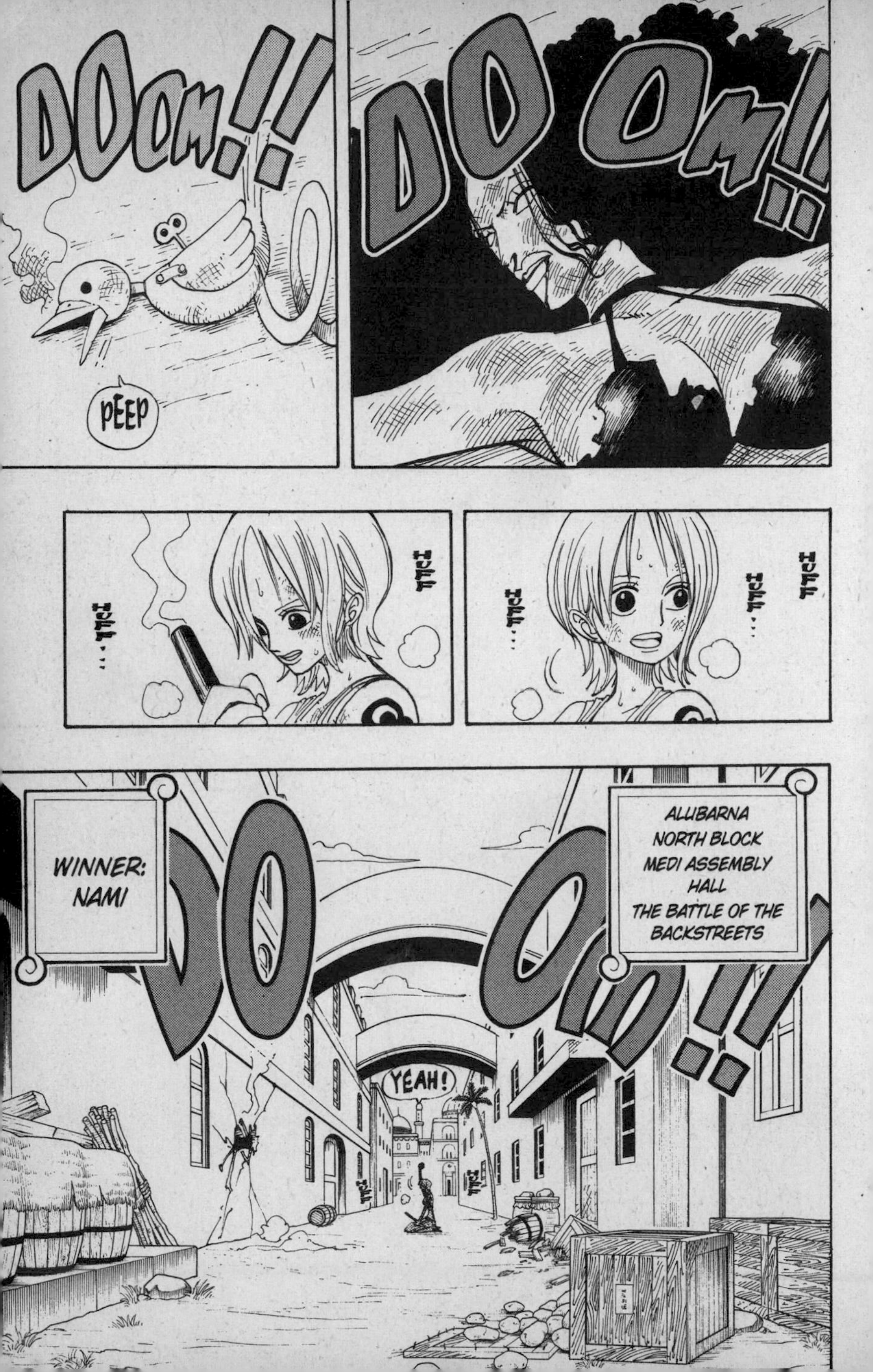
DOOM!!
DOOM!!
PEEP
HUFF
HUFF...
HUFF...
HUFF
HUFF...
ALUBARNA NORTH BLOCK MEDI ASSEMBLY HALL THE BATTLE OF THE BACKSTREETS
DOOM!!
WINNER: NAMI
YEAH!
HUFF
HUFF

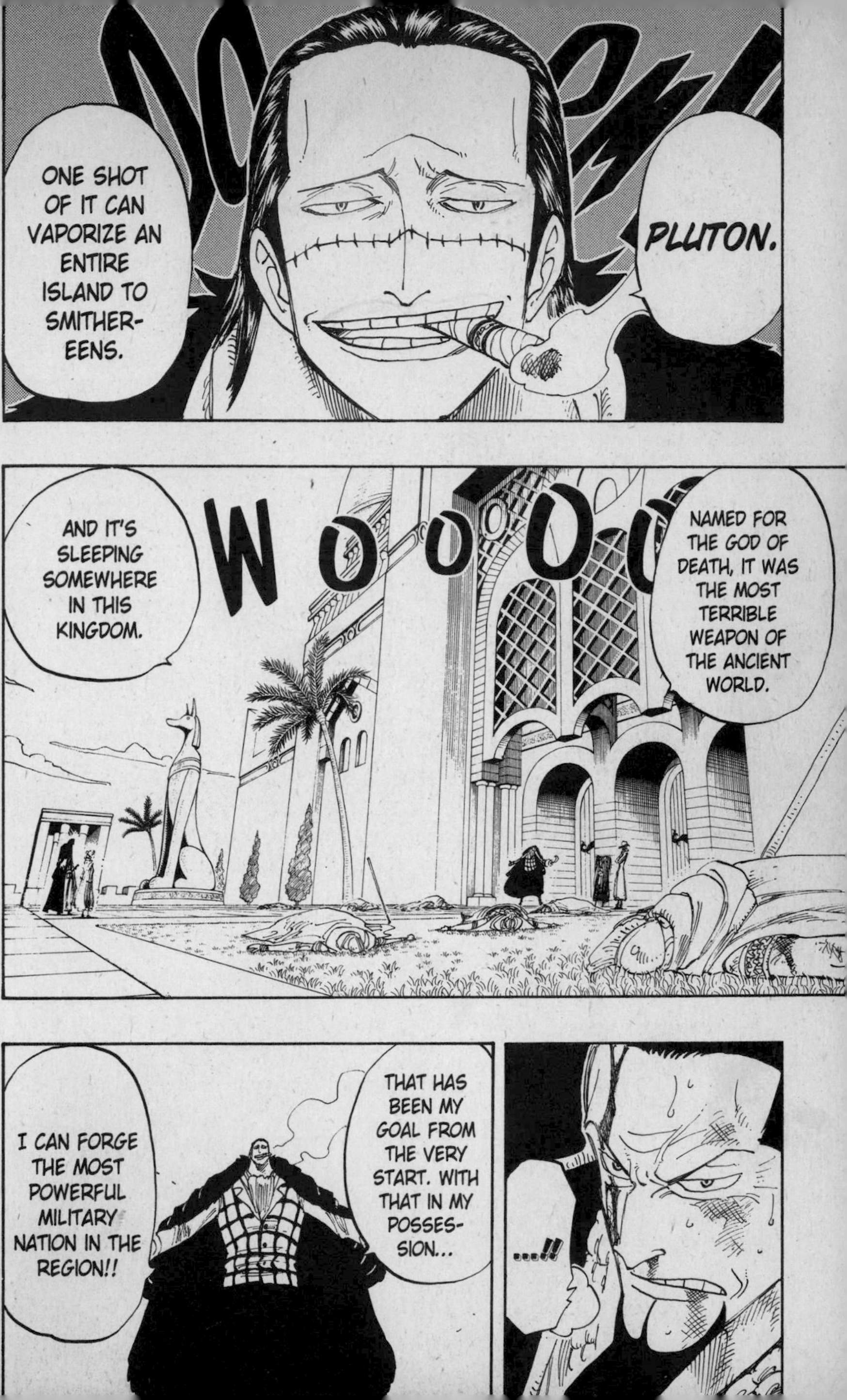
PLUTON.
ONE SHOT OF IT CAN VAPORIZE AN ENTIRE ISLAND TO SMITHER-EENS.
NAMED FOR THE GOD OF DEATH, IT WAS THE MOST TERRIBLE WEAPON OF THE ANCIENT WORLD.
AND IT'S SLEEPING SOMEWHERE IN THIS KINGDOM.
...!!
THAT HAS BEEN MY GOAL FROM THE VERY START. WITH THAT IN MY POSSES-SION...
I CAN FORGE THE MOST POWERFUL MILITARY NATION IN THE REGION!!

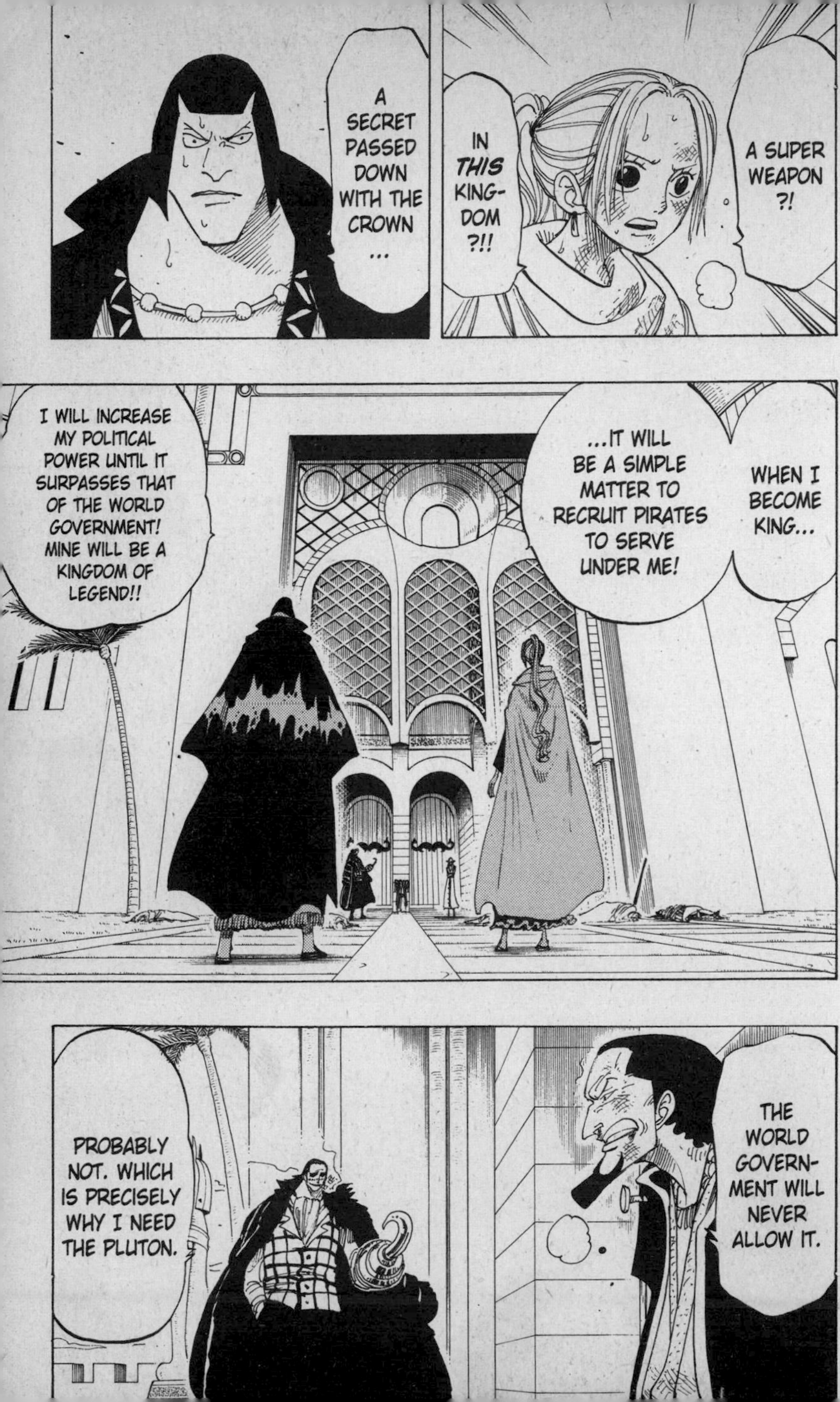
A SUPER WEAPON ?!
IN THIS KINGDOM ?!!
A SECRET PASSED DOWN WITH THE CROWN ...
WHEN I BECOME KING...
...IT WILL BE A SIMPLE MATTER TO RECRUIT PIRATES TO SERVE UNDER ME!
I WILL INCREASE MY POLITICAL POWER UNTIL IT SURPASSES THAT OF THE WORLD GOVERNMENT! MINE WILL BE A KINGDOM OF LEGEND!!
THE WORLD GOVERNMENT WILL NEVER ALLOW IT.
PROBABLY NOT. WHICH IS PRECISELY WHY I NEED THE PLUTON.

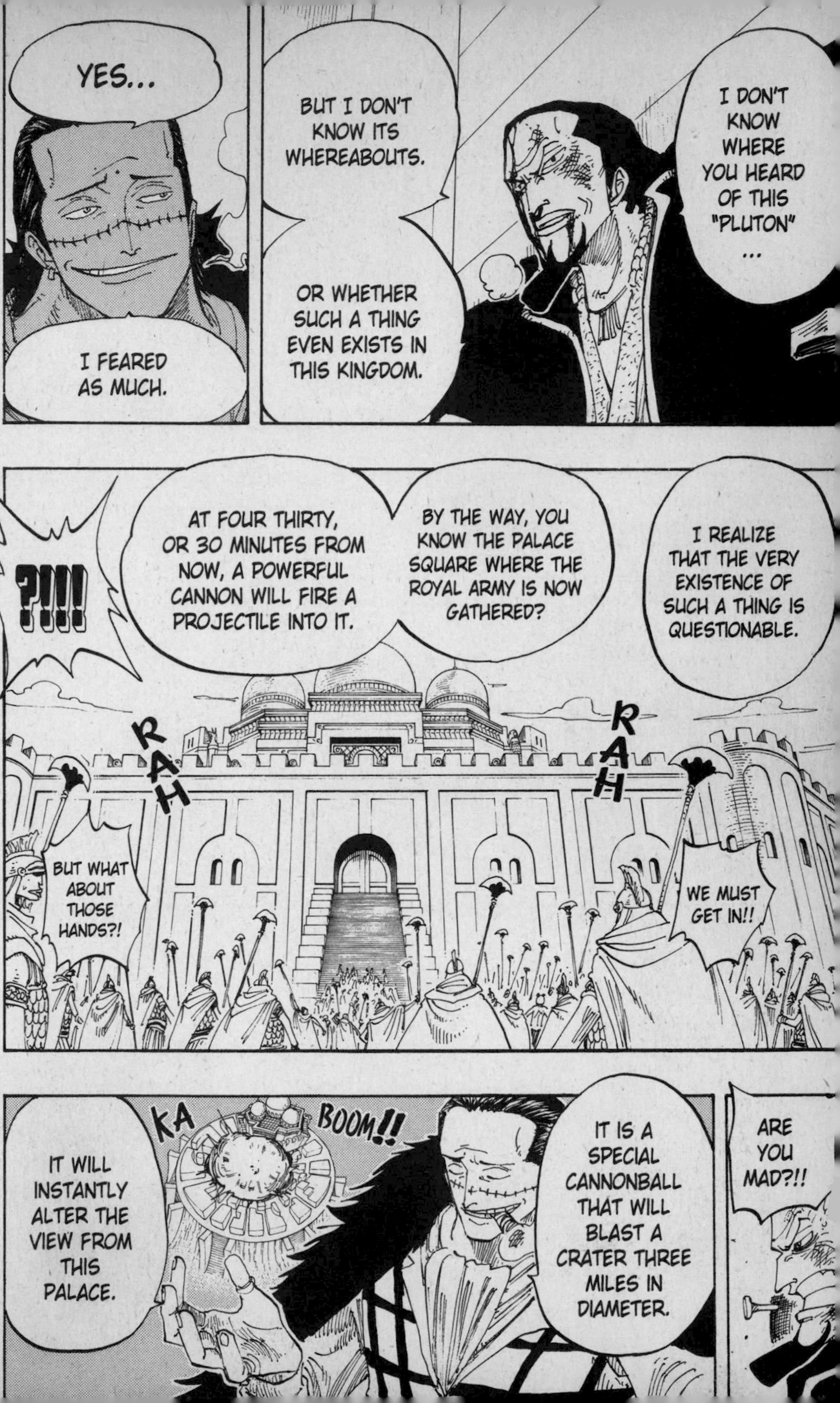

I DON'T KNOW WHERE YOU HEARD OF THIS "PLUTON"...
BUT I DON'T KNOW ITS WHEREABOUTS.
OR WHETHER SUCH A THING EVEN EXISTS IN THIS KINGDOM.
YES...
I FEARED AS MUCH.
I REALIZE THAT THE VERY EXISTENCE OF SUCH A THING IS QUESTIONABLE.
BY THE WAY, YOU KNOW THE PALACE SQUARE WHERE THE ROYAL ARMY IS NOW GATHERED?
AT FOUR THIRTY, OR 30 MINUTES FROM NOW, A POWERFUL CANNON WILL FIRE A PROJECTILE INTO IT.
?!!!
RAH
WE MUST GET IN!!
BUT WHAT ABOUT THOSE HANDS?!
RAH
ARE YOU MAD?!!
IT IS A SPECIAL CANNONBALL THAT WILL BLAST A CRATER THREE MILES IN DIAMETER.
KA BOOM!!
IT WILL INSTANTLY ALTER THE VIEW FROM THIS PALACE.

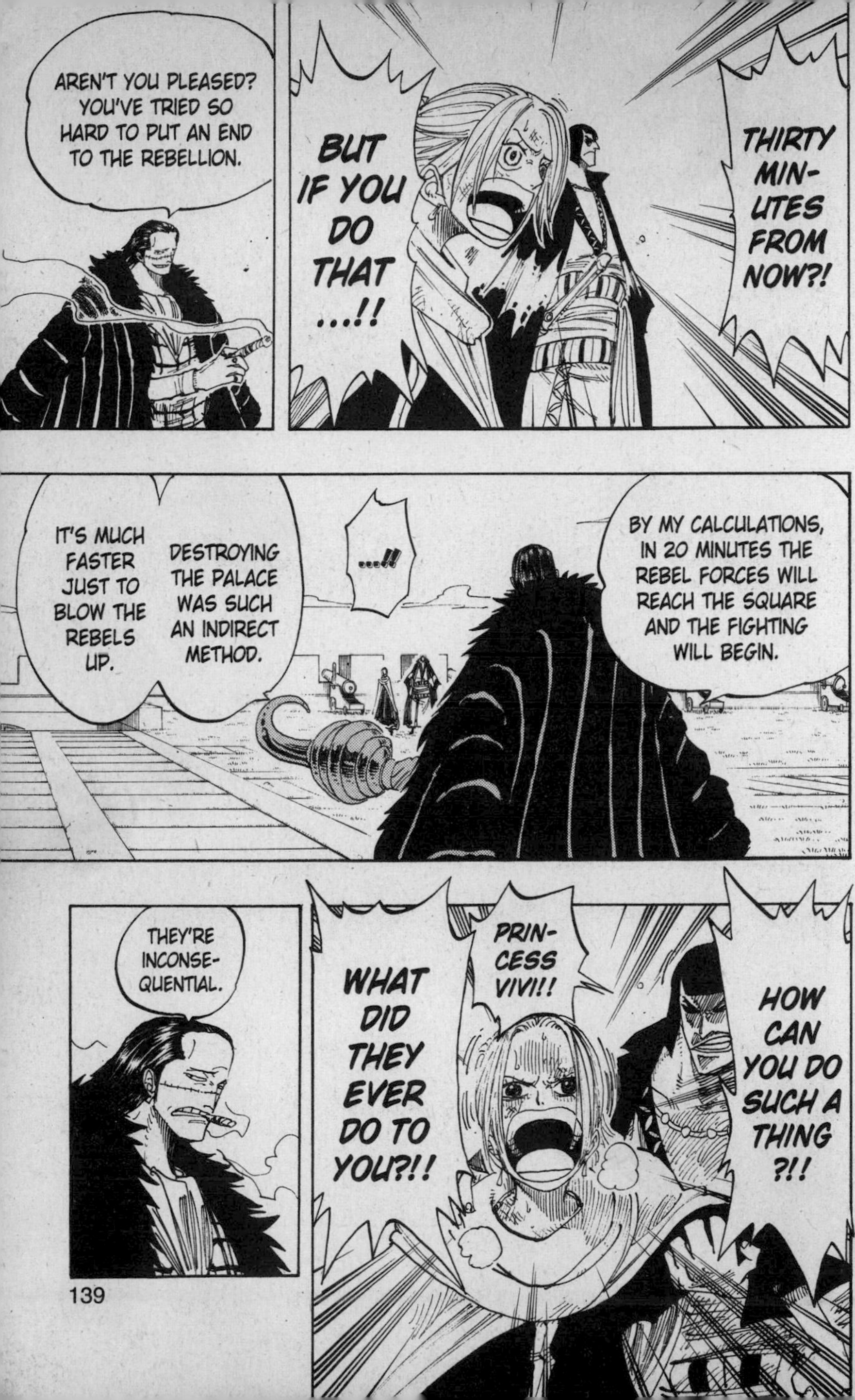
THIRTY MIN-UTES FROM NOW?!
BUT IF YOU DO THAT ...!!
AREN'T YOU PLEASED? YOU'VE TRIED SO HARD TO PUT AN END TO THE REBELLION.
BY MY CALCULATIONS, IN 20 MINUTES THE REBEL FORCES WILL REACH THE SQUARE AND THE FIGHTING WILL BEGIN.
...!!
DESTROYING THE PALACE WAS SUCH AN INDIRECT METHOD.
IT'S MUCH FASTER JUST TO BLOW THE REBELS UP.
HOW CAN YOU DO SUCH A THING?!!
PRIN-CESS VIVI!!
WHAT DID THEY EVER DO TO YOU?!!
THEY'RE INCONSE-QUENTIAL.

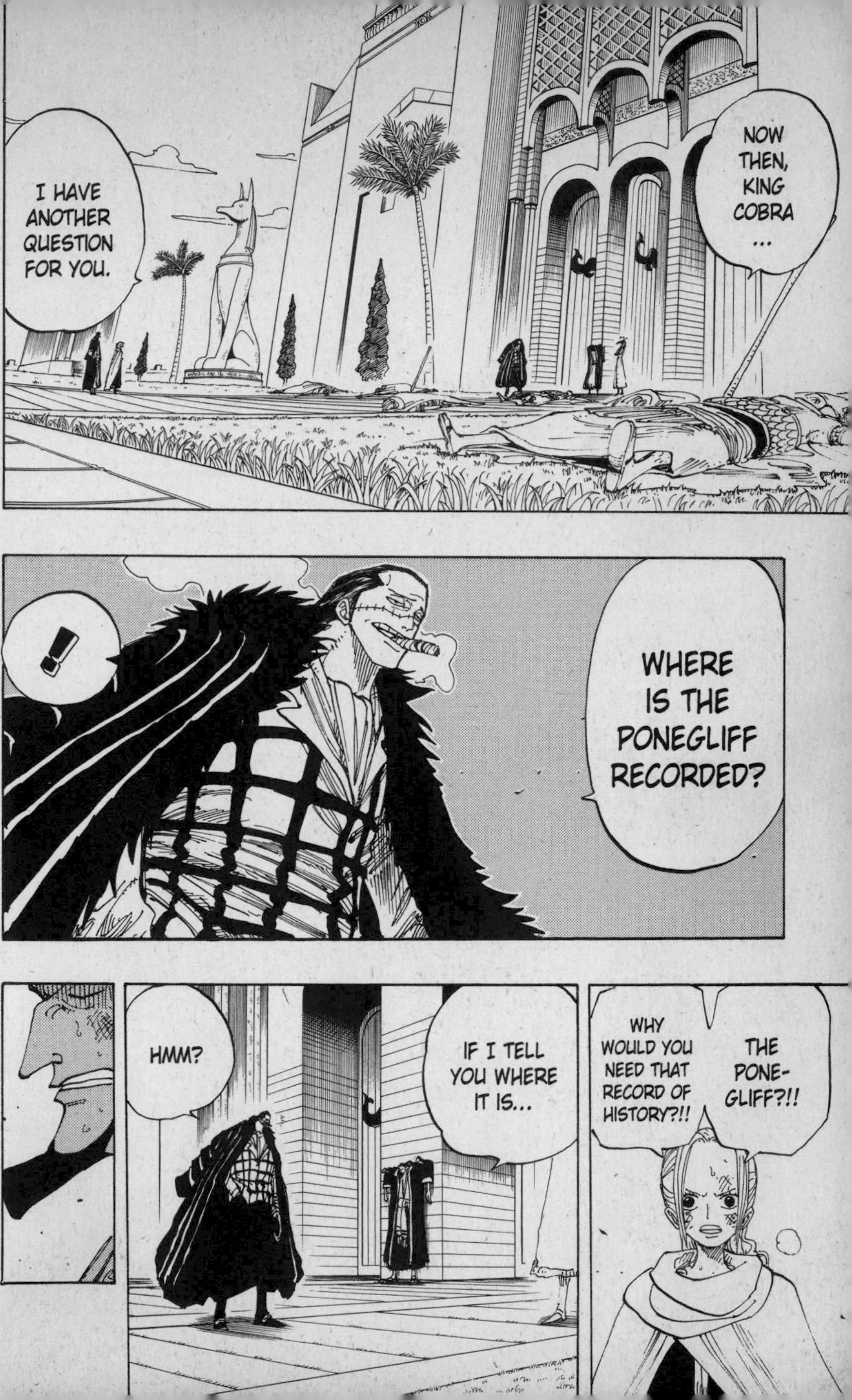
NOW THEN, KING COBRA ...
I HAVE ANOTHER QUESTION FOR YOU.
WHERE IS THE PONEGLIFF RECORDED?
!
THE PONE-GLIFF?!!
WHY WOULD YOU NEED THAT RECORD OF HISTORY?!!
IF I TELL YOU WHERE IT IS...
HMM?

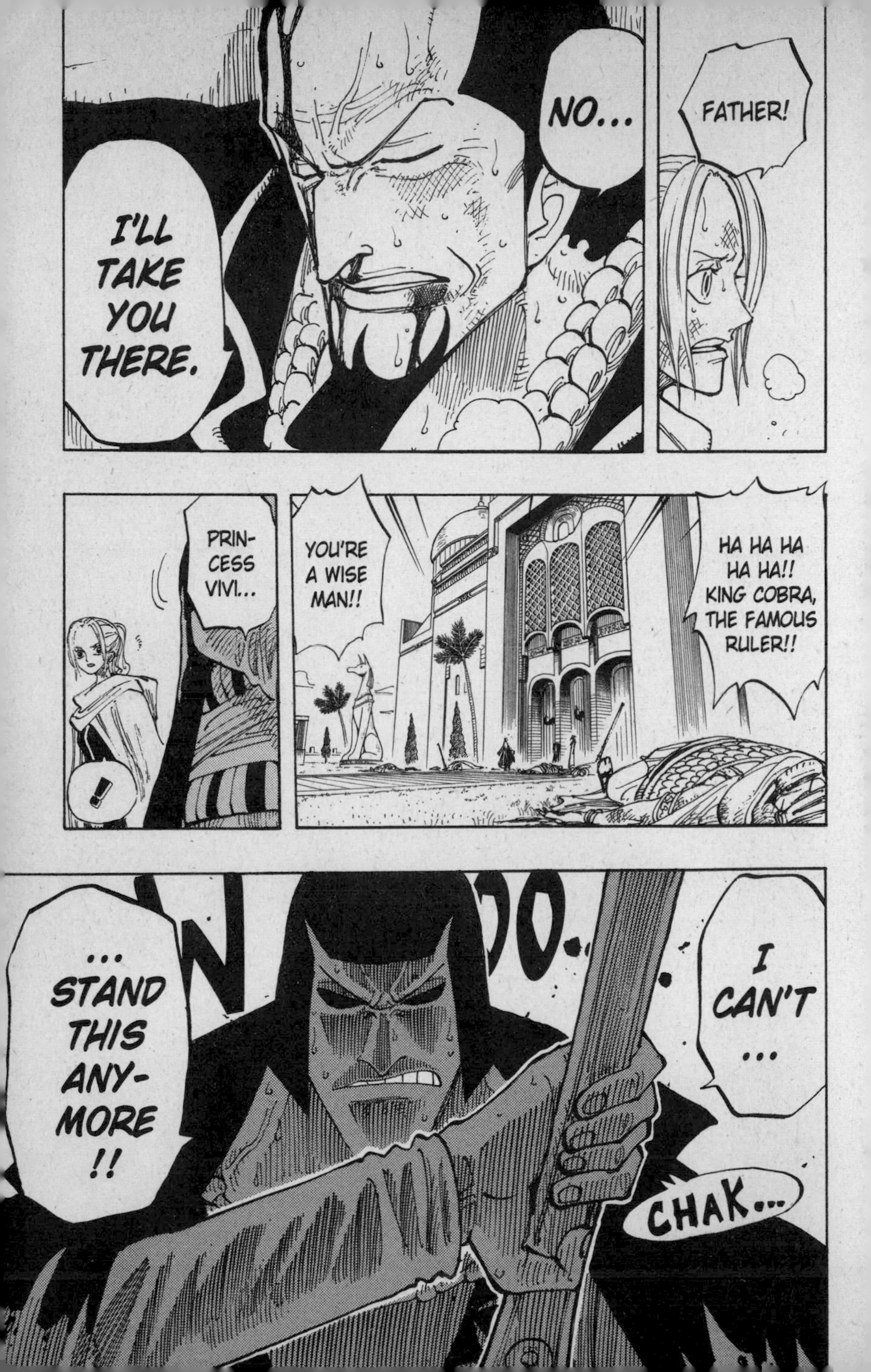
FATHER!
NO...
I'LL TAKE YOU THERE.
HA HA HA HA HA!! KING COBRA, THE FAMOUS RULER!!
YOU'RE A WISE MAN!!
PRINCESS VIVI...
!
I CAN'T ...
DO..
... STAND THIS ANYMORE !!
CHAK...

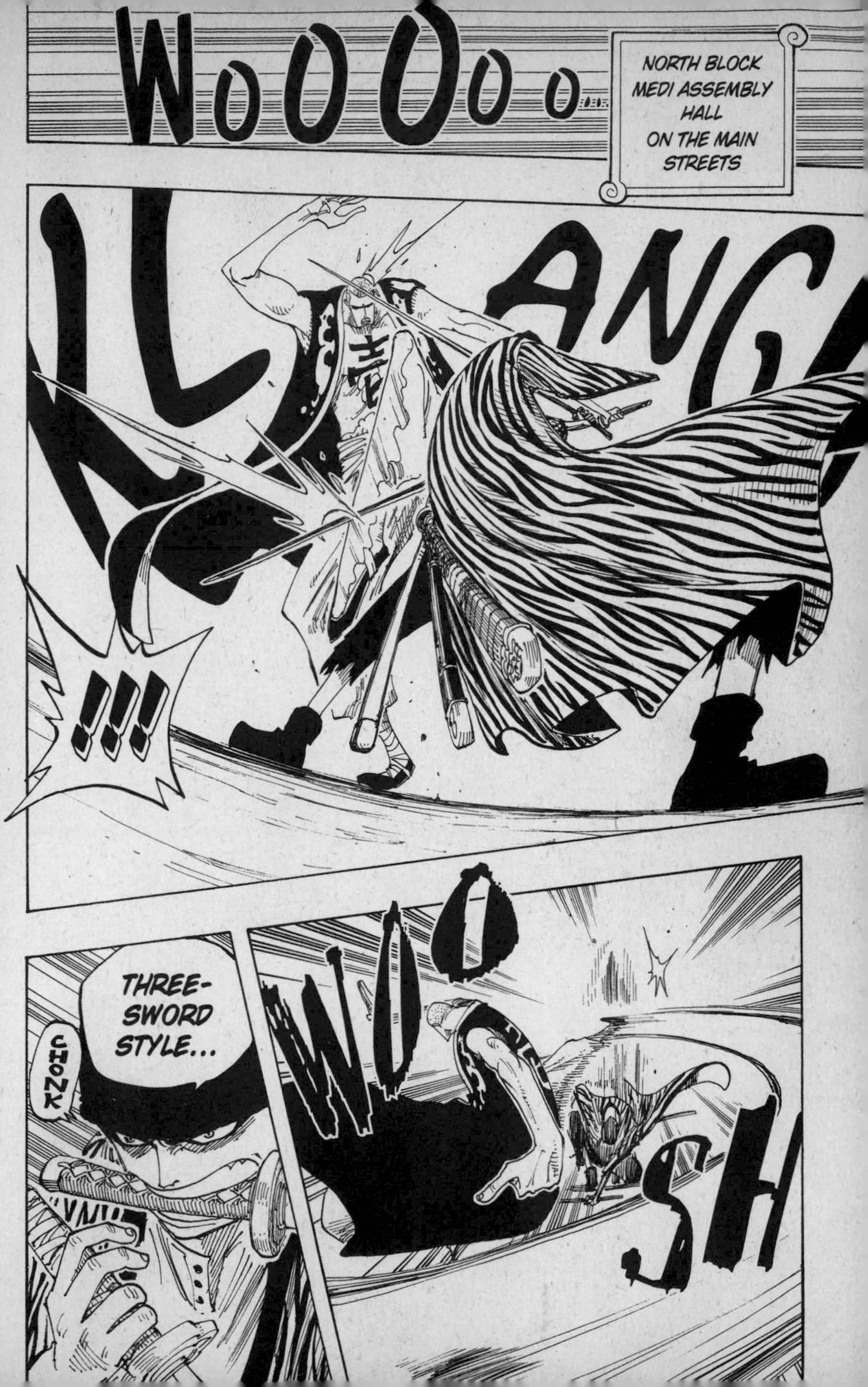
NORTH BLOCK
MEDI ASSEMBLY
HALL
ON THE MAIN
STREETS
WOOOOO O...
CLANG
!!!
WOOOSH
THREE-
SWORD
STYLE...
CHONK

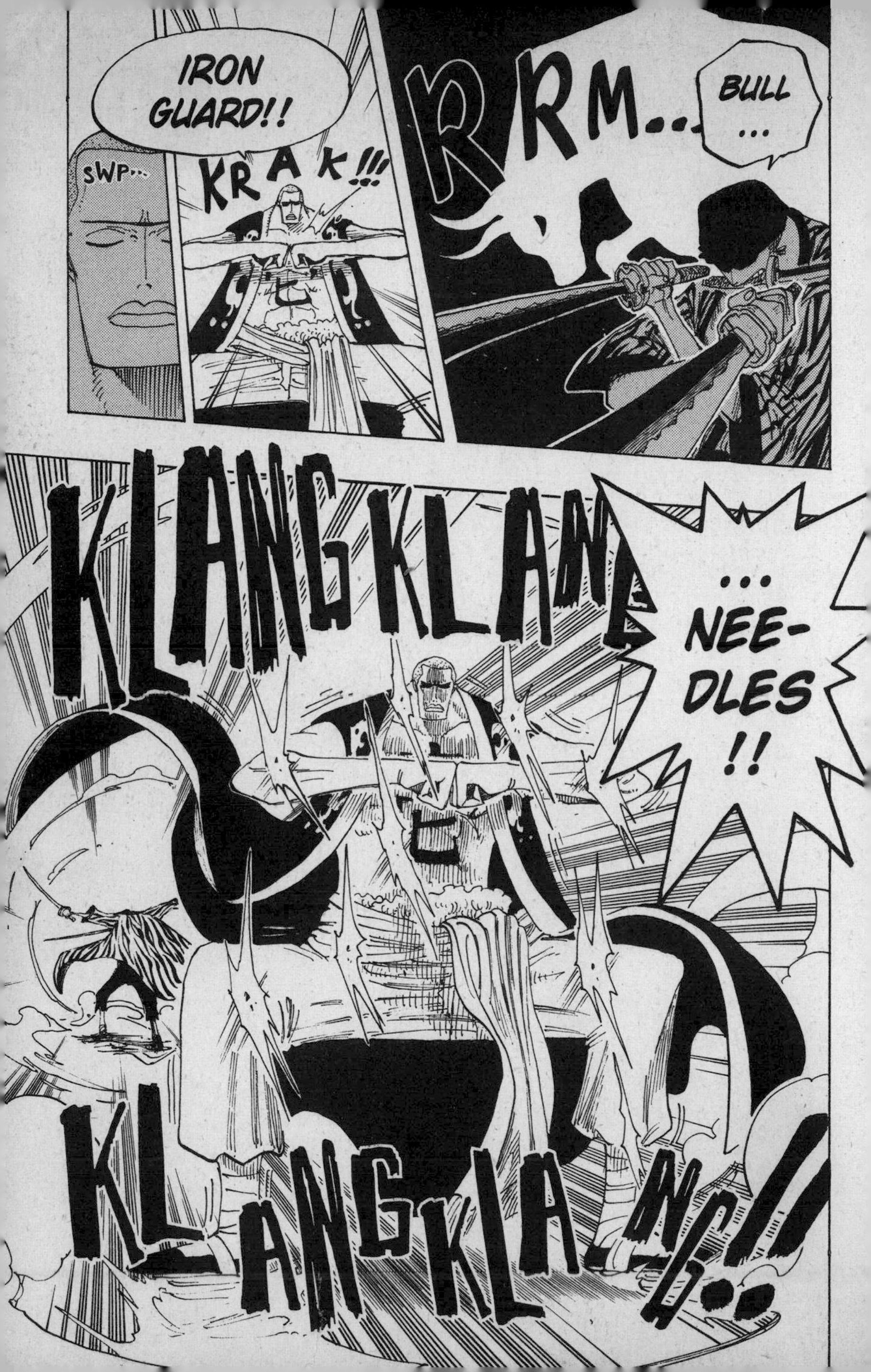
BULL ...
RRM...
IRON GUARD!!
KRAK!!!
SWP...
... NEE-DLES !!
KLANGKLANG
KLANGKLANG!!

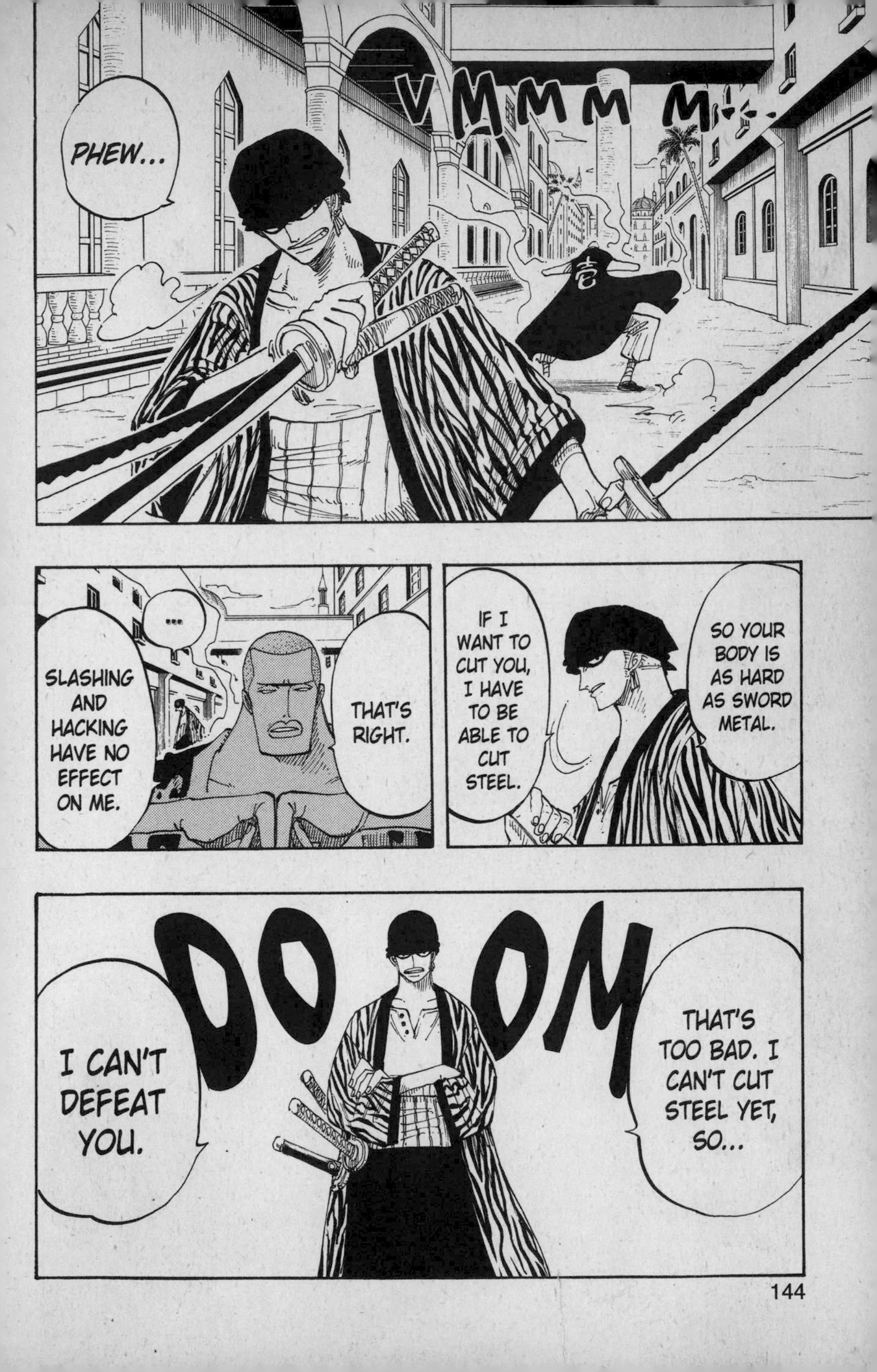
VMMMM M...
PHEW...
SO YOUR BODY IS AS HARD AS SWORD METAL.
IF I WANT TO CUT YOU, I HAVE TO BE ABLE TO CUT STEEL.
THAT'S RIGHT.
...
SLASHING AND HACKING HAVE NO EFFECT ON ME.
THAT'S TOO BAD. I CAN'T CUT STEEL YET, SO...
DOOM
I CAN'T DEFEAT YOU.

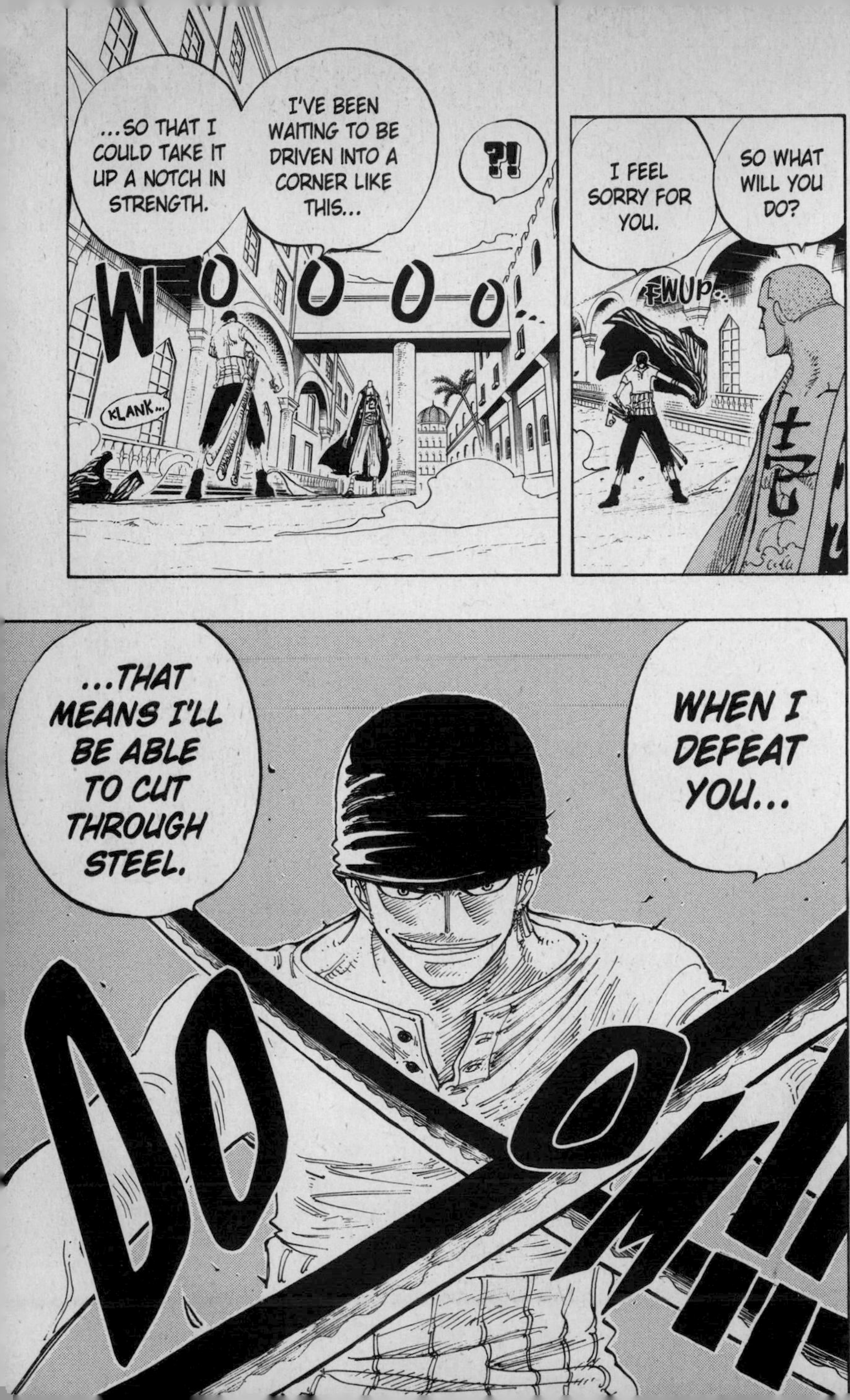
SO WHAT WILL YOU DO?
I FEEL SORRY FOR YOU.
FWUP
?!
I'VE BEEN WAITING TO BE DRIVEN INTO A CORNER LIKE THIS...
...SO THAT I COULD TAKE IT UP A NOTCH IN STRENGTH.
WOOOO!
KLANK...
WHEN I DEFEAT YOU...
...THAT MEANS I'LL BE ABLE TO CUT THROUGH STEEL.
DOM!!

NO BRAKES.

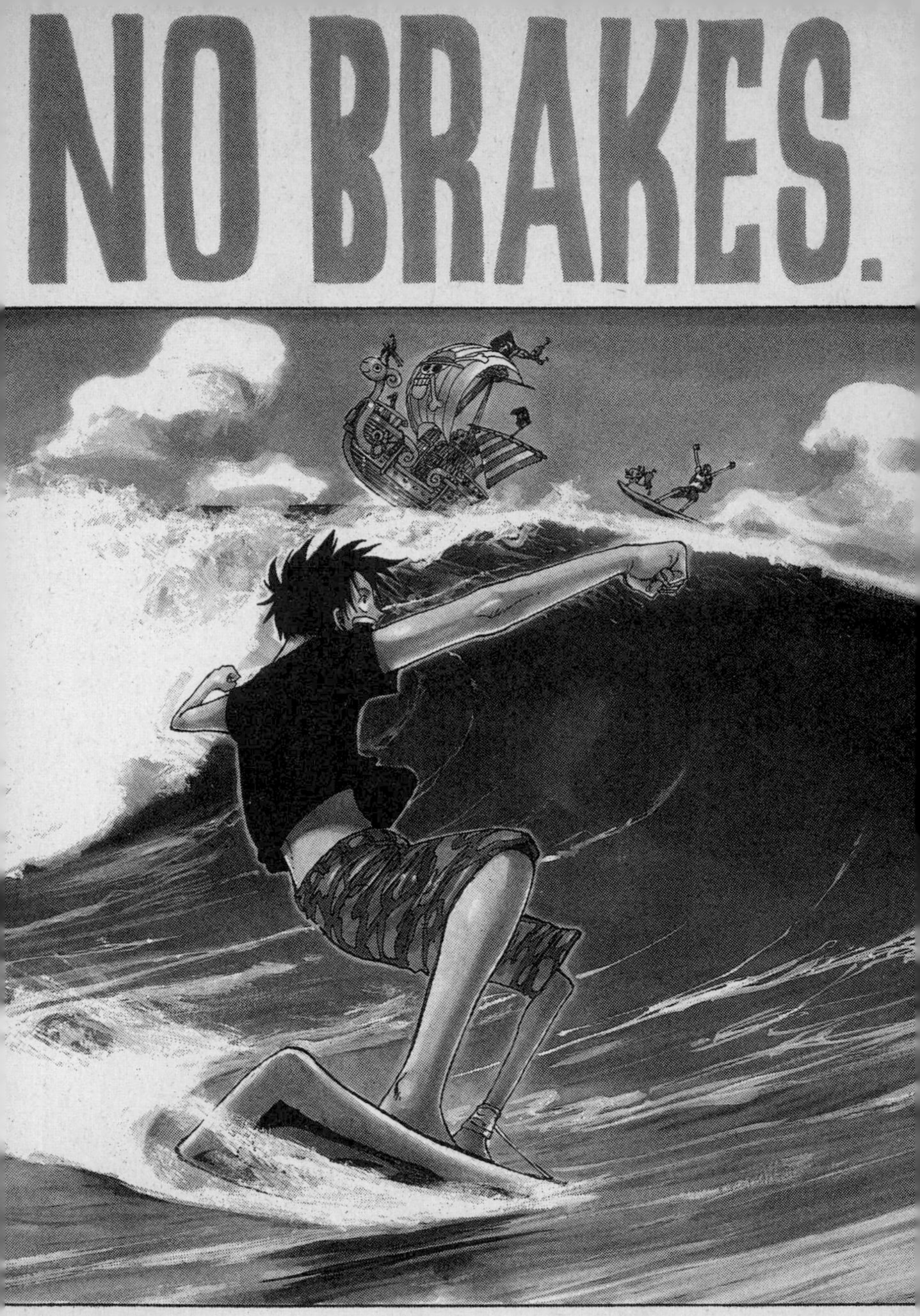

Chapter 194: CUTTING STEEL

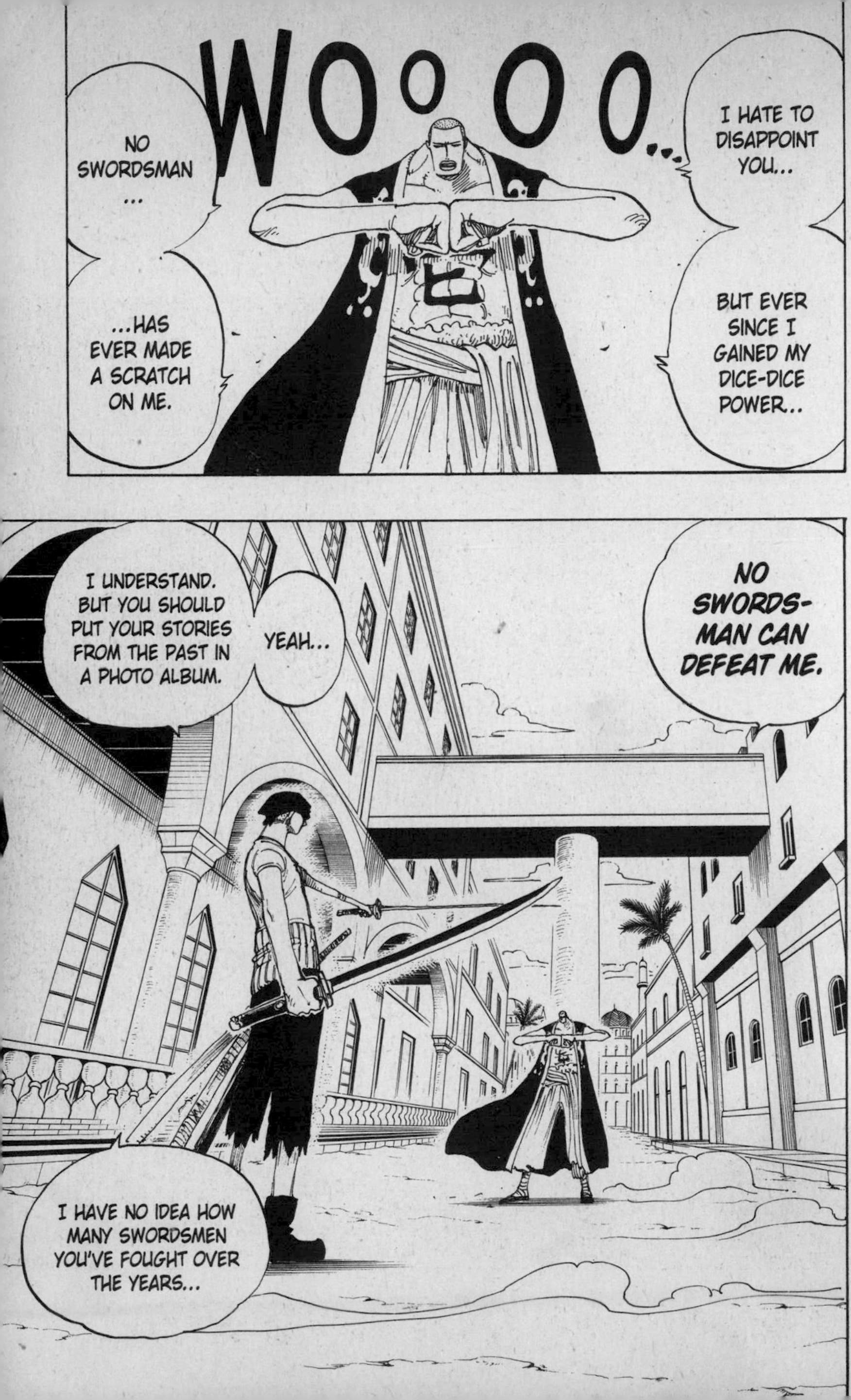
WOOOO...
I HATE TO DISAPPOINT YOU...
BUT EVER SINCE I GAINED MY DICE-DICE POWER...
NO SWORDSMAN ...
...HAS EVER MADE A SCRATCH ON ME.
NO SWORDSMAN CAN DEFEAT ME.
I HAVE NO IDEA HOW MANY SWORDSMEN YOU'VE FOUGHT OVER THE YEARS...
YEAH...
I UNDERSTAND. BUT YOU SHOULD PUT YOUR STORIES FROM THE PAST IN A PHOTO ALBUM.

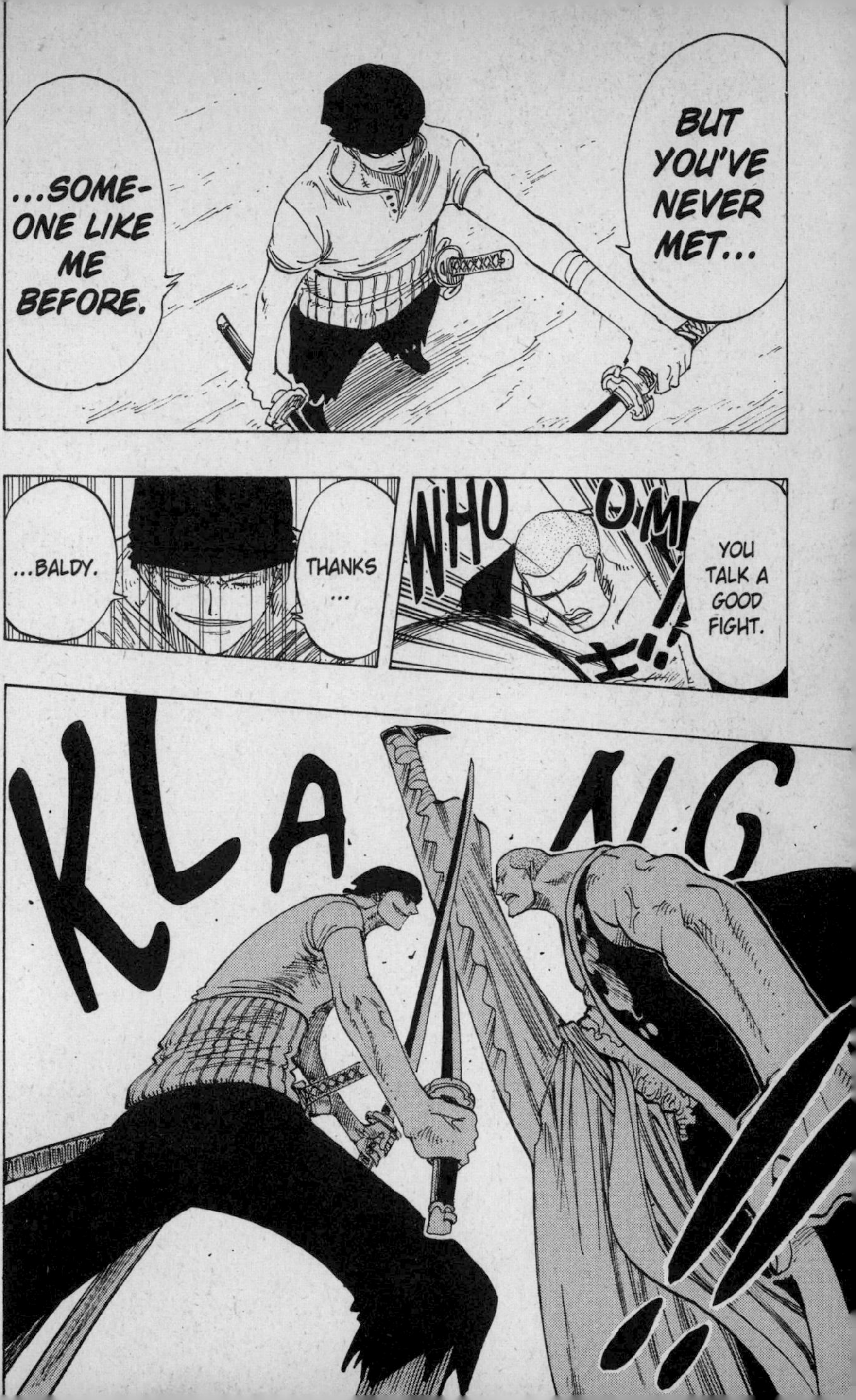
BUT YOU'VE NEVER MET...
...SOME-ONE LIKE ME BEFORE.
WHO OM
YOU TALK A GOOD FIGHT.
THANKS ...
...BALDY.
KLA NG

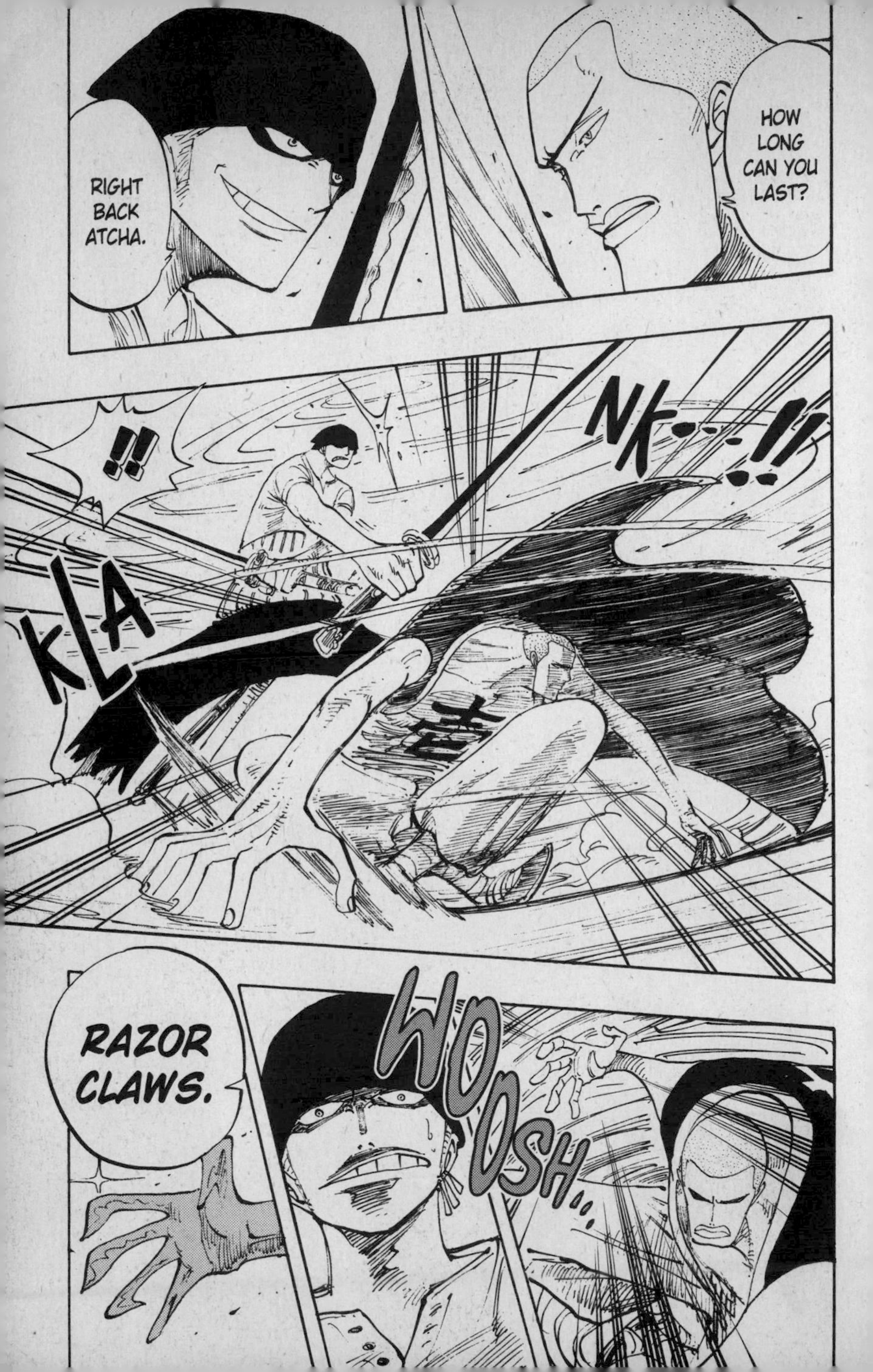
HOW LONG CAN YOU LAST?
RIGHT BACK ATCHA.
NK...!!
!!
KLA
WOOSH...
RAZOR CLAWS.

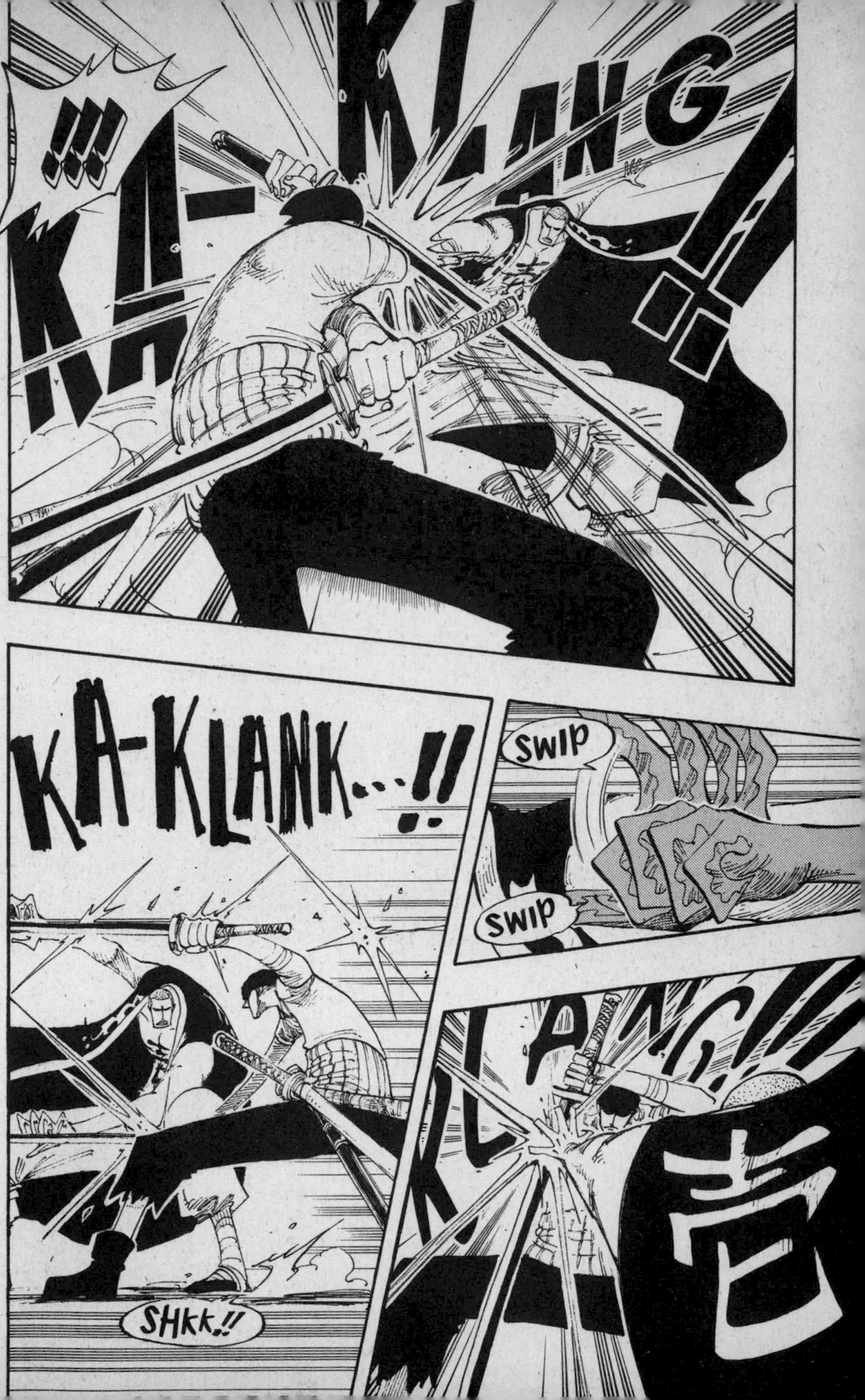
KA-KLANG!!
SWIP
SWIP
KLANG!!
KA-KLANK...!!
SHKK!!

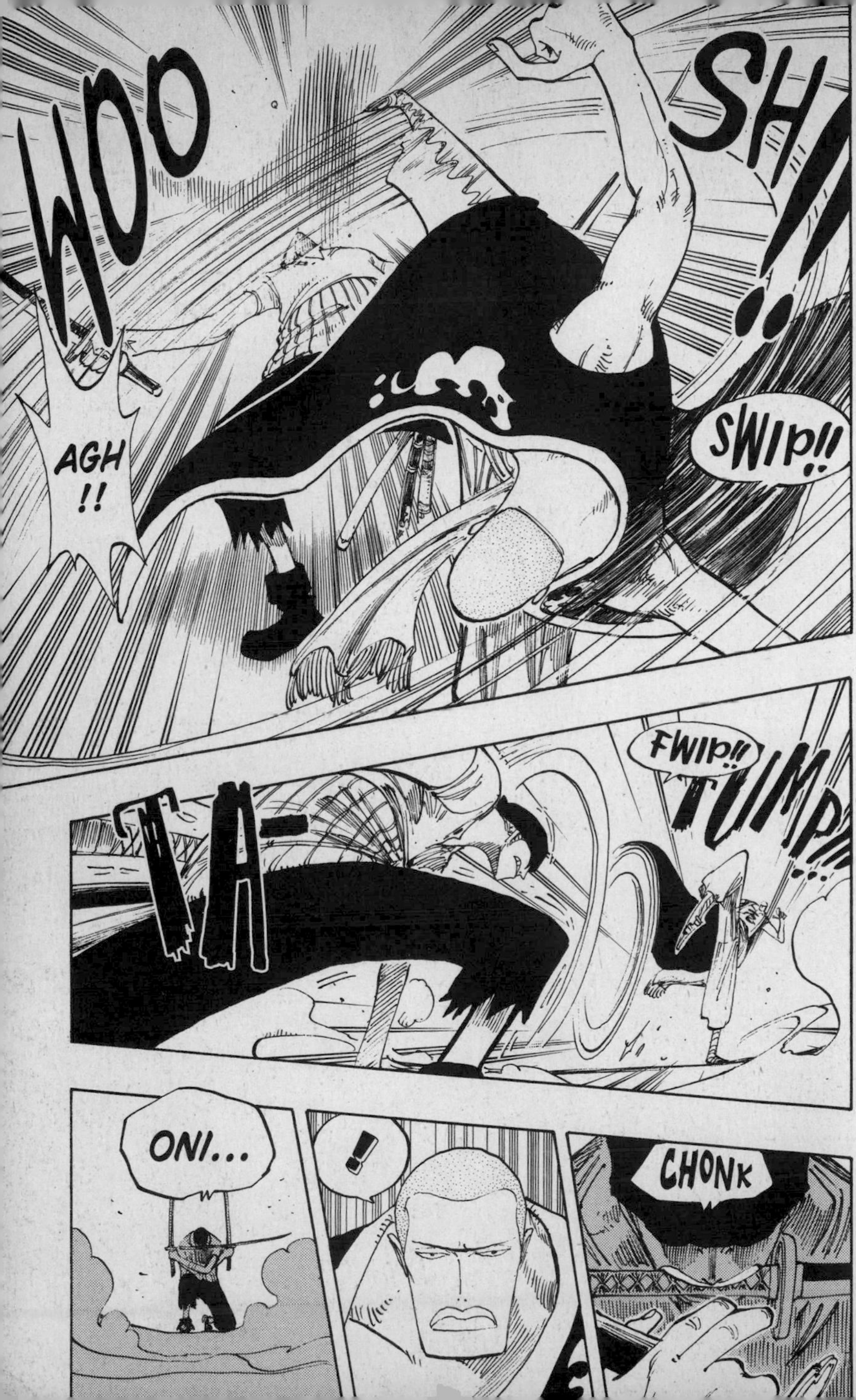
WHOOSH!!
SWIP!!
AGH!!
FWIP!!
TUMP!!...
TA-
CHONK
!
ONI...

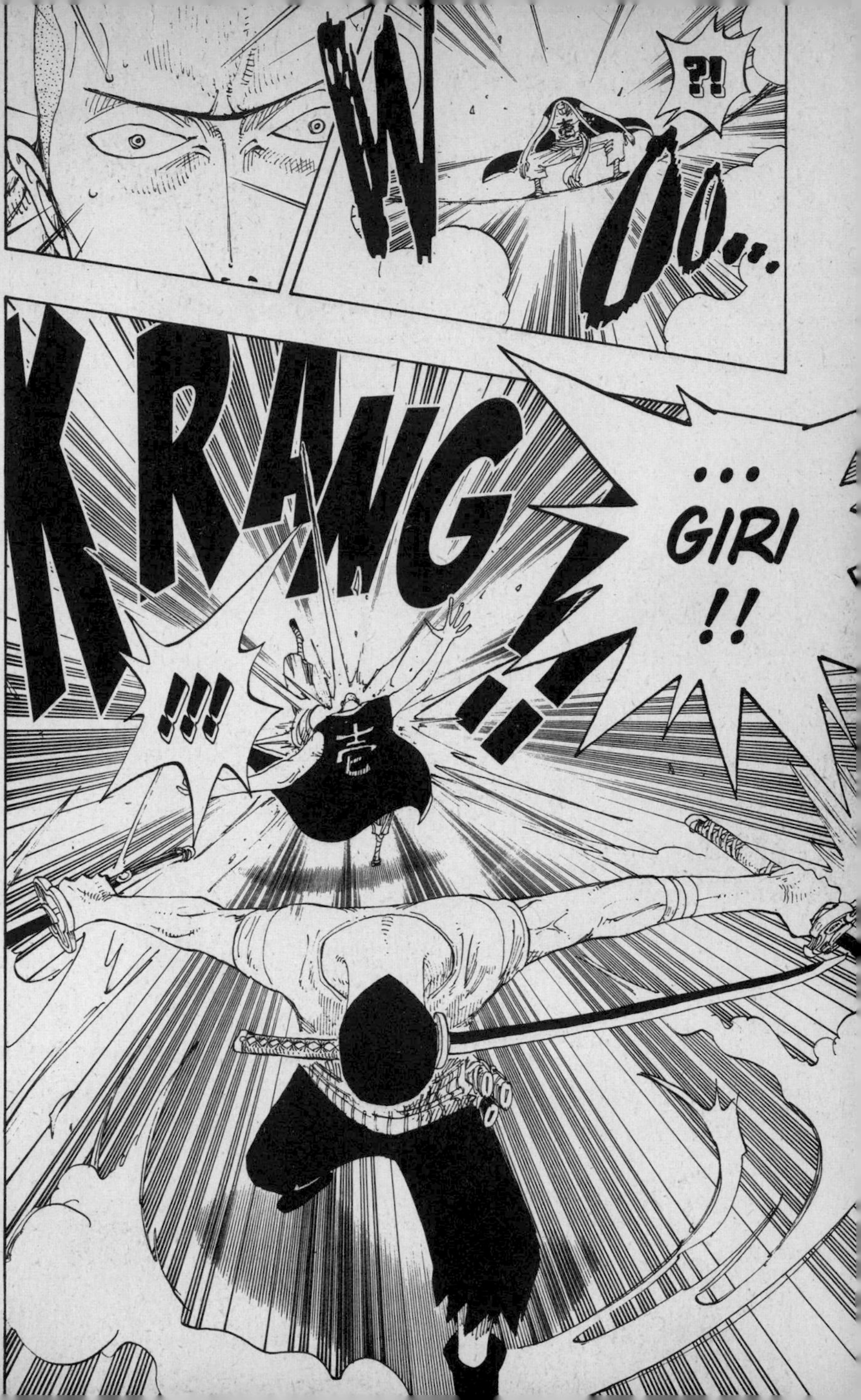
?!
WOO...
...GIRI !!
KRANG!!
!!!

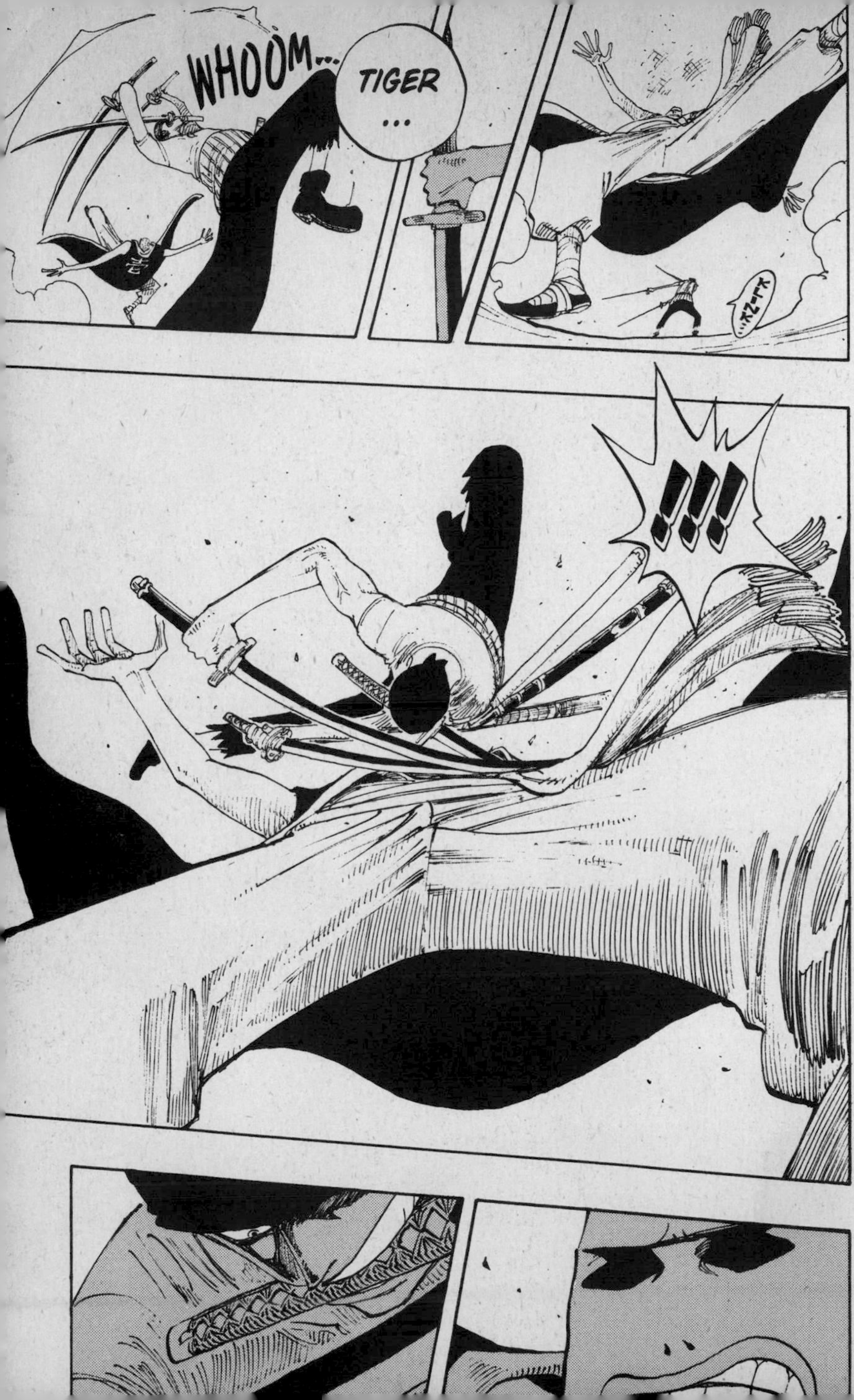
KLINK...
TIGER ...
WHOOM...
!!!

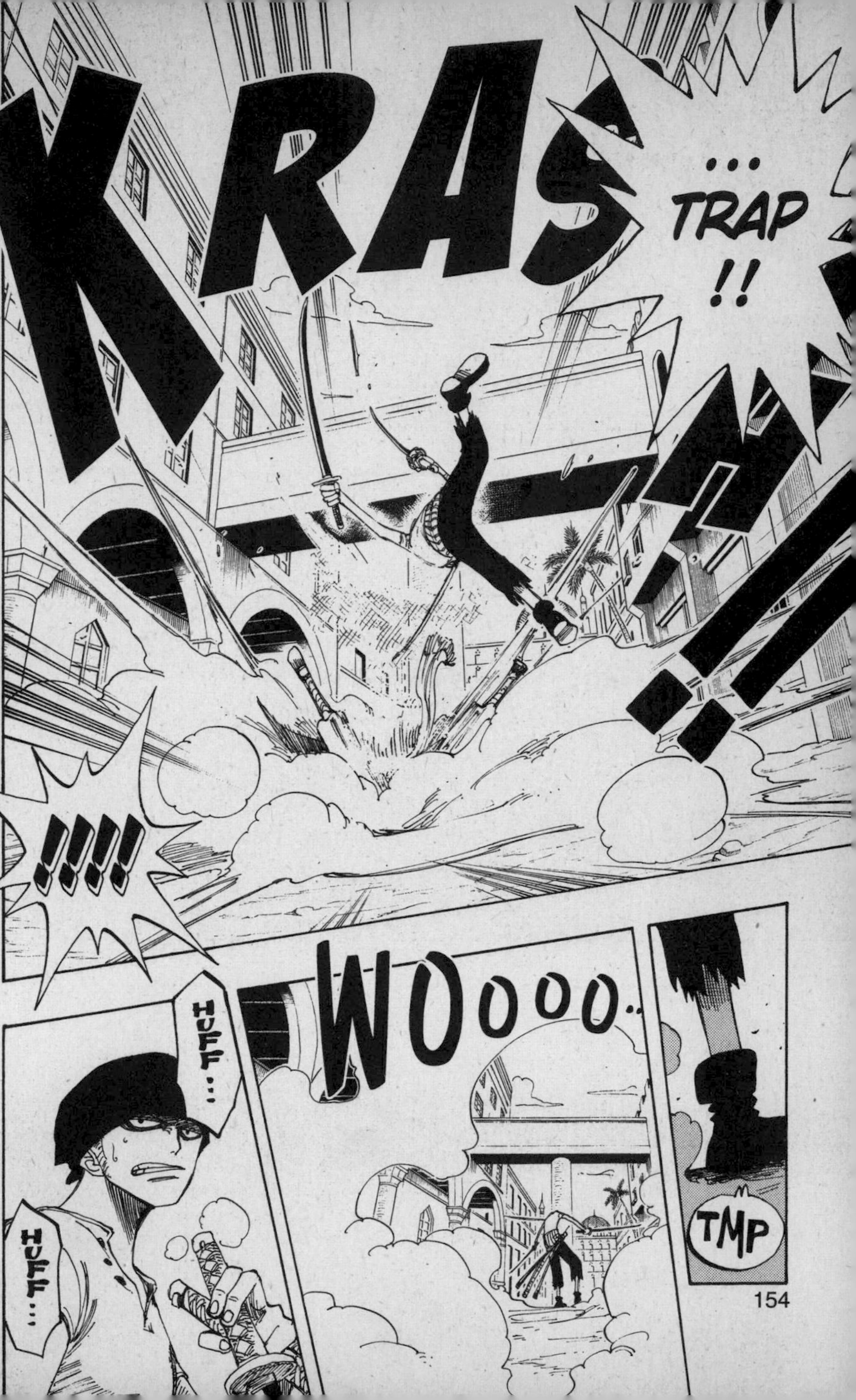
KRASH!!
...TRAP!!
!!!!
TMP
WOOOO..
HUFF...
HUFF...

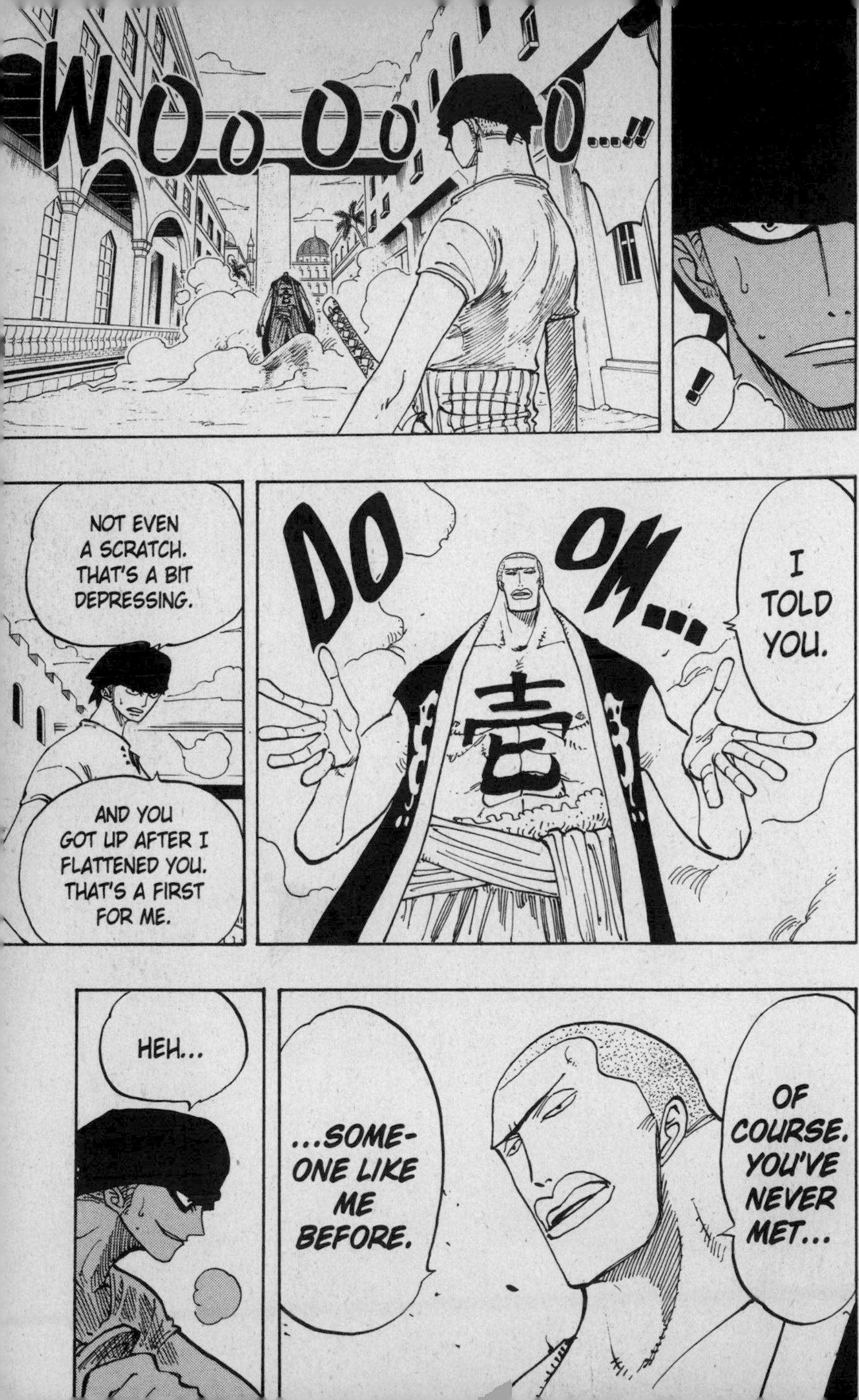
!
WOOOOOO...!!
I TOLD YOU.
DOOM...
NOT EVEN A SCRATCH. THAT'S A BIT DEPRESSING.
AND YOU GOT UP AFTER I FLATTENED YOU. THAT'S A FIRST FOR ME.
OF COURSE. YOU'VE NEVER MET...
...SOME-ONE LIKE ME BEFORE.
HEH...

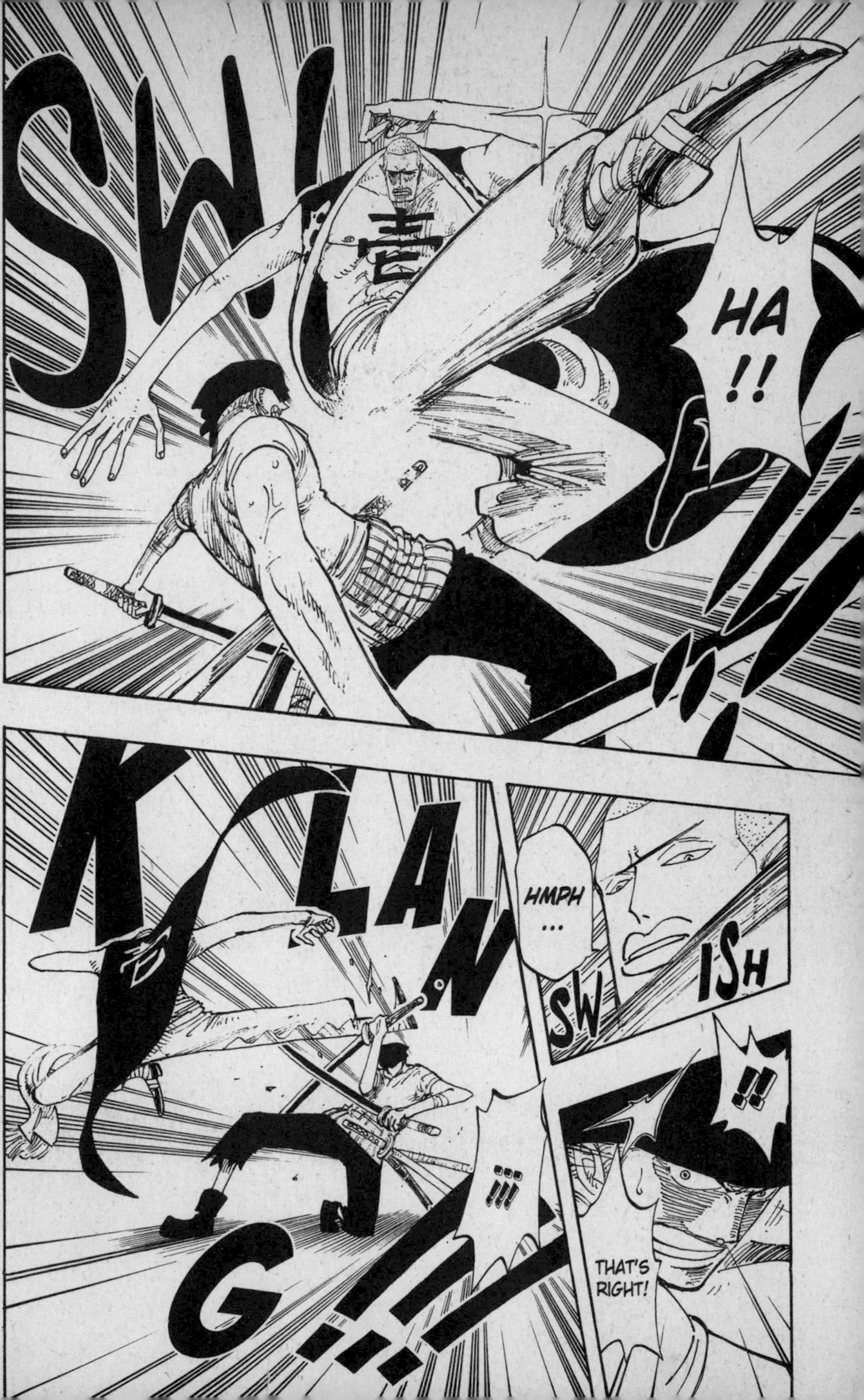
HA !!
HMPH ...
SW ISH
!!
THAT'S RIGHT!
!!!
KLANG!!!

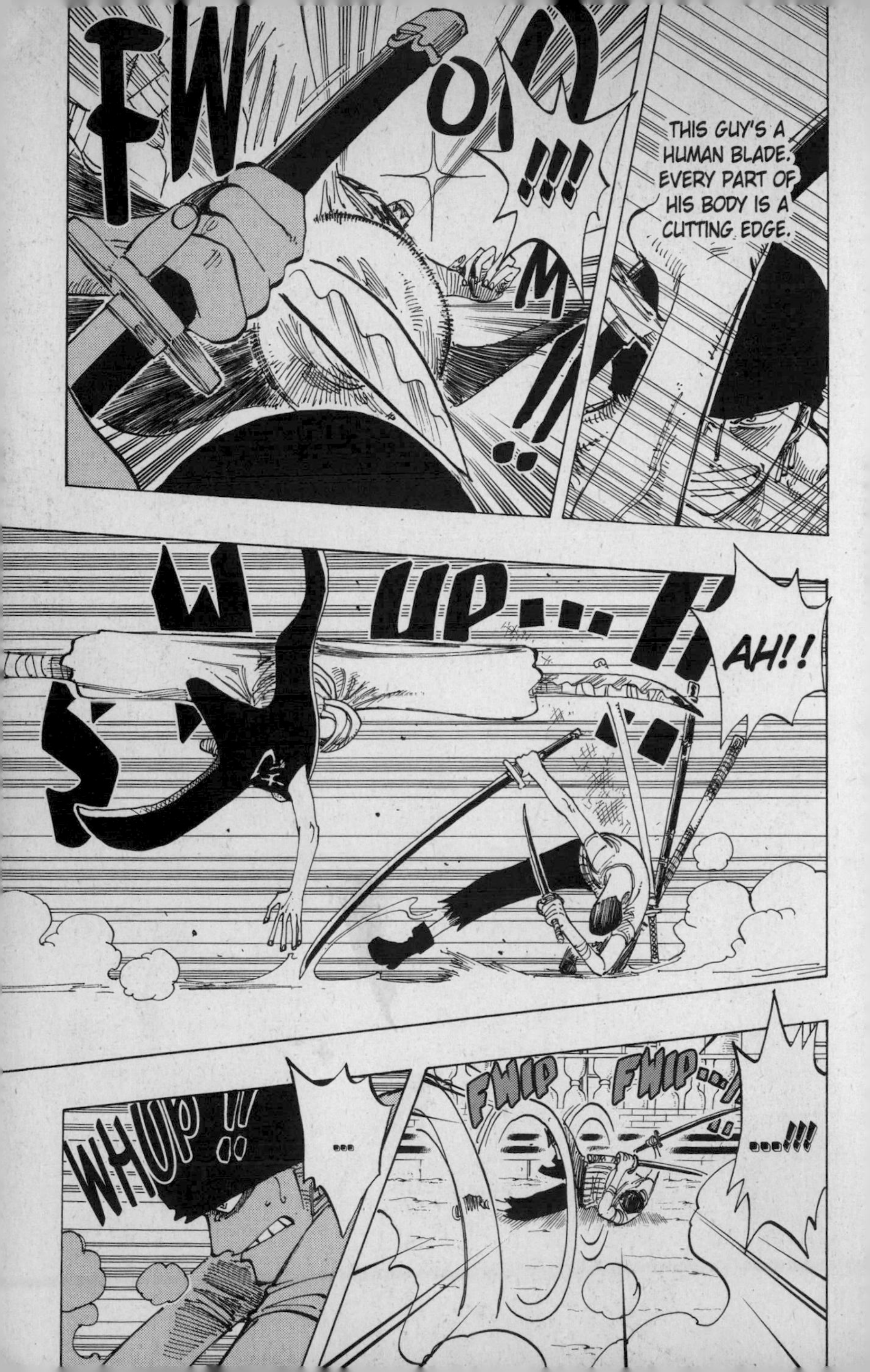
THIS GUY'S A HUMAN BLADE. EVERY PART OF HIS BODY IS A CUTTING EDGE.
FWOOM!!!
AH!!
SWUP...!!
...!!!
FWIP FWIP...!!
...
WHUP!!

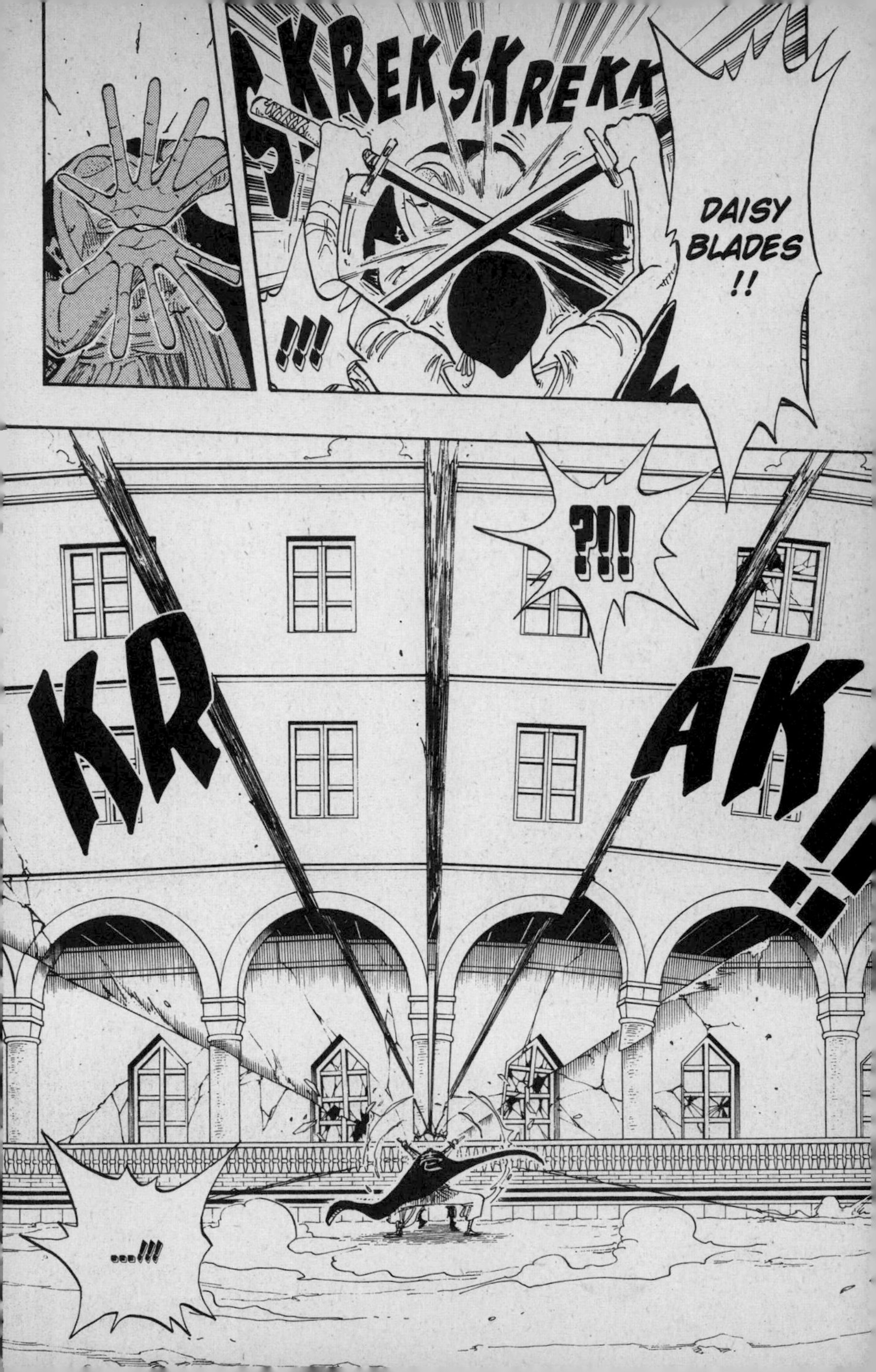
DAISY BLADES !!
SKREK SKREKK
!!!
?!!
KRAK!!!
...!!!

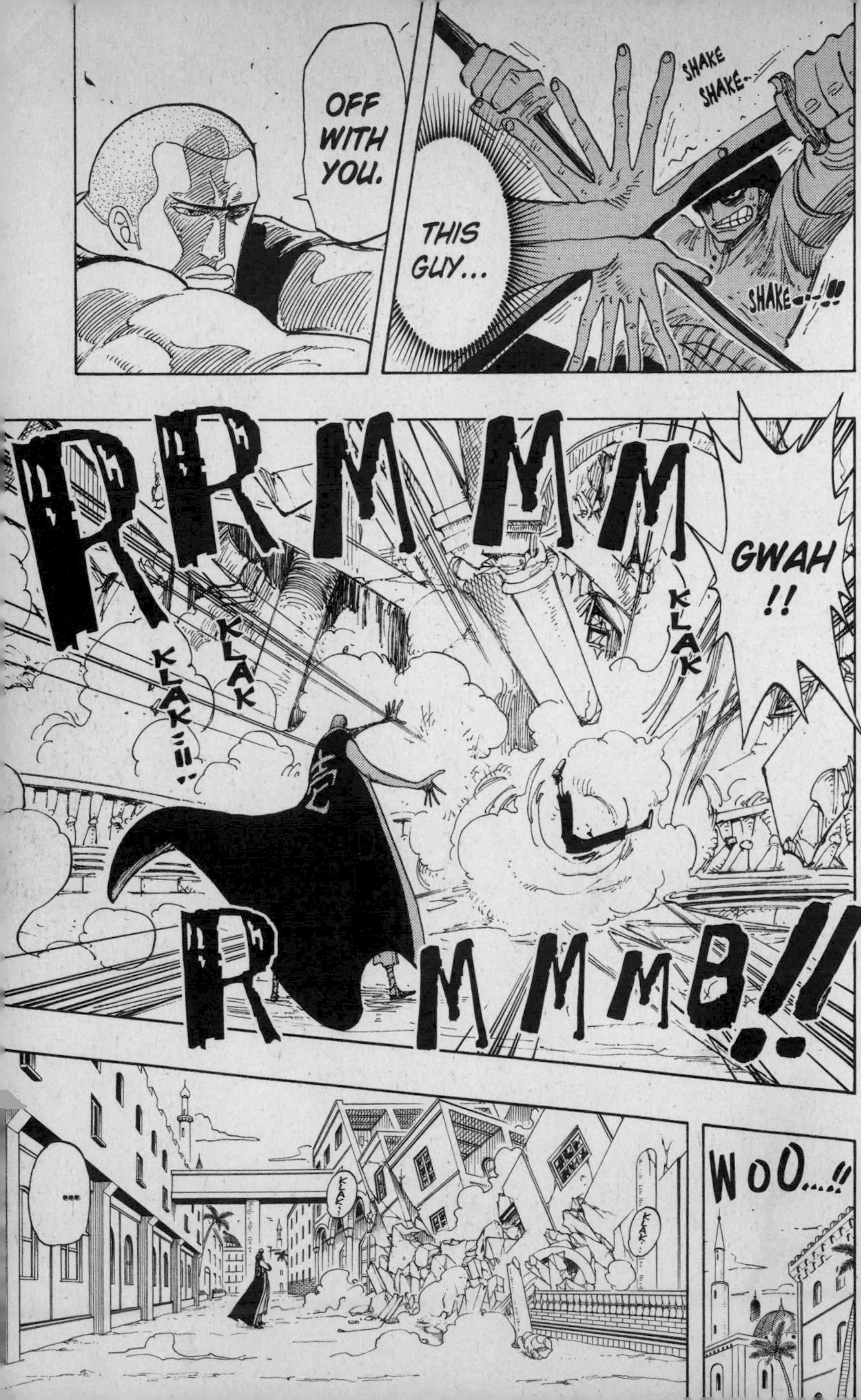
SHAKE SHAKE...
THIS GUY...
SHAKE...!!
OFF WITH YOU.
GWAH!!
KLAK
RRMMM RMMMB!!
KLAK
KLAK...!!
WOO...!!
KLAK...
KLAK...
...

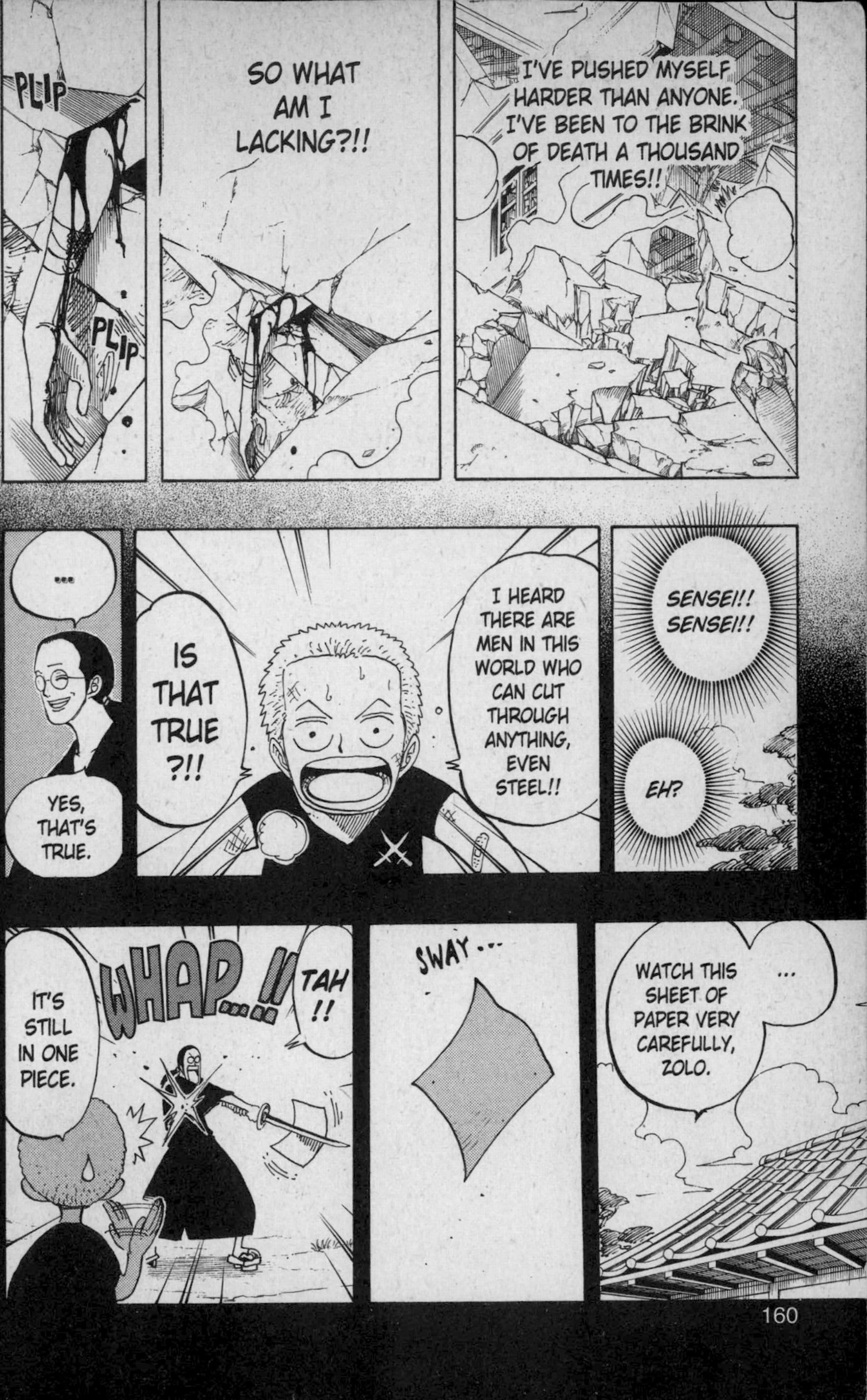
I'VE PUSHED MYSELF HARDER THAN ANYONE. I'VE BEEN TO THE BRINK OF DEATH A THOUSAND TIMES!!
SO WHAT AM I LACKING?!!
PLIP
PLIP
SENSEI!! SENSEI!!
EH?
I HEARD THERE ARE MEN IN THIS WORLD WHO CAN CUT THROUGH ANYTHING, EVEN STEEL!!
IS THAT TRUE ?!!
...
YES, THAT'S TRUE.
WATCH THIS SHEET OF PAPER VERY CAREFULLY, ZOLO.
...
SWAY...
TAH !!
WHAP...!!
IT'S STILL IN ONE PIECE.

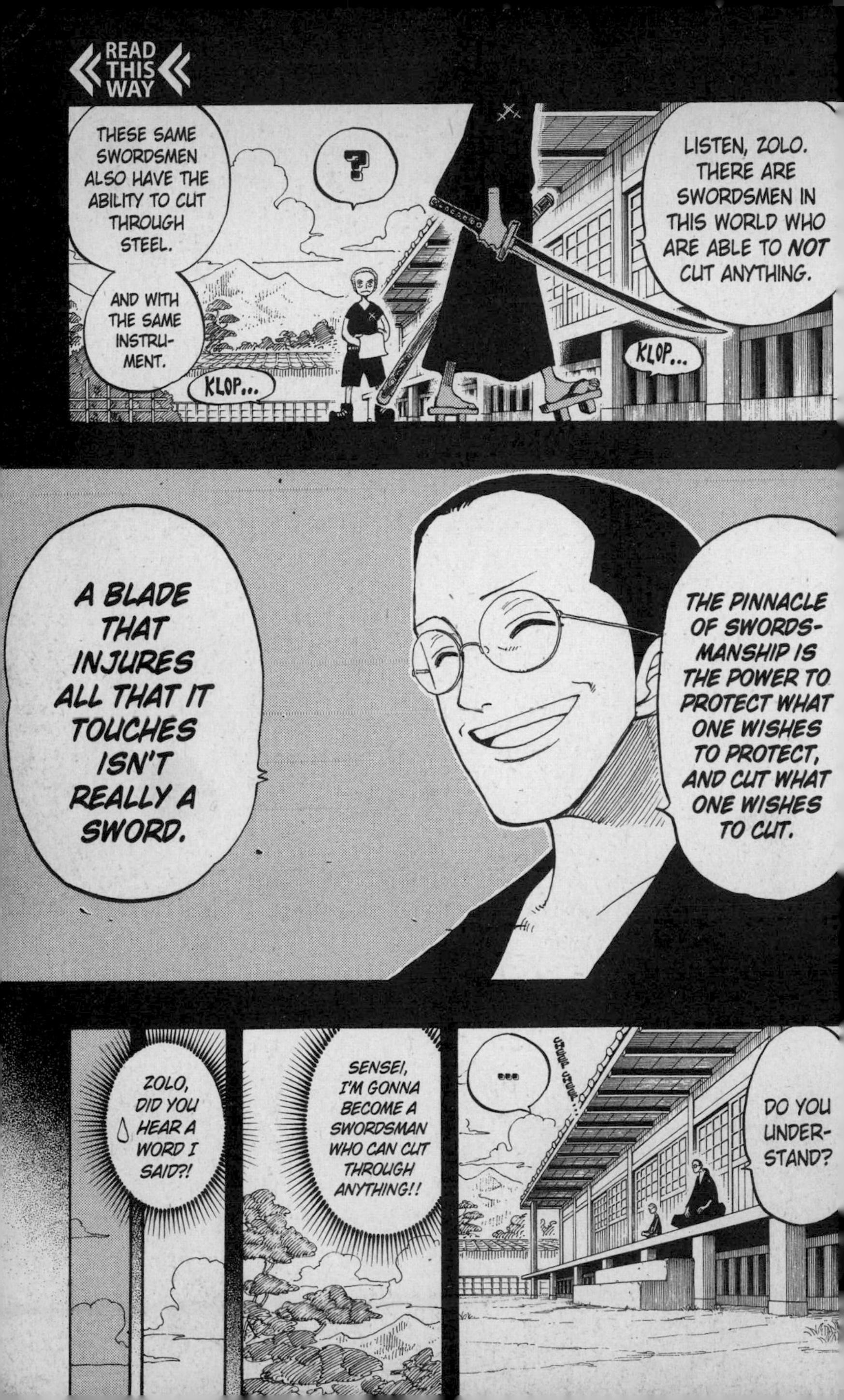
READ THIS WAY
LISTEN, ZOLO. THERE ARE SWORDSMEN IN THIS WORLD WHO ARE ABLE TO *NOT* CUT ANYTHING.
KLOP...
?
THESE SAME SWORDSMEN ALSO HAVE THE ABILITY TO CUT THROUGH STEEL.
AND WITH THE SAME INSTRUMENT.
KLOP...
THE PINNACLE OF SWORDSMANSHIP IS THE POWER TO PROTECT WHAT ONE WISHES TO PROTECT, AND CUT WHAT ONE WISHES TO CUT.
A BLADE THAT INJURES ALL THAT IT TOUCHES ISN'T REALLY A SWORD.
DO YOU UNDERSTAND?
...
SENSEI, I'M GONNA BECOME A SWORDSMAN WHO CAN CUT THROUGH ANYTHING!!
ZOLO, DID YOU HEAR A WORD I SAID?!

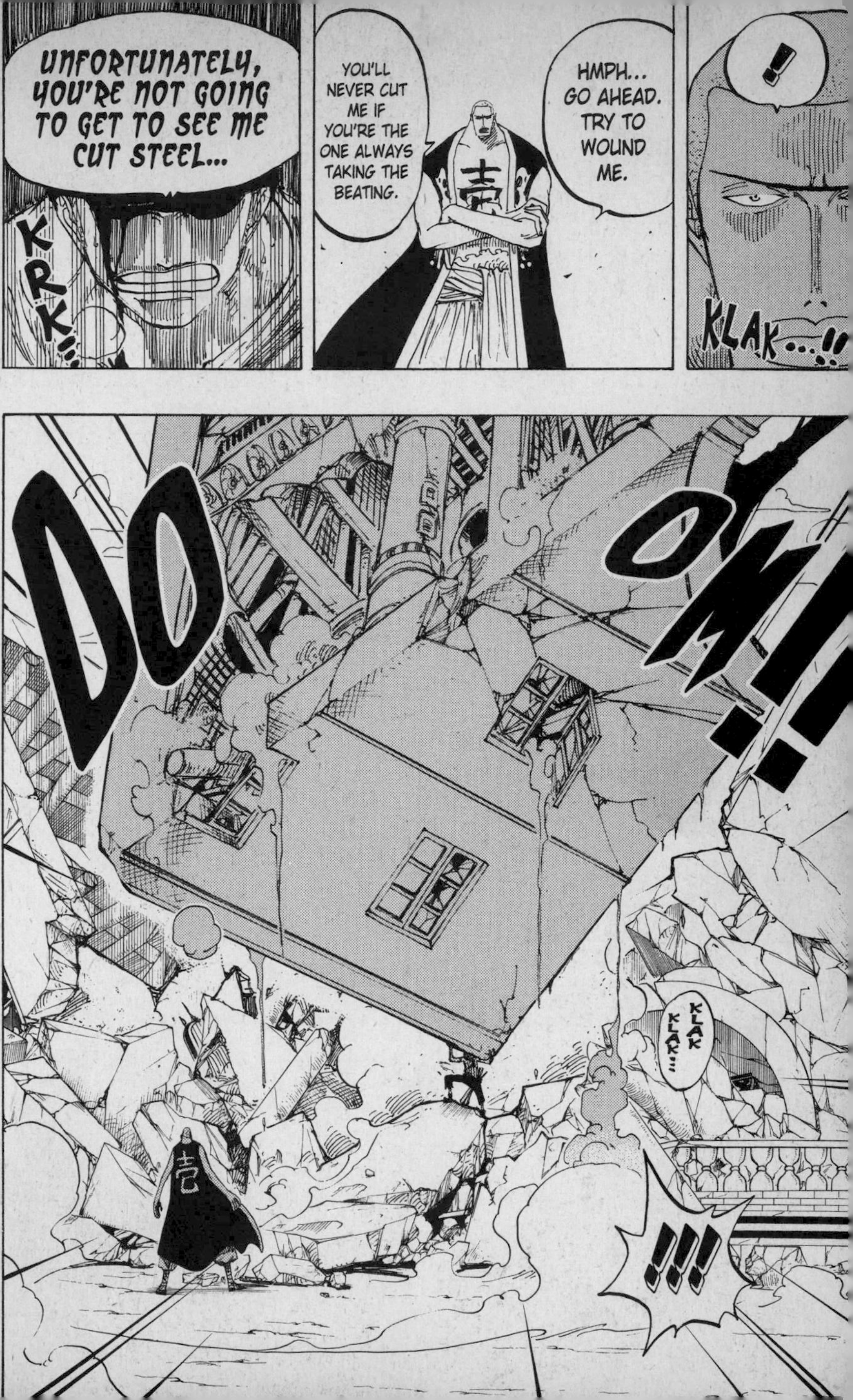
!
KLAK...!!
HMPH... GO AHEAD. TRY TO WOUND ME.
YOU'LL NEVER CUT ME IF YOU'RE THE ONE ALWAYS TAKING THE BEATING.
UNFORTUNATELY, YOU'RE NOT GOING TO GET TO SEE ME CUT STEEL...
KRK!!
OM!!
DO
KLAK KLAK...
!!!

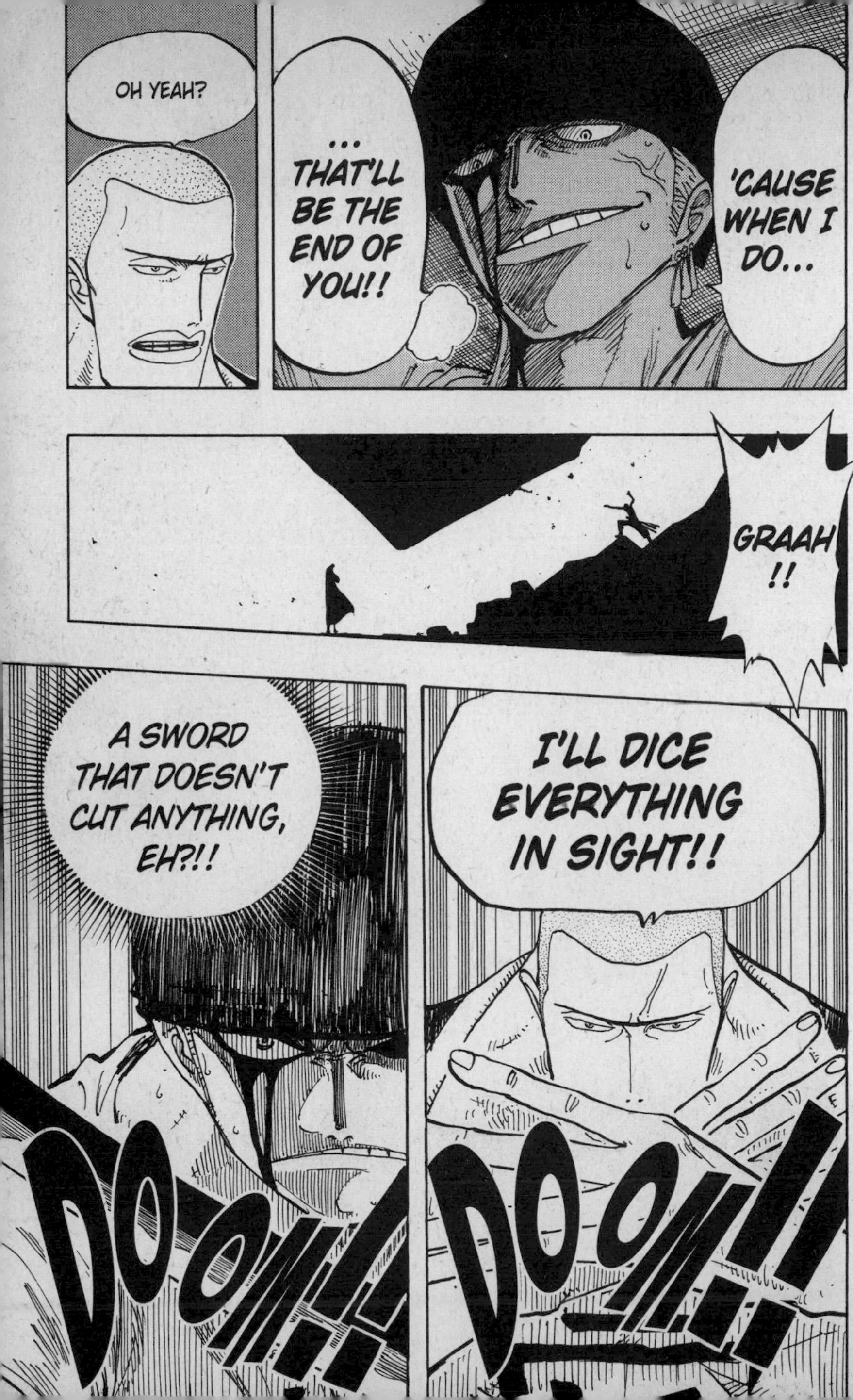
'CAUSE WHEN I DO...
... THAT'LL BE THE END OF YOU!!
OH YEAH?
GRAAH !!
I'LL DICE EVERYTHING IN SIGHT!!
DO-ON!!
A SWORD THAT DOESN'T CUT ANYTHING, EH?!!
DO-ON!!

Oda: Allow me to address a question that comes up a lot. It's about just how involved I am in the *One Piece* anime. But first I'd like you to be aware of certain facts.

1. First and foremost, I am a manga artist. I don't create anime, and that's that. But I do help out with character design for original anime stories and movies based on my manga. I don't really do much. So I have to entrust the world and characters of *One Piece*, which I created in the manga, to other people.

2. This is one name I'd like you to remember--the one and only ★Konosuke Uda.
This name always appears in the opening credits of the anime. He is the Series Director for the *One Piece* anime. In other words, he's in charge of everything. That's so cool... Series Director. (Ta-dah!)

3. The *One Piece* anime has seven different directors including Mr. Uda, and they take turns directing the episodes. That's because a 30-minute episode is impossible to make in just one week. A particular week's director is listed in the end credits under "Episode Director." And the one who oversees all the other directors is Konosuke Uda. (Wahoo!)

4. If he and I didn't see eye to eye, then Luffy would immediately become un-Luffy-like, and the world of *One Piece* would be completely different. No matter how poignant the original story is, if the director of the anime messes up, it's ruined. But that never happens. In fact, amazingly Mr. Uda and his warrior directors totally understand *One Piece*

5. Direction naturally includes the music, sound effects, voice acting, and art design--the whole package. So I'm very grateful to everyone involved with the anime. By the way, my editor Habu checks the script.

6. What I really wanted to do was to call attention to the names in the end credits. I really hope you take note of them, because all of those people work incredibly hard.

7. Umm... That may have come across a bit stiff, but Mr. Uda has a good sense of humor. Often after a meeting with him and the producer (who's also a funny guy), we go out to eat. But basically for the *One Piece* anime, I leave everything up to Mr. Uda and I enjoy watching it as much as anyone. Sometimes I even cry.

8. So that's it for the Question Corner. See you in the next volume!

Chapter 195:

MR. BUSHIDO

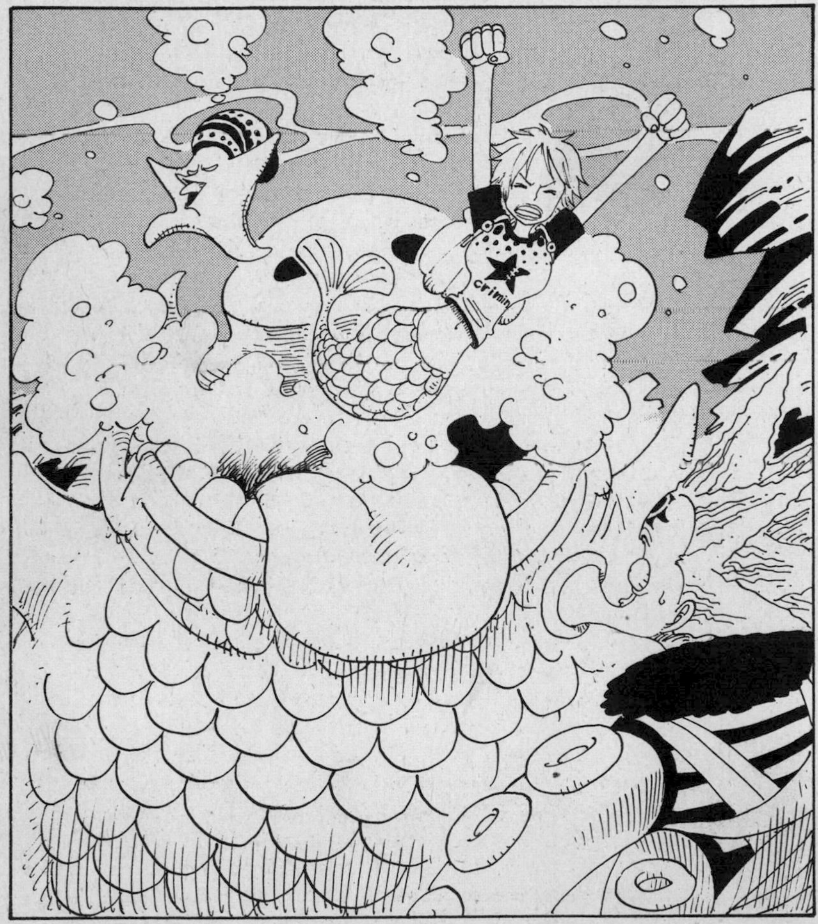

HACHI'S WALK ON THE SEAFLOOR, VOL. 12:
"CAMIE THE MERMAID AND STARFISH PAPPAGU"

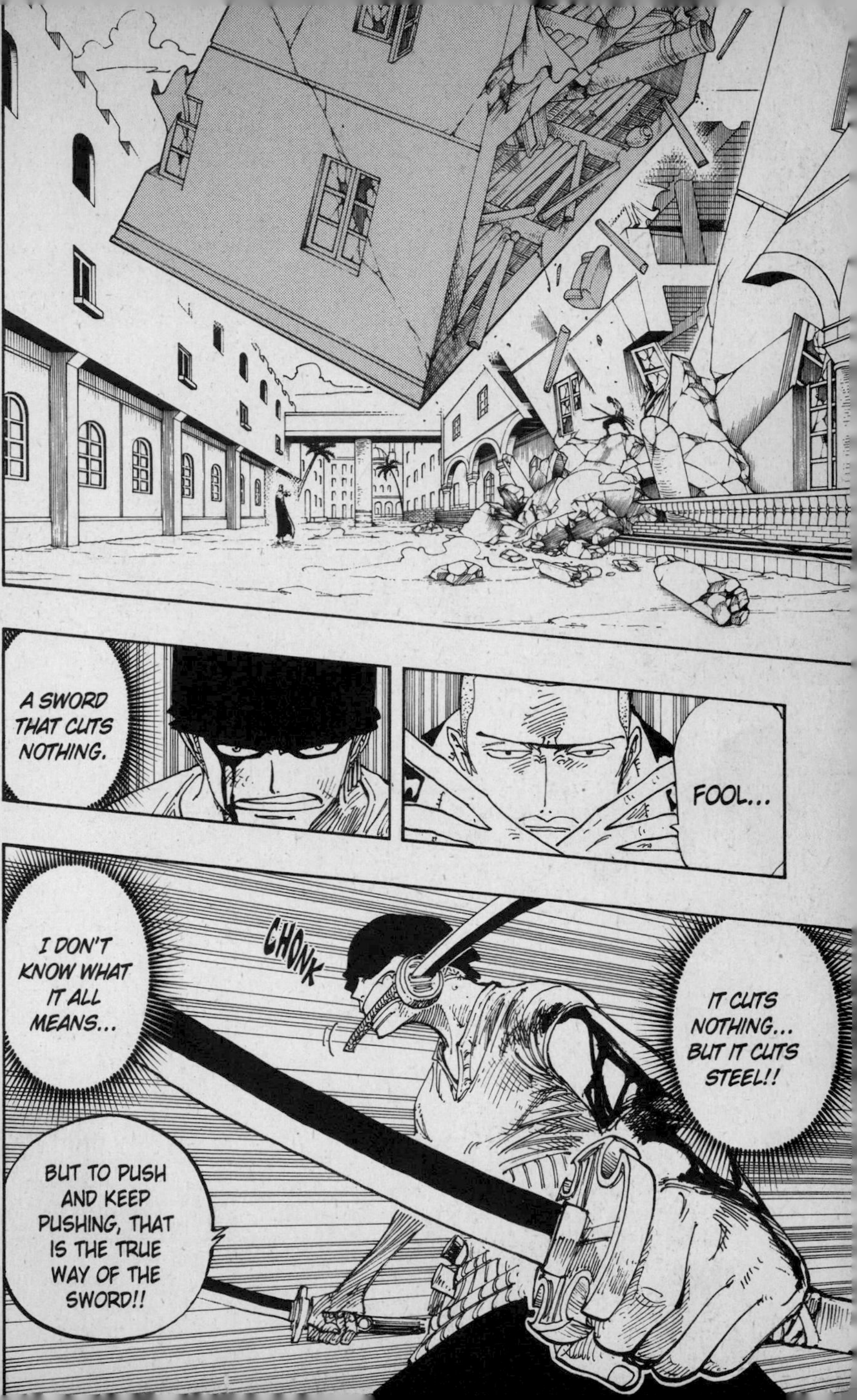
FOOL...
A SWORD THAT CUTS NOTHING.
IT CUTS NOTHING... BUT IT CUTS STEEL!!
CHONK
I DON'T KNOW WHAT IT ALL MEANS...
BUT TO PUSH AND KEEP PUSHING, THAT IS THE TRUE WAY OF THE SWORD!!

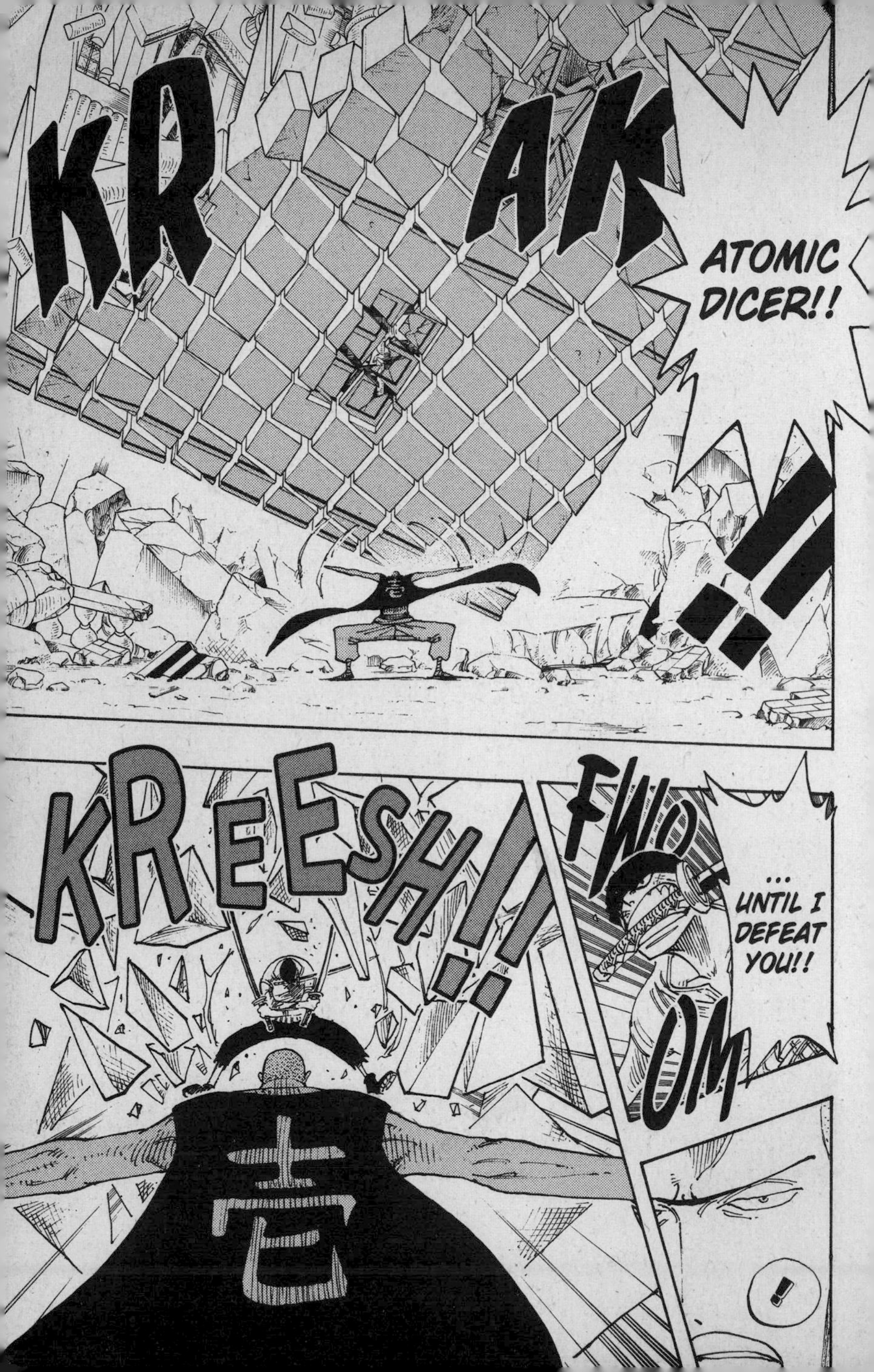

ATOMIC DICER!!
KRAK
!!
FWOOM
... UNTIL I DEFEAT YOU!!
!
KREESH!!

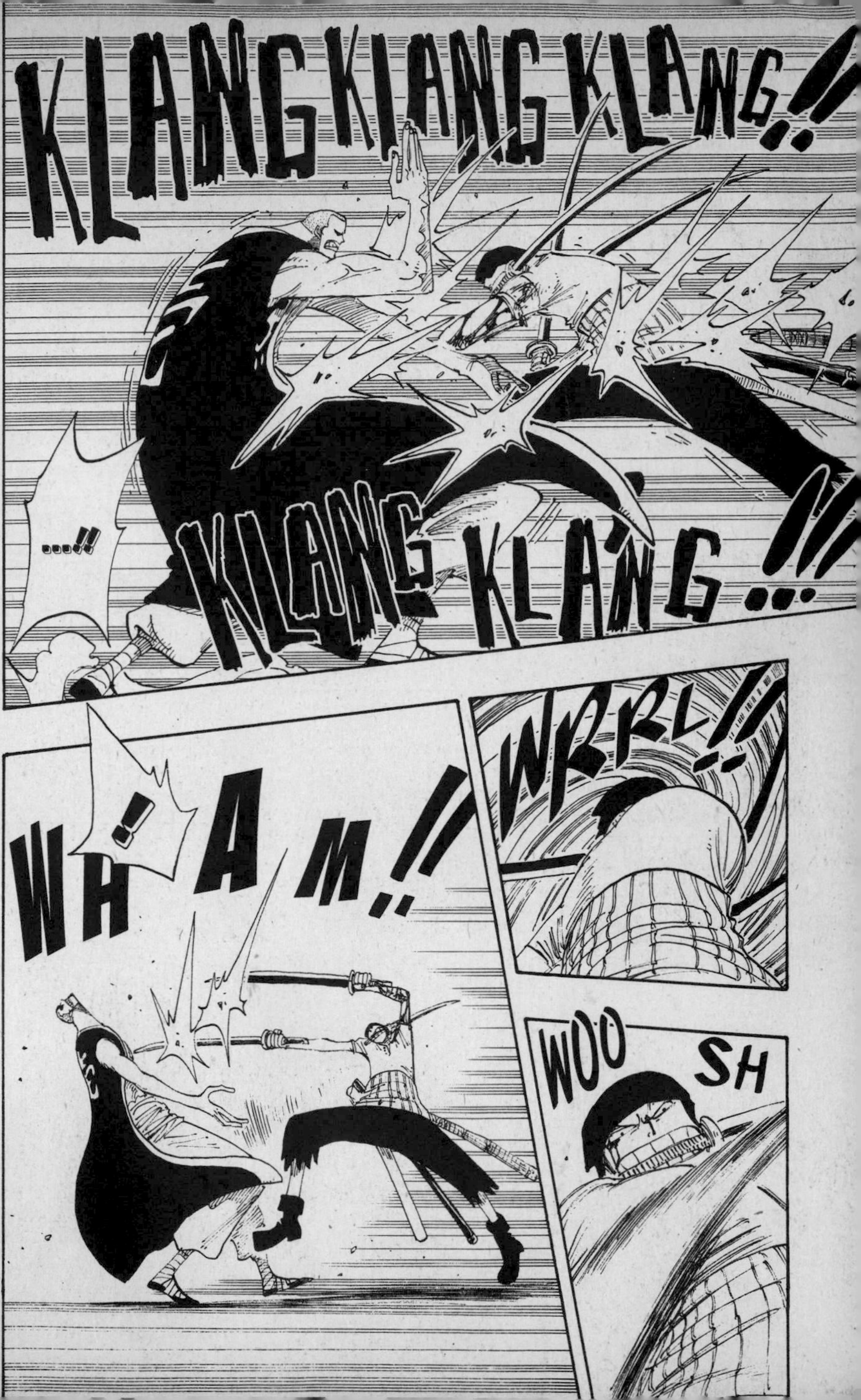
KLANG KLANG KLANG!!
...!!
KLANG KLANG...!!!
WRRL!!
WOOSH
!
WHAM!!

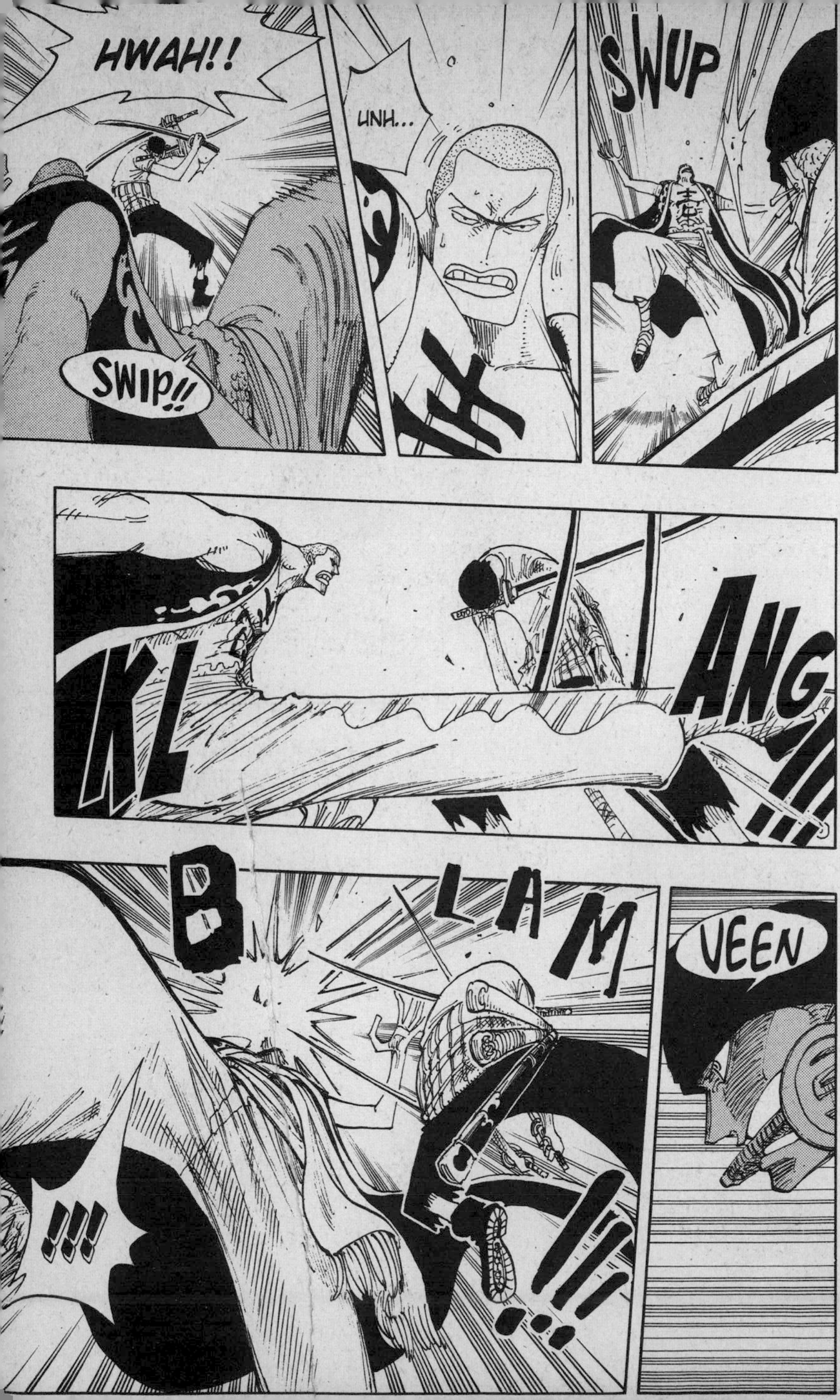
SWUP
UNH...
HWAH!!
SWIP!!
KL ANG!!!
VEEN
BLAM
!!!
!!!

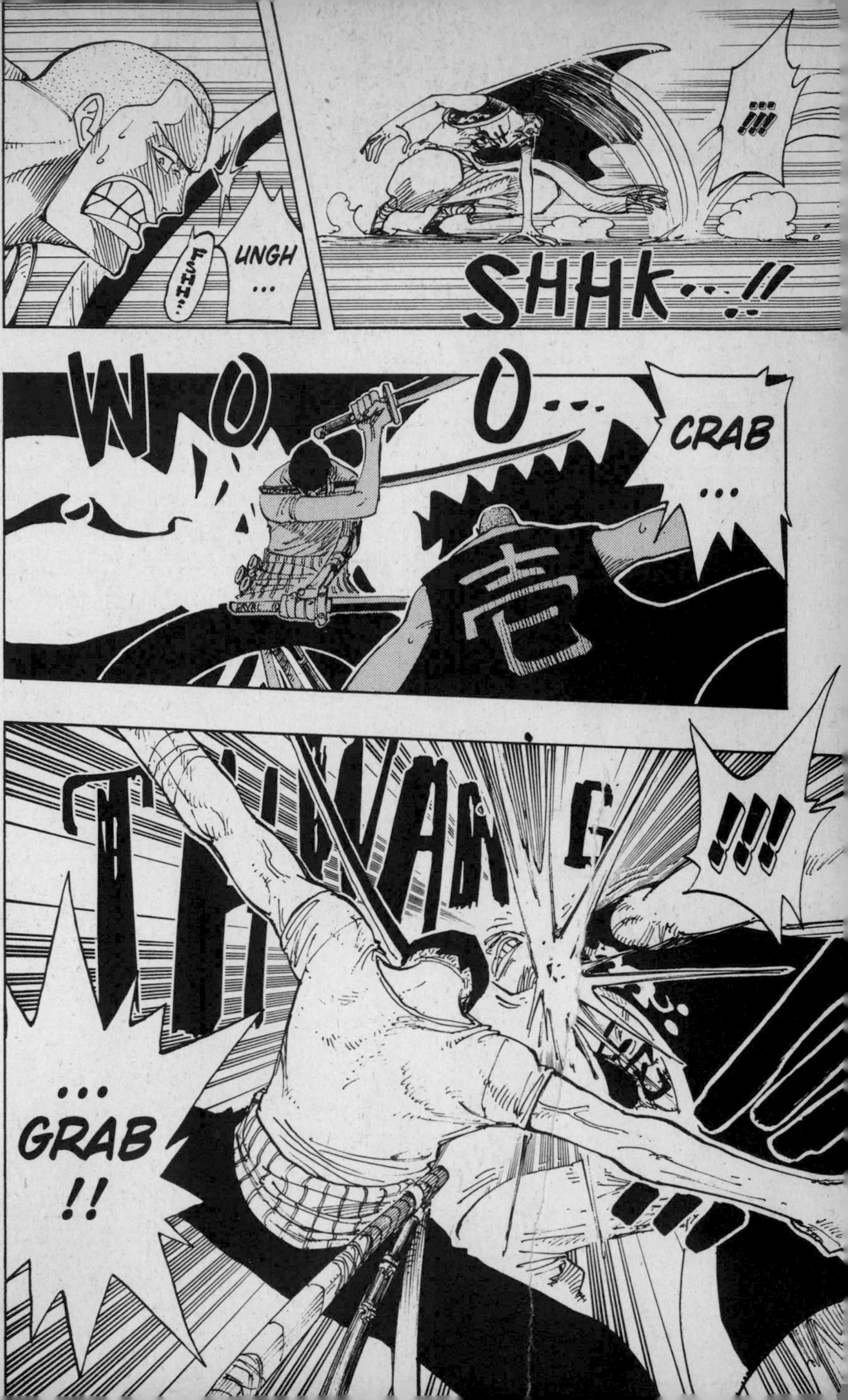
!!!
SHHK...!!
UNGH ...
FSHH...
CRAB ...
WO O...
!!!
THWANG
... GRAB !!

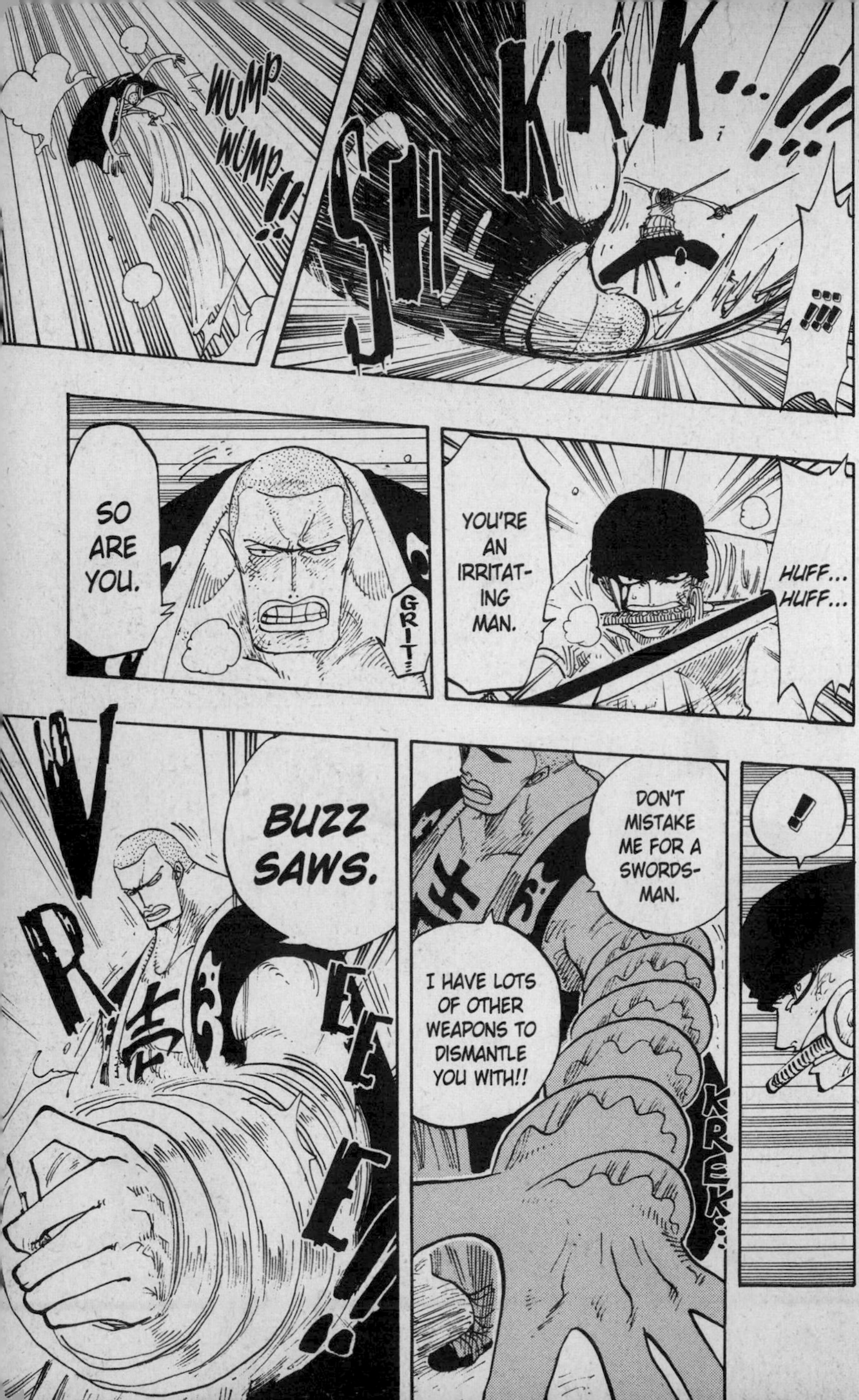
SHKKK...!!
!!!
WUMP WUMP!!
HUFF... HUFF...
YOU'RE AN IRRITAT-ING MAN.
SO ARE YOU.
GRIT
!
DON'T MISTAKE ME FOR A SWORDS-MAN.
I HAVE LOTS OF OTHER WEAPONS TO DISMANTLE YOU WITH!!
KREK...
BUZZ SAWS.
VREEEE

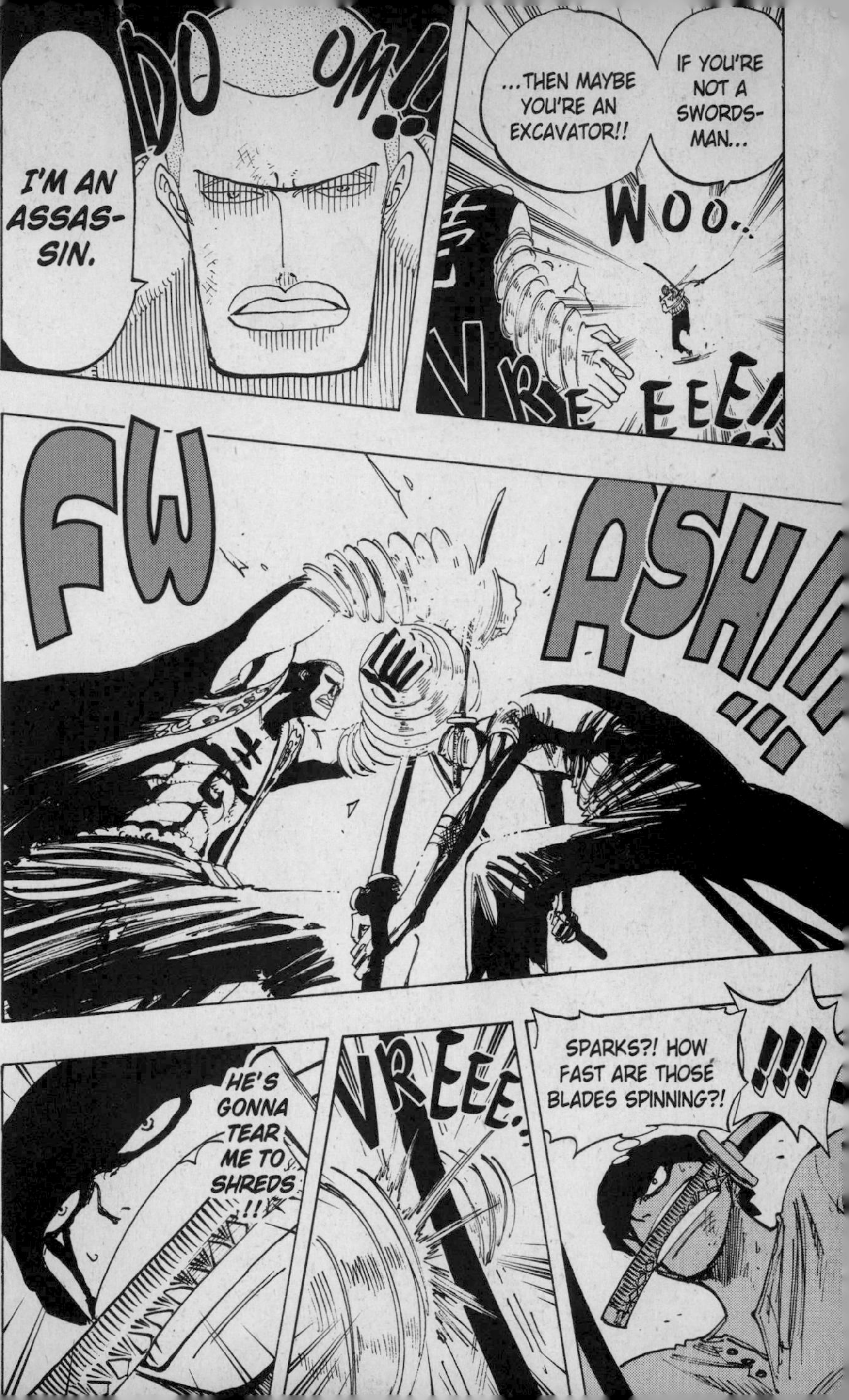
IF YOU'RE NOT A SWORDS-MAN...
...THEN MAYBE YOU'RE AN EXCAVATOR!!
WOO..
VREEEE!!
DOOM!!
I'M AN ASSAS-SIN.
FWASH!!!
!!!
SPARKS?! HOW FAST ARE THOSE BLADES SPINNING?!
VREEE..
HE'S GONNA TEAR ME TO SHREDS!!

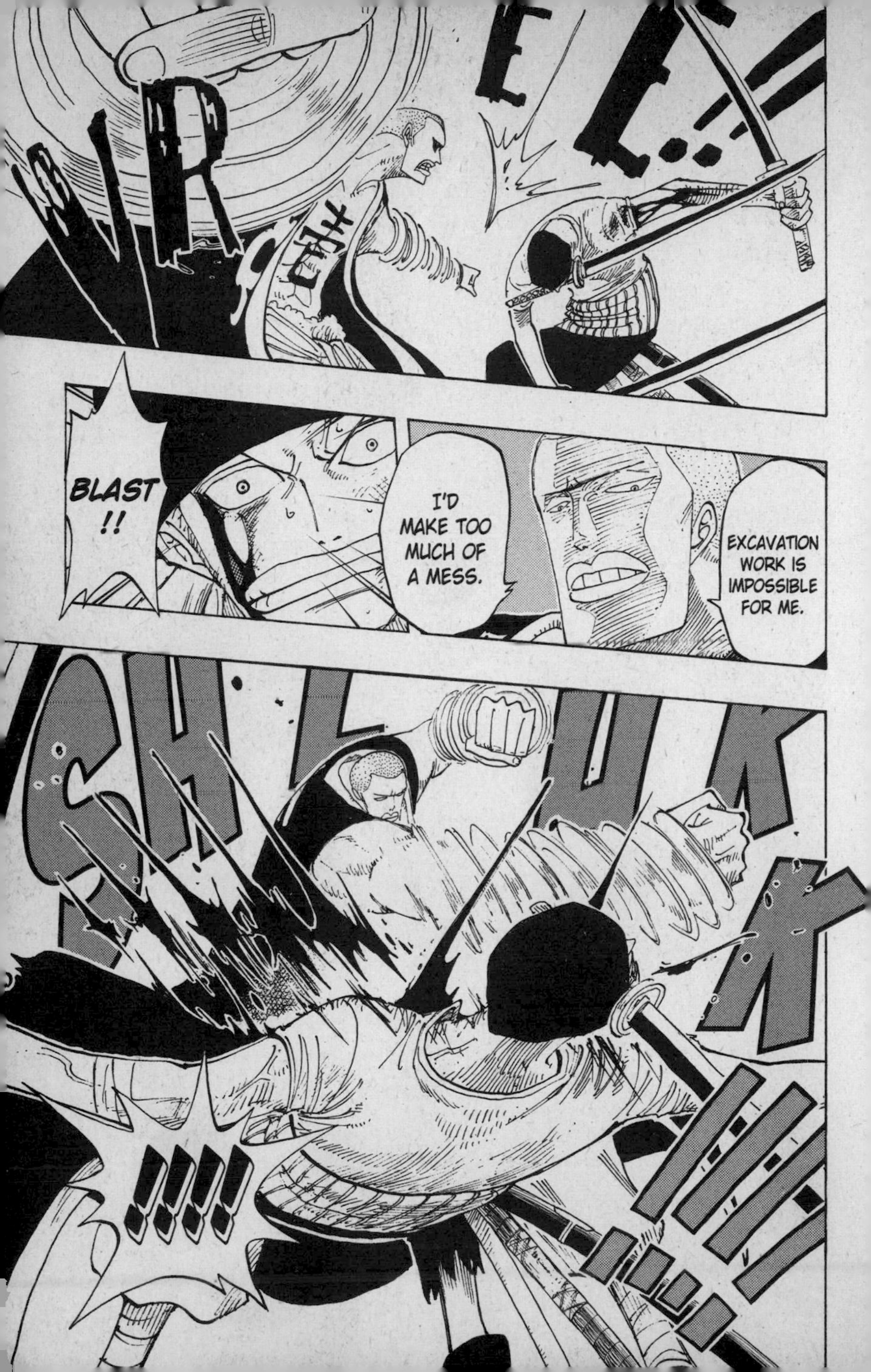
EXCAVATION WORK IS IMPOSSIBLE FOR ME.
I'D MAKE TOO MUCH OF A MESS.
BLAST!!

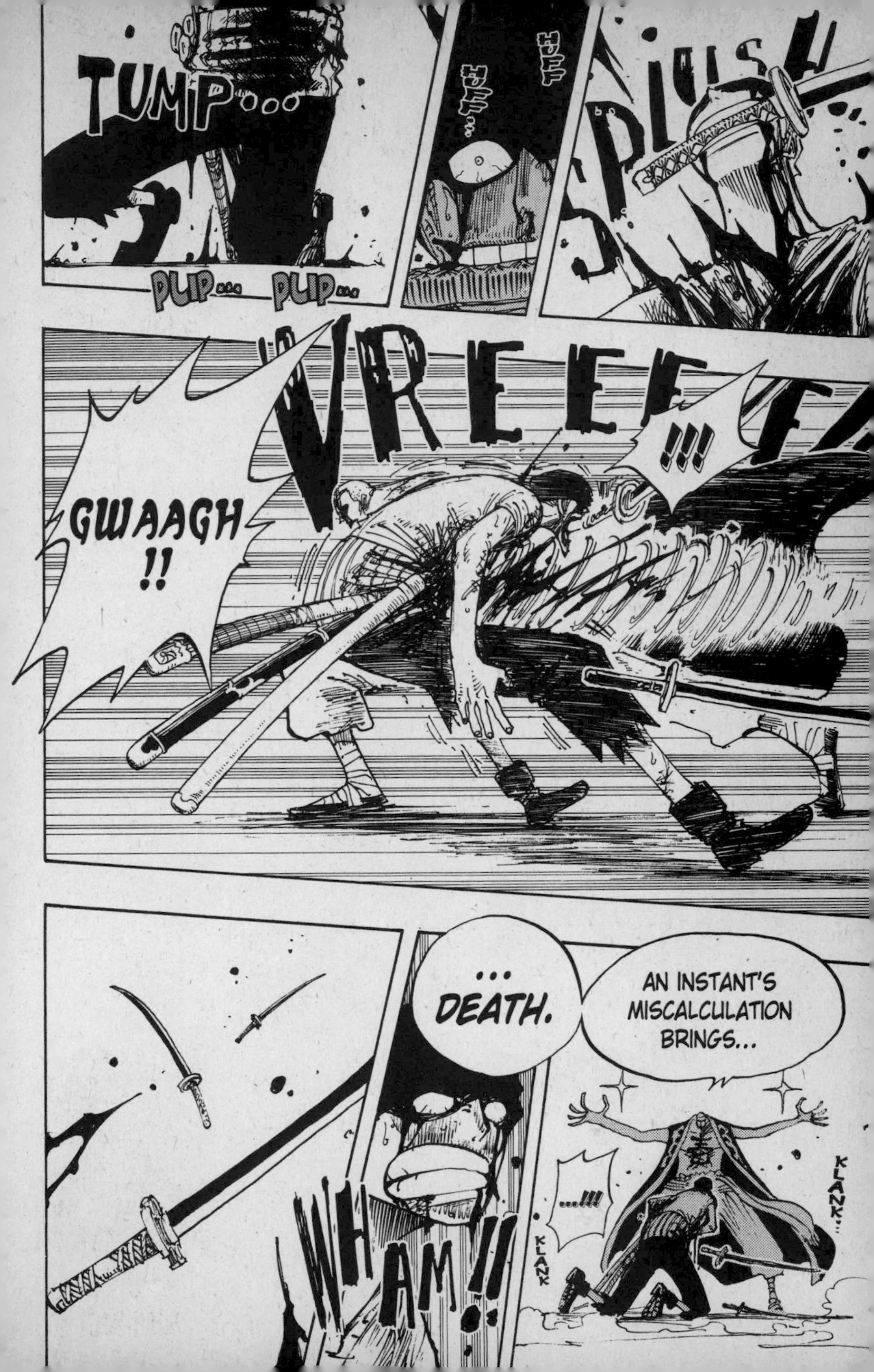
SPLUSH
HUFF...
HUFF
TUMP...
PLIP...
PLIP...
!!!
VREEF
GWAAGH!!
AN INSTANT'S MISCALCULATION BRINGS...
...DEATH.
...!!!
KLANK...
KLANK
WHAM!!

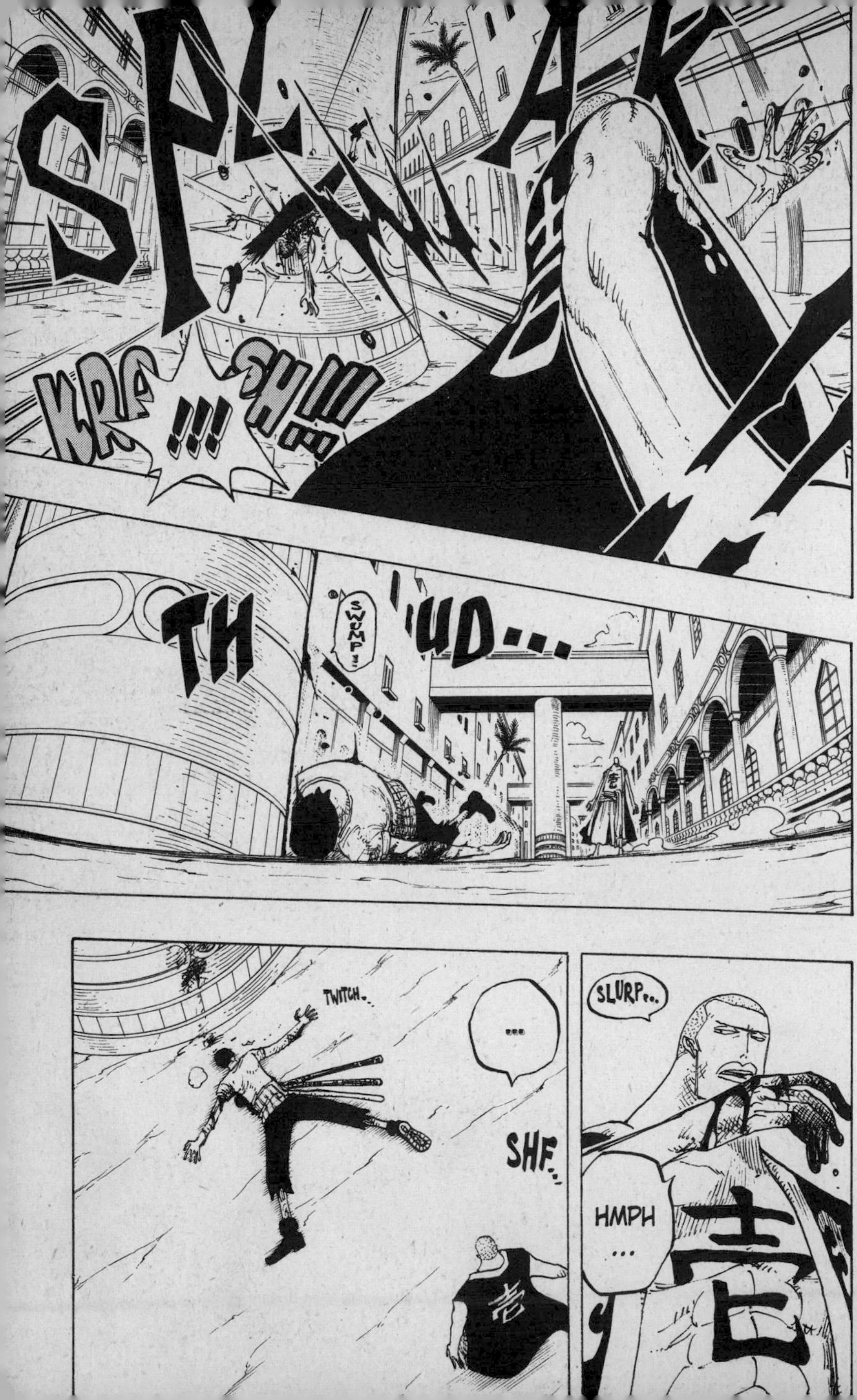
SPLAK
KRE!!! SH!!!
TH UD...
SWUMP!!
SLURP...
HMPH ...
TWITCH..
...
SHF..

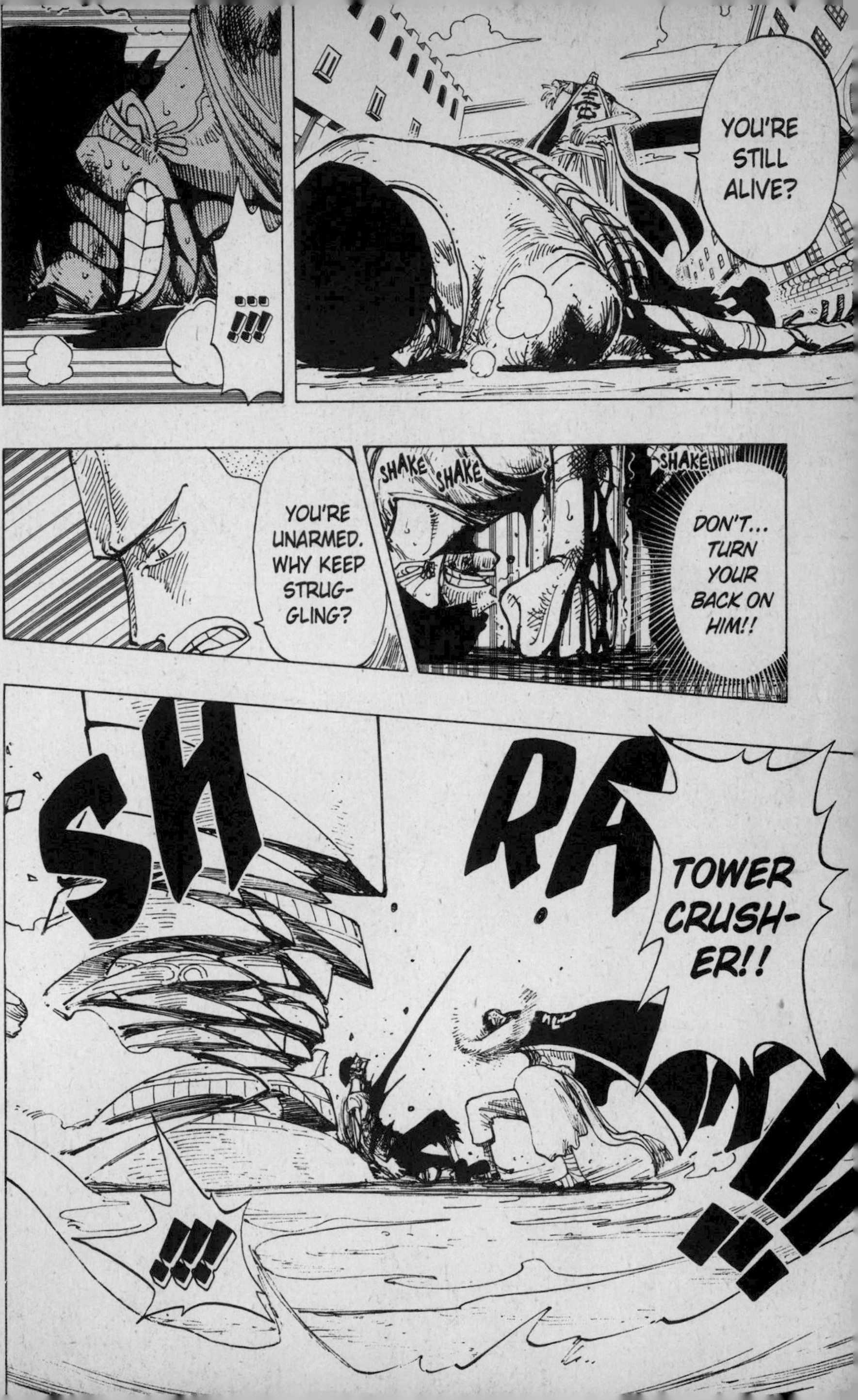
YOU'RE STILL ALIVE?
...!!!
SHAKE
SHAKE
SHAKE
DON'T... TURN YOUR BACK ON HIM!!
YOU'RE UNARMED. WHY KEEP STRUG-GLING?
TOWER CRUSH-ER!!
SH
RA
!!!

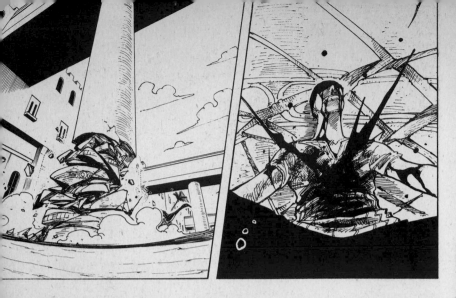

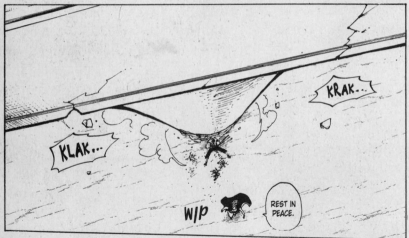

KRAK...

KLAK...

W/P

REST IN PEACE.

KLAK

KREK

KLAK

KLAK

K'REK

KLAK

I'M HAVING BAD LUCK WITH STONE TODAY.

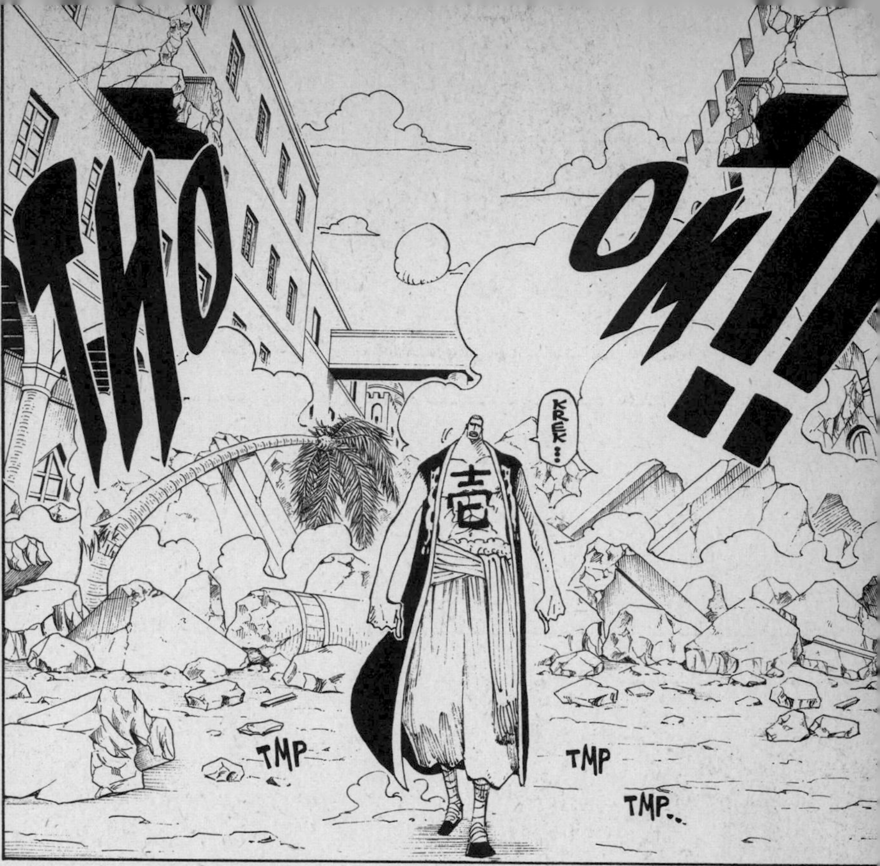
THOOM!!!
KREK...
TMP
TMP
TMP...

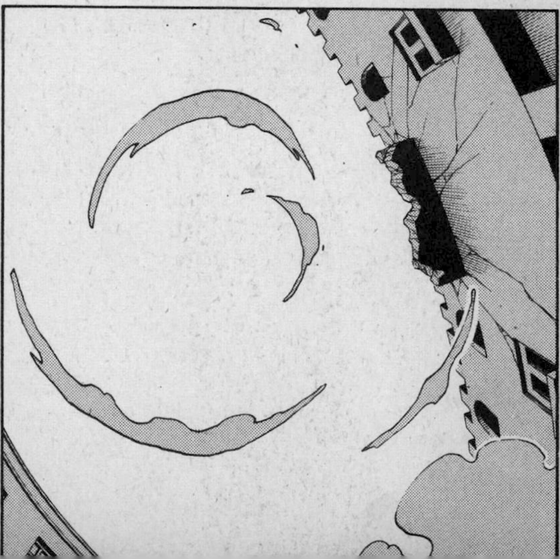

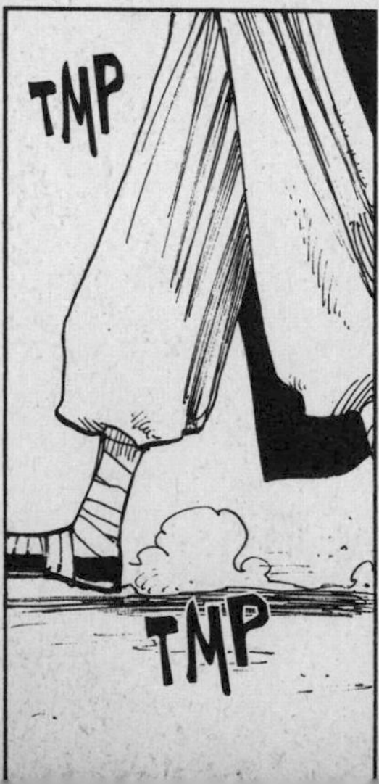
TMP
TMP

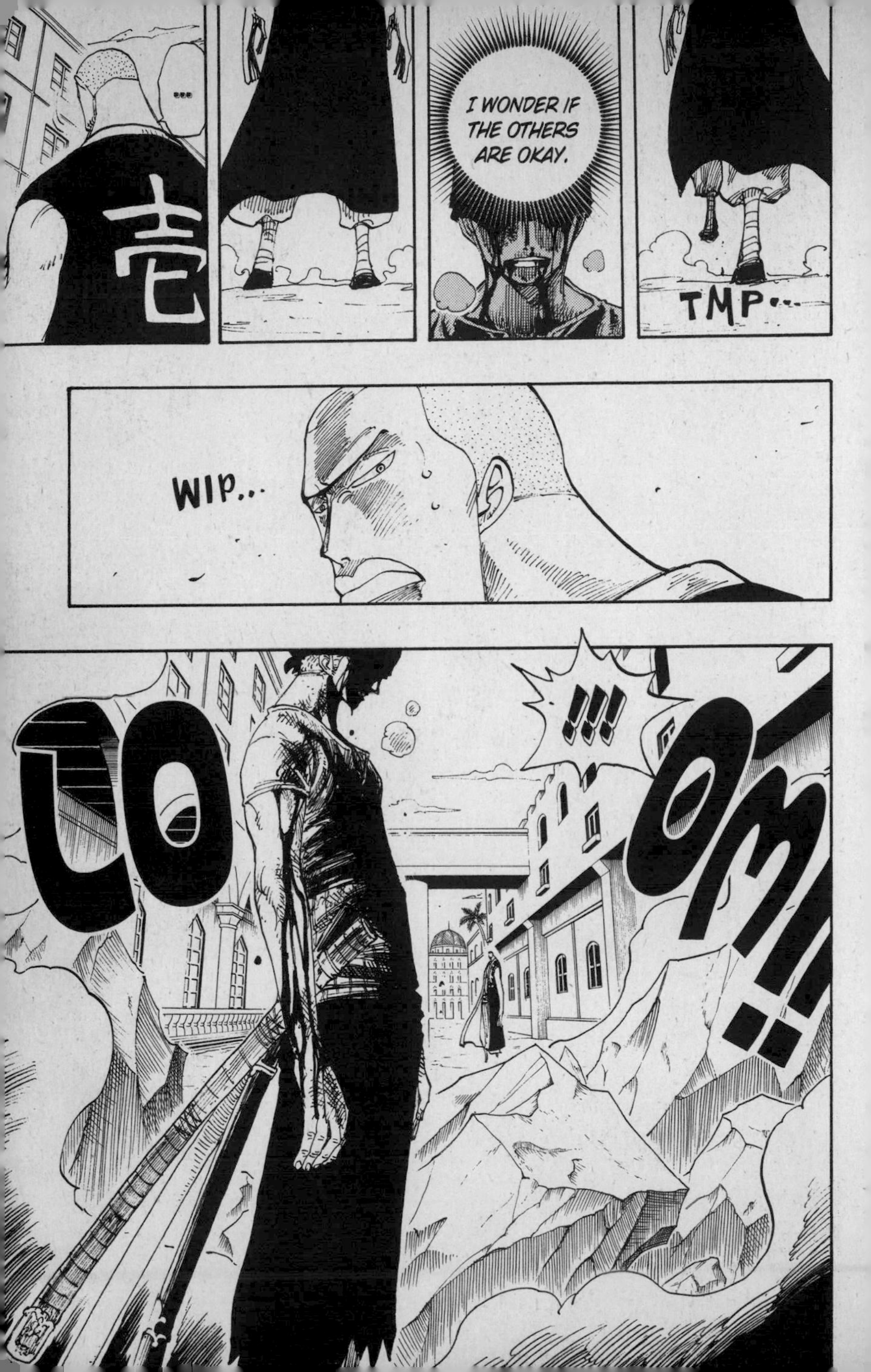
TMP...
I WONDER IF THE OTHERS ARE OKAY.
...
WIP...
!!!
CO
OM!!

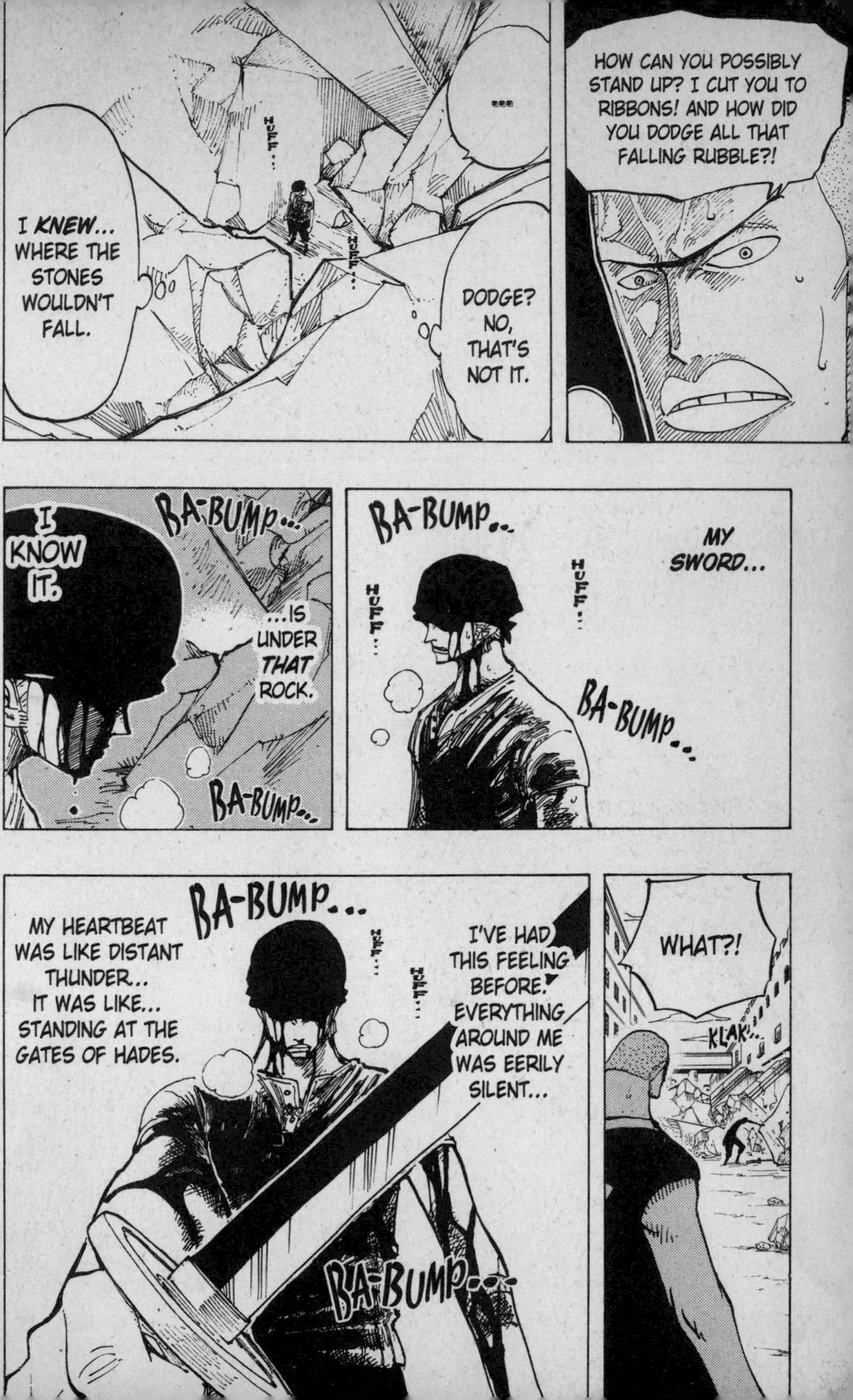
HOW CAN YOU POSSIBLY STAND UP? I CUT YOU TO RIBBONS! AND HOW DID YOU DODGE ALL THAT FALLING RUBBLE?!
...
HUFF...
HUFF...
DODGE? NO, THAT'S NOT IT.
I *KNEW*... WHERE THE STONES WOULDN'T FALL.
BA-BUMP...
MY SWORD...
HUFF...
HUFF...
BA-BUMP...
BA-BUMP...
I KNOW IT.
...IS UNDER *THAT* ROCK.
BA-BUMP...
WHAT?!
KLAK...
BA-BUMP...
HUFF...
HUFF...
I'VE HAD THIS FEELING BEFORE. EVERYTHING AROUND ME WAS EERILY SILENT...
MY HEARTBEAT WAS LIKE DISTANT THUNDER... IT WAS LIKE... STANDING AT THE GATES OF HADES.
BA-BUMP...

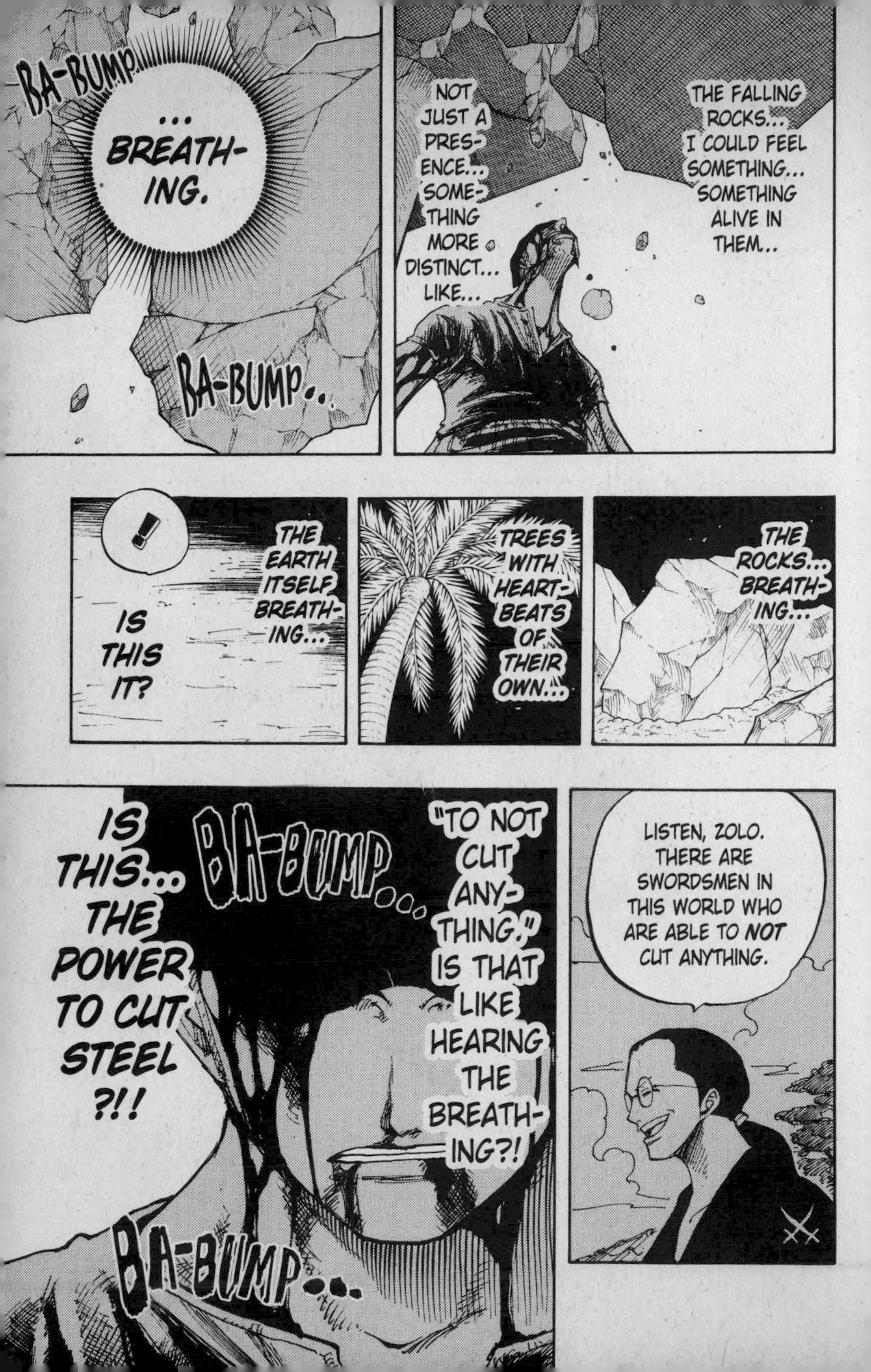
THE FALLING ROCKS... I COULD FEEL SOMETHING... SOMETHING ALIVE IN THEM...
NOT JUST A PRESENCE... SOMETHING MORE DISTINCT... LIKE...
BA-BUMP
... BREATHING.
BA-BUMP...
THE ROCKS... BREATHING...
TREES WITH HEARTBEATS OF THEIR OWN...
!
THE EARTH ITSELF BREATHING...
IS THIS IT?
LISTEN, ZOLO. THERE ARE SWORDSMEN IN THIS WORLD WHO ARE ABLE TO NOT CUT ANYTHING.
"TO NOT CUT ANYTHING." IS THAT LIKE HEARING THE BREATHING?!
BA-BUMP...
IS THIS... THE POWER TO CUT STEEL ?!!
BA-BUMP...

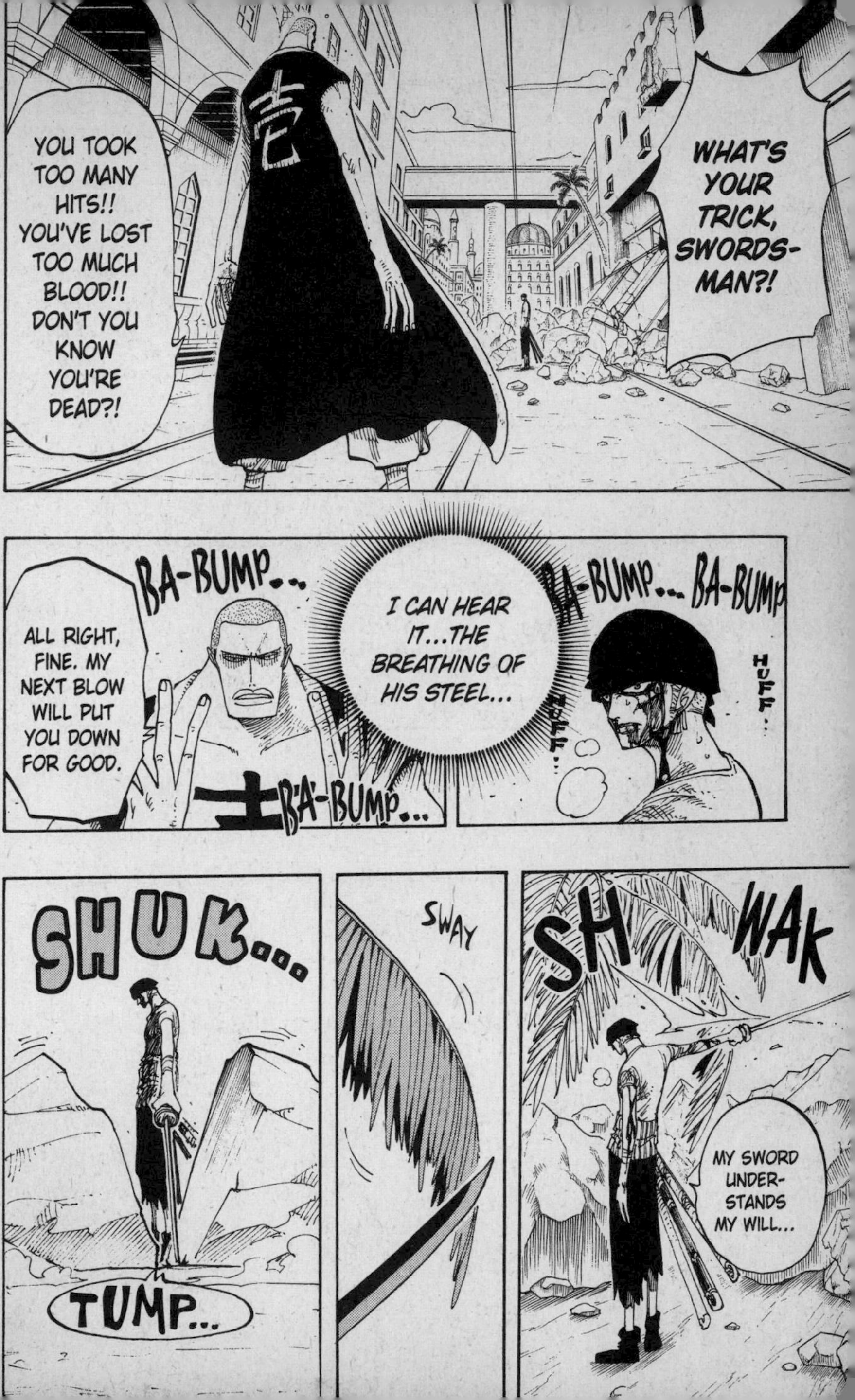
WHAT'S YOUR TRICK, SWORDSMAN?!
YOU TOOK TOO MANY HITS!! YOU'VE LOST TOO MUCH BLOOD!! DON'T YOU KNOW YOU'RE DEAD?!
BA-BUMP... BA-BUMP
HUFF...
HUFF...
I CAN HEAR IT...THE BREATHING OF HIS STEEL...
BA-BUMP...
ALL RIGHT, FINE. MY NEXT BLOW WILL PUT YOU DOWN FOR GOOD.
BA-BUMP...
SHWAK
MY SWORD UNDERSTANDS MY WILL...
SWAY
SHUK...
TUMP...

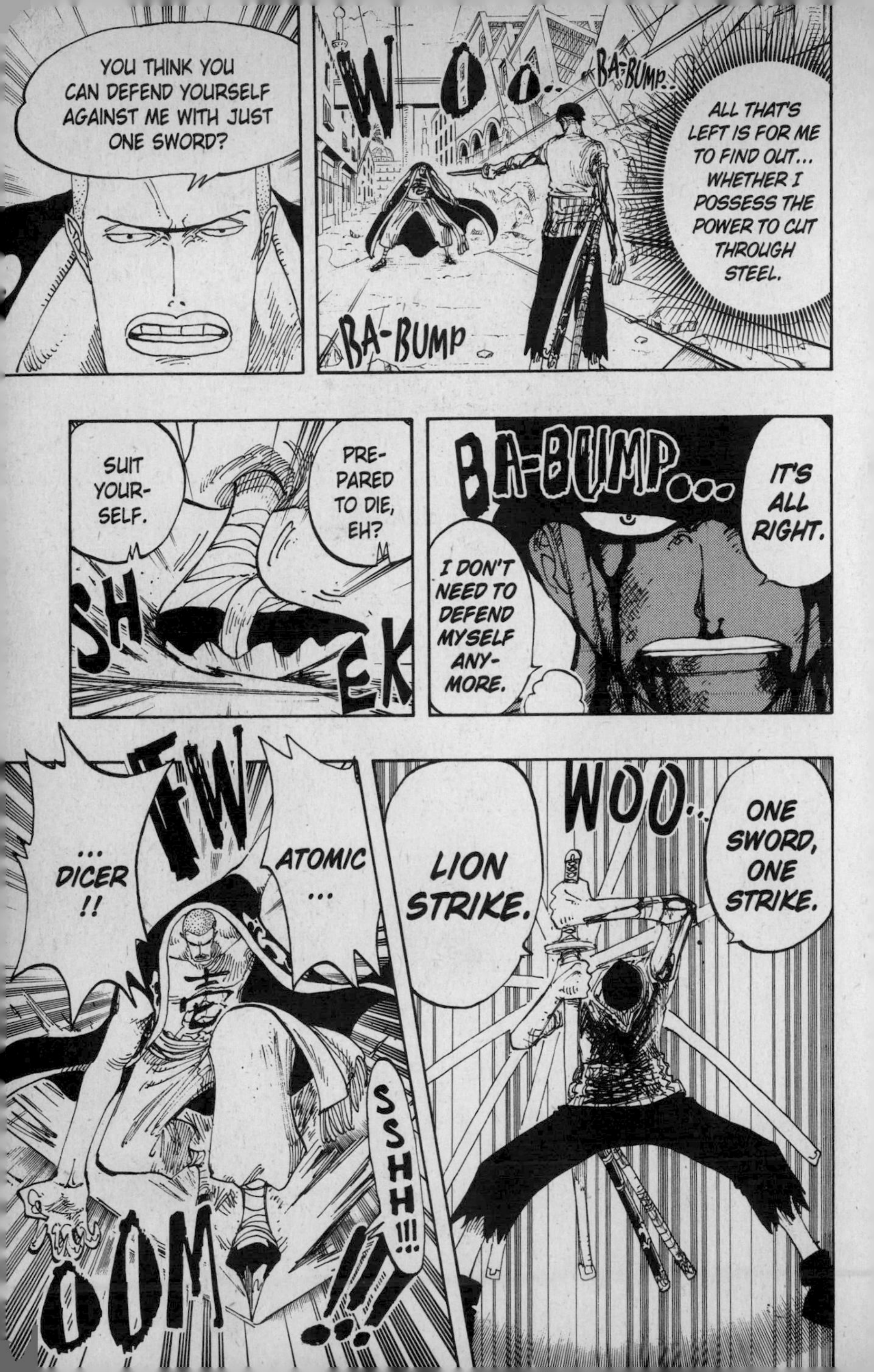
WOO..
BA-BUMP...
ALL THAT'S LEFT IS FOR ME TO FIND OUT... WHETHER I POSSESS THE POWER TO CUT THROUGH STEEL.
BA-BUMP
YOU THINK YOU CAN DEFEND YOURSELF AGAINST ME WITH JUST ONE SWORD?
BA-BUMP...
IT'S ALL RIGHT.
I DON'T NEED TO DEFEND MYSELF ANYMORE.
PRE-PARED TO DIE, EH?
SUIT YOUR-SELF.
SHEK
WOO..
ONE SWORD, ONE STRIKE.
LION STRIKE.
ATOMIC ...
... DICER !!
FWOOM!!
SSHH!!!

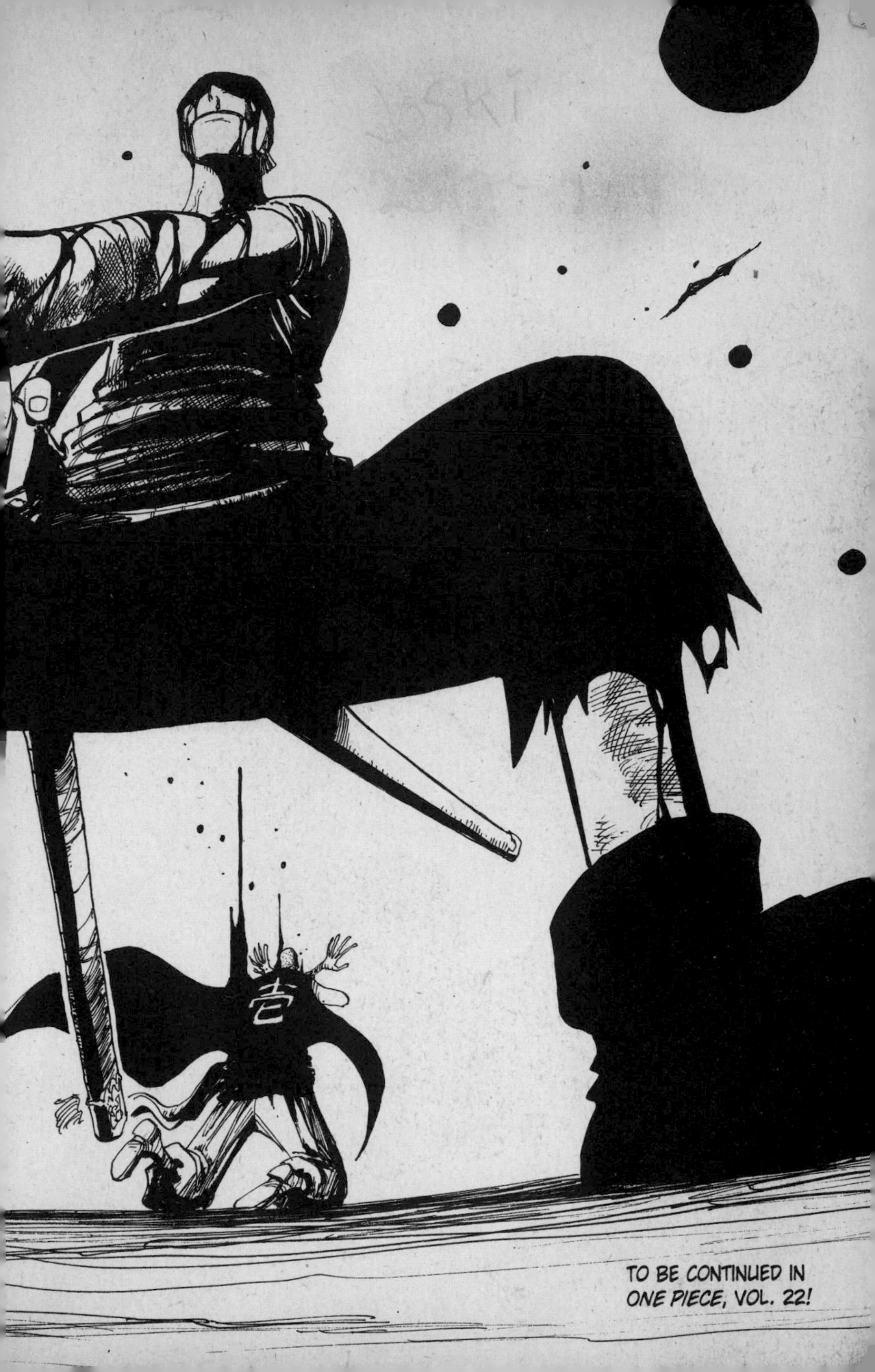
壱
TO BE CONTINUED IN
ONE PIECE, VOL. 22!

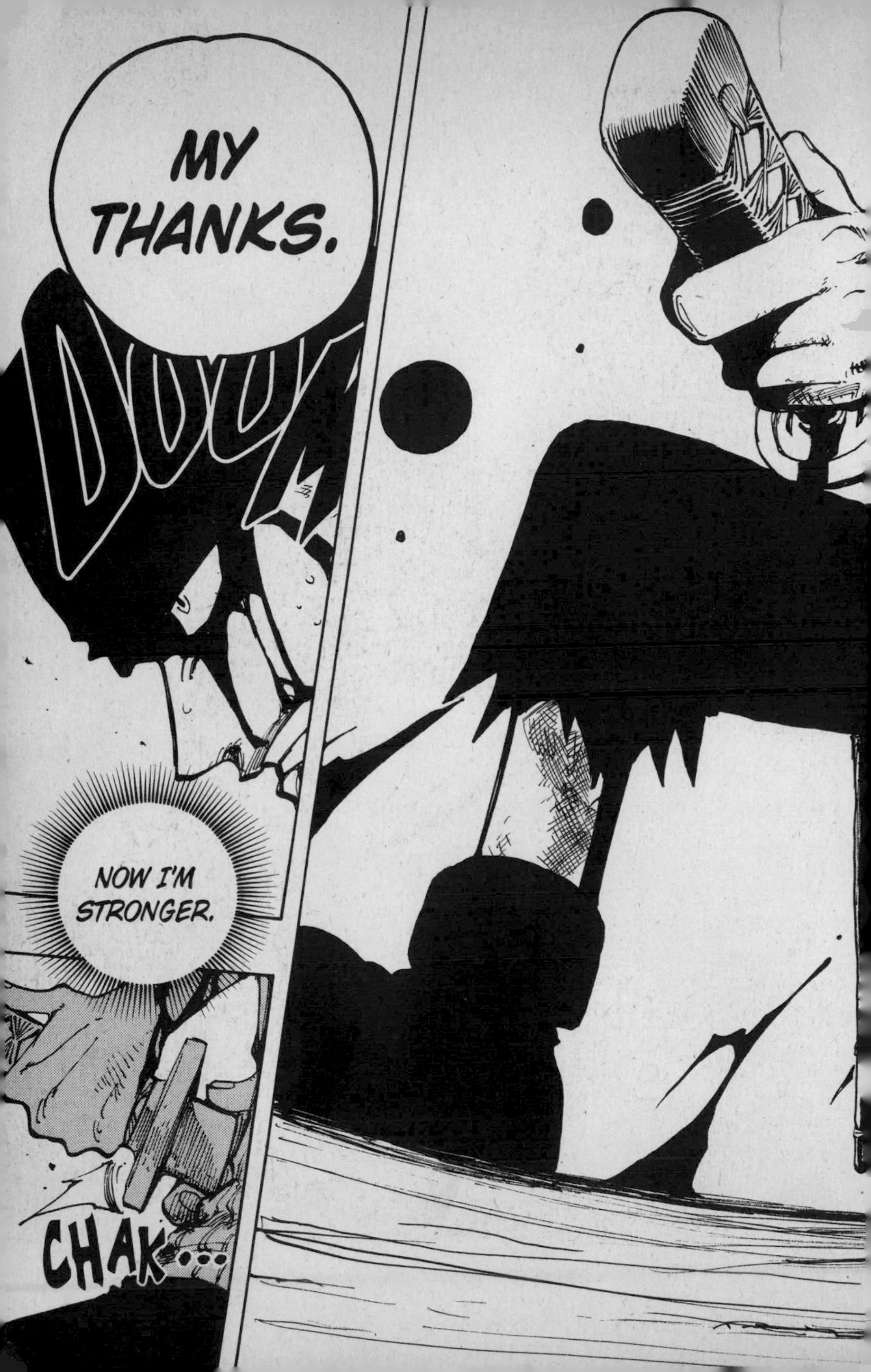
MY THANKS.
NOW I'M STRONGER.
CHAK...

COMING NEXT VOLUME:

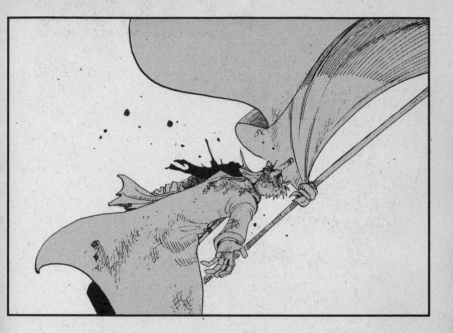

When Crocodile's evildoing is exposed to the leaders of both sides, the rebellion that will destroy Alabasta just might be averted... But the Baroque Works will do everything in their power to make sure that doesn't happen—even if they have to kill Princess Vivi! The Straw Hats are in for the fight of their lives to keep this evil Croc from getting his way!

ON SALE OCTOBER 2009!
Read it first in SHONEN JUMP magazine!

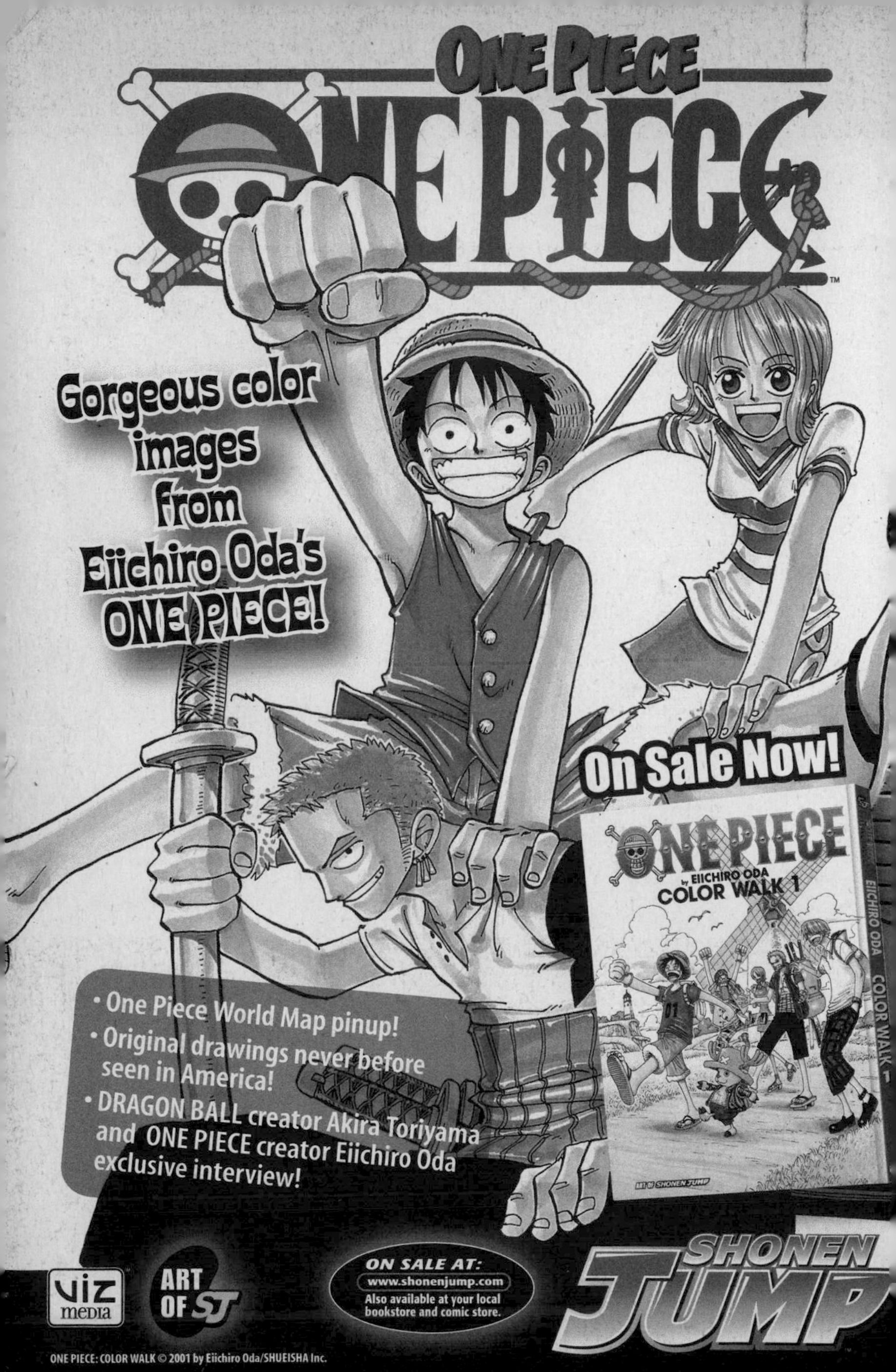

ONE PIECE
ONE PIECE
Gorgeous color images from Eiichiro Oda's ONE PIECE!
On Sale Now!
ONE PIECE
by EIICHIRO ODA
COLOR WALK 1
SHONEN JUMP
EIICHIRO ODA COLOR WALK 1
• One Piece World Map pinup!
• Original drawings never before seen in America!
• DRAGON BALL creator Akira Toriyama and ONE PIECE creator Eiichiro Oda exclusive interview!
viz media
ART OF SJ
ON SALE AT:
www.shonenjump.com
Also available at your local bookstore and comic store.
SHONEN JUMP

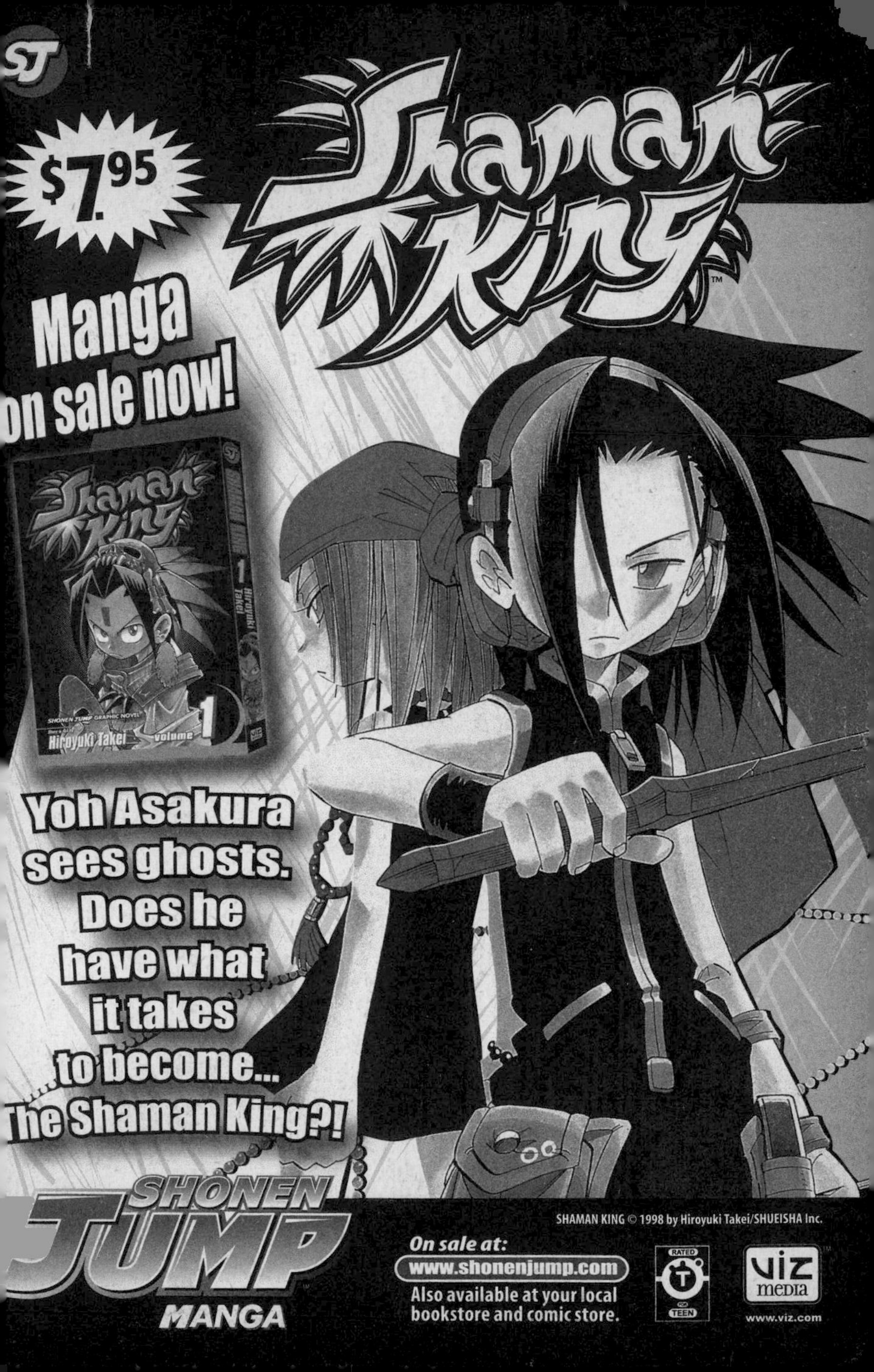
SJ
$7.95
Shaman King™
Manga on sale now!
Shaman King
SHONEN JUMP GRAPHIC NOVEL
Hiroyuki Takei
volume 1
Yoh Asakura sees ghosts. Does he have what it takes to become... The Shaman King?!
SHONEN JUMP MANGA
SHAMAN KING © 1998 by Hiroyuki Takei/SHUEISHA Inc.
On sale at:
www.shonenjump.com
Also available at your local bookstore and comic store.
RATED T TEEN
VIZ media
www.viz.com

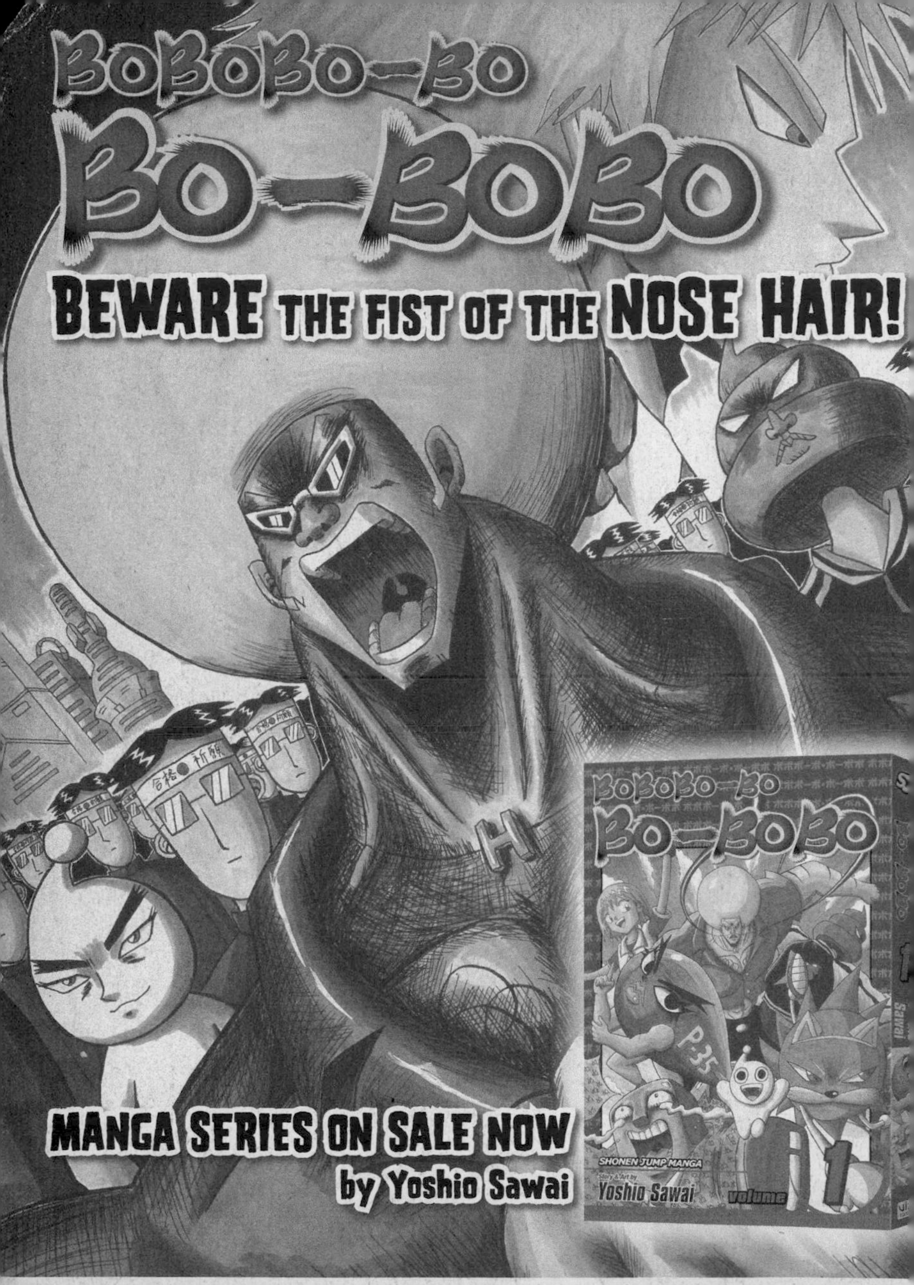
BOBOBO-BO
BO-BOBO
BEWARE THE FIST OF THE NOSE HAIR!
MANGA SERIES ON SALE NOW
by Yoshio Sawai
BOBOBO-BO BO-BOBO
SHONEN JUMP MANGA
Story & Art by Yoshio Sawai
volume 1

Tell us what you think about SHONEN JUMP manga!

Our survey is now available online.
Go to: www.**SHONENJUMP**.com/mangasurvey

Help us make our product offering better!